France: Empire and Republic,
1850-1940

A volume
in
THE DOCUMENTARY HISTORY
of
WESTERN CIVILIZATION

FRANCE:
EMPIRE AND REPUBLIC, 1850-1940

Historical Documents

Selected and Introduced by
DAVID THOMSON

WALKER AND COMPANY
New York

FRANCE: EMPIRE AND REPUBLIC, 1850-1940
Introduction, Preface, editorial notes,
bibliography, chronology, translations
by the editor, and compilation
Copyright © 1968 by David Thomson.

Library of Congress Catalog Card Number: 68-27380.

Printed in the United States of America.

Published in the United States of America in
1968 by Walker and Company, a division of the
Walker Publishing Company, Inc.

Published simultaneously in Canada by
The Ryerson Press, Toronto.

Volumes in this series are published in association
with Harper & Row, Publishers, Inc., from
whom paperback editions are available in Harper
Torchbooks.

Contents

Preface

Having studied the history of modern France for some thirty years, I am still surprised by its deeper subtleties and its inexhaustible intellectual interest. These qualities make its study one of the most rewarding media of historical education. But they may elude the student unless he is brought into direct contact with the nuances of attitude and frictions of social life which, within the framework of national institutions and outlooks, explain much of what has happened in France. The purpose of this book is to expose him to them.

I have, therefore, chosen and arranged the documents and excerpts from documents so as to elicit some of the most important of these nuances and frictions. Chronological sequence, preserved within each section, has been subordinated to a functional design which emphasizes the interplay between State and Society. To document formal institutions, whether political, economic, or social, without showing the tussles of men and movements to overthrow, change, or appropriate them in their own interests, would be barren indeed.

In the translation and presentation of the French documents, my wife's linguistic knowledge and expertise, and her unsparing help, have put me even more than usual in her debt. To her I dedicate this book.

Sidney Sussex College   D.T.
Cambridge

Introduction

The theme of this volume is the historical development of France from the middle of the last century until her defeat by Germany in the summer of 1940. It spans, in political terms, two of the ten régimes France has known since the beginning of the nineteenth century: the Second Empire of Napoleon III and the Third Republic. But its theme is not limited to the constitutional or political aspects of French development in these years, nor even to the military, diplomatic, economic, or social aspects. It comprises whatever significant events in any and all of these aspects of national life and activity most help to explain the over-all fortunes of France between 1850 and 1940. Since its scope is so multilateral, and the interplay of the various aspects of national change so intricate, choice of material for a volume such as this must be made on certain firm principles if it is to be kept within tolerable limits of size, expense, and utility. For the sheer quantity of available "documents" relating to this theme is dauntingly vast, as even hasty reflection will suggest.

Georges Clemenceau, France's greatest national leader and "Father of Victory" in the First World War, was born in 1841 and died in 1929. Marshal Pétain, France's "Hero of Verdun" in the First World War and maker of the Armistice with Hitler in 1940, was born in 1856 and lived on until 1951. Although their lifetimes overlapped by more than seventy years within the period which is our concern, their actual lives extended well beyond it at both ends. Clemenceau was a boy of ten when Louis Napoleon carried out his *coup d'état* at the end of 1851; Pétain, who was born only five years later, lived to see the Fourth French Republic bitterly attacked by General de Gaulle in 1951. Two such long lifetimes of momentous changes and intensely dramatic happenings could, in themselves, merit many volumes of documentation. They are only two names of many scores which throng these years of French history. Clearly, then, any one person's selection of materials is certain to be intrinsically an individual judgment, exposed to all the hazards, preferences, prejudices, and disputable choices of any individual judgment.

Yet it remains true that, although others might have produced a volume of materials somewhat different in range and often different in precise choice, and although they might have arranged and even interpreted them in other ways, there are many documents in this volume which no adequate selection could reasonably omit. Some have undeniable importance and relevance, as laying the basis for long-term developments. Such are the written Constitution of 1852, or the Commercial Treaty with England of 1860, or the Constitutional Laws of 1875. These and other indispensable documents have been given in full. Others, again, have come to be recognized by a common consensus, as measured by the frequency with which they are referred to or quoted (and sometimes misquoted) by historians, to have a basic importance. Such are Léon Gambetta's appeal for "war to the end" in October, 1870, or Karl Marx's remarkable contemporary assessment of the Paris Commune in 1871, or Émile Zola's article "*J'Accuse*" of January, 1898. The whole of the relevant sections of these famous statements have been quoted in this volume.

Yet others are expressions of policies (party manifestoes or declarations of principle by national leaders), or statements of prevalent attitudes or interests (of sectional or pressure groups), which have definable importance or which convey, in concise form, forces and ideas that have clearly mattered in the life and thought of these years. Here, again, the whole or the most relevant sections of the documents have been given, with conscious effort to avoid the disjointed snippets which sometimes masquerade as "documents." In this third category, however, there is more room for personal choice as to which statements are left out or put in.

The volume contains yet a fourth category of documents, the inclusion of which would have caused mild surprise to historians brought up in the older French (and Anglo-American) school of historiography, which drew excessively sharp and clear distinctions between "primary" and "secondary" sources. These range from the passage quoted from Anatole France's *L'Île des pingouins*, to the personal records of trips into the villages of central France by the historian Daniel Halévy. Inclusion of such extracts in a volume of "documents" is in tune with modern notions of the serious and scholarly study of history, and is justifiable on two main grounds: they present some of the more elusive and intangible aspects of national life which are ill represented by more formal documents but which no historian can afford to neglect; and, as extracts from the writings of eminent and influential literary men of the time, they serve to remind the student that contemporary literature, provided it be cautiously used and interpreted, may itself provide highly revealing documentation for the historian.

It is to be regretted that many more examples could not be included of the immensely lively intellectual activity of France in these years, notably in philosophy, political theory, and scientific discovery. But to attempt such coverage would demand a further volume. The guiding principle which has governed the selection of material has been, in virtually every instance, the fact that the writer was either an eye-witness, as with Georges Clemenceau's account of the outbreak of the Paris Commune on March 18, 1871, (Document 50), or a participant, as with the comment on the Dreyfus Affair by Charles Péguy (Document 60).

In 1898 two distinguished French historians, Charles Langlois and Charles Seignobos, published an *Introduction to the Study of History* in which they stated, in conformity with the rigid positivist views of historiography then in vogue, that:

> The historian works with documents. Documents are the traces which have been left by the thoughts and actions of men of former times. . . . For want of documents the history of immense periods in the past of humanity is destined to remain for ever unknown. For there is no substitute for documents: no documents, no history.[1]

Since they wrote, the study of history has advanced rapidly along two lines. Techniques of interpreting documents and computerizing the data extracted from them have reached a stage of finesse unimagined in the nineteenth century; and ways of eliciting historical truths from a wide variety of relics of the past other than documents have been ingeniously developed. The second development alone makes the doctrine of Langlois and Seignobos quite inadequate. The discoveries of archeology and of anthropology, the work of historians of art, science, and technology, have disproved the dictum, "No documents, no history." What is true, of

[1] C. V. Langlois and C. Seignobos, *Introduction to the Study of History* (London, 1898, trans. G. G. Berry, reprinted New York, 1966), p. 17.

course, is that historians can work only with *surviving evidence* of the past, and this must be culled from *relics* of the past; but such relics can be many things other than documents. They can be pieces of stone or wood, buildings or paintings, coins or skeletons. All of which is a salutary reminder that this volume attempts to deal with only one species of historical evidence out of many possible kinds. It deals with what for some reason got written down and survived. It may have been written down (and possibly printed and published as most of these documents eventually were) for various reasons: because it was an official and formal text of a law or decree, or because it was a speech in parliament or in the country, or it was a personal letter or journal, or the writer wished to expound and record an idea, attitude, argument, opinion, or belief. Since French history in these decades was packed with action and French society beset with often violent controversy, the tone of much that got written was highly polemical, exhortatory, and excited. If the reader gains an impression of excessive rhetoric and portentous declamation, let him be assured that this was the authentic flavor of French life. And he has been spared more than 99 per cent of it.

Just as a selection of documents, in the sense described above, is basically different from an anthology of "readings," which could properly include secondary writings by other than eye-witnesses or participants, so it can never be a substitute for professionally written historical accounts or explanations. Documents are the raw materials of historiography (though not the only ones), and a selection of them can be a useful supplement to historical study, illustrating incidents or generalizations, making the story more vivid and the explanation more intelligible. But it is of little value apart from the historian's balanced account. It is not to be thought of as a "Do it yourself kit" for the amateur historian or student of history. It is at best an aid to study, a medium of instruction, an exemplification of what kinds of raw material are grist to the historian's mill and of the problems he is liable to encounter in correlating evidence. It can be very valuable for all these purposes. It is a device increasingly used as such in universities and colleges. But there should be no assumption that "history in the raw" is somehow more objective or more authentic than the finished product of the historian. It may, for reasons mentioned above, reflect just as much of the personal taste, tendentiousness, and idiosyncrasy of the individual compiling it as can any textbook or monograph. Its objectivity will be no greater, but also no less, than that of the man who makes it.

Its coherence, indeed, can come only from a whole set of presuppositions and decisions by the compiler about the pattern of national development he wishes to convey. And any such pattern is disputable, open to subsequent revision and correction, as much as any other general interpretation of historical events. The rest of this Introduction can, therefore, be most profitably devoted to a brief account of the pattern which emerges from the events between 1850 and 1940 and which, in turn, gives coherence to the selection of documentary sources here presented.

* * *

The dominant feature of the period 1850–1940 is also a feature of the whole period of French history since 1789: turbulence. It opens with the fragile and deadlocked Second Republic, destroyed by a *coup d'état* carried out by its own elected President, Louis Napoleon Bonaparte. It moves into an era of wars between major European powers, beginning with the Crimean War of 1854 to 1856, which broke the long period of peace that had followed 1815. The European wars reached their culmination in the Franco-Prussian War of 1870, in which the French armies were routed or taken prisoner and Napoleon III had to abdicate. Attempts to frame a treaty of peace were interrupted first by Gambetta's war of national defense, then by the lurid outbreak of the Paris Commune of 1871 correctly labeled by Karl Marx as "the civil war in France." Slowly and painfully a new parliamentary constitution was devised. It became the Third Republic, the longest-lived experiment in parliamentary government France has ever known. It lasted sixty-five years — an average man's lifetime.

But under even this relatively stabilized régime considerable turbulence persisted. French history was punctuated by violent upheavals, internal or external. The agitation of Boulangism was followed, at the turn of the century, by the Dreyfus Affair. The First World War and the world economic crisis shattered French life, as they affected other European countries; though in general the war shattered France more than any other country except Russia, and the Depression affected France later and less than most others. Between the two world wars France experienced many tensions, between liberal-democratic parties and totalitarian movements, as well as between communist and fascist activists. In 1940 the nation plunged into defeat in which the Third Republic was submerged, never to reappear. The disturbing consequences of these successive crises were aggravated by two further circumstances more peculiar to France: the nation passed through a period of declining birth rate and demographic stagnation, especially in the twentieth century, which seemed to be symptomatic of a deep-seated national malaise; and the parliamentary system produced chronic governmental instability which, especially after 1918, weakened authority and intensified periods of national crisis.

For all these reasons the country which, in 1850, had still been one of the dominant powers in Europe and a torchbearer of revolutionary and emancipating ideas, had by 1940 come to look more like "the sick man of Europe" and a nation obsessed with anxieties about security and stability. This dramatic transformation of spirit and of image is one of the inescapable themes of the history of these years.

Perhaps one clue to an explanation of that transformation lies in the very nomenclature of the successive régimes: the Second Republic, the Second Empire, the Third Republic. In trancelike ways the French went on re-enacting their own past, restlessly experimenting with enigma variations on old tunes. The pattern of development of these years is, as already suggested, part of a larger pattern. After 1815 the French repeated, in the same sequence, the cycle of political experiments they had conducted between 1789 and 1815. Beginning with a legitimist Bourbon monarchy (Louis XVIII and Charles X) they moved on to a more constitutional monarchy under Louis Philippe (1830–1848) as previously under Louis XVI (1789–1792). This was succeeded by the short-lived Second Republic, and it by the Second Empire (1852–1870). The sequence Monarchy-Republic-Empire was as it had been between 1789 and 1815. Each Monarchy had ended with raising of barricades in the Paris streets; each Republic, with a military *coup d'état* by a Bonaparte; each Empire, with defeat in a foreign war, at Waterloo and at Sedan.

For a time, in 1871, it looked as if yet a third cycle might be beginning. Adolphe Thiers, the veteran statesman entrusted with executive power, was known to favor a constitutional monarchy. The Bordeaux Assembly, with which he had to work between

1871 and 1875, contained at first a big majority of monarchists. The royalists were strenuously trying to produce a "fusion" of legitimists and Orleanists so as to place the Bourbon pretender, the Comte de Chambord, on the throne. But Chambord destroyed their hopes and his own chances, and never again was monarchy to be a serious rival to the Republic. France settled, a third time, for a very "conservative republic."

The posture of looking backward and the habit of numbering Republics and Empires as if they were kings characterize the other side of the coin. France, instead of being really revolutionary as she had been between 1789 and 1848, had acquired a "revolutionary tradition"; and traditions—even of revolution—are nostalgic, backward-looking, conservative influences.[2] It is in this sense that Karl Marx's interpretation of the Paris Commune of 1871 was, in the end, as wrong as it could be; for he thought it was the model of a new-style proletarian revolution, whereas it was only the last dying flicker of the old Jacobin revolutionary tradition. It was an irresistible upsurge of the people of Paris, fighting nobly but vainly on the barricades for their ideals. Never again, not even in the resistance movements between 1940 and 1945, was the city of Paris to regain the militant leadership of revolution it had displayed before 1871. The Paris Riots of February, 1934, the most serious challenge to political authority in France between the two world wars, roused no audible echoes elsewhere. It is fashionable to attribute the decline of Paris in revolutionary leadership to the replanning of the city by Baron Haussmann during the Second Empire. Certainly the clearance of the central working-class districts and the making of long, wide, straight boulevards facilitated the keeping of order in the streets. They were intended to do so. But the changing role of Paris, its establishment as a center of administrative authority rather than of revolutionary inspiration, was brought about by many other factors. Not least of these was the growth of a more positive and active State, in which nevertheless strong forces of regionalism combined with the eternal provincialism of France to resist the ascendancy of the capital.

[2] For elaboration of the idea see the present writer's *Democracy in France Since 1870* (London, New York, Toronto, 1946; 4th edn., 1964), Chapter I.

* * *

The changes of régime, even the changing impact of the "revolutionary tradition," form one facet of national development in these years, but only one. The period was also, *par excellence*, the age of the industrial revolution in France. It has been suggested that the clue to much that happened is that France was simultaneously experiencing two different revolutions. The first was the political revolution, whose ferment and aftermath left many with a sense that the ideals of individual liberty were still unfulfilled and that equality had still to be pursued. This merged and mingled with the consequences of the commercial and industrial revolution, which, by 1850, had made slower progress in France than in Britain or Belgium.

The rate of economic growth was uneven, both in time and place. The Second Empire was, in general, a period of high prices and (especially after 1860) of active commercial and colonial expansion. A period of predominantly low prices began in 1873 and lasted until 1896. And the expansion, which had been interrupted between 1870 and 1880, was resumed under the Third Republic and continued until the end of the century. Just as the monarchy had been a time of economic growth and of active road and canal construction, so the Second Empire was identified with the "heroic age" of banking and of railroad building. In fact, there was real continuity in the whole process. Bankers and financiers—the Laffittes, Péreires, and Rothschilds—were no less important in national life under the Second Empire and Third Republic than they had been under Louis Philippe. Charles Freycinet in the 1880's continued and built upon the program of public works begun by Napoleon III. When the first boom in railways came to an end in 1847, the projected trunk lines were still far from complete. By 1850 only some 3,000 kilometers of line were open to traffic; another 14,500 kilometers were added during the Second Empire, and then by 1890 that figure was more than doubled again.

In commercial and colonial policy, too, continuity was considerable. The traditional protectionism of the régimes before 1850 was modified by the Second Empire, whose free-trade propensities reached a climax in the Chevalier-Cobden Treaty with Britain in 1860. Although the Third Republic revived protectionist tendencies, and several attempts were made to modify the free-trade agreements which had proliferated during the 1860's, it was not until the later 1880's that the so-called "Méline Tariffs" substantially replaced the Napoleonic arrangements (see Part II, B below).

Modern French colonialism began with the conquest of Algeria by Charles X and Louis Philippe, ran to quixotic forms in Napoleon's Mexican expedition, and found its most successful champion in Jules Ferry under the Third Republic. The only feature more striking than the number and the variety of régimes in modern France is the way in which both economic forces and national policies persist throughout, almost regardless of the constitutional variations.

Part of the explanation for this deep-seated continuity is the slowness of the transformation brought about within French society. Its most resilient feature was that agriculture remained, throughout the period, the major national industry and a livelihood for more French families than any other occupation. Though big towns were few, small and medium-sized rural communities were legion. Most French families lived in a rural or semi-rural environment and in relatively small, compact communities. Official statistics are notoriously misleading, but no amount of reclassification or readjustment of them can escape from these ineluctable facts. Population figures rest on the arbitrary (and increasingly misleading) definition of "rural population" as all those living in communes whose chief center contained fewer than 2,000 inhabitants. This clearly included many whose occupation was not farming. Just as clearly it omitted many others, living in towns slightly larger than 2,000 inhabitants, whose occupation was farming. So "rural" cannot be equated with "agricultural" in handling such figures, although erroneous inclusions and omissions no doubt often nearly cancel out. But round figures on even this rough basis give the following rate of change, which is reliable enough as an index of the shift of emphasis.

	Total Population	Rural Population	Percentage
1846	35,400,000*	26,750,000*	75.6
1876	36,900,000	24,900,000	67.6
1906	39,250,000	22,700,000	57.9
1936	41,900,000	19,900,000	47.6

* The totals in 1846 included Alsace-Lorraine

The broad picture was that before 1846 the main increase in total population had been an increase in rural population; between 1846 and 1872 the rural population remained almost stationary; after

1876 it declined absolutely as well as relatively. Since French farmers, collectively, could amply feed the whole nation, with a surplus to export in payment of manufactured goods, industry until
the First World War remained to a considerable extent small-
scale and widely dispersed. France became a predominantly
industrial state only between the two world wars. This basic self-
sufficiency and belated industrialization proved a benefit, in that the
world economic depression hit France later and less severely, measured in terms of mass unemployment, than it hit other more highly
industrialized economies. Since farming itself was based largely
on the unit of the small and medium-sized peasant holding, the
"farming lobby" of the Third Republic was always its largest and
often its most effective. Most deputies represented rural constituencies, and the Senate blatantly over-represented the countryside
as against the towns.

Given the economic and political importance of the French
countryside, and of agriculture in particular, it was natural that
much attention should be paid nationally to the interests and problems of the land. A recession in farming, a run of bad harvests
and epidemics, was treated as a token of national disaster and even
national decline. Most public issues—military conscription, public
education, fiscal and commercial policies, major public works—
were seen first, and at times exclusively, in relation to the interests
of the "rural population." Economists, sociologists, even moralists,
debated tirelessly the merits of the small and medium-sized farming
unit as against the large, more highly capitalized unit. The 38,000
communes of France—each with its mayor and municipal council
—were the social and, in many ways, the political unit of French
national life. During the Third Republic more than 30,000 of them
had populations of less than 1,500. Yet each had one senatorial
elector (representing it on electoral colleges), while Paris had
only thirty senatorial electors to represent its population of around
three million. Domestic politics never lost something of the flavor
of parish-pump politics.

The coincidence in time of political and economic revolutions
helped to produce and to perpetuate the multi-party system. Old
issues went unsettled (anticlericalism) side by side with new issues
raised by industrialism (relations of capital and labor). As there
was no necessary or inherent connection between such issues as
anticlericalism in education and socialism in industry, no clear-cut
or simple party alignment was possible. Live political issues cut

across one another, making a kaleidoscope of shifting patterns rather than any durable alignments. These were the years when modern French political parties were taking shape, building up local organizations, and seeking ideological definition (see Part III, D). And the consequent multi-party spectrum, together with an incorrigible propensity toward fragmentation and "independence," compelled the parliamentary representative system to work in a particular way. Ministries were at the mercy of temporary party coalitions within the assemblies, and were overthrown mercilessly whenever one of the marginal groups participating in the majority coalition decided to abandon it. Ministries lived for an average of nine months each before 1920, only six months each after 1920. No devices of proportional representation or obligatory dissolution could much improve the system. It was the consequence of having many differing standpoints about the burning issues of politics. For that reason, Part III has been devoted to "Conflicts within Society."

As regards the notorious ministerial instability of the Third Republic, however, two qualifications must be added. Frequent ministerial changes, far from being invented by the Republic, had been almost equally common under the monarchy before and after 1789, and had even been a feature of the Second Empire. And modern research has shown certain built-in compensatory elements even during the interwar years. As ministries fell more often, the same names reappeared in them more inevitably, so that the balance of "stability" was redressed.[3] Secondly, partly as a consequence of cabinet fragility, executive power tended to be increased by other means—by grants of plenary or emergency powers, authority to issue decree-laws, and greater dependence on the permanent civil service. However regrettable were such trends from the point of view of theories of representative government, it must not be assumed that the power at the disposal of governments was thereby diminished. As William Pickles has remarked, "The powers of the French executive *as a whole* have steadily increased under every regime, not excluding that of the Fourth Republic."[4]

It was characteristic that the largest sectional interests seldom

---

[3] J. Ollé-Laprune, *La stabilité des ministres sous la troisième république 1879–1940* (Paris, 1962), p. 73.
[4] W. Pickles, *The French Constitution, October 4, 1958* (London, 1960), p. 47.

coincided with particular parties. The Radical and Radical-Socialist Party took pride in representing the "little man" in farming,
industry, and trade. It did so neither inclusively nor exclusively.
Just as factory workers might support the Radicals or parties still
further to the "Right," rather than the Socialists or Communists,
so small peasant proprietors might vote Socialist or Communist.
The stubborn refusal of Frenchmen to make class and political
divisions coincide, in part a consequence of the double and simultaneous "revolution" taking place, was in some respects a source
of great strength to the parliamentary system. The intellectual
Socialist leader, Léon Blum, was deputy for Narbonne, a constituency of wine-growers and well-to-do peasant landowners. But if
clashes of sectional economic interest were thus prevented from
being too stark, the penalty was that, being blurred, they were
too seldom or too belatedly resolved. Hence, among other reasons,
the notorious *immobilisme* of the Third Republic.

In French industry the traditions and outlooks of the artisan and
the skilled craftsman survived surprisingly long. Only after the
concentrated industrialization caused by urgent national needs
during the First World War did the French fully develop their
mining and metallurgical industries. The silent social revolution
of 1914 to 1918 was the displacement of the prewar industrial
worker, technically skilled, alertly intelligent, and politically indi-
vidualist, by the "hands" of mass production, herded into the big
towns and including in their ranks many thousands of foreign
immigrants. Even so, in fine craftsmanship and versatile individual
precision work, France remained one of the great workshops of
the world. Labor organizations, reflecting the fissiparous tendencies
of French life as a whole, failed to find the cohesion and mass basis
which alone could have enabled them to offset the inherent bias
of the constitutional and administrative system in favor of the
peasantry and of the countryside.

Nevertheless, under the combined pressure of the new Left,
the experience of economic depressions and deep social hardship,
and paternalist habits of *étatisme*, the State in France in the twentieth century increasingly assumed responsibility for setting up and
running social services and promoting greater social security. Part
III, D illustrates some of the aims and the means adopted to achieve
them. Since social legislation is often immensely detailed and cum-
bersome, it has been possible to give only the main operative articles

of some laws; but they usually state the purpose and method aptly enough. The "Popular Front" Program of 1936 was sensational only because it could list so many important objectives of this kind still unrealized, and because the victory of the *Rassemblement populaire* in the general elections betokened that the reforms listed would be carried out. It is noteworthy that not one of the reforms then introduced, other than the 40-hour working week, was subsequently undone. It is equally important that many can be traced back to the early years of the century, when Georges Clemenceau played the role in French welfare legislation which David Lloyd George played in Britain of the same years. But the reforms most effectively implemented were those taken up by the powerful administrative bureaucracy, and these were inevitably limited in scope and purpose.[5]

* * *

The questions which preoccupied public debate as burning issues inevitably changed drastically after 1871, and again after 1918. After the Bonapartist *coup* of 1851 the theme of opposition to the régime was mainly constitutional, with monarchist opposition increasingly giving way to republican. So strong was the undercurrent of republicanism that "the Republic under the Empire," the positivist world of intellectuals and *salons*, became almost an entity in itself. But it was so unpractical and idealized an entity that later, in the disillusioned days of Gambettist "opportunism," it was possible to exclaim, "How beautiful was the Republic—under the Empire!" The harsh realities of the Government of National Defense, and of the protracted struggle to define the institutions of the new Republic between 1871 and 1875, may help to explain why the new régime did, in the end, survive longer than any other since 1789.

After 1871 the dominant motif of public sentiment was revenge —and recovery of the lost provinces of Alsace and Lorraine, which Bismarck annexed in the Treaty of Frankfurt. Military reorganization, public finance, even the new educational system were all strongly influenced by the burning desire to reverse the fortunes of 1870 and 1871. For the next two decades at least, this mood was so prevalent that the theatrical General Boulanger could

[5] For the whole range see J. M. Jeanneney and M. Perrot, *Textes de droit économique et social français, 1789-1957* (Paris, 1957).

ride the wave of public enthusiasm as *"Général Revanche,"* and could attain a personal following large and alarming enough to menace parliamentary government. Moralists like Ernest Renan ruminated gloomily on the lessons to be learned from France's defeat by Germany, and men of letters indulged in one of those periodic heart-searchings which national crisis commonly elicits in France (see Part III, D).

They had hardly emerged from this when the much fiercer storm of the Dreyfus Affair burst upon the land. The issues of the Affair were many. They ranged from the first single issue of whether an innocent man had been wrongfully condemned to a frontal collision between the military power and the claim of civilian society that injustice must not be tolerated even in the name of national security or the "honor of the Army." Boulangists and anti-Dreyfusards were alike products of a system of compulsory military service, which rested on the French revolutionary doctrine of "the Nation in Arms." This system, justified on the traditional Jacobin grounds that every citizen of the Republic has the duty to defend the nation when it is in danger and therefore must be subjected to extended periods of compulsory military training and service in the reserves, lent itself to great abuse. It placed excessive power in the hands of the High Command and the General Staff. In reaction, Republicans of the Left began to denounce the wastefulness and demoralization of the barracks, and the Socialist leader Jean Jaurès pointed to the attractive example of the Swiss system (Document 56). The holocaust of 1914 seemed, however, to prove the need for mass armies, and only the occasional critic, such as Charles de Gaulle (Document 57), questioned their adequacy.

Closely interwoven with the disputes about military power and its limits were reinvigorated versions of the conflicts between clericalism and anticlericalism which had beset every régime since the Civil Constitution of the Clergy of 1790. Under the Second Empire, Napoleon's foreign policy had been repeatedly under the necessity of trying to placate both Roman Catholics and Liberals simultaneously. Napoleon's decline and fall were largely due to the proven impossibility of this task: the "Roman Question" proved insoluble. Establishment of the Italian Kingdom, with Rome as its capital, and the outcome of the Vatican Council of 1870 made for a permanent split between the Church and any liberal State, not least the Third Republic. After 1879, when the "Republic of the Republicans" came into being (in the sense that President, Senate, and Chamber first came simultaneously into the control of the Republican Party), France experienced its counterpart to the contemporary *Kulturkampf* in Germany. The laws setting up secular education and attacking clerical influence over the young provoked bitter and vulgar controversy on both sides. The village *curé* and the village schoolteacher became symbols of a revived national schism, striking deep into the heart of French society. The attacks on the religious orders, and the eventual separation of Church and State in 1905, seemed an almost natural continuation of the process (Part III, C). Rash participation of leading churchmen on the army side in the Dreyfus Affair contributed to the final breach.

The more far-reaching industrial changes mentioned above, and the intense national tragedy of the First World War, produced some reunification of spirit. The notion of *union sacrée* might, conceivably, have survived the war itself had not a new force of division appeared—communism. The ranks of parliamentary socialism, newly and fragilely united by Jaurès shortly before the outbreak of war and his own assassination in 1914, were now confronted with the famous "Twenty-One Conditions" of orthodox Bolshevik communism (Document 75). The irreparable breach between socialism and communism, then affirmed, was permanently to weaken the Left between the wars in its resistance to the new menace of paramilitary leagues and fascist activists. Even the Popular Front was only a working electoral alliance between Communists and the other parties of the Left and Left-Center, and in 1936 no Communists assumed ministerial office under Blum.

Although the prevalent burning issues in this way changed over the years, there was usually some linkage between them. Memories of the Paris Commune of 1871, and of excesses perpetrated by both *communards* and the governmental troops, persisted during the decades of *revanche;* and the question of an amnesty for exiled or imprisoned *communards* kept those memories alive throughout the 1870's. Socialists and Communists were almost inevitably anticlericals, despite the *Ralliement* and the rise of small "Social Catholic" movements sharing in socialistic ideals. These considerations are a warning against loose use of the fateful labels "Left" and "Right" in these years.

In important ways the two labels even exchanged general con-
notations. In the 1890's the Right was anti-Semitic on the grounds
that Jews (e.g., Dreyfus) betrayed secrets to the Germans, or
brought financial disaster to French investors (e.g., Cornelius
Herz in the Panama scandal). In the 1930's the Right showed itself anti-Semitic again, but for quite different reasons: it was opposed to communism and by now it believed in *rapprochement*
with Germany. In the 1870's the Left set the pace in passionate
revanchard politics, and Boulanger was a "good republican" general. In the 1920's the Left was in part pacifistic, seeking international pacification and conciliation, and the very opposite of
intransigent and chauvinistic. Even eminent individuals underwent
a sea-change. Charles Maurras, voice of the *Action française*, was
militantly anti-Dreyfusard and anti-German in 1900: in 1940 he
supported Marshal Pétain in making an Armistice with Germany
and backed Vichy's so-called "National Revolution." Pierre Laval,
who entered politics on the extreme Left and was the youngest
Socialist in the new Chamber of 1914, in 1940 became a key figure
in the régime at Vichy.

André Siegfried has spoken of the *toujours à gauche* of French
political life—others of its *sinistrisme* or Leftward drift, as manifest
in the affection of conservative parties for left-wing labels. Republicans are the Conservatives, Radicals the moderate Liberals,
Socialists the S.F.I.O. or "French Section of the Workers' International," and so on. If we look behind labels to the contents, we
might more aptly speak of the *dextrisme*, or Rightward drift. The
"moderate" party of each generation, once satisfied, tended to join
the ranks of the Conservatives and so moved to the "Right." The
Republicans of the 1870's, content with the new parliamentary
system, became the Conservatives of the next decade. The Radicals of the 1880's, satisfied by the triumphs of anticlericalism
and anti-militarism, became the Conservatives of the early years
of the twentieth century. The Radical-Socialists, satisfied with
the mild social reforms of the prewar years, joined the Right-
Center of the interwar period. This accumulative recruitment of
moderates to the forces resisting further change, while not peculiar
to France, has been a strikingly recurrent process there. No
doubt it acted as a reinforcement of the propensity for inertia and
immobilisme. The documents on political parties do not attempt
to do more than illustrate shifts of emphasis in their programs

and manifestoes that reveal such tendencies. To deal with all parties exhaustively, or with any one exhaustively, would transcend the purpose of this volume.

* * *

More must be said about French foreign policy in these years. Except for the first two decades, when the Italian Question loomed larger in French concern, by far the dominant anxiety was the power and purposes of Germany. The unification of Italy and Germany by 1871 fundamentally changed the distribution and balance of power in Europe. Thenceforth, as Bismarck foresaw, the two new states of central Europe, instead of constituting in some measure a power vacuum within which the policies of the major powers could operate to their own advantage, could now themselves manipulate the balance of power. With the overriding aim of securing his gains and preventing France from finding allies in her plans for a war of revenge, Bismarck operated on the principle he expounded to the Russian Ambassador Saburov: "Nobody wants to be in a minority. All politics reduce themselves to this formula: try to be à trois in a world governed by five Powers." The five, as he saw them in the 1870's, were Russia, Austria-Hungary, Germany, Italy, and France. He accepted the likelihood of British isolation. His League of Three Emperors (the Dreikaiserbund), which he forged in 1873, was designed to rally Russia and Austria-Hungary to his side and achieve this most desirable unbalance in his favor. Despite his further Dual Alliance with Austria-Hungary in 1879, the Dreikaiserbund broke down, and in 1893 Russia entered into an entente with France.

Italy, with which he made a treaty in 1882, was a weak and unreliable substitute for Russia, and by 1907 France, Russia, and Great Britain had formed the Triple Entente, aligned against the Triple Alliance of Germany, Austria-Hungary, and Italy. Far from being à trois in a world of five powers, Germany was now the heart of one of two rival and nearly equal Great Power alliances, engaged in feverish competition and beset with anxieties. The system of rival alliances, which led straight to the War of 1914, had not been intended by anyone. It was the outcome of the interaction of Bismarckian policies for isolating France with skillful French diplomacy working to prevent such isolation. It was so directly the consequence of the terms of the Treaty of

Frankfurt of 1871 that the text of this Treaty is given in full (Document 85).

After the ordeal and losses of the First World War, which nevertheless restored Alsace and Lorraine to France (this had been the eighth of President Woodrow Wilson's Fourteen Points), French policy was concerned above all with establishing security. Deprived of the material guarantee for which Marshal Foch had pressed—possession of the left bank of the Rhine—and also of the diplomatic guarantees from the United States and Britain, in expectation of which the claim to the Rhineland had been abandoned, the French remained restlessly and nervously the chief "consumers of security" in Europe. Alliances with Poland and the states of the Little Entente (Czechoslovakia, Yugoslavia and Rumania), Locarno Pacts, League of Nations provisions, all these still left her incorrigibly anxious. By insisting that greater security must precede substantial disarmament, against the favorite British thesis that security was unobtainable without greater disarmament, France strained the working relationship with Britain upon which the success of her European policies—as indeed of the League of Nations itself—depended. Yet they remained allies throughout the ordeals of the Spanish Civil War and of the Munich Agreement, into war itself in 1939.

In June, 1940, faced with the collapse of her armies before the invading German forces, France withdrew from the war. The government of Marshal Pétain signed an Armistice with Germany on June 22, and with Italy on June 24. The rump of the National Assembly, meeting at Vichy on July 10, agreed by 569 votes against 80, with 50 absentions, to confer power on Pétain to promulgate "the new Constitution of the French State." This was the end of the Third Republic and the foundation of the Vichy Government, which, under the terms of the Armistice, remained the nominal government of France during the German occupation.

The seventy-year span of the Third Republic thus had a curiously rounded existence. Born of the German victory at Sedan and the abdication of the Emperor Napoleon III in September, 1870, it died after another German breakthrough at Sedan in May, 1940, which led to the abdication of the last government of the Republic. It was born and it died amid the sound of gunfire at Sedan, amid cries of betrayal and abdication, in an agony of national humiliation. Just as doctrines of "a Nation in Arms" and preparations for war haunted its development, so wars punctuated its history.

The sense that foreign policy and national security were of crucial importance led to two remarkable phenomena which modified the generalizations usually made about the system of government. One was that changes of régime and frequent changes of ministry did not prevent great continuity in foreign policy. One or two foreign ministers of the Second Empire—a Drouyn de Lhuys and a Count Walewski—held the office for a run of years, but overriding continuity was provided by the emperor himself and (though more disputably) the influence of the empress. The Third Republic displayed two remarkable instances. During the critical years between 1898 and 1905, when the domestic scene was dominated by the Dreyfus turmoil and the Church-State controversy, six ministries succeeded one another; but throughout the whole period Théophile Delcassé remained at the Foreign Office, forging the Franco-British Entente. Again, from April, 1925, until January, 1932, despite fourteen ministerial reshuffles, Aristide Briand was at the Quai d'Orsay continuously except for four days, and strove to solve the problems of national security in a world setting. Seven years may not be a long spell for one minister to control foreign policy, but it is very much longer than the general political record of the Republic would superficially suggest, and comparisons with Britain or the United States show few examples of greater continuity. Continuity came also, it should be added, from the long services of Quai d'Orsay officials, such as Alexis Saint-Léger, who entered the foreign ministry in 1904 and was its Secretary-General from 1933 until 1940.

The other phenomenon was that three times over, in moments of acute national crisis, France turned for salvation to a veteran father-figure. In 1871 it was to Adolphe Thiers, then seventy-three, who governed the nation with so much vigor that he paid off the indemnity and got German troops of occupation off French soil some two years early. In 1917 it was to Georges Clemenceau, aged seventy-six, who forthwith reinvigorated the whole war effort and became, by general acclaim, the Father of Victory. In 1940 it was to Marshal Pétain, aged eighty-four, who lent the aura of the Hero of Verdun to the Armistice arrangements and the Vichy Government. A régime chronically short of reserves of credit and esteem invoked, in the final resort, the only reserve of national credit left to it—esteem for a well-known veteran statesman or soldier. In so doing, it achieved astonishing feats of continuity, for by exalting to decisive power in time of crisis men who personified the past, they inevitably brought the past to bear upon the future. Thiers worked for a "conservative republic" because he clung to Orleanist parliamentary ideas. Clemenceau, presiding over the Paris Conference in 1919, was vindictive to Germany because he personally remembered 1870. Pétain in 1940 was defeatist because he not only remembered 1914, but 1870 as well—he had been a boy of fourteen at the time of the first Sedan.

Is the story then one of defeats and losses, decline and fall, of a once great nation overreaching its grasp? French history as a whole does not support this view. Its systematic refutation would require examination of many aspects of national life and achievement barely touched on in these documents and lying beyond their scope. The Second Empire enchanted Europe with its gaiety and wit, dazzled it with its technology and public works, but much of the creative work of the time came from the rebels and critics—Victor Hugo in exile, Baudelaire and Flaubert, Daumier and Manet. Its taste may be condemned, in general, as philistine, especially in music and painting. But the Third Republic brought remarkable cultural and artistic efflorescence in many different fields. In science, there were Marcellin Berthelot and the Curies, Louis Pasteur and Claude Bernard, all of whose work brought much help to suffering humanity; in painting, the whole impressionist school, which had come to birth under the Empire, in music the galaxy of Debussy, Ravel, and Fauré, in poetry the symbolists. These names betokened a society unusually rich in vitality and creativeness, in what its most illustrious philosopher, Henri Bergson, called *élan vital*. It was a society vibrating with energy, full of character and color, the very opposite of the hesitant, nervous entity sometimes depicted. It had undeniable qualities of greatness and of durable civilization.

But refutation of despondent estimates of twentieth-century France lies even closer at hand—in its speedy and ebullient resurgence since the middle of the century.

France, which from the 1920's until the 1950's could be regarded as "the sick man of Europe," became by the 1960's one of the most dynamic, purposeful, and successful states in western Europe. This dramatic reversal of fortunes, which lies beyond the scope of this volume, should serve as warning enough against easy judgments about this most volatile of nations. From the 1860's onwards, it may be said, Europe "grew away" from France, in the sense that France began to lose all the advantages she had previously enjoyed *vis-à-vis* her European neighbors. Germany, in particular, developed at a rate and on economic foundations so vastly superior to the French that the balance of power was upset. In the eventual armed conflict, France was saved partly by her own sacrifices but also by the redressing of the balance by intervention of the two great flanking powers of Europe, the British Commonwealth and Russia, and ultimately by help from the United States. The new balance could be held against German resurgence only by a continuing and active concert of the victorious powers. This was prevented by a whole series of events: the Bolshevik Revolution, United States isolationism, cross-purposes with Britain, decline in French national *élan* and power, the upsurge of Nazism. When the unbalance was fully operative, France was among its first victims, accompanied by Czechoslovakia, Poland, the Netherlands, Belgium, Denmark, and Norway, and nearly accompanied by the United Kingdom.

War, diplomacy, and the balance of power in Europe so greatly dominated the evolution of France in these years that there are few issues of domestic politics which do not link up with those of foreign affairs. Yet it would be wrong to neglect the tussles on the home front that were fought for their own sakes. The Liberal L. A. Prévost-Paradol, writing in 1868, suggested that since 1789 France had been a democratic society in search of a democratic form of government.[6] It was certainly not as simple as that. Yet there was a constant antiphony in the interaction between State and Society in these years which, it is hoped, the arrangement of these documents may help to demonstrate. The State sometimes takes the initiative (under pressure or persuasion)—as in passing Laws of Associations, or setting up a Ministry of Agriculture (Documents 35 and 45). At other moments occupational or interest groups engage in self-help (Documents 37 and 41). At still other moments, State and Society combine and cooperate to common ends (Documents 36 and 49). Other excerpts have been included chiefly to exemplify particular attitudes (e.g., Documents

[6] L. A. Prévost-Paradol, *La France nouvelle* (Paris, 1868); a book much read and discussed by politicians and others in 1870 after Sedan.

51, 55, 61, 70), for the fragmentation of French public opinion was one of its most important characteristics, despite moments of fervent national unity. The imminence—or the existence—of a disloyal majority under any régime was a factor of great importance. The Third Republic remained, as it had begun, "that form of government which divides Frenchmen least."

Chronology

CHRONOLOGY 1848 – 1940

YEAR		INTERNAL EVENTS	EXTERNAL EVENTS		YEAR
1848	Dec.	Louis Napoleon elected President of Second Republic	Year of Revolutions		1848
1849	May	Legislative Assembly elected	Fall of Roman Republic	July	1849
1850	Mar.	Falloux Law on Education	Repression in Italy, Germany, Austria-Hungary		1850
	May	Electoral Law reduces electorate			
1851	Dec.	Louis Napoleon's *coup d'état*; endorsed by plebiscite			
1852	Jan.	Constitution modelled on First Empire			1852
		Reorganization of banking (*Crédit foncier, Crédit mobilier* founded); *Bon Marché* stores in Paris			
	Nov.	Plebiscite on Empire			
	Dec.	Empire proclaimed			
1853	Jan.	Napoleon III marries Eugénie de Montijo			1853
1854			Crimean War (–1856)	March	1854
1855		Universal Exhibition in Paris	Fall of Sebastopol	Sept.	1855
1856			Congress and Treaty of Paris	March	1856
1857					1857
1858	Jan.	Orsini bomb plot	Pact of Plombieres (Napoleon III and Cavour)	July	1858
1859			Franco-Austrian War – Villafranca	Apr.	1859
			Ferdinand de Lesseps begins making Suez Canal		
1860			Chevalier-Cobden Commercial Treaty	Jan.	1860
			France annexes Savoy and Nice		
1861			Mexican War (–1867)	Oct.	1861
1862			Occupation of Cochin-China, Cambodia (–1867)		1862

GENERAL TRENDS

ECONOMIC

POLITICAL — Government (1857–1870); Autocratic Government (1851–1857)

SOCIAL — 1890: Great Exhibitions

COLONIAL — Interests (1855–1870)

FOREIGN POLICY — Assertions of Prestige and European Influence; End of Age

INTERNATIONAL — European Wars (1854–1870); of Revolutions

Timeline chart (1863–1874)

Date	Events (international)
1863	Polish Revolt against Russia
1864	First International founded; Prussian-Danish War (Schleswig-Holstein)
1865	Occupation of Saigon
1866	Austro-Prussian War; Sadowa alarms France
1867	French troops leave Mexico; Maximilian shot
1868	
1869	Suez Canal opened
July 1870	Franco-Prussian War
Sept. 1870	Battle of Sedan
Jan. 1871	Armistice with Bismarck
Feb. 1871	Preliminary Treaty of Peace
May 1871	Treaty of Frankfurt; loss of Alsace-Lorraine
1872	
June 1873	Bismarck's "Dreikaiserbund"
March 1874	Protectorate over Annam

Phase o —————————→ ←—————————

Little Overseas Interest (1870–1879) ←———— ————→ Active Colonial Expansion — Overseas

Policies of Public Works, Paternalist Expenditure, Etc. (1848–

Increasingly Libera... ←———— ————→ Provisional Regimes (1870–1875)

Period of Economic Expansion; High Prices (1853–1874) ————————→

Date	Events (domestic France)
Oct. 1863	Rouher replaces Persigny as minister; Crédit lyonnais
1864	Comité des forges formed
1865	Educational reforms; Victor Duruy
1866	
1867	Universal Exhibition in Paris; Crisis of Crédit mobilier
1868	Press laws relaxed
Jan. 1869	Emile Ollivier forms government ("Liberal Empire")
May 1870	Gambetta's Belleville Manifesto
May 1870	Plebiscite on constitutional changes
Sept. 1870	Napoleon III abdicates; Republic proclaimed; Provisional Government set up in Paris
Feb. 1871	Elections for National Assembly
Feb. 1871	Thiers made "Chief of the Executive Power"
Mar. 1871	Paris Commune
Aug. 1871	Rivet Law creates title, "President of the French Republic"
1872	
Jan. 1873	Death of Napoleon III; German troops leave France as indemnity is paid
May 1873	Marshal MacMahon succeeds Thiers (Septennate)
Oct. 1873	Letter of Comte de Chambord, renouncing tricolor
1874	

YEAR	EXTERNAL EVENTS
1875	War scare
1876	
1877	
1878	Congress of Berlin
1879	
1880	
1881	Treaty of Bardo; Protectorate over Tunisia; Protectorate over Upper Niger
1882	
1883	Protectorate over Tonkin
1884	Protectorate over Tonkin

GENERAL TRENDS

INTERNATIONAL ——— Period of General Peace, Occasional Tensions (1871–1890)

FOREIGN POLICY — and Revenge for 1871 (1871–1890) (Fear of Diplomatic Isolation)

COLONIAL

SOCIAL

POLITICAL — Republic on Trial (1876–1879) — Republicanism (1879–1895)

ECONOMIC — (1875–1896)

YEAR		INTERNAL EVENTS
1875		Constitutional Laws creating Third Republic
1876	Feb.–Mar.	Republican gains in general elections
1877	May	Crisis of *Seize mai* (President MacMahon)
	June	Chamber of Deputies dissolved
	Sept.	Death of Adolphe Thiers
	Oct.	Republicans keep a majority in Chamber elections
	Dec.	President MacMahon's letter of surrender
1878		Universal Exhibition in Paris; *Union générale* founded; Louis Pasteur's work on vaccines
1879	Jan.	Republicans win Senate elections; President MacMahon resigns; Jules Grévy President
1880		Amnesty for *communards*: Jesuits expelled
1881		Laws establish free primary education; freedom of press and public meeting extended
1882	Feb.	Collapse of *Union générale*; *Ligue des patriotes* founded
	Dec.	Death of Léon Gambetta
1883		Congress of Mutual Aid Societies (Lyons)
	Aug.	Death of Comte de Chambord
1884		Laws on Associations

Timeline Chart, 1885–1895

Foreign and Colonial Affairs

1885	Treaty of Tientsin with China
1886	
1887	Indochinese Union formed
1888	
1889	Second International founded
1890	Treaty with Britain—Lake Chad
1891	Protectorate over Madagascar; Papal Encyclical *Rerum novarum* (Leo XIII)
1892	Annexation of Ivory Coast (Dahomey)
1893	Entente with Russia
1894	Capture of Timbuktu
1895	Alliance with Russia; French West Africa set up

Period Bars

- Rivalry and Mounting Fears (1890–1918)
- Preparedness (1890–1914)* — National Recovery*
- Very Active Colonial Expansion; Scramble for Africa and Far East (1879–1911)
- Syndicalist, Socialist; Dreyfus (1890–1914)
- "Republic of the Republicans" — Moderate "Opportunist"
- Period of Slow Economic Growth; Low Prices

Domestic Affairs

1885		Protective Tariffs; Electoral Law (*scrutin de liste*)
1886		First *Bourse du travail* in Paris; Strikes at Decazeville and Vierzon; Pasteur Institute founded in Paris
1887	Jan.	Boulangist agitation
	Dec.	President Grévy resigns—"Wilson scandal"; Sadi Carnot elected President
1888		
1889		Universal Exhibition in Paris (Eiffel Tower)
	Oct.	End of Boulangist agitation; Republican gains in general elections
1890	Nov.	*Ralliement* begins: Cardinal Lavigerie's toast
1891		Big strikes, anarchist outrages
1892		Méline Tariffs; Mineowners' Central Committee formed; National Federation of *Bourses du travail*
	Nov.	Panama Canal scandal
1893		49 Radical-Socialists and Socialists elected
1894	June	President Sadi Carnot assassinated; Casimir-Périer elected President; Lumière brothers make first films
	Dec.	Dreyfus Affair begins
1895	Jan.	President Casimir-Périer resigns; Félix Faure elected President; *Confédération générale du travail* (C.G.T.) formed
	June	

EXTERNAL EVENTS

YEAR		EXTERNAL EVENTS
1896		Agreement with Britain about Siam
		Annexation of Madagascar
1897		Franco-German Convention about Togo
1898	June	Delcassé becomes Foreign Minister
		Anglo-French Convention about Nigeria
		Lease of Kwangchow Wan from China
1899	Sept.	Fashoda incident
1900		Emile Loubet elected President
1901		Secret Treaty with Italy
1902		
1903		
1904	Apr.	Anglo-French Entente
1905	June	Delcassé resigns as Foreign Minister
1906		Conference of Algeciras
1907		Anglo-Russian Entente
1908		Austria annexes Bosnia-Herzegovina
1909		
1910	Jan.	French Equatorial Africa set up
1911		Agadir Crisis

GENERAL TRENDS

INTERNATIONAL — System of Rival Alliances, Phase of

FOREIGN POLICY — Making of Alliances, Military

COLONIAL

SOCIAL — Violent Social Schism—Anticlerical,

POLITICAL — Radical Republicanism; Anticlericalism; Dreyfus
Rise of Socialist Movements (1895–1913)

ECONOMIC — Moderate Economic Growth; High Prices (1896–1913)

INTERNAL EVENTS

YEAR		INTERNAL EVENTS
1896		St. Mandé Program
1897	Dec.	"Cadenas Law" on Bank of France
1898	Jan.	Émile Zola's "J'accuse" letter
		Comité de l'Action française formed
1899	Feb.	Emile Loubet elected President
	June	Waldeck-Rousseau ministry formed
1901	July	Law concerning Contract of
		Associations
		First Radical Party Congress
1902	May	Electoral gains of Bloc républicain;
		Combes ministry
1903		Shipowners' Central Committee formed
1904		L'Humanité founded as Socialist organ
		Ten-hour Day Law
1905		Socialist Party (S.F.I.O.) founded
	Dec.	Law of Separation of Church and State
1906		Charter of Amiens
		Rehabilitation of Dreyfus:
		end of Dreyfus Affair
1907		Radical Congress at Nancy:
		aims redefined
1908		Georges Sorel's Réflexions sur la violence
		Anatole France's L'île des pingouins
1909		Extensive strikes
1910		Railway strikes; labor agitation
1911		Jean Jaurès' L'Armée nouvelle

Mar. 1912	Protectorate over Morocco
1913	
Aug. 1914	First World War begins
1915	
1916	
1917	Bolshevik Revolution; entry of U.S.A. into war
Jan. 1918	Wilson's Fourteen Points
Nov.	Armistice with Germany
1919	Paris Conference; Treaties of Peace Covenant of League of Nations
1920	
Feb. 1921	Treaty of Alliance with Poland
Feb. 1922	Washington Conference: naval disarmament
Apr.	Treaty of Rapallo: Germany and Soviet Union
Jan. 1923	Occupation of Ruhr
July	Treaty of Lausanne with Turkey

Sacrifice for Victory

Increasing Strains of War

Union Sacrée; Wartime Government

New Industries; High Prices; Franc Weak — *Rapid Industrial Growth (War Needs)*

1912	Jan.	Poincaré ministry formed
1913	July	Law of Secret Ballot
	Aug.	Three-years' military service required
1914	June	Viviani ministry formed
	July	Jean Jaurès assassinated; general mobilization
	Sept.	Battle of the Marne
1915	Oct.	Aristide Briand ministry formed
1916	Feb.	Battle of Verdun begins
	July	Battle of Somme
1917		Strikes and mutinies
		Income tax introduced
	Nov.	Georges Clemenceau forms ministry — "I make war"
1918		
1919	Nov.	Victory of *Bloc national* at elections General Confederation of French Production formed
1920	Jan.	Paul Deschanel elected President
	Sept.	Alexandre Millerand elected President, on Deschanel's illness
	Dec.	Conference of Tours; Communist Party splits from Socialist Party (Twenty-One Conditions)
1921	Dec.	C.G.T.U. splits from C.G.T.
1922	Jan.	Poincaré forms ministry
1923		

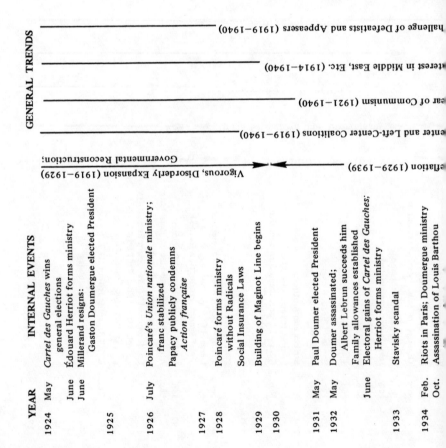

YEAR	INTERNAL EVENTS	GENERAL TRENDS	EXTERNAL EVENTS	YEAR
1924 May	Cartel des Gauches wins general elections		Treaty of Alliance with Czechoslovakia	Jan. 1924
June	Édouard Herriot forms ministry			
June	Millerand resigns: Gaston Doumergue elected President			
1925			Evacuation of Ruhr / Revolt in Syria / Locarno Pacts	1925 / Dec.
1926 July	Poincaré's Union nationale ministry; franc stabilized / Papacy publicly condemns Action française		Treaty of Alliance with Rumania	June 1926
1927			Treaty of Alliance with Yugoslavia	Nov. 1927
1928	Poincaré forms ministry without Radicals / Social Insurance Laws		Briand-Kellogg Pact	Aug. 1928
1929	Building of Maginot Line begins		World economic crisis breaks	1929
1930			Briand's Memorandum on European Union / Evacuation of Rhineland	May 1930 / June
1931 May	Paul Doumer elected President		Japanese attack on Manchuria	Sept. 1931
1932 May	Doumer assassinated; Albert Lebrun succeeds him / Family allowances established		Stresa Conference / Franco-Soviet Non-Aggression Pact	Sept. 1932 / Nov.
June	Electoral gains of Cartel des Gauches; Herriot forms ministry			
1933	Stavisky scandal		Hitler becomes Chancellor of German Reich	Jan. 1933
1934 Feb.	Riots in Paris; Doumergue ministry		Soviet Union admitted to League of Nations	Sept. 1934
Oct.	Assassination of Louis Barthou			

General Trends (spanning bands):

- First, Bolshevism, then Fascism (1919–1940)
- Challenge of Defeatists and Appeasers (1919–1940)
- Interest in Middle East, Etc. (1914–1940)
- Fear of Communism (1921–1940)
- Center and Left-Center Coalitions (1919–1940)
- Inflation (1929–1939)
- Vigorous, Disorderly Expansion (1919–1929); Governmental Reconstruction;

International (right column)

Jan. 1935	Saar plebiscite in favor of Germany
Mar.	Germany abrogates Part V of Treaty of Versailles
May	Franco-Soviet Pact
Oct.	Italian attack on Abyssinia; sanctions invoked
Dec.	Hoare-Laval proposals for appeasement of Italy
Mar. 1936	Germany remilitarizes Rhineland
May	Italy annexes Abyssinia
July	Civil War begins in Spain – "Nonintervention"
July 1937	Japan attacks China
Mar. 1938	German *Anschluss* with Austria
Sept.	Munich Agreement about Czechoslovakia
Mar. 1939	Germany occupies Bohemia and Moravia Spanish Civil War ends; Italy occupies Albania
Apr.	
Sept.	Second World War begins; *drôle de guerre* in West Poland divided between Germany and U.S.S.R.
June 1940	General de Gaulle emerges to lead "Free French"
June	Armistice with Germany and Italy Battle of Britain

Category bands

INTERNATIONAL ——— Increasing Collapse of System of Collective Security; Fears of

FOREIGN POLICY ——— Anxiety for "Security"; Maginot Line:

COLONIAL ——— Pride in Overseas Possessions-

SOCIAL ——— Increasing Tensions Between Right and Left:

POLITICAL — Right-Center Government | Popular Front (1936-1938) | Alternating Right-

ECONOMIC ——— Economic Depression:

France (left column)

1935 June	Pierre Laval ministry
1936 Mar.	C.G.T. and C.G.T.U. combine at Congress of Toulouse
May	Popular Front wins elections; Léon Blum ministry – "stay-in strikes"
June	Matignon Agreements
1937	Paris Exhibition: Cagoulard Plot exposed
1938 Apr.	Édouard Daladier forms ministry
1939	Daladier granted plenary powers Albert Lebrun re-elected President
Apr.	
Sept.	Daladier makes Communist Party illegal
1940 Mar.	Paul Reynaud succeeds Daladier; end of "phony war"
May	Battle of France begins; Dunkirk evacuation
June	Germans enter Paris; Reynaud succeeded by Pétain
July	National Assembly votes full power to Pétain; Vichy Government created

Part I: The State and Its Foundations

Section A:

Establishment of the Second Empire

The French state in 1850 was a Republic. Founded as recently as November, 1848, it had commonly been numbered as the Second in order to emphasize its affinity with the First Republic of 1792. The fashion of harking back to earlier régimes, of reenacting earlier epics, was well set. The Bourbon monarchs, Louis XVIII and Charles X, who came to the throne after the fall of Napoleon, had been "restored Bourbons" whose restoration ended abruptly in 1830 in favor of the upstart liberal "Orleanist" king, Louis Philippe. So, in 1848, when he in turn was overthrown, like his predecessors, by Paris intrigues and riots, there had been simple reversion to a Second Republic.

It was based on universal adult male suffrage, for a decree of the Provisional Government on March 5 suddenly increased the electorate from some 250,000 to some 9,000,000. It also separately attributed law-making power to a single elected National Assembly, and independent executive power to a popularly elected President. The legislature was the response to fears of returning to an absolute monarchy, the Presidency was prompted by the other dominant fear, of "Red" revolution and anarchy.

Had the makers of the new Republic been less blinded by these twin fears, they might have been more conscious of the inherent danger that a National Assembly and a President so separated in their functions and powers would almost certainly collide. Since each authority could claim to enjoy the expressed sanction of the sovereign electorate, conflict would almost certainly produce deadlock. The temptation to end deadlock by a *coup*, carried out by an ambitious President elected for four years at the expense of a divided parliamentary Assembly elected for three, when the President controlled the armed forces, could easily be foreseen. But the two doctrines of popular sovereignty and separation of powers—uneasily co-existing as long ago as the Declaration of the Rights of Man and of the Citizen of August, 1789—remained uneasy bedfellows in Chapter III of the Constitution of 1848:

Article 18. All public powers, whatever they may be, come from the people. They cannot be delegated by heredity.

Article 19.   The separation of powers is the first condition of a free
government.

In the first Presidential elections on December 10, 1848, Louis Napoleon, nephew of the great Napoleon, won 5,434,226 votes, well over
half the whole electorate and a majority of much more than double
that of all the other five candidates together. From the moment that a
Bonaparte was placed in this situation, it could be only a matter of
tactics and timing before a "Second Empire" replaced the ill-fated
"Second Republic." In the event, it took less than four years. An
electoral law of May 30, 1850, reduced the electorate again by some
three million. On December 2, 1851, Louis carried out an armed *coup*
which gained him virtually dictatorial power. A year later he completed
the transformation and was crowned Emperor Napoleon III.

The relative certainty with which these changes came about must be
explained by three main factors: the skill in propaganda and tactics of
Louis Napoleon himself; the misjudgments of him, and of the situation,
by his opponents, both monarchist and republican; and the social and
economic crises which led various classes to support his bid for power.
The documents which follow illustrate these three factors.

Document No. 1 is an extract from Louis Napoleon's exposition of
"Napoleonic Ideas," written in 1839 amid the wave of Bonapartist sentiment born of disillusion with the Orleanist monarchy of Louis Philippe,
in time for the transfer of the great Napoleon's ashes from St. Helena to
Paris. Document 2 expresses the conservative monarchist attitude of
the Duc de Broglie toward the *coup* of 1851, while Document 3 expresses the Marxist view. Both of these, it should be noted, attribute
much to the prevalent social and economic distress of the preceding
year. Document 4 is the text of the Constitution of June, 1852, which
resulted from these events and was the basic structure of the Second
Empire.

1. *"Napoleonic Ideas": Louis Napoleon (1839)*

Louis Napoleon (1808–1873), son of Napoleon's brother Louis, became head of the Bonaparte family in 1832 on the death of the Duke of
Reichstadt. In 1839 he wrote an exposition of the Bonapartist aims and
traditions, as part of his persistent campaign to restore the dynasty to
power in France. Fully exploiting the growing discontent with the
corrupt and cynical government of Louis Philippe and the signs of reviving nostalgic memories of imperial glory, he there outlined the
changes in the system of government which he believed France needed
and wanted. In 1840, seizing the opportunity offered by the king's decision to transfer the ashes of Napoleon from St. Helena to the In-
valides, Louis Napoleon published a new edition of the work, headed
from *Londres, 1840.* The extract contains his main account of the political reorganization he envisages. The Preamble to the eventual Con-

stitution of January, 1852 (December 4), has been described as "like a brief summary of *Des idées napoléoniennes*." The work, which went through many editions, was one of the cleverest pieces of political sales talk produced in the nineteenth century. The extract is from the edition of 1860 (Paris, Amyôt et Plon) pp. 92–100.

THE IDEA predominant in all the Emperor's internal establishments was the desire to found a civil order. France is surrounded by powerful neighbors. Since Henry IV she has been exposed to jealousy in Europe. She must have a large standing army in order to maintain her independence. This army is organized; it has colonels, generals, and marshals: but the rest of the nation is not, and besides this military hierarchy, besides these dignities to which fame brings such honor, there should also be civil dignities which have the same importance; otherwise, the government would always be liable to fall into the hands of some fortunate soldier. The United States provides a striking example of the drawbacks caused by weakness on the part of the civil authority. Although in that country there are none of the ferments of discord which will simmer for a long time still in Europe, yet because the central civil power there is weak, every independent organization gives rise to alarm, and to a feeling of being menaced. Not only military power is feared, but also the power of money, the Bank; hence there is party strife. The governor of the Bank could have more influence than the President; what is more, a victorious general would soon eclipse civil power. In the Italian republics, as well as in England, the aristocracy was the organized civil order; but since France has fortunately no longer any privileged bodies, one could achieve the same advantages through a democratic hierarchy without offending the principles of equality.

Let us examine from this point of view the constitutions of the Empire.

The principles on which the imperial laws were based are:

Civil equality, in accordance with the democratic principle.

Hierarchy, in accordance with the principles of order and stability.

Napoleon was the supreme Head of the State, the elected of the people, the representative of the nation. In his public acts the Emperor gloried in owing all to the French people alone. When, at the foot of the Pyrenees, surrounded by kings paying homage he meted out thrones and empires, he vigorously claimed the title of first representative of the people, although that had been expected to be the exclusive prerogative of the Legislative Body.

Imperial power alone is transmitted by hereditary right. There is no other hereditary post in France; all others are awarded on election or merit.

There are two Chambers: the Senate and the Legislative Body.

The Senate, more popular as a name than the Chamber of Peers, is composed of members proposed by the electoral colleges; one third only is left for nomination by the Emperor. It is presided over by a member appointed by the head of State; he watches over the maintenance of the constitution; he is the guarantor of individual freedom and liberty of the press. Since the Senate was, after the sovereign, the first power in the State, the Emperor had endeavoured, as far as circumstances permitted, to give it great importance; for when the influence exerted by the constituent bodies does not follow the order of their political hierarchy, it is evident proof that the constitution is not in harmony with public feeling; it is then like a machine in which the wheels do not rotate in the right order.

Moreover, in order to give the Senate influence, the idea of the Emperor was not to make it solely a court of justice, nor a refuge for all the ministers whom public opinion has condemned, but on the contrary to compose it from among all the leading men, and to make it the guardian and guarantor of all the freedoms of the nation.

In order to make the senators independent and to keep them closely connected with the provinces, there were established, in each district of the court of appeal, senatorial estates which yielded to the occupying senator a rent of 20,000 to 25,000 livres for life.

The Legislative Body is returned by the electoral colleges of the *départements;* the members of this body receive remuneration during its sessions.

It is essential at this point to describe the method of election introduced by Napoleon. In the constitution of the year VIII Sieyès[1] had invented a system of notabilities which removed all participation in the elections from the people. Although Sieyès, a former member of the Constituent Assembly, of the Convention and of the Directory, was a friend of liberty, he was obliged to act in this way through force of circumstance and in order to maintain

[1] Abbé Sieyès (1748–1836), famous constitution-monger of the Revolution.

the Republic; for, before 18 Fructidor, the electors returned Royalists to the Legislative Body: on that day they were driven out. Then came the turn of the Jacobins: 20 Floréal swept them aside. At the following elections they appeared to maintain their position and prepared to dispatch their rivals. So nothing was stable: each year brought the triumph of one party, as Thibaudeau himself said.

But the firm, national progress of the Consulate had already created a strong, compact France, and the vessel of State ran less risk of foundering on the two reefs which were always to be feared: the Terror and the Ancien Régime.

Napoleon, created life-consul, abolished Sieyès's lists of notabilities, and established cantonal assemblies composed of all the citizens domiciled in the canton. These assemblies appointed the members of the electoral colleges of *arrondissement* and *département*. Those eligible for the electoral colleges were to be the highest tax-payers in the *département*; but they could add ten members to the colleges of *arrondissement* and twenty members to the colleges of *département* who were not property owners, but selected from members of the Legion of Honour, or men who had rendered public services. The colleges presented two candidates for the vacant places in the Legislative Body; only the colleges of *département* proposed candidates for senators' places; one of the two candidates had to be chosen from outside the college which presented him.

In examining the spirit behind these laws, at a time when we were emerging from violent dissensions and when there was still the threat of war, at a time when the sincerest friends of liberty saw the need to restrict electoral rights, one is forced to recognize that the Emperor's intention was to re-establish elections on the widest possible basis; and the following words of the government spokesman of the time confirm this impression: "The electoral colleges link the high authorities with the people, and *vice-versa*; they are the intermediary bodies between power and the people; it is a classification of citizens, an organization of the nation. In this classification it was necessary to combine the opposing interests of property owners and proletariat, since property is the fundamental basis of every political association; it was necessary also to include non-property owners, so as not to close careers to talent and genius."

The Council of State was one of the first mechanisms of the

Empire.[2] Composed of the most distinguished men, it formed the privy council of the sovereign. The men who belonged to it, being free from all restraint, not aiming at attracting attention, and stimulated by the presence of the sovereign, elaborated laws with no other preoccupation than that of the interests of France. The spokesmen of the Council of State had to submit for acceptance by the Chambers those laws which had been prepared in private.

The Emperor created juniors (*auditeurs*) at the Council of State; their number was fixed at three hundred and fifty; they were divided into three classes, and attached to all administrative departments. The Council of State thus provided a nursery of educated, enlightened men, well capable of administering the country. Being familiar with all the great political problems, they received from the government important missions.

This institution filled a long-felt want; for if a country has schools for the art of the jurisconsult, for the art of healing, for the art of war, for theology, etc., is it not shocking that there is nothing for the art of government? It is certainly the most difficult art of all, for it embraces all the exact sciences, political and moral.

2. *The* Coup d'État *of 1851: Duc Albert de Broglie*

The noble family of de Broglie (pronounced as if it were spelled de Breuil) came from Italy and has often been likened to the aristocratic Whig families of England, such as the Sidneys or Russells. As regards the eminent roles successive generations played in national life and their characteristic liberal-conservative (or Right-Center) outlook in politics, the comparison is apt. Duke Victor de Broglie (1785–1870) served Louis Philippe as Foreign Minister and Prime Minister from 1835 to 1836. His son, Duke Albert de Broglie (1821–1901), was, like his father, elected to the Academy for his literary work and was twice to become Prime Minister in the formative years of the Third Republic (in 1873 and 1877). As leader of the Right-Center, he was in part responsible for the shaping of the Laws of 1875, which founded the Third Republic. His mother Albertine was daughter of Mme. de Staël and a pious Swiss Protestant. His father, Duke Victor, was a very broadminded Catholic. Duke Albert became an active member of the Liberal Catholic group, fighting the despotic State in 1840 and the despotic Papacy in 1870. A friend of Falloux, Dupanloup, and Montalembert, and a contributor to the *Correspondent*, he cut a somewhat aloof and disdainful figure in parliamentary politics. His explanation of the *coup* should be compared closely with that of Marx (Document 3). The

[2] See below, Document 29.

Mémoires du duc de Broglie having appeared in parts in the *Revue des deux Mondes* in the 1920's, were published in collected form in 1938, with a Preface by his grandson by Calmann-Lévy Paris: the following extracts from volume 1, pages 229–233 appear in translation here by permission of the publishers, Calmann-Lévy.

I HAVE told by what mixture of good and bad reasons the leaders of the conservative party in the Constituent Assembly persuaded us to give our votes for the Presidency of the Republic to the nephew and heir of the first Emperor. By taking this course, and by ourselves helping him to get eight million votes which would raise him to a position in which he would have at his disposal an army of five hundred thousand men and all the resources of executive power, none of us could pretend that he would not try to make use of this combined force and popularity to place on his head the crown to which he felt entitled through his birth and all the memories which were connected with his name. I do not think that any of us doubted that he would try to become Emperor, least of all would I insult M. Thiers, who had advised us to support him, by implying that he had not anticipated such a natural eventuality. He simply thought, and we thought the same, that once we had made use of the popularity of his name to overthrow the revolutionary usurpers of February 1848 and restabilize the bases of a disturbed society, we should retain the influence to prevent him whenever he tried to transform the power which had been entrusted to him for the public weal into an instrument of personal aggrandizement.

We had no right therefore to be surprised, still less to cry "Traitor," when once he had gone along with us at first and handed over our common enemies, we saw that he was evidently aiming at something better than the temporary and limited authority of a republican president. The question was how we could prevent him from using force to seize power other than that conferred on him by republican legality.

It is probable that it would have been a very simple matter if the President Prince had been such as his exploits at Boulogne and Strasburg had led us to suppose,[1] and such as he had been judged by those of our leaders who had known him on the benches of

---

[1] Louis had made two abortive and somewhat ludicrous attempts at *coups* in 1836 and 1840, the second of which, at Boulogne, led to his imprisonment at Ham.

the Constituent Assembly, an adventurer who was both mad and incapable, with the confidence of a visionary in his imperial star, but lacking experience, knowledge or reliable resources of character and intelligence. Such a man who had been put to the test for three years, and submitted to the flood of light on his power which so few reputations and popular figures survive, would have been rapidly discredited. Once he had reached the end of his mandate and attempted to prolong it illegally, he would not have found any support in the sane and sensible section of the population. It was evidently on this that those people had been relying who, by supporting his candidature, had consented to bestow power for a few years into his hands.

But it must be conceded that their illusion was complete and that, far from being diminished and weakened during his three years' Presidency, on the contrary the Prince had increased the public's esteem and confidence in him; and it was becoming much more difficult to bring him down from power than if we had tried to prevent his attaining it. There were now added, to the blind votes of the crowd who had placed him over us, the support of all the commercial and industrial interests which had been thrown into confusion by the February crisis, and which could breathe again since he had taken the reins of government. What qualities did he possess which enabled him to achieve the very rare distinction of being still more popular after his trial period than beforehand? It was somewhat difficult to say, and our friends in particular, knowing that he was devoid of those talents which had made the fortune of public men under the parliamentary régime—eloquence, administrative ability, wide knowledge and a cultivated mind—were at a loss to understand. He had qualities of a different order, patient skill, the art of not compromising himself between the different parties which a fortuitous coalition had grouped round him, the ability to dissimulate his thoughts, and when on rare occasion he decided to speak in public, the gift of finding the right word which reflected general opinion. In short this madman, this "lout," as M. Thiers was fond of calling him, without appearing to affect anybody, had made play with all those who had laughed at him.

We were slow to admit that we had been mistaken; nobody likes to confess that he has been caught out, but we realized that an army of four hundred thousand men, and all the resources which the administration in France provides for the man in power, joined to immense popularity, made of this candidate for Empire a very redoubtable adversary for those who remained faithful to liberal and constitutional principles. Did we at least have the resources to stand up to him proudly on republican legality, and to declare that he would not be allowed to overstep the limits of his constitutional attributions at any price or on any pretext?

Alas, no: by bad luck the Constituent Assembly had saddled us with such an absurd constitution, so contrary to all the rules of good sense and prudence, that to try and condemn the country to remain with it would, almost certainly, lay it open to all the hazards of a revolutionary cataclysm.

To give some idea of the dangers which the country was forced to run through the imprudence of this constitutional system, and which surpassed the bounds of reason, suffice it to say that, not content with leaving two powers each stemming from universal suffrage face to face for two years, with no legal means of settling their differences, our constituent members had carefully arranged that these two powers should come to an end at an interval of three weeks from each other, one on April 28, the other on May 10, 1852, so that we should have had to renew the whole political machine all together, and the country would have remained for these three weeks completely without a government. This period was approaching, and its arrival was viewed with terror. Business which had just started to revive since the commotion in February came to a halt, and commerce which was still ailing was horror-struck. Yet it was those who wanted to surround France with legality who were condemning her to this tacit death. It is not surprising that the President let it be understood that he would free the country and was listened to eagerly, and that this sort of talk made a great number of converts. It was not the Imperial candidate nor his friends who produced successful propaganda in favor of the Empire and a *coup d'état*, but the stupidity of the Constitution of 1848.

The way to stop the Bonapartist current was not—as events have proved—to try to get it to break up against the frail rampart of constitutional legality. One succeeded only in giving society the alternative of either submitting to an Empire or again running all the risks of a revolutionary venture.

It was the fear of being caught in this dilemma, between absolute power resuscitated in the person of a nephew of the first Napoleon, having neither his glory nor his genius, or the return of anarchy from which we had just emerged, which suggested the idea to a whole section of the majority of the Assembly that by trying to make a better Constitution than the one which had been bequeathed to us, we could at least stem the torrent which we could not stop completely. To revise the Constitution so as to give society the guarantees missing in that of 1848, and to acquire by this revision legal grounds on which we could defend ourselves against usurpation as against revolution, this was the idea—one could say, if you like, the dream—of a whole group of deputies who were called "the meeting of the Pyramids" after the place where they assembled. My father, M. Daru, M. Buffet, my childhood friend who is still the friend of my old age, M. de Montalembert himself, and lastly my comrades in arms Mérode and Moustier, were all members. I associated myself with their efforts from my retreat, where I was quite powerless; but since I was still imbued with much ambition and high hopes, I wrote an article on these lines for the *Revue des deux Mondes*.

3. *The* Coup d'État *of 1851: Karl Marx (1852)*

Karl Marx (1818–1883) studied the course of events in France with as much care as he studied economic conditions in Britain, with the common purpose of explaining how events squared with his analysis of history and social change. Having examined the events of 1848 to 1850 in *The Class Struggles in France*, he produced also, in 1852, *The Eighteenth Brumaire of Louis Bonaparte*. The *coup* now effected by the nephew was, he argued, a farcical burlesque version of the device by which Napoleon had gained power in 1799: "the social revolution of the nineteenth century cannot draw its poetry from the past, but only from the future." Offering his own economic and sociological explanation of the events, he proposes his satirical variants of *Des idées napoléoniennes*. The most convenient text of the whole pamphlet is to be found in Karl Marx and Frederick Engels, *Selected Works* (2 vols., Moscow, Foreign Languages Publishing House, 1951), Vol. I, pp. 221–311. The extracts are from pp. 291–3 and 305–7 of this edition.

(a) IN THE YEAR 1851, France, to be sure, had passed through a kind of minor trade crisis. The end of February showed a decline in exports compared with 1850; in March trade suffered and factories closed down; in April the position of the industrial Departments appeared as desperate as after the February days; in May business had still not revived; as late as June 28 the holdings of the Bank of France showed, by the enormous growth of deposits and the equally great decrease in advances on bills of exchange, that production was at a standstill, and it was not until the middle of October that a progressive improvement of business again set in. The French bourgeoisie attributed this trade stagnation to purely political causes, to the struggle between parliament and the executive power, to the precariousness of a merely provisional form of state, to the terrifying prospect of the second Sunday in May 1852.[1] I will not deny that all these circumstances had a depressing effect on some branches of industry in Paris and the Departments. But in any case this influence of the political conditions was only local and inconsiderable. Does this require further proof than the fact that the improvement of trade set in towards the middle of October, at the very moment when the political situation grew worse, the political horizon darkened and a thunderbolt from Elysium was expected at any moment? For the rest, the French bourgeois, whose "skill, knowledge, spiritual insight and intellectual resources" reach no further than his nose, could throughout the period of the Industrial Exhibition in London have found the cause of his commercial misery right under his nose. While in France factories were closed down, in England commercial bankruptcies broke out. While in April and May the industrial panic reached a climax in France, in April and May the commercial panic reached a climax in England. Like the French woollen industry, so the English woollen industry suffered, and as French silk manufacture, so did English silk manufacture. True, the English cotton mills continued working, but no longer at the same profits as in 1849 and 1850. The only difference was that the crisis in France was industrial, in England commercial; that while in France the factories stood idle, in England they extended operations, but under less favorable conditions than in preceding years; that in France it was exports, in England imports which were hardest hit. The common cause, which is naturally not to be sought within the bounds of the French political horizon, was obvious. The years 1849 and 1850 were years of the greatest material prosperity and of an overproduction that appeared as such only in 1851. At the beginning of this year it was given a further impetus by the prospect of the Industrial Exhibition. In addition there were the following special circumstances: first, the partial failure

[1] There was widespread fear of collapse if elections to both Assembly and Presidency should coincide in May 1852: cf. the previous document.

of the cotton crop in 1850 and 1851, then the certainty of a bigger cotton crop than had been expected; first the rise, then the sudden fall, in short, the fluctuations in the price of cotton. The crop of raw silk, in France at least, had turned out to be even below the average yield. Woollen manufacture, finally, had expanded so much since 1848 that the production of wool could not keep pace with it and the price of raw wool rose out of all proportion to the price of woollen manufactures. Here, then, in the raw material of three industries for the world market, we have already threefold material for a stagnation in trade.

Apart from these special circumstances, the apparent crisis of 1851 was nothing else but the halt which overproduction and overspeculation invariably make in describing the industrial cycle, before they summon all their strength in order to rush feverishly through the final phase of this cycle and arrive once more at their starting point, the *general trade crisis*. During such intervals in the history of trade commercial bankruptcies break out in England, while in France industry itself is reduced to idleness, being partly forced into retreat by the competition, just then becoming intolerable, of the English in all markets, and being partly singled out for attack as a luxury industry by every business stagnation. . . .

Now picture to yourself the French bourgeois, how in the throes of this business panic his trade-sick brain is tortured, set in a whirl and stunned by rumours of *coups d'état* and the restoration of universal suffrage, by the struggle between parliament and the executive power, by the Fronde war between Orleanists and Legitimists, by the communist conspiracies in the south of France, by alleged *Jacqueries* in the Departments of Nièvre and Cher, by the advertisements of the different candidates for the presidency, by the cheapjack slogans of the journals, by the threats of the republicans to uphold the Constitution and universal suffrage by force of arms, by the gospel-preaching émigré heroes *in partibus*, who announced that the world would come to an end on the second Sunday in May, 1852—think of all this and you will comprehend why in this unspeakable, uproarious confusion of fusion, revision, prorogation, constitution, conspiration, coalition, emigration, usurpation and revolution, the bourgeois madly snorts at his parliamentary republic: "Rather an end with terror than terror without end!"

Bonaparte understood this cry. His power of comprehension was sharpened by the growing turbulence of creditors who, with each sunset which brought settling day, the second Sunday in May 1852, nearer, saw a movement of the stars protesting their earthly bills of exchange. They had become veritable astrologers. . . .

(b) After the first revolution had transformed the peasants from semi-villeins into freeholders, Napoleon confirmed and regulated the conditions on which they could exploit undisturbed the soil of France which had only just fallen to their lot and slake their youthful passion for property. But what is now causing the ruin of the French peasant is his small holding itself, the division of the land, the form of property which Napoleon consolidated in France. It is precisely the material conditions which made the feudal peasant into a small-holding peasant and Napoleon into an emperor. Two generations have sufficed to produce the inevitable result: progressive deterioration of agriculture, progressive indebtedness of the agriculturist. The "Napoleonic" form of property, which at the beginning of the nineteenth century was the condition for the liberation and enrichment of the French country folk, has developed in the course of this century into the law of their enslavement and pauperization. And precisely this law is the first of the *idées napoléoniennes* which the second Bonaparte has to uphold. If he still shares with the peasants the illusion that the cause of their ruin is to be sought, not in this small-holding property itself, but outside it, in the influence of secondary circumstances, his experiments will burst like soap bubbles when they come in contact with the relations of production.

The economic development of small-holding property has radically changed the relation of the peasants to the other classes of society. Under Napoleon, the fragmentation of the land in the countryside supplemented free competition and the beginning of big industry in the towns. The peasant class was the ubiquitous protest against the landed aristocracy which had just been overthrown. The roots that small-holding property struck in French soil deprived feudalism of all nutriment. Its landmarks formed the natural fortifications of the bourgeoisie against any surprise attack on the part of its old overlords. But in the course of the nineteenth century the feudal lords were replaced by urban usurers; the feudal obligation that went with the land was replaced by the mortgage; aristocratic landed property was replaced by bourgeois capital. The small holding of the peasant is now only the pretext that allows the capitalist to draw profits, interest and rent from the soil, while leaving it to the tiller of the soil himself to see how he can extract his wages. The mortgage debt burdening the soil of France imposes on the French peasantry payment of an amount of interest equal to the annual interest on the entire British national debt. Small-holding property, in this enslavement by capital to which its development inevitably pushes forward, has transformed the mass of the French nation into troglodytes. Sixteen million peasants (including women and children) dwell in hovels, a large number of which have but one opening, others only two and the most favoured only three. And windows are to a house what the five senses are to the head. The bourgeois order, which at the beginning of the century set the state to stand guard over the newly arisen small holding and manured it with laurels, has become a vampire that sucks out its blood and marrow and throws them into the alchemistic cauldron of capital. The *Code Napoléon* is now nothing but a *codex* of distraints, forced sales and compulsory auctions. To the four million (including children etc.) officially recognized paupers, vagabonds, criminals and prostitutes in France must be added five million who hover on the margin of existence and either have their haunts in the countryside itself or, with their rags and their children, continually desert the countryside for the towns and the towns for the countryside. The interests of the peasants, therefore, are no longer, as under Napoleon, in accord with, but in opposition to the interests of the bourgeoisie, to capital. Hence the peasants find their natural ally and leader in the *urban proletariat*, whose task is the overthrow of the bourgeois order. But *strong and unlimited government* —and this is the second *idée napoléonienne*, which the second Napoleon has to carry out—is called upon to defend this "material" order by force. This *ordre matériel* also serves as the catchword in all of Bonaparte's proclamations against the rebellious peasants.

Besides the mortgage which capital imposes on it, the small holding is burdened by *taxes*. Taxes are the source of life for the bureaucracy, the army, the priests and the court, in short for the whole apparatus of the executive power. Strong government and heavy taxes are identical. By its very nature, small-holding property forms a suitable basis for an all-powerful and innumerable bureaucracy. It creates a uniform level of relationships and persons over the whole surface of the land. Hence it also permits of uniform action from a supreme centre on all points of this uniform mass. It annihilates the aristocratic intermediate grades between the mass of the people and the state power. On all sides, therefore, it calls forth the direct interference of this state power and the interposition of its immediate organs. Finally, it produces an unemployed surplus population for which there is no place either on the land or in the towns, and which accordingly reaches out for state offices as a sort of respectable alms, and provokes the creation of state posts. By the new markets which he opened at the point of the bayonet, by·the plundering of the Continent, Napoleon repaid the compulsory taxes with interest. These taxes were a spur to the industry of the peasant, whereas now they rob his industry of its last resources and complete his inability to resist pauperism. And an enormous bureaucracy, well gallooned and well fed, is the *idée napoléonienne* which is most congenial of all to the second Bonaparte. How could it be otherwise, seeing that alongside the actual classes of society he is forced to create an artificial caste, for which the maintenance of his regime becomes a bread-and-butter question? Accordingly, one of his first financial operations was the raising of officials' salaries to their old level and the creation of new sinecures. . . .

4. *The Constitution of January 14, 1852*

If French history between 1789 and 1870 is regarded as a series of variations on the theme of insurrections and resurrections, the Constitution which Louis Napoleon instituted after his *coup d'état* is one of the clearest examples of a resurrection. It was essentially a return to the Constitution of the Year VIII (1800), which had made Napoleon First Consul, and again it was intended to be the prelude to Empire. Less than three weeks after the *coup*, Louis Napoleon held a plebiscite on the question "Do the French people desire Louis Bonaparte's authority to be maintained, and delegate to him the powers necessary to establish a Constitution on the lines laid down in the proclamation?" Only 600,000 said "No"; some 7,500,000 said "Yes." The proclamation now to be implemented had outlined political organization such as had been previously laid down in his *Napoleonic Ideas*.

The principles were avowedly highly authoritarian, as is plain from the Preamble, and still more from the powers allotted to the President of the Republic in Articles 5 to 18 (below). It was a document republican only in form; in spirit and intention it was highly monarchical. Louis moved from the Elysée Palace to the royal palace of the Tuileries, and in other ways assumed at once a semi-royal state. The Senate was a body of *ex officio* or nominated dignitaries. The Legislative Body, reduced to a mere 260 deputies, was indeed elected by universal suffrage but was deprived of any freedom of discussion or of any action independent of the executive power. They met for only three months a year, and ministers could not be members (Articles 41 and 44). Although much was said on paper about the role of "the people," the administrative power of the Ministry of the Interior, working through prefects, mayors, and police, was mobilized to "guide" the people in their voting. By Article 58, Presidential decrees had the force of law until the elections in March, 1852, and he made full use of this lawmaking power. The National Guard was abolished, new press controls were decreed, even university teachers were disciplined. All the machinery of the Empire came into being again, before the elections produced a vast and docile majority, and before a still bigger majority in the plebiscite of November (some 7,800,000) approved his becoming emperor. On December 1, 1852, he assumed the title of Napoleon III; and next day, on the anniversary of Austerlitz and of his own *coup* the year before, he made his formal entry into the capital city of the French Empire.

Details of the Constitution were, of course, changed in later years, usually in response to pressures from liberals and republicans. The political system which evolved during the next eighteen years had features peculiarly its own, and these may be studied in Dr. Theodore Zeldin's stimulating little study *The Political System of Napoleon III* (1958). Even when the institutions were not formally changed, they could sometimes be made to work in new ways, especially in response to new social and economic pressures. The system evolved in close relation to the fact that the Second Empire was the high noon of the industrial and commercial revolutions in France (see below, Part II, C).

French text of the Constitution is in *Bulletin des lois de la république française*, X série, Vol. 11, No. 3522, and in Léon Duguit, H. Monnier, and R. Bonnard, *Les constitutions et les principales lois politiques de la France depuis 1789* (5th edn. Paris, 1932).

The President of the Republic,

Whereas the French people has been called upon to pronounce on the following resolution: "The People wish to maintain the authority of Louis-Napoleon Bonaparte, and give him the necessary powers to make a constitution according to the principles laid down in his proclamation of December 2."

Whereas the principles proposed for acceptance by the People were:

1. A responsible head appointed for ten years;

2. Ministers dependent on the Executive Power alone;
3. A Council of State drawn from the most eminent men, to prepare laws and uphold them before the Legislative Body;
4. A Legislative Body to discuss and vote the laws, returned by universal suffrage, without a second ballot which falsifies the election;
5. A Second Assembly drawn from all the people of note in the country, to be a stabilizing power, guardian of the fundamental compact and of the public freedom;

Whereas the people have replied in the affirmative by seven million five hundred votes:

PROMULGATES THE CONSTITUTION in the following terms:

Title I

Article 1—The Constitution recognizes, confirms and guarantees the great principles proclaimed in 1789, which are the basis of French public law.

Title II: Forms of Government of the Republic

Article 2—The Government of the French Republic is entrusted for ten years to Prince Louis-Napoleon Bonaparte, the existing President of the Republic.

Article 3—The President of the Republic governs by means of the Ministers, the Council of State, the Senate, and the Legislative Body.

Article 4—Legislative authority is exercised collectively by the President of the Republic, the Senate, and the Legislative Body.

Title III: The President of the Republic

Article 5—The President of the Republic is responsible to the French People, to whom he always has the right to appeal.

Article 6—The President of the Republic is the Head of the State; he commands the forces on land and at sea, declares war, makes treaties of peace, alliance and commerce, appoints to all posts, makes the regulations and decrees necessary for the execution of the laws.

Article 7—Justice is administered in his name.

Article 8—He alone can initiate laws.

Article 9—He has the right to pardon.

Article 10—He sanctions and promulgates the laws and the *sénatus-consultes*.

Article 11—Every year he presents to the Senate and to the Legislative Body a message on the state of the Republic.

Article 12—He has the right to declare a state of siege in one or several *départements*, provided that it is reported to the Senate within the shortest time possible. The consequences of the state of siege are regulated by law.

Article 13—Ministers are dependent only on the Head of State; they are not responsible, except each for his own concern, for the acts of the Government; they are not jointly responsible, and they cannot be arraigned by the Senate.

Article 14—The Ministers, members of the Senate, of the Legislative Body, and of the Council of State, the officers in the army and the navy, the magistrates and the civil servants shall take the oath as follows:

"I swear obedience to the Constitution and allegiance to the President."

Article 15—A *sénatus-consulte* fixes the sum allowed annually to the President of the Republic for the whole duration of his office.

Article 16—If the President of the Republic dies before the expiration of his mandate, the Senate invites the Nation to proceed to a new election.

Article 17—The Head of State has the right, in a secret document deposited in the Senate archives, to designate the name of the citizen whom he recommends, in the interests of France, to the confidence and votes of the People.

Article 18—Until the election of the new President of the Republic, the President of the Senate governs with the help of the ministers in power, who form themselves into a Council of Government, and make decisions by majority vote.

Title IV: The Senate

Article 19—The number of Senators shall not exceed one hundred and fifty: it is limited for the first year to eighty.

Article 20—The Senate is composed of:

1. The Cardinals, the Marshals and the Admirals.
2. Citizens whom the President of the Republic deems suitable to raise to the dignity of senator.

Article 21—Senators are irremovable and appointed for life.

Article 22—The office of senator is unpaid; nevertheless, the President of the Republic, by reason of services rendered, or of their financial position, may grant to senators a personal remuneration which shall not exceed thirty thousand francs per year.

Article 23—The president and vice-presidents of the Senate are appointed by the President of the Republic and chosen from among the senators. They are appointed for one year. The salary of the president of the Senate is fixed by decree.

Article 24—The President of the Republic summons and prorogues the Senate. He fixes the duration of its sessions by decree. The sessions of the Senate are not public.

Article 25—The Senate is the guardian of the fundamental compact and of public freedoms. No law can be promulgated before being submitted to it.

Article 26—The Senate shall oppose the promulgation:

1. Of laws which would be contrary to, or which would derogate from the Constitution, religion, morality, freedom of worship, freedom of the individual, equality of citizens before the law, inviolability of property and the principle of irremovability of the magistrature;
2. Of those laws which could endanger the defense of the territory.

Article 27—The Senate regulates by a *sénatus-consulte:*

1. The constitution of the colonies and of Algeria;
2. All that has not been provided for by the Constitution and which is necessary for its functioning;
3. The meaning of articles of the Constitution which give rise to different interpretations.

Article 28—These *sénatus-consultes* will be submitted for the sanction of the President and promulgated by him.

Article 29—The Senate maintains or annuls all acts which are referred to it by the Government as unconstitutional, or denounced as such by petition of the citizens.

Article 30—The Senate may, in a report addressed to the President of the Republic, lay down the principles of a government bill of major national interest.

Article 31—It can likewise propose modifications to the Constitution. If the proposition is adopted by the Executive Power, it is enacted by a *sénatus-consulte.*

Article 32—Nevertheless, every modification of the basic principles of the Constitution, as they were laid down in the proclamation of December 2 and adopted by the French People, shall be submitted to universal suffrage.

Article 33—In the case of the dissolution of the Legislative Body, and until a new one has been convened, the Senate, on the proposition of the President of the Republic, provides by emergency measures all means necessary for the functioning of Government.

Title V: The Legislative Body

Article 34—Election is based on the population.

Article 35—There shall be one deputy in the Legislative Body for every thirty-five thousand electors.

Article 36—The deputies are elected by universal suffrage without a second ballot.

Article 37—They receive no salary.

Article 38—They are elected for six years.

Article 39—The Legislative Body discusses and votes government bills and taxation.

Article 40—Every amendment adopted by the committee empowered to examine a government bill shall be sent by the president of the Legislative Body to the Council of State, without discussion—if the amendment is not adopted by the Council of State, it cannot be submitted for discussion by the Legislative Body.

Article 41—Ordinary sessions of the Legislative Body sit for three months; its meetings are public; but at the request of five members it may move into Secret Committee.

Article 42—Reports on meetings of the Legislative Body by newspapers or any other method of publication shall be limited to reproduction of the minutes drawn up, at the end of each session, under the supervision of the president of the Legislative Body.

Article 43—The president and vice-presidents of the Legislative Body are appointed by the President of the Republic for one year; they are chosen from among the deputies. The salary of the president of the Legislative Body is fixed by decree.

Article 44—Ministers may not be members of the Legislative Body.

Article 45—Petitions may be brought to the Senate. No petition can be addressed to the Legislative Body.

Article 46—The President of the Republic convokes, adjourns, prorogues and dissolves the Legislative Body. In the case of dissolution, the President of the Republic must convoke a new one within six months.

Title VI: The Council of State

Article 47—The number of Councilors of State in regular service is between forty and fifty.

Article 48—The Councilors of State are appointed by the President of the Republic and dismissed by him.

Article 49—The Council of State is presided over by the President of the Republic and, in his absence, by the person whom he designates as vice-president of the Council of State.

Article 50—The Council of State is entrusted, under the chairmanship of the President of the Republic, to draft government bills and regulations for public administration, and to resolve difficulties that arise in the matter of administration.

Article 51—It conducts, on the Government's behalf, the discussion of government bills in the Senate and the Legislative Body. The Councilors of State entrusted to speak for the Government are nominated by the President of the Republic.

Article 52—The salary of each Councilor of State is twenty-five thousand francs.

Article 53—Ministers are entitled to rank, to a seat and to a vote in the Council of State.

Title VII: The High Court of Justice

Article 54—A High Court of Justice passes judgment, without right of appeal, or of judicial revision, on all persons brought before it accused of crimes, criminal intent or conspiracy against the President of the Republic and against the internal or external security of the State. The Court cannot sit except by virtue of a decree by the President of the Republic.

Article 55—A *sénatus-consulte* will determine the organization of this High Court.

Title VIII: General and Transitional Provisions

Article 56—The provisions of codes, laws and existing regulations, which are not contrary to the present Constitution, remain in force until they are legally revoked.

Article 57—A law shall determine municipal organization. Mayors are appointed by the Executive Power, and may be chosen from outside the municipal council.

Article 58—The present Constitution shall come into force from the date when the chief bodies of the State which it is organizing shall be constituted. The decrees issued by the President of the Republic, from December 2 until this date, shall have the force of law.

SECTION B:
ESTABLISHMENT OF THE THIRD REPUBLIC

It has sometimes been said that France advanced backwards into the Third Republic. Certainly, the new régime took shape slowly and piecemeal, with considerable pauses and hesitancies, and decisions about it were often taken by marginal votes or by dint of fine balances of opposing forces, neither of which much wanted the arrangement that eventually proved to be durable. The establishment of the Third Republic therefore involves three types of document, all of which are illustrated below: parliamentary resolutions, formal constitutional laws, and personal letters.

First (Documents 5 to 9) came a series of ad hoc decisions taken by the National Assembly, which had been elected in February, 1871, primarily in order to make peace with Germany, but also in order to devise a new republican régime. As a large majority of its members, to begin with, were monarchists and not republicans in sympathy, they naturally hesitated to take irrevocable steps; and when they took them, they did so with one eye on the possibility of a future monarchical restoration. Yet almost in spite of themselves—though also because by-elections reinforced the ranks of republicans and because monarchist intrigues were rendered futile by the Comte de Chambord (Document 14)—the deputies eventually settled for a "conservative republic" as "that form of government which divides Frenchmen least."

Second, there were the definitive Constitutional Laws themselves, substantially five in number, of which the four main ones are given here (Documents 10 to 13). (The Law of August 2, 1875, on the election of senators, is not given, partly because its complex arrangements for indirect election of senators by means of electoral colleges would not justify the space they would here occupy, and partly also because they were then changed in 1884, 1898, and 1908.) The history of all these constitutional changes can be studied in Maurice Deslandres, *Histoire constitutionnelle de la France: L'avènement de la troisième république: La Constitution de 1875* (Paris, 1937).

Thirdly, there was reaffirmation of the *de facto* working existence of the Third Republic by the capitulation of the forces of royalism, first by the Comte de Chambord himself, then by the royalist President Marshal MacMahon, as the result of the famous constitutional and political crisis known as "the Sixteenth of May," 1877 (Documents 15 to 19).

The Third Republic, which was thus in one sense "proclaimed" on September 4, 1870, immediately after the abdication of Napoleon III, did not emerge fully fledged as the "Republic of the Republicans" until January, 1879. Its establishment was influenced by the crisis of the Paris Commune of 1871, in ways which will be illustrated later (Part III, A). See also David Thomson, *Democracy in France Since 1870* (1964), Chapter III.

§(a) The Republic of M. Thiers (1870–1873)

Although, as Document 5 shows, Adolphe Thiers was not among the group of Paris deputies who proclaimed the Republic on September 4, 1870, the first phase of its growth has aptly been labeled "the Republic of M. Thiers." Not only was he the only national figure to whom the Assembly could turn, in February, 1871, with enough credit to wield the supreme executive power, but also his own great skill in handling the Assembly (and his statesmanship in handling the delicate diplomacy of making and implementing the Treaty of Frankfurt, Document 85) earned him the title bestowed on him in 1873, "Liberator of his country." The five documents below illustrate the stages by which his own powers *vis-à-vis* the National Assembly were defined, definitions which in themselves accustomed France to a parliamentary government and predisposed the Assembly to frame the Constitutional Laws as it did. See F. H. Brabant, *The Beginning of the Third Republic in France: A History of the National Assembly (February–September 1871)* (London, 1940).

When Thiers fell from power on May 24, 1873, all his initial undertakings had been successfully carried out. Marshal MacMahon, a veteran soldier of Rightist opinions as against the Left-Center position of Thiers, was elected to succeed him by 391 out of 392 votes, because the Left in the Assembly abstained from voting. Thiers had been a completely political animal; MacMahon did not feel that politics were his business. The change was of great importance for the future of the Presidency. It became in MacMahon's hands first the instrument of a party—the Right-Center groups led by the Duc de Broglie—and then little more than honorific. Effective executive power shifted from the Presidency (in the time of Thiers) to the man who was vice president of the Council of Ministers, an office first instituted on September 2, 1871, to take the place of the President in convoking and chairing the Council of Ministers when the President was unable to be present.

Again, politicians were predisposed to accept working arrangements as permanent, and the arrangements were embodied in the Laws of 1875. French texts of Document 5 in *Enquête parlementaire sur les actes du Gouvernement de la Défense nationale*, Rapports III. (Versailles, 1873), 1416B, pp. 64–65; and of Documents 6–9 in Duguit, Mounier, Bonnard, *op. cit.*, pp. 314–319.

5. *The Republic Proclaimed, September 4, 1870*

FRENCHMEN!

The people has forestalled the Chamber which was wavering. To save the Nation in danger, it has asked for the Republic. It has put its representatives not in power, but in peril.

The Republic was victorious against the invasion of 1792: the Republic is proclaimed.

The Revolution has been carried out in the name of the right of public safety.

Citizens, watch over the City which is entrusted to you; tomorrow, along with the army, you shall avenge the Nation!

Emmanuel Arago	Garnier Pagès
Crémieux	Magnin
Dorian	Ordinaire
Jules Favre	E. Pelletan
Jules Ferry	Ernest Picard
Guyot-Montpayroux	Jules Simon
Léon Gambetta	

Hôtel-de-Ville, Septembre 5 1870

6. *Resolution of February 17, 1871*

THE NATIONAL ASSEMBLY, depository of national sovereignty, considering it important, until the institutions of France are constituted, to make immediate provision for the necessities of government and the conduct of negotiations, decrees:

M. Thiers is named Chief of the Executive Power of the French Republic: he shall carry out his functions, under the authority of the National Assembly, with the concurrence of ministers whom he shall choose and over whom he shall preside.

7. *The Rivet Law, August 31, 1871*

Article 1—The Chief of the Executive Power shall take the title of President of the French Republic, and shall continue to carry out, under the authority of the National Assembly for so long as it shall not have finished its tasks, the functions which were delegated to him by the Decree of February 17, 1871.

Article 2—The President of the Republic promulgates laws as soon as they are passed to him by the President of the National Assembly. He ensures and superintends the execution of laws. He resides where the Assembly is in session. He is heard by the National Assembly whenever he deems it necessary, after he has informed the President of the Assembly of his intention. He appoints and dismisses ministers. The Council of Ministers and the ministers are responsible before the Assembly. Every act of the President of the Republic must be countersigned by a minister. The President of the Republic is responsible before the Assembly.

8. *Law of March 13, 1873*

REGULATING THE attributions of the Public Powers and the conditions of ministerial responsibility

The National Assembly, reserving in its integrity the constituent power which belongs to it, but wishing to effect improvements in the attributions of Public Powers,
DECREES:
Article 1—The Law of August 31, 1871, is modified as follows:
   The President of the Republic communicates with the Assembly by means of messages which, except for those which open sessions, are read at the tribune by a minister. Nevertheless, he will be heard by the Assembly in the discussion of laws when he deems it necessary, after informing it by a message of his intention. The debate on the occasion when the President of the Republic wishes to speak is suspended after the message is received, and the President will be heard on the following day, unless it is decided by a special vote that it shall be on the same day. The sitting is adjourned after he has been heard, and the debate is resumed only at a later

sitting. The decision is reached in the absence of the President of the Republic.

Article 2—The President of the Republic promulgates laws declared to be urgent within three days, and laws not urgent within one month, after the vote of the Assembly. Within three days, where a law not submitted for three readings is concerned, the President of the Republic shall have the right, in a message stating his reasons, to ask for fresh consideration. For laws submitted to the formality of three readings, the President of the Republic shall have the right, after the second reading, to ask that the third reading shall be put on the agenda only after an interval of two months.

Article 3—The provisions of the preceding Article shall not apply to acts by which the National Assembly shall exercise the constituent power which is reserved for it in the preamble of the present Law.

Article 4—Interpellations[1] can be addressed only to ministers, and not to the President of the Republic. When interpellations addressed to ministers or petitions sent to the Assembly are concerned with external affairs, the President of the Republic shall have the right to be heard. When such interpellations or petitions have bearing on internal affairs, ministers alone shall reply about acts which concern them. Nevertheless if, by a special resolution, communicated to the Assembly before the opening of the debate by the vice president of the Council of Ministers, the Council declares that the questions raised are connected with the general policy of the Government, and thus involve the responsibility of the President of the Republic, then the President shall have the right to be heard in accordance with the procedure laid down in Article 1. After hearing the vice president of the Council, the Assembly fixes the date for the debate.

Article 5—The National Assembly shall not dissolve before it has legislated (i) on the organization and mode of transmission of the legislative and executive powers; (ii) on the creation and the attributions of a Second Chamber not due to enter upon its duties until after the dissolution of the present Assembly; (iii) on the

---

[1] The procedure by which ministers could be forced to explain their actions in the Chamber, and which could be followed by an adverse vote, had begun in 1791 but had been suspended from 1852 to 1869.

electoral law. The Government shall submit to the Assembly bills on the matters here enumerated.

9. *Law of the Septennate, November 20, 1873*

Article 1—The executive power is entrusted for seven years to Marshal MacMahon, Duke of Magenta, as from the promulgation of this Law; such power shall continue to be exercised under the title of President of the Republic and in current conditions until modifications may be made in them by the Constitutional Laws.

Article 2—Within three days after the promulgation of this Law a Commission of Thirty will be appointed in open session and by *scrutin de liste*[1] to examine the Constitutional Laws.

§ (b) The Constitutional Laws (1875)

The definitive Constitutional Laws, passed by the National Assembly during the year 1875, were debated at great length and it may be said that the presiding influence upon them—other than the sheer experience of the deputies themselves and affection for working arrangements they had found practicable—was that of the conservative Right-Center, which was partly monarchist (if wistfully so after 1873). But the forces of republicanism were by then, too, of considerable strength, and they exerted effective pressure at certain points. The new régime was thus a complex compromise, in the making of which many men had some share, ranging from Thiers and Gambetta on one side to MacMahon and Broglie on the other.

The crucial initial step is commonly regarded as being the passing of the so-called "Wallon Amendment" which appears as part of Article 2 of the Law of February 25 concerning the organization of the Public Powers. It states simply that "The President of the Republic is elected by an absolute majority of votes by the Senate and the Chamber of Deputies meeting as the National Assembly." This statement envisaged the perpetuation of a structure basically similar to that which the existing National Assembly knew, and it spoke of "the Republic." The amendment was passed by 353 votes to 352—a majority of one vote, which brought forth the usual stories that one fat man had been counted twice, and consequently there had really been complete deadlock. But by then the presuppositions of a Republic were more substantial and more widespread in France than such legends would imply.

[1] Voting for a list of candidates, as opposed to *scrutin uninominal,* voting for a single candidate.

Thiers had shown that a Republic could be conservative, and Gambetta had won over new sectors of the electorate to faith in republicanism. The monarchists, moreover, had failed to convince even themselves of their prospects. French texts of Documents 10–13 in *Bulletin des lois* . . . XII série, vol. 10, No. 3953; vol. 11, No. 4270; vol. 10, No. 3954; and vol. 11, No. 4740.

10. *Law of February 25, 1875, relating to organization of the Public Powers*

Article 1—The legislative power is exercised by two Assemblies: the Chamber of Deputies and the Senate. The Chamber of Deputies is chosen by universal suffrage, in conditions determined by the electoral law. The composition, method of nomination and attributions of the Senate will be regulated by a special law.

Article 2—The President of the Republic is elected by an absolute majority of votes by the Senate and the Chamber of Deputies meeting as the National Assembly. He is appointed for seven years. He is re-eligible.

Article 3—The President of the Republic has the initiative in proposing legislation, concurrently with members of the two Chambers: he promulgates laws when they have been voted by the two Chambers: he superintends and ensures their execution. He has the right of pardon; amnesties can be granted only by a law. He has direction of the armed forces. He appoints to all civil and military posts. He presides on state occasions; envoys and embassadors of foreign powers are accredited to him. Every act of the President of the Republic must be countersigned by a minister.

Article 4—Gradually, as vacancies occur after the promulgation of the present law, the President of the Council appoints, in the Council of Ministers, Councilors of State in ordinary service.[1] The Councilors of State thus appointed can be dismissed only by a decree passed in the Council of Ministers. Councilors of State appointed under the Law of May 24, 1872, can be dismissed before the expiry of their powers only in the way laid down in this Law. After the dissolution of the National Assembly, dismissal can be effected only by a resolution of the Senate.

Article 5—The President of the Republic can, with the agreement

[1] See Document 29.

of the Senate, dissolve the Chamber of Deputies before the legal expiry of its mandate. In this case the electoral colleges are convoked for new elections within three months.

Article 6—Ministers are collectively responsible before the Chambers for the general policy of the Government, and individually for their personal acts. The President of the Republic is responsible only in the case of high treason.

Article 7—In the event of a vacancy by death or any other cause, the two Chambers meeting together proceed immediately to the election of a new President. In the interval the Council of Ministers is invested with executive power.

Article 8—The Chambers shall have the right, by separate decisions taken by an absolute majority of each, either spontaneously or at the request of the President of the Republic, to declare that there is need to revise the Constitutional Laws. After each of the two Chambers shall have passed this resolution, they shall meet together as the National Assembly to proceed to the revision. Decisions carrying out revision of the Constitutional Laws, in whole or in part, must be taken by an absolute majority of the members composing the National Assembly. Nevertheless, for the duration of the powers conferred by the Law of November 20, 1873, on Marshal MacMahon, such revision can take place only when it is initiated by the President of the Republic.

Article 9—The seat of the executive powers and of the two Chambers is at Versailles.[2]

11. *Constitutional Law of July 16, 1875, on relations between the Public Powers*

Article 1—The Senate and the Chamber of Deputies meet every year on the second Tuesday in January, unless convoked earlier by the President of the Republic. The two Chambers must sit for at least five months each year. The session of one begins and ends at the same times as that of the other. On the Sunday after the opening of Parliament, public prayers shall be addressed to God in churches and chapels, to invoke His blessing on the work of the Assemblies.

[2] This Article was repealed by Laws of June 21 and July 22, 1879, restoring the government and the Assemblies to Paris.

Article 2—The President of the Republic declares the session closed. He has the right to convoke the Chambers for an extraordinary session. He must convoke them, if requested, in the interval between sessions, by an absolute majority of the members composing each Chamber. The President can adjourn the Chambers. Nevertheless, adjournment may not exceed the period of one month, and may not occur more than twice in one session.

Article 3—At least one month before the legal termination of the powers of the President of the Republic, the Chambers must meet together as the National Assembly to proceed to the election of a new President. If the Chambers are not convoked, this meeting may take place with full legality on the fifteenth day before the expiry of these powers. In the event of the death or resignation of the President of the Republic, the two Chambers meet immediately and with full legality. In the event that, by application of the Law of February 25, 1875, the Chamber of Deputies should be dissolved at the moment when the Presidency of the Republic becomes vacant, the electoral colleges[1] should be summoned at once, and the Senate should meet with full legality.

Article 4—Any meeting of either Chamber held outside the period of common session is illicit and not of full legality, except in the event foreseen in the preceding Article, and when the Senate meets as a court of justice: and, in this latter event, it may exercise only judicial functions.

Article 5—The sittings of the Senate and those of the Chamber of Deputies are public. Nevertheless each Chamber may form itself into secret committee, on the request of a certain number of its members fixed by standing orders. It then decides, by an absolute majority, whether the sitting shall be held again in public on the same subject.

Article 6—The President of the Republic communicates with the Chambers by messages, which are read at the tribune by a minister. Ministers have entry to both Chambers and must be heard when they so ask. They may have the assistance of commissioners, appointed by decree of the President of the Republic, for the debate on any given bill.

Article 7—The President of the Republic promulgates laws within one month after transmission to the Government of the law definitively adopted. He must promulgate within three days laws whose

[1] See Document 12.

promulgation has been declared urgent by a specific vote in each of the two Chambers. Before the date fixed for promulgation the President of the Republic may, by a message giving his reasons, ask the two Chambers to reconsider them, and they cannot refuse.

Article 8—The President of the Republic negotiates and ratifies treaties. He makes them known to the Chambers as soon as the interest and security of the State permit. Treaties of peace, of commerce, treaties involving State finance, those which have bearing upon personal rights and the property rights of Frenchmen abroad, are operative only after they have been voted upon by the two Chambers. No cession, exchange or acquisition of territory can take place except by virtue of a law.

Article 9—The President of the Republic cannot declare war without the previous assent of the two Chambers.

Article 10—Each Chamber is judge of the eligibility of its members and of the regularity of their election; it alone can receive their resignation.

Article 11—The *bureau* of each of the two Chambers is elected each year for the duration of the session, and for any extraordinary session which may take place before the ordinary session of the following year. When the two Chambers meet together as the National Assembly, their *bureau* consists of the President, Vice-Presidents and Secretaries of the Senate.

Article 12—The President of the Republic cannot be proceeded against except by the Chamber of Deputies, and cannot be judged except by the Senate. Ministers can be proceeded against by the Chamber of Deputies for crimes committed in the exercise of their functions. In this event, they are judged by the Senate. The Senate can be constituted a Court of Justice by a decree of the President of the Republic, issued in the Council of Ministers, to judge any person charged with an attempt against the security of the State. If the preliminary investigation has started in an ordinary court, the decree convoking the Senate can be framed to include the decision to transfer the case. A Law shall determine the method of procedure for bringing the charge, the preliminary investigation, and the judgment.

Article 13—No member of either Chamber can be prosecuted or harassed by the police because of opinions expressed or votes given by him in the exercise of his functions.

Article 14—No member of either Chamber can, during a parliamentary session, be prosecuted or arrested for a criminal or a minor offense except on the authority of the Chamber of which he is a member, unless he be caught in the act. The detention or prosecution of a member of either Chamber is suspended during a session, and for its whole duration, if the Chamber so requires.

12. *Law of February 24, 1875, relating to organization of the Senate*

Article 1—The Senate is composed of 300 members: 225 elected by the *départements* and colonies, and 75 elected by the National Assembly.

Article 2—The *départements* of the Seine and the Nord shall each elect 5 senators. The *départements* of Seine-Inférieure, Pas-de-Calais, Gironde, Rhône, Finistère, Côtes-du-Nord, shall each elect 4 senators. Loire-Inférieure, Saône-et-Loire, Ille-et-Vilaine, Seine-et-Oise, Isère, Puy-de-Dôme, Somme, Bouches-du-Rhône, Aisne, Loire, Manche, Maine-et-Loire, Morbihan, Dordogne, Haute-Garonne, Charente-Inférieure, Calvados, Sarthe, Hérault, Basses-Pyrénées, Gard, Aveyron, Vendée, Orne, Oise, Vosges, Allier, shall each elect 3 senators. All other *départements* shall elect 2 each. The territory of Belfort, the three *départements* of Algeria, the four colonies of Martinique, Guadeloupe, Réunion and French India shall each elect 1 senator.

Article 3—No one can be a senator unless he is French, at least forty years old, and possesses all his civil and political rights.

Article 4—Senators of the *départements* and colonies are elected by an absolute majority, and when need be by *scrutin de liste* by an electoral college meeting in the chief town of the *département* or colony and composed of: (i) the deputies (ii) general councilors; (iii) the councilors of the *arrondissement;* (iv) delegates chosen, one by each municipal council, from among the electors of the commune. In French India the members of the colonial council or of local councils shall be substituted for the general councilors, councilors of the *arrondissement* and delegates of the municipal councils. They vote in the chief town of each settlement.

Article 5—Senators appointed by the Assembly are elected by *scrutin de liste* and by an absolute majority of votes.

Article 6—Senators of the *départements* and colonies are elected for nine years and are renewable, one third at a time, every three years. At the beginning of the first session the *départements* will be divided into three groups each containing an equal number of senators. It will be determined, by drawing lots, which of the groups will be renewed at the end of the first three-year period and which at the end of the second.

Article 7—Senators elected by the Assembly are irremovable. In the event of a vacancy arising from death, resignation or any other cause, replacement will be arranged, within two months, by the Senate itself.

Article 8—The Senate has, concurrently with the Chamber of Deputies, the right of initiative and drafting in lawmaking. Finance bills, however, must in the first instance be presented in the Chamber of Deputies and voted upon by it.

Article 9—The Senate can be constituted a Court of Justice to judge either the President of the Republic or ministers, and to take cognizance of attempts against the security of the State.

Article 10—Election of the Senate will be proceeded with one month before the date fixed by the National Assembly for its dissolution. The Senate shall enter upon its functions and shall be constituted on the day when the National Assembly dissolves.

Article 11—The present Law shall be promulgated only after the decisive vote on the Law of the Public Powers.

13. *Organic Law of November 30, 1875, on the Election of Deputies*

Article 1—Deputies shall be chosen by the electors registered: (i) on the lists drawn up in conformity with the Law of July 7, 1874; (ii) on the complementary list comprising those who have resided in the commune for six months. Inscription on the complementary list will take place, in accordance with the laws and regulations which already govern political electoral rolls, by the commissions and following the procedures established in Articles 1, 2, 3, and 4 of the Law of July 7, 1874. Petitions to invalidate the formation and revision of either of the two lists will go directly to the civil division of the *Cour de Cassation*.[1] The electoral lists drawn up on March 31, 1875, shall hold good until March 31, 1876.

[1] The supreme court for revising judgments of all lower courts on matters of law, and so for resolving conflicts of legal decisions.

Article 2—Regular soldiers and conscripts of all ranks and arms in the army and navy take no part in any voting when they are with their units, on duty or carrying out their functions. Those who, at the time of the election, are on leave, not on active service, or in possession of a regulation pass, can vote in the commune on the electoral lists of which they are regularly registered. This last rule applies equally to officers and conscripts who are on half-pay or in the cadre of reserves.

Article 3—Throughout the period of elections, circulars and programs signed by candidates, posters and electoral manifestoes signed by one or more electors can, after a copy has been sent to the Public Prosecutor's office, be posted up and distributed without previous authorization. Distribution of ballot papers is not subject to the formality of their being sent to the Public Prosecutor's office. It is forbidden for any agent of a public or municipal authority to distribute ballot papers, programs and circulars for candidates. The regulations of Article 19 of the Organic Law of August 2, 1875, on elections of senators, shall be applicable to elections of deputies.[2]

Article 4—The poll shall last only one day. Voting takes place in the chief place of the commune; nevertheless, each commune can be divided, by decree of the Prefect, into as many sections as local circumstances and the number of electors demand. The second ballot shall continue to take place on the second Sunday after the day of the announcement of the result of the first ballot, in accordance with the provisions of Article 65 of the Law of March 15, 1849.

Article 5—The process of voting shall be in conformity with the provisions of the Organic and Regulating Decrees of February 2, 1852. The vote is secret. The lists of expenses of each section, signed by the president and the secretary, shall be kept deposited for a week with the secretariat of the mayor, where they will be shown to any elector who wishes.

[2] In the Law of August 2, 1875, on elections of senators, not included here, the Article 19 referred to lays down: "Any attempt at corruption by using the means specified in Articles 177 and following of the Penal Code, to influence the vote of an elector or to cause him to abstain from voting, shall be punished by imprisonment for a term of between three months and two years and a fine of 50 to 500 francs, or by one of these penalties alone. Article 463 of the Penal Code applies to the penalties imposed by the present Article."

Article 6—Every elector is eligible to be a candidate, without property qualification, when he is over the age of twenty-five.

Article 7—No soldier or sailor, forming part of the active armed forces on land or sea, can be elected a member of the Chamber of Deputies, no matter what his rank or his functions. This rule applies to soldiers and sailors on half-pay or not on active service; but it does not extend to officers in the second section of the cadre of the general staff, nor to those who, kept in the first section as having been commander-in-chief against the enemy, have ceased to be employed on active service, nor to officers who, having acquired retirement rights, have been sent home or kept at home pending the settlement of their pension. The decision whereby the officer shall have been entitled to claim his retirement rights shall become, in this event, irrevocable. The rule stated in the first paragraph of the present Article does not apply either to the reserve of the regular army or to the territorial army.

Article 8—The exercise of public duties paid for by the State is incompatible with a deputy's mandate. In consequence, any *fonctionnaire* elected a deputy shall be dismissed from his post unless, within eight days after the verification of the returns, he makes it known that he does not accept the deputy's mandate. The above rules do not apply to the functions of a minister, under-secretary of State, ambassador, plenipotentiary, the Prefect of the Seine, the Prefect of Police, the First Presidents of the *Cour de Cassation, Cour des Comptes, Cour d'Appel de Paris*, the *Procureurs généraux* attached to the *Cour de Cassation, Cour des Comptes* or the *Cour d'Appel de Paris*, Archbishops and Bishops, the Pastor-Presidents of the Consistory in consistorial areas where the chief town has two or more pastors, the Grand Rabbi of the Central Consistory, the Grand Rabbi of the Consistory of Paris.

Article 9—Equally exempted from the rules of Article 8 are: (i) The titular professors of chairs which are filled by competition or by presentation of the bodies where the vacancy has occurred; (ii) persons on temporary secondment. Any secondment that has lasted more than six months ceases to be temporary and is governed by Article 8 above.

Article 10—The *fonctionnaire* preserves the rights he has acquired to a retirement pension, and can, after the expiry of his mandate, be restored to his office. The civil *fonctionnaire* who, having had twenty years' service at the date when he accepts a deputy's mandate, will become fifty years of age when his mandate ceases, can claim his rights to a special retirement pension. This pension will be determined in conformity with the third paragraph of Article 12 of the Law of June 9, 1853. If the *fonctionnaire* returns to his post after his mandate ceases, the rules laid down in Article 3, paragraph 2, and Article 28 of the Law of June 9, 1853, shall apply to him. In duties where the grade is distinct from the post the *fonctionnaire*, in accepting a deputy's mandate, gives up the post and keeps only the grade.

Article 11—Any deputy appointed or promoted to a salaried public office ceases to belong to the Chamber by the very fact of accepting it: but he can be re-elected, if the office which he holds is compatible with a deputy's mandate. Deputies who are appointed ministers or undersecretaries of State need not be re-elected.

Article 12—The following cannot be elected by *arrondissements* or colonies falling entirely or partly within their province, during the exercise of their duties and for six months after their duties have come to an end by reason of resignation, dismissal, change of residence or for any other cause: (i) the First Presidents, Presidents and members of the prosecuting staff of the *Cour d'Appel;* (ii) the Presidents, Vice Presidents, titular judges, examining magistrates, and prosecuting staff of the courts of first instance; (iii) the Prefect of Police, the Prefects and the Secretaries-General of prefectures, the Governors, Directors and Secretaries-General of colonies; (iv) the chief engineers and surveyors and those of each *arrondissement;* (v) the Rectors and Inspectors of each Academy; (vi) Inspectors of primary schools; (vii) the Archbishops, Bishops and Vicars-General; (viii) the Treasurers, Paymasters and District Collectors of Finance; (ix) the Directors of Direct and Indirect Taxes, of Registration, Estates and Posts; (x) the Conservators and Inspectors of Forests. The Under-Prefects cannot be elected in any of the *arrondissements* of the *département* in which they hold office.

Article 13—Pledges exacted beforehand from candidates (*mandat impératif*) are null and void.

Article 14—Members of the Chamber of Deputies are elected by individual voting. Each administrative *arrondissement* shall elect one deputy. *Arrondissements* whose population exceeds one hundred thousand inhabitants shall elect one further deputy for every hundred-thousand inhabitants or less. In this event the *arrondisse-ments* shall be divided into constituencies whose boundaries shall be determined by a Law and can be modified only by a Law.

Article 15—Deputies are elected for four years. The Chamber is all renewed simultaneously.

Article 16—In the event of a vacancy by death, resignation or otherwise the election shall take place within three months, count-ing from the day when the vacancy began. Where the vacancy is due to the exercise of option, it must be filled within one month.

Article 17—Deputies are paid. This pay is fixed by the regula-tions in Articles 96 and 97 of the Law of March 15, 1849, and by those of the Law of February 16, 1872.

Article 18—No one is elected on the first ballot unless he has won (i) an absolute majority of the votes cast; (ii) a number of votes equal to a quarter of the electors on the register. At the second ballot a relative majority is sufficient. When votes are equal, the eldest candidate is elected.

Article 19—Each *département* of Algeria elects one deputy.

Article 20—Electors in Algeria who reside in a locality not formed into a commune shall be added to the electoral rolls of the nearest commune. When the time comes to set up electoral units, either by grouping together mixed communes in each of which there would not be sufficient electors, or by combining together electors resident in localities not yet communes, the orders fixing the seat of these units will be made by the Governor-General, on the recommendation of the Prefect or of the general in command.

Article 21—Each of the four colonies, to which senators have been accorded by the Law of February 24, 1875, relating to the organ-ization of the Senate, returns one deputy.

Article 22—Any breach of the matters forbidden in Article 3, paragraph 3, of this Law will be punished by a fine of between 16 and 300 francs. Nevertheless the court of summary jurisdiction can apply Article 463 of the Penal Code. The rules of Article 6 of the Law of July 7, 1874, shall apply to the political electoral rolls. The Decree of January 29, 1871, and the Laws of April 10, 1871, of May 2, 1871, and of February 18, 1873, are rescinded. Similarly rescinded is paragraph 11 of Article 15 of the Organic Decree of February 2, 1852, insofar as it refers to the Law of May 21, 1836, on lotteries, save that it is for the courts to apply to those convicted Article 42 of the Penal Code. There shall remain in full force the provisions of those Laws and Decrees now in force which the present Law does not rescind.

Article 23—The provision of Article 12, by which six months must elapse between the time when his duties cease and the date of his election, shall not apply to *fonctionnaires*, other than Prefects and Under-Prefects, whose duties shall have ceased either before the promulgation of this Law, or within twenty days after it.

§(c) The Royalist Débâcle (1871–1879)

What reaffirmed and consolidated the Republic was the débâcle of royalism—a slow and complex process, which is here represented by the attitude of the legitimist Bourbon claimant to the throne, Henry Comte de Chambord, grandson of Charles X, and by the constitutional crisis of 1877 known as "the Sixteenth of May."

It was a permanent and fatal weakness of monarchism after 1830 that the legitimists could never forgive the Orleanists, who seized power under Louis Philippe. The Orleanists of the 1870's had their own pretender to the throne in the person of Louis Philippe's grandson, the Comte de Paris. Moderate men of the royalist Right, like Charles Chesnelong and Falloux, worked hard and persistently to bring about a "fusion" of the two parties. They proposed that, since Chambord was older (fifty-one as against thirty-three) and had no heir, the Orleanists should support moves to restore Chambord to the throne first, in return for legitimist support to ensure that the Comte de Paris should then succeed him. This sensible scheme was entirely frustrated by Chambord's refusal to accept as his royal standard the tricolor flag of the Revolution, rather than the so-called white flag of the Bourbons (In fact, the white flag had been invented only in 1815 by the returned *émigrés*, and the traditional dynastic emblem had been the blue banner with golden lilies. So even the Count's history was somewhat shaky). His "Manifesto" of July 5, 1871, threw the monarchists into great disarray. His further letter of October 27, 1873, written from Salzburg and published in the legitimist newspaper *L'Union* on October 31, was simply to reaffirm the stand taken in 1871. The French texts of both letters are reprinted in the Comte de Falloux, *Mémoires d'un royaliste*, Vol. III (Paris, Perrin, 1925), pp. 235–8 and 324–7. Only the first is here translated (Document 14).

When a republic appeared unavoidable, moderate royalists, led by the Duc de Broglie, concentrated on devising a conservative constitutional and political system of a kind which might eventually make a royalist restoration possible. They ensured that the royalist but unpolitical old soldier Marshal MacMahon should hold the Presidency for a tenure of seven years (Document 9), and encouraged him to act as a bulwark against radical republicanism. The conjunction of inherent constitutional dilemmas with clashing personalities and political forces produced the first major constitutional crisis of the new régime. The five letters reproduced below, three from MacMahon, two from his most powerful antagonist, Léon Gambetta (1838–1882), are key documents in the crisis and reflect its personal character.

The Law of the Septennate was in some respects discordant with the Constitutional Laws of 1875. MacMahon had accepted office on the same terms as Thiers—i.e., with Presidential powers as defined in the Resolution of February 17 and the Rivet Law of March 13, 1871 (Documents 6 and 7), and the Law of March 13, 1873 (Document 8). The Law of the Septennate affirmed these powers only "until modifications may be made in them by the Constitutional Laws" (Art. 1). The Constitutional Laws of 1875 did not specifically diminish Presidential powers, although the implications of Article 6 of the Law of February 25, declaring ministers "collectively responsible before the Chambers for the general policy of the Government" and making the President of the Republic "responsible only in the case of high treason," could reasonably be taken to imply that a government would be expected to resign as a whole if it were defeated on major policy issues by one of the Chambers. In that event, what was the position of the President of the Republic, who could still plausibly claim to "appoint and dismiss ministers," and who was elected President until 1880?

President MacMahon unwittingly put himself into this dilemma in particularly awkward circumstances when, on May 16, 1877, he rose early, summoned his orderly officer, and dictated a letter to Jules Simon, President of the Council of Ministers. It was signed and dispatched immediately, without consultation (Document 15). Simon, uncomfortably leading a ministry that was uneasily balanced between moderate Republican Left and moderate Conservative Right, welcomed an opportunity to escape from his problems without loss of political credit. He at once wrote a letter of resignation, insisting that MacMahon's letter "imposes on me the duty of giving you my resignation." The Republicans could now go to the country, if the President should dissolve the Chamber, with the cry that he had unconstitutionally forced a government out of office while it had the confidence of the Chamber. Mac-Mahon as champion of the Conservatives had lost the first round.

The two letters from Gambetta (Documents 16 and 17)—one to his mistress, the other to his friend Arthur Ranc, exiled on the charge of assisting the Paris Commune—reveal his characteristic calculations and his shrewd judgment of MacMahon. The detailed story of the crisis of *Seize mai* is told in French by Daniel Halévy in *La République des ducs* (Paris, 1937) and in English by Guy Chapman in *The Third Republic of France: The First Phase, 1871–1894* (London, 1962). After dissolution of the Chamber in October the electorate returned a smaller, but still substantial Republican majority, despite the intense administrative pressure exercised during the elections on behalf of the Conservatives. MacMahon's dilemma was now worse than ever. In August, Gambetta had warned that "when France has made her sovereign voice heard, one must either give in or give up" (*soumettre ou démettre*).

In the end, MacMahon did both, as is indicated in his statements of December 14, 1877, and of January 30, 1879 (Documents 18 and 19). By the first he "gave in" and signed away further Presidential claims to determine policy. By the second he also "gave up"; for, in face of a new political deadlock between himself and the majority in the Chamber, he resigned before reaching the end of his Septennate. The Presidential right to dissolve the Chambers remained, but it was never again exercised. Its disuse has often been blamed for the instability and brevity of ministries under the Third Republic. But these persistent characteristics of French political life (by no means peculiar to the Third Republic) were more substantially due to the operations of the multiparty system. The lesson correctly learned from the crisis of May 16 was that, where no party can hope to secure an independent majority in the Chamber, the exercise of a power of dissolution can produce political exasperation rather than clarification.

The French texts of President MacMahon's statements are conveniently published in Charles de Freycinet, *Souvenirs, 1848–1878* (Paris, Charles Delagrave, 1912) pp. 355–6, and his *Souvenirs, 1878–1893* (Paris, Charles Delagrave, 1913), pp. 3–4 and 58–9. Gambetta's letters are collected in D. Halévy and E. Pillias, *Lettres de Gambetta, 1868–1882* (Paris, Grasset, 1938). Letters 309 and 327 are here reproduced by kind permission of the publisher, Bernard Grasset.

14. *Royalist Manifesto, 1871*

PEOPLE OF FRANCE:

I am among you. You have opened the doors of France to me, and I could not refuse the happiness of again seeing my country, but I do not wish by staying longer to give new pretexts for excitement in times as troubled as these.

I am therefore leaving this Château of Chambord which you gave me, and from which I took the name borne proudly for forty years along the exile's path.

In going, I must tell you that I am not parting from you; France knows I belong to her.

I cannot forget that royal legality is the heritage of the nation, nor can I refuse those duties to the nation which it imposes upon me.

These duties I shall fulfill, on my word as an honest man and as King.

With God's help we shall found together, whenever you wish, a government conforming to the real needs of the country, broadly based on administrative decentralization and local liberties.

As a guarantee of these public liberties to which every Christian people has a right, we shall grant universal suffrage honestly practiced, and authority to two Chambers; and we shall resume, restoring its true character, the national movement of the end of last century.

A minority in revolt against the country's wishes made it the beginning of a period of demoralization by falsehood and of disorganization by violence. Their criminal schemes inflicted revolution on a nation which asked only for reform, and since then has driven it into an abyss in which, recently, it would have perished but for the heroic effort of our army.

It is the laboring classes, these workers in field and town whose lot has been the subject of my liveliest concern and my dearest studies, who have suffered most from this social disorder.

But France, cruelly disabused by these unparalleled disasters, will understand that one cannot return to the truth by an exchange of errors; that eternal necessities cannot be evaded by expedients.

She will recall me and I shall come to her intact—with devotion, my principle and my flag.

As regards the flag, it has been said that there are conditions to which I cannot submit.

People of France! I am ready to do everything to help my country to rise again from its ruins and to regain her position in the world; the only sacrifice I cannot make for her is sacrifice of my honor.

I belong, and want to belong, to my time: I pay sincere homage to all its greatness and, under whatever color flag our soldiers marched, I have admired their heroism and thanked God for all that their courage added to the treasure-house of France's glory.

Between you and me there must be no misunderstanding, no mental reservations.

No, I shall not—because ignorance and credulity have spoken of privilege, absolutism or intolerance, and I know not what else, of tithes, feudal rights, phantoms which the most daring bad faith is trying to raise before your eyes—I shall not permit the standard of Henry IV, of Francis I, and of Joan of Arc, to be snatched from my hands.

It was under this flag that national unity was achieved, that your fathers, led by mine, conquered Alsace and Lorraine, whose fidelity to us is still a consolation in our grief.

It conquered barbarism in that land of Africa, witness to the first feats of arms of the princes of my family: it will conquer the new barbarism that is menacing the world!

I shall entrust it without fear to the valor of our army. It has always followed, as they know, only the path of honor.

I received it as a sacred trust from the old King, my grandfather, when he died in exile. It has always been, for me, inseparable from the memory of my absent fatherland. It floated over my cradle: may it overshadow my grave.

In the glorious folds of this unsullied standard I shall bring you order and liberty.

People of France! Henry V cannot abandon the white flag of Henry IV.

Chambord, July 5 1871   Henry

15. *President MacMahon to Jules Simon, May 16, 1877*

MR. PRESIDENT OF THE COUNCIL,

I have just read in the *Journal Officiel* the report of yesterday's sitting. I saw with surprise that neither you, nor the Keeper of the Seals, had given due emphasis in the debate to all the serious arguments which might have prevented the abrogation of the law on the press, which was passed less than two years ago on the motion of M. Dufaure, and which quite recently you yourself asked should be applied in the courts, and yet, during several discussions in the Council of Ministers, even yesterday morning, it had been decided that the President of the Council, together with the Keeper of the Seals, should be responsible for opposing the abrogation.

It was already astonishing enough that in its recent meetings the Chamber of Deputies should have debated a whole municipal law, and even adopted some clauses which you yourself had admitted in the Council of Ministers were dangerous, such as the publicity of municipal councils, and yet the Minister of the Interior took no part in the discussion.

This attitude on the part of the Head of the Cabinet makes one ask if he has retained the influence needed in the Chamber to make his views prevail.

An explanation about this is indispensable, for if I am not, as you are, responsible to Parliament, I have a responsibility to France which must now, more than ever, be my concern.

I remain,

Yours sincerely,
Marshal de MacMahon
President of the Republic

16. *Léon Gambetta to Léonie Léon, May 16, 1877*

[Paris, Wednesday] 16th May 1877

MY DEAR CHILD,

War is declared and we are even challenged to fight. I have accepted, for I hold positions that are impregnable. We occupy the heights of the law, from which we can machine-gun just as we like the wretched troops of the Reaction floundering in the plain. You will see from the newspaper how I have arranged my battle order: but you won't find the tumultuous reception of the people of Paris gathered round the Grand Hotel. I was nearly stifled by the enthusiastic crowd; shouts of *"Long live the Republic, long live Gambetta!"* filled the air. As usual, I preached moderation and calm, and I had great difficulty in getting them to go away quietly, after assuring them that the right was in good hands and that their aspirations would in the end be crowned with triumph.

I see in your journey this morning a further sign of the good star which guides us; for if I had been far away, nothing could have been decided or prepared. Thank you again for your unfailing instinct.

I am going to Versailles tomorrow, where we shall be met, perhaps, by a Ministry of Reaction, and the suspension of our meetings. I still hope to see you Friday, unless you hear to the contrary tomorrow evening. I can't tell you the happiness you gave me yesterday evening: it was the source of all my strength and clear thinking today.

You are always my good angel and my joy. Here is a kiss.

17. *Léon Gambetta to Arthur Ranc, August 20, 1877*

Paris, Monday, 20th August 1877

My DEAR FRIEND,

I have owed you for some time two or three answers to the excellent letters you have been sending me. You know only too well my crushing burden of work, and also my worries about the post, and will excuse this involuntary delay. I am taking advantage today of the reliable Coquelin as an intermediary, to write to you and make up in one swoop for my sins of omission.

I shall not dwell on general political ideas, as my speeches and the newspapers have given you ample information on this subject. I would rather let you know what I think will happen after the election. There is no point in repeating to you once more that the Republicans will be successful. That battle is already won, but what will our opponents do, and what shall we do ourselves? I imagine that these are the two questions in your mind.

We have two kinds of opponents, the Ministers and the Marshal. The first of them will resign. They are saying as much to their intimates, and are already trying to play down their personal responsibility for the crisis. They are blaming everything on the impulsiveness of the old soldier, and point out that the famous letter which started all the trouble was not signed by any of them. They found themselves in a false position, and out of sheer heroism they rushed to save the person of the Head of State. I heard all this from a reliable source, and numerous signs that have been noted among their associates do no more than confirm this family information.

As for the Marshal, it is quite a different matter. He would much prefer not to go, to shift the terrible responsibility incurred onto the Ministers, to submit to parliamentary conditions again and to finish his septennate as well as he can. His reasons for this line of conduct would be purely material. There are several expedients open to him: they will at least occur to him, even if they are not feasible.

1. Attempt a show of strength. I don't believe he will, for very good reasons which I don't need to list to you, but the chief one is this: the army is loyal and its *leaders* very divided, so it is impossible to risk such a step without being sure of being obeyed by

all. So they will circulate these rumors, but not even the most timid people will be taken in by them. You can be sure that we have taken even stronger precautions than in 1873 to foil such an attempt, if it were made.

2. Try to patch up the differences between the Left-Center and Right-Center, so as to look like constitutional repentance. This expedient is more disquieting than the first, but thanks to the animosity of M. Thiers, and his authority over the section of the Left which might weaken, there is no serious cause for fear; from which it should be plain to you, apart from other excellent reasons, how important it was to promote M. Thiers as candidate for the Presidency.

3. Capitulate and submit to all the conditions of the new majority. An improbable solution, but one which certain people do not regard as impossible.

4. Resign. I think it will be this, in spite of all appearances, for I am convinced that the effect of the elections will be overwhelming and menacing for him. We, for our part, must at the earliest possible moment vigorously recall the message and indicate that the leader of the coalition cannot remain in power. For, as he said himself, his honor and his conscience will not allow him to carry out the policy that France desires, and in all sincerity, neither we nor the country can tolerate his presence in public affairs. We need the right sort of delegation to inform him of this decision, refusal to vote the budget, and a demand for a Congress. We can get all these things if we lose not an hour or a vote. For example, we must make use of the plenary session, which is the supreme instrument of discipline and power.

And then? Organize a strong Ministry, including representatives of the four shades of opinion. Sweep away ruthlessly, and with no hesitation, the upper and lower levels of the various departments.

And then? You will say, wait patiently for laws and reforms, for M. Thiers is always M. Thiers. But we will arrange a short amnesty, to prepare the way for the big one.

I had an opportunity of talking about you, as you may suppose, and I can tell you, the famous old man said most readily that he had always thought the way in which you have been persecuted was flagrant injustice, and he would gladly use his influence to make amends. So, as I go on saying, the chief result of May 16 will have been to put an end to your suffering. I look forward to seeing you here before Christmas. I am confident, then, and hope you will soon be notified that you will shortly be set free.

Best wishes,

Yours,

Léon Gambetta

18. *President MacMahon to the Presidents of the Chambers, December 14, 1877*

SIRS,

The elections of October 14 have once more confirmed the confidence of the country in its Republican institutions.

In obedience to parliamentary rules, I have formed a Cabinet chosen from both Chambers, composed of men who are determined to uphold and maintain these institutions by wholehearted application of the Constitutional Laws.

It is imperative in the interests of the country that the present crisis should be resolved; it is no less imperative that the crisis should not occur again.

Exercise of the right of dissolution is, after all, no more than a method of final consultation with a judge from whom there is no appeal, and could not develop into a system of government. I have felt bound to avail myself of this right, and I am complying with the country's answer.

The Constitution of 1875 established a parliamentary Republic by laying down my nonresponsibility, whereas it instituted the collective and individual responsibility of ministers. Thus our respective duties and our rights are determined for us; the independence of ministers is the precondition of their responsibility. These principles derive from the Constitution and are those of my Government.

The end of this crisis will be the beginning of a new era of prosperity. All the public powers will cooperate to encourage its development. The agreement that has been reached between the Senate and the Chamber of Deputies (which can now be confident of reaching the end of its mandate in accordance with the regulations) will enable the important legislative business required in the public interest to be completed.

The Universal Exhibition will soon be opened; commerce and industry will make rapid strides and we shall provide the world with further testimony of the vitality of our country, which has always recovered by hard work, thrift, and our deep respect for the ideas of conservation, order and liberty.

Marshal de MacMahon

19. *President MacMahon to Jules Grévy, January 30, 1879*

MR. PRESIDENT OF THE CHAMBER OF DEPUTIES,

Since the beginning of this session, the Government has presented a number of laws which it thought could be passed without endangering the security and good administration of the country, while at the same time satisfying public opinion. Setting aside my own ideas, I had given these laws my approval for I was not making sacrifice of any of the principles to which my conscience required me to remain faithful.

Today, in the belief that it is responding to a majority opinion in both Chambers, the Government is proposing general measures concerning the higher military commands which I consider harmful to the interests of the army, and consequently, to the country. I cannot support them.

Confronted with this refusal, the ministry is retiring. Any other ministry appointed from the majority party in the assemblies would impose the same conditions on me.

I believe that I should straightway cut short the length of the mandate entrusted to me by the National Assembly. I tender my resignation as President of the Republic.

In retiring from power, I find consolation in the thought that, during the fifty-three years I have spent in the service of my country as soldier and citizen, I have never been guided by feelings other than those of honor and duty and by absolute devotion to the country.

Mr. President, I request you to communicate my decision to the Chamber of Deputies.

I am, Sir,

Yours very truly,
Marshal de MacMahon

SECTION C: VOICES OF OPPOSITION

Each French régime set up after 1789 was confronted with a disloyal opposition, in the sense of a substantial movement seeking to overthrow the existing régime. The Second Empire and the Third Republic were no exceptions. Often there were two or more disloyal oppositions, normally seeking different ends but liable to combine when the régime ran into crisis and so conspiring to intensify the crisis. The evolution of the dictatorship of Napoleon III into the latter-day "Liberal Empire" as conceived by Émile Ollivier (1825–1913) and the evolution of the parliamentary system after 1879 each represented a process by which the rivalries of parties in agreement upon certain basic political principles replaced these more bitter and insurrectionist movements aimed at overthrowing not merely a government, but a constitution. The nature of the party system itself will be examined later (Part III, D): the present section is concerned with the attitudes and activities of the "disloyal oppositions," and with how they were countered. Monarchist oppositions (both legitimist and Orleanist) survived under the Second Empire, just as a Bonapartist opposition continued, for a decade or more, under the Third Republic. Although these oppositions were essentially disloyal, they will not be documented here because neither produced significant historical effects. Attention is concentrated on their rivals, which had considerable historical significance: the Republican opposition to the Empire, and the authoritarian challenges to the Third Republic.

§ (a) Voices of Opposition to the Second Empire

The three main forms of attack on the Empire are illustrated by excerpts from the liberal opposition as voiced by Adolphe Thiers; the radical republican attack, embodied in Léon Gambetta; and the wild but highly effective onslaught of popular ridicule, expressed by Henri Rochefort. In their contrasts, no less than their common target, these documentary excerpts help to recapture the mood of those convinced of the iniquity and the ultimate vulnerability of Louis Napoleon's dictatorship.

Thiers had joined enthusiastically in the creation of the July Monarchy of 1830, and he remained by inclination a conservative constitutionalist, distrusting the extremes of either legitimist monarchy or radical republicanism, and hankering after the English style of constitutional monarchy. Along with several Republicans, Thiers made one of his greatest mistakes in supporting Louis Napoleon for the Presidency of the Second Republic in 1848. Arrested and exiled immediately after the *coup* of 1851, Thiers eventually returned to public life in 1863 as a deputy for Paris in the Legislative Body. In January, 1864, he delivered in the Chamber a famous speech demanding the "indispensable freedoms," the essential part of which is translated as Document 20. He was to oppose the war in 1870, as he had opposed most of the foreign policies of the emperor; and when twenty-six constituencies simultaneously chose him to represent them in the National Assembly of 1871, it was his whole record as a champion of liberalism that earned him the executive power previously described (Documents 6 to 8); French text in *Annales du Sénat et du Corps Législatif* (December 6, 1863, to January 13, 1864), pp. 308–9.

Léon Gambetta, who emerged as the most eloquent spokesman of the Republican Left-Center corresponding to Thiers as the recognized spokesman of the Center, conducted even more vigorous attacks against the existing régime. He won eminence first as a champion of Republicans in the law courts, then as a writer and speaker. Edmond and Juliette Adam, who began their political *salon* in Paris in the fall of 1869, opened for him an opportunity to become the center of the most influential Republican coterie. When he stood as Republican candidate for the working-class constituency of Belleville he scored a victory over Hippolyte Carnot, son of the "organizer of victory" in the French Revolution. In an open letter to his constituents he set out his policy in memorable form, which came to be known as the Belleville Manifesto (Document 21). It derived from the policy outlined by Jules Simon in *La politique radicale* (Paris, 1868), and became in turn the basis of many subsequent Radical manifestoes. French text in J. Reinach, *Discours et plaidoyeurs politiques* (11 vols., Paris, G. Charpentier, 1881–85), vol. 1, p. 422.

Meanwhile, the French press, freed from its earlier restrictions, seized upon its freedom with both hands and lent itself to scurrilous and often brilliant abuse of the imperial court. Foremost among opposition journalists was Henri Rochefort (1830–1913), the authentic voice of the Paris boulevards, turbulent and full of verve. He began *La Lanterne*, pamphlets against the Empire, in 1868. The first issue sold 120,000 copies; the second was seized by the police; the third cost Rochefort thirteen months in prison. The extract (Document 22) comes from the first issue. Being temperamentally against all authority, he was also to oppose the Third Republic—as a supporter of Boulanger and an opponent of Dreyfus.

20. *The Indispensable Freedoms: Adolphe Thiers, January 11, 1864*

. . . I KNOW quite well that the word "Liberty" leaves nobody unmoved. It arouses unlimited desires in some, fantastic fears in others. But, gentlemen, if we will only consult experience, stopping short at what is incontestable and indisputable, is it not possible to find out, to decide what I shall call, as regards liberty, *indispensable?*

Yes, gentlemen, indispensable; you may go to Vienna, Berlin, The Hague, Madrid, or Turin, today, nobody will dispute the point any more. Yes, there is an indispensable liberty, and today it is beyond argument for enlightened men. I beg you to allow me to expound as briefly as I can this indispensable liberty. And I hasten to add that fortunately it can be perfectly reconciled with our existing institutions provided, of course, that the blessed spring from which came the Decree of November 24 is not dried up. (*Varied reactions*)

In my view, gentlemen, there are five conditions which make up what are termed the indispensable freedoms. The first is the condition which ensures the safety of the citizen. The citizen must be able to stay quietly at home, or travel all over the state without being in danger from any arbitrary action. Why do men group themselves in society? To ensure their safety. But if, when they are sheltered from individual violence, they then became victims of arbitrary actions from the power that was meant to protect them, they would have failed in their aim. The citizen must be protected against individual violence and against any arbitrary action by those in power. Thus, in respect of individual liberty, I will say no more, for it certainly deserves to be held incontestable and indispensable. But when a citizen has obtained this security it is not enough. If he went off to sleep in peaceful indolence, he would not preserve this security for very long. The citizen must keep watch over the common weal. In that case he must think about it, and he ought not to think alone, for he would then only reach an individual opinion; his fellow citizens must think along with him, they must all exchange ideas together and reach that communal thought which is called public opinion; that is only possible through the press. The press, then, should be free, but when I say freedom I do not mean impunity. Just as the individual freedom of the citizen exists on condition that he does not provoke prosecution by the law, so freedom of the press assumes that the writer will not attack the honor of citizens or disturb the peace of the country. (*Signs of approval*)

So, for me, the second indispensable freedom is that freedom in the exchange of ideas which forms public opinion. But when this opinion has been produced, it must not be idle rumor, it must achieve some result. Men must be chosen to bring expression of that opinion here, to the center of the State—which presupposes freedom of election—and by freedom of the electors I do not mean that the Government which is responsible for the laws has no role to play; that the Government, which is composed of citizens, has no opinion: I am simply saying that it must not be able to dictate who is chosen and to impose its will in the elections. That is what I call electoral freedom.

But that is not all, gentlemen. When these men come here as elected representatives to express public opinion, they must enjoy complete freedom. They must be able—and you will appreciate, gentlemen, the implications of what I am saying here—they must be able to exercise real control, and at the right time, over all actions of those in power. This control must not come too late, leaving only irreparable mistakes to be deplored. That is freedom of national representation which I shall deal with later. That freedom, in my view, is the fourth of the indispensable freedoms.

Now we come to the last one—not the most important, for they are all equally important, but the last one, whose aim is this: to see that public opinion, as stated here by the majority, actually directs the actions of the Government. (*Noise*)

Gentlemen, in order to achieve this freedom, men have conceived two systems, the Republic and the Monarchy.

In a Republic, the method is quite simple: the Head of State changes every four, six or eight years, according to the text of the Constitution.

But the supporters of the Monarchy want to be as free as if they were under a Republic; so what system did they invent? Instead of bringing the effect of public opinion to bear upon the Head of State, they brought it to bear on the depositories of his authority, to engage the debate not with the Sovereign, but with the depositories of his authority. In this way the Sovereign does not change, and the continuity of power is thus ensured, but something else does change: politics, and so we have the admirable situation of a country under a monarch who remains above our debates, a country which governs itself according to its own ideas and its own opinions. (*Prolonged and varied reaction*)

Well, those are the five conditions for freedom which I con-

sider necessary, incontestable and indispensable; of those five conditions, which have we got already? And which remain to be
acquired? Which can we have? I repeat—all of them. (*Noise*) . . .

21. *The Belleville Manifesto: Léon Gambetta, 1869*

1. The "*Cahiers*" of the Electors:

IN THE NAME of universal suffrage, basis of every political and
social organization, let us instruct our deputy to reaffirm the
principles of radical democracy and to demand with vigor: the
most radical application of universal suffrage, both for the election
of mayors and municipal councilors, with no local differentiation,
and for the election of deputies; re-partitioning of constituencies
according to the actual number of electors entitled to vote and
not according to the number of electors on the register; individual
liberty to be in future protected by the law and not left at the
mercy of arbitrary administrators; repeal of the Law of General
Security; suppression of Article 75 of the Constitution of the
Year VIII, and the direct responsibility of all *fonctionnaires*;[1]
trial by jury for every kind of political offense; complete freedom
of the press unrestricted by stamp duty and caution money; suppression of licensing of printers and publishers; freedom of meeting without let or hindrance, with liberty to discuss all religious,
philosophical, political and social affairs; repeal of Article 291 of
the Penal Code;[2] full and complete freedom of association; suppression of the ecclesiastical budget and separation of Church and
State; free, compulsory, secular primary education with competitive examinations for children of greatest intelligence for admission
to higher education, which shall likewise be free; suppression of
town dues, suppression of high salaries and pluralities, and modification of our system of taxation; appointment of all public *fonctionnaires* by election; suppression of standing armies, the cause
of ruin to the nation's finances and business, a source of hatred
between peoples and of distrust at home; abolition of privileges and

[1] Article 75 of the Constitution of the Consulate (1800) had perpetuated the
provision of a Law of August 1790 prohibiting the ordinary courts from
trying cases in which the public administration or its agents were involved.
It remained law until 1870.
[2] See Part II, D, below.

monopolies which we define in these words: "a bonus to idleness"; economic reforms are connected with the social problem, the solution of which—although subordinate to political change—must be constantly studied and sought in the name of the principles of justice and social equality. Indeed this principle alone, put into general application, can cause social antagonism to disappear and give complete reality to our slogan: Liberty, Equality, Fraternity!

2. Gambetta's reply

Citizen Electors—I accept this mandate.

On these conditions I shall be especially proud to represent you because this election will have been conducted in conformity with the true principles of universal suffrage. The electors will have freely chosen their candidate. The electors will have determined the political program of their delegate. This method seems to me at once right and in line with the traditions of the early days of the French Revolution.

I therefore in my turn adhere freely to the declaration of principles and the rightful claims which you commission me to press at the tribune.

With you, I think that there is no other sovereign but the people, and that universal suffrage, the instrument of this sovereignty, has no value and basis and carries no obligation, unless it be radically free.

The most urgent reform must therefore be to free universal suffrage from every tutelage, every shackle, every pressure, every corruption.

With you, I think that universal suffrage, once made the master, would suffice to sweep away all the things which your program demands, and to establish all the freedoms, all the institutions which we are seeking to bring about.

With you, I think that France, the home of indestructible democracy, will know liberty, peace, order, justice, material prosperity and moral greatness only through the triumph of the principles of the French Revolution.

With you, I think that a legal and loyal democracy is the political system *par excellence* which achieves most promptly and certainly the moral and material emancipation of the greatest number, and best ensures social equality in laws, actions and customs.

But—with you also—I consider that the progressive achievement of these reforms depends absolutely on the political régime and on political reforms, and it is for me axiomatic in these matters that the form involves and determines the substance.

It is, furthermore, this sequence and order of priority which our fathers have indicated and fixed in the profound and comprehensive slogan beyond which there is no safety: Liberty, Equality, Fraternity. We are thus in mutual agreement. Our contract is completed. I am at once your delegate and your trustee.

I go further than signifying agreement. I give you my vow: I swear obedience to this present contract and fidelity to the sovereign people.

22. *Henri Rochefort on "The Deceased Older Parties," 1868*

THERE WAS for a while talk of extending indulgence as far as a general amnesty for all offenses by the press; but, everything considered, it was decided that they would take up this plan again when the "older parties" had disbanded. There is nothing finer than this phrase "older parties" with which they have held up everything for the last fifteen years. It was in the name of the older parties that *Ruy Blas* was banned. When somebody asks if he can start a shop for plums and Chinese oranges, he is told that permission will not be given until the older parties, who might choose his shop as a meeting place, have begun to disband. If I had the slightest influence with the older parties I should advise them to take a step which would embarrass the Government terribly: it would be to write this solemn letter to the papers:

Dear Mr. Editor,
Sir,
　　The Government has promised so many things for the day on which we agree to disband, that we have decided to do so. We have not so much as a dessert knife on our premises, therefore let the State cease restraining itself from granting us those reforms which it is burning to press upon us, such as liberty of the press, reduction of taxes, abolition of censorship and so many other favors which the older parties have up till now prevented from being showered upon us.

Yours etc.
Signed: The deceased older parties

. . .

With their backs now to the wall, the civil servants would not know what on earth to do, and would end by hiring characters from American quarries, at forty sous a day, to impersonate the older parties, since it would become increasingly impossible to do without them.

I myself, when I went to the Ministry of the Interior, to ask what was likely to be the answer to my request for authorization of *La Lanterne,* was accused, by the senior official who received me, of being a self-declared enemy of the present state of affairs and a supporter of the famous older parties.

This insinuation was even less well founded, since (I have no need to hide the fact here) I am a convinced Bonapartist. I should like to be allowed, nevertheless, to choose my favorite in the dynasty. Among the legitimists some prefer Louis XVIII, others Louis XVI, while others bestow all their sympathies on the head of Charles X. As a Bonapartist, I prefer Napoleon II; it is my right.

I would even add that he represents for me the ideal sovereign. Nobody will deny that he occupied the throne, since his successor is called Napoleon III. What a reign, my friends, what a reign! Not one tax, no useless wars, with the taxes which follow; none of those distant expeditions in which they spend six hundred millions in order to make a claim for fifteen francs, no consuming civil lists, no ministers each accumulating five or six posts at a hundred thousand francs apiece; that's the sort of monarch I understand. Oh yes, Napoleon II, I love thee, and admire thee without reserve! Who will now dare to maintain that I am not a sincere Bonapartist?

(*La Lanterne,* No. 1. May 1, 1868)

§(b) Voices of Opposition to the Third Republic

In some respects the Third Republic was fortunate in its enemies. Marshal MacMahon was no political genius, General Boulanger was something of a mountebank, and Charles Maurras, who was undoubtedly unbalanced, fell foul of the Roman Church, whose support might have made him more formidable. Hence, perhaps, its relative longevity as French régimes go. The following section of documents illustrates four widely different angles of attack.

First, the attack of Boulangism, which derived some of its seriousness from the growing mood of disillusionment and discontent with the scandals and squalid tone of public life and which, for a time, rallied a formidable array of anti-republican forces. Georges Boulanger (1837–1891) became Minister of War in January, 1886, in the third ministry of that good Gambettist Republican, Charles Freycinet. The appointment was made on the recommendation of Georges Clemenceau, who regarded him as a reliably "republican general." His reforms of the army made him immensely popular, and after his first great review at Longchamps on Bastille Day, 1886, he became a street idol. The music halls began to sing his praises. His appeal had a sharp nationalistic edge, in that he represented the desire for a war of revenge against Germany (see Documents 85 and 86); when Bismarck, in January, 1887, named Boulanger as the greatest obstacle to good Franco-German relations, his popularity in France was doubly certain. Backed by the League of Patriots and other chauvinistic forces, he sponsored the demand for revision of the Constitution, as well as for revenge against Germany. When Daniel Wilson, son-in-law of Jules Grévy, the Republican President since 1879, was discovered in 1887 to have conducted a prosperous traffic in honors and decorations, a political crisis broke. Both monarchists and Bonapartists rallied to Boulanger's cause, and in January, 1889, he was elected for Paris and staged a *coup d'état*. Document 23 is a translation of his electoral address, and summarizes his appeal at that moment. As the plot involved his turning an election into a plebiscite by standing in every constituency at the forthcoming general elections—an odd procedure which the existing electoral laws made possible—the government foiled it by hastily changing the law so as to prohibit multiple candidatures (Document 24). Boulanger lost his nerve at all the crucial moments, and shot himself two years later. French texts in Charles Chincholle, *Le Général Boulanger* (Paris, Savine, 1889) pp. 310–12 and *Bulletin des Lois*, XII série, vol. XXXIX, No. 21142.

Secondly, there was repeated criticism from the many elements in French national life which resented and resisted the supremacy of Paris and the power of the central administration. These ranged from Rightist monarchist and traditional elements, which cherished local diversities of the *ancien régime*, and sheer peasant provincialism and parish-pump outlooks, to the philosophical anarchism of a Pierre-Joseph Proudhon, which valued the small community above all (in the manner of Rousseau), and even the insurrectionist *communard* tradition (not unrelated to Proudhonism), which demanded wider local autonomy. Centripetal forces of all kinds were liable to arise in protest against the intense centralization of the administration. By the beginning of the twentieth century these forces—tamed of former excesses—nevertheless contrived a common front to demand a whole program of internal reforms in the municipal elections of 1904. That program is given as Document 25, French text in J. Charles-Brun, *Le Régionalisme* (Paris, Bloud, 1911), pp. 281–4. The author is able (p. 39) to cite an impressive array of great names which had, at some time, lent their support to the cause of decentralization or regionalism, including Chambord, Maurras, de Broglie, Montalembert, Simon, Favre, Proudhon, and so on across the whole political spectrum.

Thirdly, there was the criticism of Charles Péguy, mystic believer, idealistic socialist, enthusiastic Dreyfusard, whose career as a poet and thinker was tragically cut short in 1914 (Document 26). In his *Notre jeunesse* (Our Youth) of 1910 he made his famous distinction between republicanism as a *mystique* and as a *politique*, a distinction which experience of the "Republic of Pals" was then making highly significant. "How beautiful was the Republic—under the Empire" had become more than a joke. French text in *Oeuvres complètes*, 4 vols. (Paris, Gallimard, 1916), vol. IV, pp. 50–61.

Finally, there was the voice—shrill and sharp—of Charles Maurras, preaching the doctrine of integral nationalism and of "France alone" in opposition to the values of civilian parliamentary purposes. The declaration that was signed by members of his League of *Action française* (Document 27) epitomizes this attack. The attack was weakened after 1926 by the fact that some of his works, and the *Action française* itself as a journal, were publicly condemned by the Papacy (Document 28). But by then, other activist and militant anti-republican groups had arisen, including the *Croix de feu* and avowedly pro-fascist leagues, to reinforce the attack; and, under the Vichy Government of 1940 to 1944, Maurras and his supporters came at last into their own, preaching the National Revolution and the end of democracy (Document 78). French texts are conveniently reprinted in 'Mermeix' (Gabriel Terrail), *Le Ralliement et l'Action Française* (Paris, Fayard, 1927), pp. 324, 456–8.

23. *General Boulanger's Address, 1889*

Electors of the Seine,

The parliamentarians, who have done all they could to prevent my standing for election, are panic-stricken today at the idea of seeing me elected. My sword upset them. They took it away from me. And now they are more anxious than when I was still wearing it.

In reality, it is not me they are frightened of, but universal suffrage, whose repeated decisions testify to the disgust the country feels at the state of degeneracy to which their incapacity, low intrigues, and tedious debates have brought the Republic.

It is in fact more convenient to make me responsible for the discredit into which they have fallen than to attribute it to their egoism and their indifference to the interest and sufferings of the people.

In order not to be forced to accuse themselves, they accuse me, by alleging that I have the most unlikely dictatorial plans. For they dismissed me as minister on the pretext that I was for war, and they attack me as a candidate on the pretext that I am for dictatorship.

Dictatorship! Were we not subjected to it in all its forms? Does a day pass without some proposal to invent exceptional laws for our electors and for me?

If the thought of playing at being dictator had occurred to me, I think it would have done so when, as Minister for War, I had the whole army in my grasp. Did anything in my attitude then justify this insulting suspicion? No! I accepted the sympathy of all without thinking of touting for popularity from anybody. What is there dictatorial in a program which advocates constitutional revision by the most democratic system, by means of a Constituent Assembly, where each deputy will have every opportunity to defend and win acceptance for his opinions?

The leaders of the Republican Party had relied upon my Republicanism when they opened the doors of the ministry to me. Give me one single act, one single profession of faith, in which I have not clearly pledged my word.

But I want, and France wants, a Republic composed of something other than a collection of ambitions and greed.

What can we hope from men who, on their own admission, have deceived you for fifteen years, and now dare to present themselves to you and ask once more for your confidence?

Electors of the Seine,

France today is eager for justice, rectitude, and unselfishness.

I want to serve her once more by trying, with you, to cut out the wastage which is exhausting her and the rivalries that degrade her.

La Patrie is our patrimony, for all of us. You will prevent it from becoming the prey of a few.

Long live France!

Long live the Republic!

General Boulanger

24. *Boulangism: Law of July 17, 1889, concerning multiple candidatures*

Article 1—Nobody can stand as candidate in more than one constituency.

Article 2—Any citizen who presents himself, or is presented, for

general or by-elections, must make known in which constituency
he intends to stand as candidate, by a declaration signed or countersigned by him and duly legalized. This declaration is deposited at
the prefecture of the appropriate *département* on the fifth day at
the latest before the date of the poll and a temporary receipt will
be issued. A final receipt will be delivered within twenty-four
hours.

Article 3—Any declaration made in violation of Article 1 of the
present Law is void and of no effect. If the declarations are sent in
by the same citizen to more than one constituency, the one with
the earliest date is alone valid. If they bear the same date, none is
valid.

Article 4—It is forbidden to sign or post bills, send or distribute
voting papers, circulars or statements of policy for the benefit of
a candidate who has not conformed to the requirements of the
present Law.

Article 5—Voting papers in the name of a citizen whose candidature has been presented in violation of the present Law are not
taken into account in the results of the voting. Bills, placards,
statements of policy, voting papers, posted up or distributed in
support of a candidature in a constituency where it cannot legally
be presented, will be removed and confiscated.

Article 6—Any candidate contravening the provisions of the present Law will be punished by a fine of ten thousand francs (10,000
fr.), and any person who acts in violation of Article 4 of the
present Law will be fined from one thousand to five thousand
francs (1,000 to 5,000 fr.).

25. *Regionalism: Program for the Municipal Elections, 1904*

THE FRENCH REGIONALIST FEDERATION, which unites in a common
interest artists anxious to see the rebirth of local life and politicians
who support communal autonomy, wishes to take advantage of
the opportunity offered by the municipal elections to remind the
public of its program and to show that Regionalism is not the
empty dream of a Utopian, but a definite scheme for the solution
of the most pressing and varied problems. Desirous of limiting its
proposals to urgent cases, the facts of which will almost certainly

be presented for decisions by the municipal councils, or to reforms necessitated by present conditions, the Regionalist Federation has decided to present the electors with nothing but a clear,
short, precise program.

There are, therefore, two types of questions which have been
deliberately omitted for the time being. First, those in which
decentralizers and federalists on one side, and on the other side
regionalists belonging to the parties of the Left and those belonging to parties of the Right, could be divided, such as the municipal
organization of Paris, and the right of the communes to organize
and control education. Next, the fundamental reforms of the
organization itself of the commune. The first type of question
could be laid claim to by one political party to the exclusion of
another, and the F.R.F. remains outside all parties. The second,
by their very complexity and extensiveness, are not suitable for
inclusion within the narrow limits of a program and cannot come
before municipal assemblies for either decisions or votes. They
should, however, receive the attention of all those who are interested in *self-government*. Local freedoms are, in fact, subordinate
to the good organization of local powers. Institutions which, by
their nature, function badly, make nonsense of the goodwill of
those men who attempt to direct them; the men are directed by the
institutions. A bad local constitution invites not liberty but tutelage, and makes intervention by the central power desirable and
necessary. These principles receive their confirmation in the facts.
Our country, isolated in the midst of modern nations by its rigid
centralization, is also isolated by the unusual nature of its communal organization. This is as different from the institutions of
ancient France as those of the peoples that surround us. This organization is uniform over the length and breadth of the land, the
same for town and country, and for all the communes in France,
and does not suit any one of them. It is imposed on communal
life by the central power, and does not seem to understand it.
The mayor is the center of all activity. Chance alone makes a
place in the deliberating assemblies for technical experts or representatives of groups with special interests. Finally, the ill-defined
limits between the business of the commune and the business of
the State, and the organization of each of them, deprive the community of a sense of its own individuality.

In order to remedy these defects there must be:

1. Differentiation between rural and urban communes;
2. Collegiality of the municipal executive power;
3. Introduction of technical expertise in the municipalities;
4. Partial establishment of professional representation in the large towns;
5. Distinction between political electoral law and municipal electoral law;
6. Separation of communal interests from political interests.

These are the reforms, of prime necessity, for which we solicit the consideration of the electors; so that they may be convinced that on their realization depends the fate of the more modest reforms for which the Regionalist Federation invites the candidates to declare their support.

Program

LEGAL REFORMS

1. Abolition of the restrictions by the present administrative laws on the autonomy of the communes concerning the method of running the public services (water, gas, electricity, transport, cheap housing, public health, etc.).
2. Greater freedom for the communes in their selection of budgetary taxes (town dues, etc.) and the gradual replacement of prefectoral control by control by the departmental commission.
3. Referendum for the sanction of initiatives involving new budgetary charges.

EXERCISE OF COMMUNAL POWERS

4. The formation of syndicates of communes, as provided for by the Law of March 22, 1890, particularly between rural communes, as soon as there is a common interest;
5. Encouragement of local initiative in intellectual matters (popular education, museums, exhibitions, libraries, and preservation of monuments, sites, places of historical interest and local traditions); the establishment of local education wherever possible, in all three grades of school;
6. Encouragement to the setting up of syndicates, friendly societies, cooperatives, and federations of them all.

The French Regionalist Federation, 1904

26. *The Republic: Charles Péguy, 1910*

I AM APPALLED when I see . . . how far removed our young men have become from all that was meant by the very thought and the *mystique* of Republicanism. It is very striking that thoughts which to us really were thoughts have for them become ideas. What for us was organic has for them become logical. . . . When a régime which was organic has become logical, and far from being alive is now historical, then that régime has fallen.

Today, the Republic is a matter for proof, for demonstration. When it was alive there was no need for proof. It was a way of living. When a régime is demonstrated easily, conveniently and triumphantly, then it is hollow, it has fallen. . . .

"What does it matter?" say the professional politicians. "What does it matter to us?" answer the politicians. "How can it affect us? We have very good prefects, so how can it affect us? It all works very well. We are no longer republicans, it is true, but we know how to govern. In fact we are better able to govern, far better than when we were republicans. . . . We have unlearned the Republic, but we have learned how to govern. Look at the elections. They are fine. They are always fine. They will be better. And they will be all the better because it is we who make them, and we are beginning to know how to make them." . . . The government makes the elections and the elections make the government. It is give and take. The government makes the electors. The electors make the government. The government makes the deputies. The deputies make the government. It is all very friendly. The masses look on. The country is requested to pay. The government makes the Chamber. The Chamber makes the government. It is not a vicious circle as you might think. It is not at all vicious. It is just a circle, a closed circuit, a closed circle. All circles are closed. Otherwise they would not be circles. It is not quite what our founders had intended. But then our founders did not do very well anyhow. And after all one cannot go on founding for ever. That would be tiring. The proof that it can last and that it can hold together is that it has already lasted forty years. It can go on for forty centuries. The first forty years are the hardest. It is the first forty years that matter most. After that one has got used to it. A country, a régime does not need you. It has no need of mystics, of a *mystique*, or of its own *mystique*. That would be an encumbrance. For so great a journey, it needs a good policy, that is to say a real government policy.

They are wrong. These politicians are wrong. From the heights of the Republic forty centuries (in the future) do not look down on them. If the Republic has been functioning for forty years, it is because everything has functioned for forty years. If the Republic is well founded in France, it is not because the Republic is well founded in France, it is because everything is well founded everywhere. In modern history, for modern peoples there occur great waves of crises, generally originating in France (1789–1815, 1830, 1848), which cause tremors from end to end of the world. There are intermissions more or less long, dead calms, lulls which pacify all things for a more or less long time. There are *epochs* and there are *periods*. We are in a period. If the Republic is stable, it is not because it is the Republic, it is not because of its own virtue, it is because it exists, it is because we exist in a period of stability. The duration of the Republic no more proves the duration of the Republic than the duration of the neighboring monarchies proves the duration of the monarchy. This duration does not signify that they are durable, but that they have begun, they are in a period, a durable period. They are contemporaneous, they are steeped in the same time, the same bath of duration. They bathe in the same period. They are of the same age. That is all it proves. . . .

[Both republicans and monarchists] believe in régimes, that a régime makes or does not make peace or war, strength and virtue, health and disease, the stability, duration, and tranquillity of a people. The strength of a race. It is as though one believed that the châteaux of the Loire caused or did not cause earthquakes.

We believe, on the contrary, (in contradiction to each separately and both together) that there are forces and realities infinitely more profound, and that peoples make the strength and the weakness of régimes, far more than régimes influence peoples. . . . We believe, on the contrary, that peoples make the régimes, the peace and war, strength and weakness, sickness and health of régimes. . . .

Everything starts as *mystique* and ends as *politique*. Everything starts with the *mystique*, with a *mystique*, with its own *mystique*, and everything ends with *politique* . . . The important point, the essential problem, is that in every order and in every system, a mystique should not be devoured by the politique to which it has given birth. . . .

We are always being told of republican degradation. When one sees what clerical politics have made of the Christian *mystique*, how can one be surprised by what radical politics have made of the republican *mystique?* When one sees what the clerics have generally made of saints, how can one be surprised by what our parliamentarians have made of heroes? When one sees what the reactionaries have made of holiness, how can one be surprised by what the revolutionaries have made of heroism?

27. Action française: *Membership Oath*

FRENCH BY BIRTH, heart, reason and will, I shall fulfill the duties of a conscious patriot.

I pledge myself to fight against every republican régime. The Republic of France is the régime of the foreigner. The republican spirit disorganizes national defense and favors religious influences directly hostile to traditional Catholicism. A régime which is French must be restored to France.

Our only future lies therefore in the Monarchy, as it is personified in the heir of the forty kings who, for a thousand years, made France. Only the Monarchy ensures public safety and, in its responsibility for order, prevents the public evils which anti-Semitism and nationalism denounce. The necessary organ of all general interests, the Monarchy revives authority, liberty, prosperity and honor.

I associate myself with the work for restoration of the Monarchy.

I pledge myself to serve it by all the means in my power.

(Declaration to be signed by members of the League of *Action française*)

28. Action française: *Decree of the Holy Office condemning certain works of Charles Maurras and the "Action française"—January 29, 1914, and December 29, 1926*

AS THERE have been several requests that a diligent inquiry should be made on the thought and intention of this Apostolic See, and especially of Pius X of happy memory, concerning the deeds and writings of Charles Maurras and the periodical entitled the *Action française*, His Holiness Pope Pius XI has ordered me, the undersigned, assessor of the Holy Office, to make careful search of the actions and documents of the Holy Congregation of the Index—which, as is well known, has been joined and incorporated in the Holy Office—and to report to him.

This inquiry is now completed and the following points have been made:

I. At the preparatory Congregation held on Thursday, January 15, 1914, "All the Advisers were unanimously of the opinion that the four works of Charles Maurras: *The Path to Paradise, Anthinea, The Lovers of Venice* and *Three Political Ideas* were really evil, and therefore deserved to be prohibited; to these works they declared that there must be added the work entitled *The Future of the Intelligence.*

"Several Advisers wished that there should also be added the books entitled *Religious Politics* and *If Strong Action Is Possible.*"

II. At the Congregation held on Monday, January 26, 1914:

"The most Eminent Cardinal Prefect declared that he spoke of this matter to the Sovereign Pontiff, and that the Holy Father, by reason of the number of petitions addressed to him orally and in writing, even by persons of considerable standing, had indeed hesitated a moment; but had finally decided that the Sacred Congregation should deal with this matter in complete freedom, while reserving to himself the right to publish the Decree.

"The Most Eminent Fathers, going to the very heart of the question, declared that, without any possible doubt, the books mentioned by the Advisers were really evil and deserved censure, especially since it is very difficult to keep young people away from these books, as their author is recommended to them as an Authority, and as the leader of those from whom the salvation of the country is expected. The Most Eminent Fathers decided unanimously to proscribe, in the name of the Sacred Congregation, the books listed, but to leave the publication of the Decree to the wisdom of the Sovereign Pontiff. In so far as concerns the periodical the *Action française, a fortnightly review,* the Most Eminent Fathers considered that the same decision should be made about it as about the works of Charles Maurras."

III. January 29, 1914: "The Secretary was received in audience by the Holy Father and reported what had taken place at the last Congregation. The Sovereign Pontiff at once began to talk about the *Action française* and the works of M. Maurras, saying that he had received, from many quarters, requests asking him not to allow the interdiction of these works by the Sacred Congregation, affirming that these works are nevertheless prohibited, and must be considered as such from now on: according to the purport of the proscription made by the Sacred Congregation, the Sovereign Pontiff reserving to himself, however, the right to indicate the moment at which the Decree shall be made public, if a new occasion arises to do so, the Decree which prohibits this periodical and these books shall be promulgated as of today's date."

IV. April 14, 1915: "The Sovereign Pontiff (Benedict XV, of happy memory) questioned the Secretary about the books by Charles Maurras and the periodical the *Action française*. The Secretary related in detail to his Holiness all that the Sacred Congregation had done in this matter, and how his predecessor, Pius X, of holy memory, had ratified and approved the proscription pronounced by the Most Eminent Fathers, but had deferred the publication of the Decree until a more propitious moment. Hearing this, His Holiness declared that that moment had not yet come; for as the war was still going on, political passions prevented an equitable judgment on this act of the Holy See."

All these matters having been carefully reported to Our Very Holy Father by myself, the undersigned, assessor of the Holy Office, His Holiness deemed that it had become opportune to publish and promulgate this Decree of Pope Pius X, and decided to effect the promulgation with the date prescribed by his predecessor of happy memory, Pius X.

Moreover, in view of the articles written and published, particularly in the last few days, by the journal of the same name *Action française*, and, especially, articles by Charles Maurras and Léon Daudet, which any sensible man is obliged to recognize as being written against the Apostolic See and the Roman Pontiff himself, His Holiness has confirmed the condemnation made by his predecessor and has extended it to the aforesaid daily, *Action française*, as it is published today, so that this journal shall be held to be prohibited and condemned, and shall be inscribed on the Index of prohibited books, without prejudice in future to investigations or condemnations of the works of either writer.

Given in Rome, at the Palace of the Holy See, December 29, 1926.

By order of the Holy Father
Canali, Assessor

SECTION D: ADMINISTRATION

The French administrative system, it is repeated *ad nauseam*, dates from Napoleon I and is highly centralized. Neither generalization is correct, nor was it correct throughout most of the period under study. Administrative history offers, indeed, an impressive example of how it is possible to combine great continuity with much fluctuation. The two key institutions, the Council of State (*Conseil d'État*) and the prefects, were in some ways descendants of the *Conseil du Roi* and the *Intendants* of the *ancien régime*. Adopted and adapted by the Revolution and Napoleon, they proved too useful as agencies of power for any subsequent régime to abandon them.

The Council of State even preserved its distinction between Councilors of State and *Maîtres des requêtes*, titles which both go back to the fourteenth century. It normally combined two functions, that of technical adviser and counselor to the government in such matters as drafting legislation or decrees, and that of an administrative court, concerned with disputes in which the public authority in any form was a party. But it underwent two important changes, in 1852 and in 1872. Until 1848 its members had always been appointed by the executive. The National Assembly of the Second Republic elected them, and used the Council as a check upon the President. In 1852 Louis Napoleon reverted to the traditional usage and restored the Council as an agency of executive power (see Document 4, Articles 47 to 53).

The Council played so important and so strongly political a role in the Second Empire that it inevitably suffered from its collapse. A Decree of September 15, 1870, suspended all its existing members from their functions and replaced it by a provisional commission until the National Assembly could devise a permanent replacement. This was done by the Law of May 24, 1872, which in essence reverted to the view of the Second Republic that its legislative role should be purely advisory. Parties in the Assembly differed mainly about how Councilors of State were to be appointed. The Law (Art. 3) provided for the twenty-two Councilors to be elected by the National Assembly for a term of nine years, renewable by one-third every three years. The twenty-four *Maîtres des requêtes* were to be appointed by the President of the Republic by decree in the Council of Ministers. Thus was a balance struck between the claims of legislature and executive (Document 29). The third category, Auditors, were to be appointed by competitive examinations, though after 1879 First Class Auditors were appointed by the President of the Republic, and the examination for appointment as Second Class Auditor was made more difficult. The Law provided for fifteen "Councilors of State in special service" (*en service extraordinaire*), one drawn from each ministerial department. Their function was to link the Council's work closely with the active administration—they could not take part in its judicial work. Article 4 of the Law of February 25, 1875 (Document 10), restored appointment of Councilors in ordinary service to the Council of Ministers—i.e., the executive power.

On this basis the Council of State operated throughout the rest of the life of the Third Republic, acquiring great independence as a judicial body and gaining in esteem as the mainstay of the permanent working administrative machinery of the country. When on "detached service" its members provided the government with a reservoir of highly trained administrators (e.g., as *chef de cabinet* for a minister) while themselves acquiring varied experience.

French text in *Bulletin des lois de la république française*, XII série vol. 92, No. 1160 (1872). See also Charles E. Freedeman, *The Conseil d'État in Modern France* (New York, 1961).

29. *Law dealing with reorganization of the Council of State, May 24, 1872*

Part I

Composition of the Council of State

Article 1—The Council of State is composed of twenty-two Councilors of State on ordinary service, and fifteen Councilors of State on special service. Attached to the Council of State are:

1. Twenty-four *Maîtres des requêtes* and
2. Thirty Auditors.

A Secretary-General is appointed as the head of the bureaus of the Council.

A special secretary is attached to the Judicial Section.

Article 2—Ministers are entitled to a seat on the General Assembly of the Council of State. Each of them is entitled to speak and vote, in nonjudicial business, on matters which concern his own ministry. The Keeper of the Seals is entitled to speak and vote whenever he presides over the General Assembly or its sections.

Article 3—The Councilors of State on ordinary service are elected by the National Assembly, meeting in public, by *scrutin de liste* and absolute majority voting. After two tests, *scrutin de ballotage* takes place between those candidates who have obtained more than double the number of votes of those remaining to be elected.

Before proceeding to election, the National Assembly invites a committee of fifteen members, appointed by the bureaus, to propose a list of candidates.

This list contains the same number of names as the number of Councilors to be elected, plus half as many again; it is drawn up in alphabetical order.

The election may not take place till at least three days after the distribution and publication of the list. The Assembly may choose candidates who have not been proposed by the committee.

The members of the Council of State may not be chosen from members of the National Assembly.

Deputies who resign may not be elected within six months of their resignation.

Where a vacancy occurs, through the death or resignation of a Councilor of State, the National Assembly proceeds, within a month, to the election of a new member.

The Councilors of State on ordinary service may be suspended for a period not exceeding two months, by decree of the President of the Republic, and during the period of suspension the suspended Councilor shall be replaced by the senior *Maître des requêtes* of the section.

The National Assembly has the right to be notified of the case through the decree which has announced the suspension; at the end of the period it may retain or dismiss the Councilor of State. In case of dismissal a replacement must be appointed within a month. Councilors of State are renewed by a third every three years; retiring members are chosen by lot and are re-eligible for an indefinite period.

Article 4—The Council of State is presided over by the Keeper of the Seals, Minister for Justice, and in his absence by a Vice President. The Vice President is appointed by a decree of the President of the Republic and chosen from among the Councilors on ordinary service.

In the absence of the Keeper of the Seals and of the Vice President, the Council of State is presided over by the senior president of sections, according to the precedence of the roll.

Article 5—The Councilors of State on special service are appointed

by the President of the Republic; they lose their legal title of
Councilor of State when they cease to belong to the active administration.

The *Maîtres des requêtes*, the Secretary-General and the special
secretary of the Judicial Section are appointed by a decree of the
President of the Republic; they cannot be dismissed except by an
individual decree.

The Vice President and the presidents of sections will be asked to
send in nominations for the *Maîtres des requêtes*, the Secretary-
General and the secretary of the Judicial Section.

Decrees of dismissal shall not be delivered before the advice of
the presidents has been obtained.

The Auditors are divided into two classes, the first composed of
ten, and the second of twenty.

Second Class Auditors are chosen by competitive examination.
Its procedure and conditions shall be laid down under regulations drawn up on the responsibility of the Council of State:
Second Class Auditors remain in their functions for not more than
four years, and receive no salary.

First Class Auditors shall be chosen by competitive examination,
according to procedure laid down under the regulations of May
9, 1849. Only Second Class Auditors will be allowed to compete.

Nevertheless, all candidates between twenty-five and thirty
years of age, who fulfill the conditions laid down in Article 5 of
the regulation of May 9, 1849, shall be admitted to the tests for the
first competition for the First Class, which shall take place after the
promulgation of the present Law.

Former Auditors of the Council of State and those who have
been attached to the provisional commission set up by the Decree
of 1870 shall be exempt from the preliminary tests.

The First Class Auditors receive a salary equal to half that of
the *Maîtres des requêtes;* the period of their functions is not
limited.

At least one third of the places for *Maîtres des requêtes* shall be
reserved for First Class Auditors.

Second Class Auditors, as also First Class Auditors, may not be
dismissed except by individual decree and only after joint consultation between the Vice President of the Council of State and the
presidents of sections.

The staff of the bureaus are appointed by the Vice President of

the Council of State, on the nomination of the Secretary-General.
Article 6—No person may be appointed Councilor of State unless
he is over thirty years of age; *Maître des requêtes*, over twenty-
seven years of age; Second Class Auditor, not less than twenty-one
and not more than twenty-five; First Class Auditor, not less than
twenty-five or more than thirty.

Article 7—The functions of Councilor on ordinary service and of
Maître des requêtes are incompatible with holding any other salaried public office.

Nevertheless general or superior officers in the army, or navy, inspectors or engineers of the Highways Department, Mines or
Marine, and Professors of Higher Education, may be seconded to
the Council of State. During the period of their functions they retain the rights proper to their position, but may not receive their
salary as well as that of Councilor of State.

The functions of Councilor and *Maître des requêtes* are incompatible with those of administrator of any privileged or subsidized
company.

The Councilors of State and *Maître des requêtes*, when they relin-
quish their functions, may be made honorary Councilors or *Maîtres
des requêtes*.

The title of Auditor and *Maître des requêtes* on special service is
abolished.

Part II

Functions of the Council of State

Article 8—The Council of State gives advice: (i) on bills of parliamentary initiative which the National Assembly judges fit to send
to it; (ii) on bills of governmental initiative which a special decree
orders to be submitted to the Council of the State; (iii) on drafts
of decrees and, in general, on all questions which are submitted to
it by the President of the Republic or by the ministers. It is required to give its advice on all regulations of public administration
and on all decrees in the form of a regulation of public administration. It exercises besides, until it be otherwise ordained, all functions that were conferred on the former Council of State by laws
or regulations which have not been abrogated. Councilors of State
may be charged by the Government to defend in the Assembly
bills which have been sent to the Council for examination.

Article 9—The Council of State sits definitively on all cases in matters of administrative adjudication, and on all requests for annulment for *ultra vires* directed against the acts of the various administrative authorities.

Part III

Forms of Procedure

Article 10—The Council of State is divided into four sections, three of which are concerned with the examination of purely administrative matters, and one with the adjudication of disputes. The Judicial Section will be composed of six Councilors of State and the Vice President of the Council of State; the other sections will consist of four Councilors and a President. The presidents of the sections are appointed by decree of the President of the Republic and chosen from the Councilors on ordinary service.

The Minister of Justice has the right to preside over the sections, except for the Judicial Section. The Councilors on ordinary service are selected for each section by decrees from the President of the Republic. The Councilors on special service, the *Maîtres des requêtes*, and the Auditors are allotted to the sections by decisions of the Minister of Justice, according to the needs of the service. The Councilors on special service may not be attached to the Judicial Section.

A regulation of public administration shall decide the internal arrangement of the Council's work, the division of business between the sections, which matters should be submitted to the General Assembly, methods of rotation of members between the sections, and executive measures not provided for by the present Law.

Article 11—Councilors on special service are entitled to speak and vote in the General Assembly and in their section on matters pertaining to the ministerial department to which they belong. They have only an advisory capacity on other matters.

The *Maîtres des requêtes* are entitled to speak and vote in the General Assembly and in their section on matters for which they are the reporters and in an advisory capacity on other matters.

Auditors are entitled to speak and vote in their section and speak in an advisory capacity in the General Assembly, but only in matters for which they are the reporters . . . [The rest of Part III deals with technical procedural details]

Part IV

Conflicts and the Tribunal of Conflicts

Article 25—Conflicts of attributions between the administrative authority and the judicial authority are resolved by a special tribunal consisting of:

(1) The Keeper of the Seals, as President;
(2) Three Councilors of State on ordinary service elected by the Councilors on ordinary service;
(3) Three Councilors from the *Cour de Cassation* nominated by their colleagues;
(4) Two members and two deputies elected by the majority of the other judges named in the preceding paragraphs.

Members of the Tribunal of Conflicts must stand for re-election every three years and are re-eligible for an indefinite period.

They choose a Vice President by secret ballot and by an absolute majority of votes.

No discussion can be valid unless at least five members are present.

Article 26—Ministers have the right to bring before the Tribunal of Conflicts matters raised in the Judicial Section which do not belong to administrative disputes. However, they may not avail themselves of this jurisdiction until the Judicial Section has refused to allow the plea for justice which must first be communicated to it.

Article 27—The Law of February 4, 1850, and the regulation of October 28, 1849, on the method of procedure before the Tribunal of Conflicts are again brought into force.

Article 28—The times fixed for the judgment of conflicts shall be suspended during the period which elapses between the promulgation of the present Law and the setting up of the Tribunal of Conflicts. . . .

[Articles 29 and 30 deal with transitional matters only]

30. *The Prefect at Work: Paul Cambon, 1876–1880*

The prefects were, by tradition and by appointment, the central government's agents in the localities. Napoleon III used them entirely as such, and they were an indispensable element in his authoritarian system. There was, therefore, a wholesale removal of Bonapartist prefects after 1870, and the 1870's were an exceptionally uneasy period for them. Gambetta, Thiers, and Broglie, each in turn, replaced prefects by their

own nominees. After the crisis of May 16, 1877, when the whole machinery for "making elections" favorable to the party in power was
used at full blast against the Republicans, it became official republican
doctrine to deprecate all direct electoral pressure. But the prefects were
inevitably enmeshed in politics, both ministerial and local, and republican practice by no means conformed with the doctrine. It was the
function of the prefects (and the sub-prefects) to serve as intermediaries
between State and Society—enforcing the commands of the State,
applying its regulations and orders, keeping the government of the day
informed of conditions in the country, and, at the same time, administering patronage, keeping on working terms with the mayors and
other local dignitaries, tending local interests. Being mostly men of high
ability and great acumen, they contrived to perform these difficult tasks
with tact and good sense, and every régime relied heavily upon them.

One such was Paul Cambon (1843–1924), protégé of Jules Ferry
and his secretary-general when Ferry was Prefect of the Seine during
the Paris Commune in 1871 (see Documents 50 to 53). He became
Prefect of Aube (southeast of Paris) when the Minister of the Interior
himself, Casimir-Périer, represented that *département* in the National
Assembly, but was removed after the fall of Thiers (May 24, 1873).
In 1876 he became Prefect of Doubs (Besançon), where he was left
during the crisis of May 16, 1877; and in 1878 was made Prefect of the
Nord (Lille), where he remained for five years under Republican ministries. His subsequent career led him to be minister-resident in Tunisia
(where he clashed with General Boulanger), and, successively, ambassador in Madrid, Constantinople, and London. He held the embassy in
London for twenty-two years, retiring only after the war in 1920.

The four letters translated below, two to his brother Jules (also a
diplomatist) when he was Prefect of Doubs in 1876 and 1877 and two
to his wife when he was Prefect at Lille in 1880, express the personal irritations and attitudes of an able man compelled by circumstances to
wrestle with provincial sectarians. "God preserve us from the fanatics,"
as he wrote at the end of 1880. The year had been spent in turmoil
because of the decision to dissolve unauthorized religious congregations.
Since Madame Cambon was a Protestant, he had sympathy with those
of religious faith, but not with clericalism. French texts in Paul Cambon,
Correspondance 1870–1924, Vol. I, 1870–1898 (Paris, Bernard Grasset,
1940), here reproduced by kind permission of the publishers.

(i) Paul Cambon to Jules Cambon, Monday March 27, 1876

I THINK Besançon is better than anything else. I shan't have to deal
with the Bonapartists. The *département* is republican and clerical;
clerical society is a pretty closed one, but exerts very little influence. I got myself covered on that side by asking Bishop Ravinet
to write to the Archbishop of Besançon, and by lunching yester-

day at M. de Saint-Aignan's, with M. de Mérode and M. X. Marmier, unsuccessful candidates in the Doubs in the last elections. Mérode is a man of great wit. He will cultivate me in the hope of winning my support in the next senatorial elections.

As for the Republicans, I have their confidence. The deputies are Albert Grévy and some nonentities, one a Radical, but a personal friend of Roux.

M. Casimir-Périer has written to the Duke of Aumale,[1] who has replied very graciously. General Guépratte has seen the Duke of Nemours with whom, moreover, M. de Saint-Aignan is dining tomorrow. This will lead to my being introduced to the prince.

(ii) Paul Cambon to Jules Cambon: Besançon, February 26, 1877

I am continually angry with my deputies who are mostly stolid Comtois with whom I have no common ground. I sometimes comfort myself by upbraiding them, but I am often saddened and sick at heart. You have no idea how distrustful everybody is here. I have to watch my every act and word as never before. I detest Franche-Comté from the bottom of my heart, and my temperament is the direct opposite to that of the people round here. They are obstinate, gloomy, rude, unresponsive to any attention and false to the core. I make the best of it. These annoyances are of a higher order than yours, perhaps, but very absorbing also. What is particularly odious is that with the Francs-Comtois you are always having to begin all over again. Whether you have been here six months or twenty years, you are always a foreigner, that is to say, an enemy, and if you manage to force a smile of agreement out of them one day, by dint of much patience and care, next day they look just as morose as ever. It has been like this ever since I arrived. A very distinguished man, Dean of the Faculty of Science at Besançon, said to me a few days ago: "I have been here for eighteen years, and I have not yet been given the freedom of the city." This mayor of mine at Besançon, a senator whom I got the Marshal to decorate, and who always has to come to dinner whenever he is in trouble, makes protestations and weeps into my waistcoat, but can't say enough against me when my back is turned. Jules Ferry told me so the other day. Deputies whom I have stuffed full of Republican speeches, compliments, licences for tobacconists' and wine-

[1] Duc d'Aumale (1822–1897), fourth son of Louis Philippe, was distrusted by Republicans as uncle of the Orleanist pretender, the Comte of Paris.

shops, then write to me for no earthly reason that I am betraying the Republic. I get cross and reply, and they apologize—and that is how I go on. There are heights and depths which, taken together, are bearable on the average. To sum up, I have no major difficulties, but I am telling you about my troubles to console you for yours, and so that you need not think that the worst evils are having to obey every summons of the Director-General's bell. After all, you don't have to bother about your Director-General. I couldn't see him far enough, a fool like that, elected by ten or fifteen thousand of his countrymen!

Rumors of war are dying down. The Duke of Aumale reaches here about March 10. We shall know what line to take about all that, as I shall have a chat with him. I can certainly talk with him more freely than with anybody else I see here.

(iii) Paul Cambon to his wife: [Lille] April 23, 1880

Will the clericals make a demonstration or not? Here is a little pamphlet which is being distributed in profusion around the town by Mme Mennessier, a very excitable old lady of Lille who has a charming daughter to marry off.

There are lots of rumors flying about; the Catholic students have rented windows to hiss "Down with Ferry!" There is no end to it all. The other side have passed the word to the working-men's clubs, Socialists, Masonic lodges, etc., to bring along their bands and swamp the opposing demonstrations. It will be a real American spectacle. I am looking forward to it. I expect really that there will be not much more than a few boos and shouts of "Long live the Senate." We shall see.

I nearly forgot to tell you that yesterday I had a visit from the Count of Caulincourt, the foremost leader of the Clerical Party in Lille. He is a cousin of M. de Saint-Aignan, and has promised to use his influence to try and prevent hostile demonstrations. We talked a lot about the Decrees. We get on very well together.

On the other hand I received a visit today from my working-class General Councilor, Cheri Dumez, who is to give the signal for the sympathetic demonstrations. He told me that he could not come to my party because he had no evening dress. I advised him to get one made, and argued that it was the most democratic of costumes. "Yes, but it is an expense." He will come after all in a frock-coat, and will bring along some of his mates in the same attire.

The clericals are getting a professor of the Catholic Faculty of Law at Lyons to come on Sunday and give a lecture on the Decrees at the Hippodrome. It will be their way of protesting while Jules Ferry is making a speech a few steps away, when he lays the foundation stone for the Faculty of Medicine.

We have reached the highest pitch of irritation and excitement all around. I am beginning to wonder how we shall get on in July, with everybody convinced they are right. That is how the Wars of Religion began in days gone by. There is no danger of that now, but there will be some scuffling in a few towns, and perhaps in Lille.

(iv) Paul Cambon to his wife: [Lille] October 21, 1880

These fools of clericalists are doing all they can to attract attention to themselves. I had arranged things nicely so that the lesser orders in Lille would be left alone, but yesterday, here were 250 Gentlemen of the town going in solemn procession to say farewell to the Redemptorists, Recollects, etc. . . . . The journal *La Vraie France* did contain an article on the Recollects, saying that I had wanted to save them but M. Constans was bent on having their heads, so the Republican papers are pitching into everybody this morning. The Legitimists · obviously only want to make a commotion; they are the ones who are leading everybody on, fighting the Government on the backs of these poor monks who are helpless in the matter, but would be glad to be free of these compromising allies.

I have seen the *curé* of my parish twice today. He is my great intermediary between the Jesuits and the congregations. I told him that the articles in *La Vraie France* and the maneuvers by the Legitimists are opening up the whole question again. The poor man is very upset. He is going to tell the Cardinal this from me.

31. *Law on the Liberty of the Press of July 29, 1881*

In general the administration gained in power throughout the period. The functions and responsibilities of the prefects increased with greater State activity. But in one sphere, at least, they diminished—that of control over the press. The tendency of monarchism and of Bonapartism alike was to assert firm control, to hamper opposition, and to hem round all publication with complex restrictions. This tendency reached a height with a Decree of February 17, 1852, which required the founders and publishers of all journals dealing with "politics or social economy" to get prior permission from the Minister of the Interior, and gave the prefects power to warn, suspend, or suppress newspapers. These restrictions were freely used, and by 1865 only 250 political journals were appearing in the provinces, as compared with some 430 in 1851. Since no drawing could be published without permission of the Prefect of Police, there was direct censorship of illustrated papers.

From 1868 onward, however, the tide turned and the press won increasing freedom. One measure that inaugurated the era of the belated Liberal Empire was the Law of May 11, 1868, which abolished the requirement that official permission was needed to found a new journal, and deprived officials of the right to warn, suspend, or suppress. Many new papers appeared, including Henri Rochefort's famous *Lanterne* (see Document 22), although the hazards and restrictions remained burdensome.

With its background of defiance of authority in such matters, republicanism naturally favored wider freedom of the press, and one of the earliest acts of the Government of National Defense was, on September 10, 1870, to declare that the professions of printing and publishing were free. It was, however, a decade and more before press liberties were fully embodied in law. The Law on the Liberty of the Press of July 29, 1881 (Document 31), took five years to complete and superseded forty-two previous laws. No previous authorization or caution money was required before publication, only deposit of copies at the prefectures or the mairies, specifying the name and address of the printer and the number printed; and, in the case of journals or periodicals, a declaration by the manager (Art. 7). No power remained in the hands of the administrative or judicial authorities to suspend or suppress a newspaper or periodical. Chapter IV of the Act (not here reproduced) dealt with the matters of press offenses, the list of which was greatly reduced and all of which were to be tried by jury in the assize courts.

This important but neglected law remained the basis of all press freedoms until the end of the Third Republic. It was modified, inevitably, during the First World War, and in the 1930's it was open to the charge that it gave excessive license, for it made possible the vicious personal attacks and incitement to violence of such publications as the *Action française* (see Document 27). The French press of the 1930's certainly tolerated a degree of scurrility, violence, and financial corruption which were abuses of the freedoms laboriously won in the course of the previous century.

French text in *Bulletin des lois de la république française*, vol. 637, No. 10,850 (1881), pp. 125–38. See also Irene Collins, *The Government and the Newspaper Press in France, 1814–1881* (Oxford, 1959); G. Weill, *Histoire du parti républicain en France, 1814–1870* (Paris, new edn., 1928); and Raymond Manevy, *Histoire de la presse, 1914–1939* (Paris, 1945).

Chapter I: Printing and Publishing

Article 1—Printing and publishing are free.

Article 2—All published printed matter, with the exception of pieces of jobbing work, shall bear the name and address of the printer, under penalty of a fine between five francs and fifteen francs.

Penalty of imprisonment may be imposed if the printer has been convicted of a similar offense during the preceding twelve months.

Article 3—Upon the publication of all printed matter the printer must deposit two copies for the national copyright libraries under penalty of a fine of between sixteen and three hundred francs.

Printed matter must be deposited at the Ministry of the Interior in Paris, at the Prefecture of the chief town of a *département*, at the Sub-Prefecture of the chief town of an *arrondissement*, and at the Mairie in other towns.

Copies thus deposited must mention the title of the printed matter and the number printed.

Voting papers, business or industrial circulars and pieces of jobbing work are excepted from the above.

Article 4—The above provisions apply to all types of printed matter or reproductions intended for publication.

However, in the case of prints, music, and most reproductions other than printed matter, three copies must be deposited in conformity with the preceding Article.

Chapter II: Periodical Publications

§1. RIGHT OF PUBLICATION, MANAGEMENT, DECLARATION TO BE DEPOSITED WITH THE PUBLIC PROSECUTOR

Article 5—Any journal or periodical may be published without previous authorization or caution money after the declaration laid down in Article 7.

Article 6—Every journal or periodical shall have a manager. The manager must be French and over twenty-one years of age. He must have full civil rights and not be deprived of his civil rights by any judicial conviction.

Article 7—Before the publication of any journal or periodical a declaration must be made to the Public Prosecutor stating:

   (i) The title of the journal or periodical and its manner of publication;

(ii) The name and address of the manager;

(iii) The name of the press where it is to be printed.

Any change in the above conditions must be notified within the following five days.

Article 8—Declarations shall be made in writing on stamped paper and signed by the managers. A receipt will be given. . . .

32. *The Mayor at Work: Édouard Herriot at Lyons, 1905–1912*

By the end of the period France was divided into 90 *départements* (each of which had a prefect as its administrative head) and also into 38,104 communes, each of which had a mayor. The communes varied in population from a tiny village of a few dozen families to large cities such as Lyons or Marseilles; but the great majority were small rural communities, and only some 800 communes had a population greater than 5,000. It is, therefore, misleading to generalize about the work of mayors.

But each commune (except Paris) had an elective municipal council, and its mayor was chosen by and from this council. Each was a public corporation able to acquire and dispose of property, institute actions in the law courts, and levy rates to finance its municipal services. These could include a very wide range of activities, as the extracts from the memoirs of Édouard Herriot show (Document 32). Herriot became Mayor of Lyons on November 3, 1905, and continued until September, 1940, when he was removed by the Vichy Government. The "Radicals' Pope," he was Prime Minister on three occasions and held many ministerial posts. He was several times president of the Chamber of Deputies, and was restored to that post (as also to the Mairie at Lyons) after liberation. He was a lifelong Radical, and his early achievements at Lyons, the third city in the country, demonstrate the strong links between Radical-Socialism and Fabian municipal ("gas-and-water") Socialism. His memoirs, *Jadis* (2 vols., Paris, Flammarion, 1948), from which these extracts are taken (pp. 172–4 and 186–190), were written in the 1940's, when Herriot was already more than seventy. (They are here reproduced by kind permission of the publisher, Ernest Flammarion.) They are an old man's reminiscences, though the vigor of mind and boundless civic pride are unmistakable. It was common for mayors of important towns also to be deputies. In the Chamber of 1932 to 1936 there were sixty mayors, including those of Bordeaux, Le Havre, Lille, Amiens, Reims, Tours, Rouen, and Grenoble. As the unpaid but influential spokesmen of local interests, the mayors could form a powerful bloc, and had a national association of their own with a permanent secretariat in Paris. Administratively, they can be regarded as the counterpart to the prefects; if the prefect is a central agent having to conciliate local interests, the mayor is a local official having to implement and conform to central policies. Often what mattered to both was being able to come to terms with each other (see Document 30). See also Francis de Tarr, *The French Radical Party from Herriot to Mendès-France* (London, New York, Toronto, 1961).

THE COMMUNE is the essential cell of our country. In 1905 it still enjoyed a certain amount of liberty and possessed certain funds, whereas since the last war the mayor has become more like a civil servant obeying orders from the State.

I found myself at the head of a great administration, responsible for a budget which included 22 million (francs) in receipts and 22 millions in expenditure (a considerable sum at that time). I was in charge of a staff of 1,650 employees, to whom I at once gave guarantees and a rise in wages. I engaged in the construction of new abattoirs with the assistance of an architect, M. Tony Garnier, *grand prix de Rome*, a specialist in the study of the modern city and an undisputed authority. Garnier conceived a grandiose project, in an area of 230,000 square meters, including a station, platforms, numbering pens, numerous stables, a covered market, slaughtering rooms, mechanized plant and cold store. The market in particular is reckoned to be a masterpiece of daring and lightness.

I set about electrifying the town's services, bringing motorized transport into general use, both for fire-fighting and street-cleaning. I made plans for new bridges over the Saône and the Rhône. This part of my work was of special interest to me. I had a very learned mathematician as my chief engineer. For the structure which was to become the Wilson Bridge, he got me to adopt a new formula, the Séjourné formula which had just been utilized in the Grand Duchy of Luxemburg as well as in Toulouse. This consisted in placing the floor on two walls, without filling the space between with masonry. I learned a great deal from my conversations with Tony Garnier, who was an artist as well as a scholar, and with Auric. My chief engineer did not believe in the three dimensions of space. I begged him to admit of their existence at least during the construction which I had entrusted to him. The law on old-age assistance which had recently been passed created heavy obligations for us, although we accepted them very willingly. We also had to apply the Law of January 2, 1907, on the separation of the Churches and the State.

For the future, I was seeking methods of developing Lyons as a "turntable" for transportation. Placed at the confluence of two great waterways, one of which, the Saône, is the typical navigable river, Lyons seemed to me most suitable to become one of the great centers for France, and perhaps for Europe, of inland navigation. I had observed that the Germans made full use of their rivers. In the port of Mannheim, situated at the confluence of the Rhine and the Neckar, in conditions similar to those at Lyons, tonnage saw a yearly increase. So far there was only talk of improving the course of the lower Rhône. I tried to contribute to it. And I started negotiations with the Compagnie Paris-Lyon which were to result in the construction of Port Rambaud on the Saône. This company, with which I have since worked so often and so successfully, gradually abandoned their old hostility to competition from waterways. I persuaded them to give up a certain wharf, the use of which they had in any case already prohibited. I came up against the opposition of the botanists who collected precious specimens from the stagnating marsh.

It will be understood that I was very preoccupied with the problem of public education. My period as assistant master had given me wide experience. At this time the law laid down that the costs of education had to be met by the town in return for quite inadequate compensation. I took steps to make it possible for Lyons to revert to the communal system and finally achieved this. In spite of our paradoxical situation, we were preparing a vast program of school building.

We put up fourteen new schools, and remembering how inadequate, in spite of its glorious history, had been the lycée where I had taught, I got another one built, near the Parc de la Tête d'Or. I also made a mistake which I soon had to rectify: abolishing prize givings.

I joined the General Council of the Rhône in November 1910 following an election which had given me 3,716 votes against 2,823 for M. Albert Rosset.

I continued to take a keen interest in municipal affairs. I used to receive regularly a visiting card from a former colleague who had taken the title of "Ex-youngest Mayor of France." I little thought that the day would come when I could claim the same designation, by the grace of the most arbitrary government that

France has ever known.[1] We were setting up new school units. In May 1910, with my friend Jean Deydier, president of the Automobile Club of the Rhône, I created the airfield which was to become the civil and military aerodrome of Lyons.

We transferred our old library to the former archbishop's palace and we had set up our museum of natural history again in the Guimet Museum. I was sorry that such an original collection by an industrialist from Lyons had been housed in Paris. M. Guimet was very willing to assemble important collections for us. He was a curious man. In spite of vague scientific knowledge and somewhat exaggerated archeological pretensions, he had very intelligently devoted part of his fortune, which had been acquired in the preparation of "Guimet blue," to traveling and research in the East and Far East. He claimed that he offered us the authentic mummy of Thais. His greatest mistake was in composing a pseudo-Chinese opera in which a duo for trombone and mandoline evoked more hilarity than emotion.

I should have liked to deck Lyons with fine adornments: my fellow citizens, I thought, gave too little care to this. Such a fine town, birthplace of the rose, has yet not made the most of its admirable setting, its quays, and its hills. I would have liked gardens in front of the houses, as in Brussels. From Budapest I borrowed the idea of the "flowering street" which has since become common. I cherished Lyons as one loves a woman.

We developed our charitable aid by opening a boys' orphanage, making the municipal administration responsible for a school for the deaf, dumb and blind, and raising the rate of assistance to the aged.

The proposal for the new hospital had at last been unanimously passed by the Hospital Council, the General Council and the Municipal Council. They no longer disputed our desire to isolate infections and tubercular cases and to give gardens to the sick as well. We had in mind to make a great university center out of this establishment, which would be worthy of our famous medical tradition and endowed with vast laboratories.

In 1910 I set up Lyonnais Restaurants for nursing mothers. The idea had been given to me by a woman of good sense and warm heart, Mme. Henri Coullet, who some years earlier had opened the

[1] M. Herriot ceased to be Mayor of Lyons under the Vichy Government of 1940.

restaurant of the rue Ramponneau in a poor district of Paris with
an original capital of ten francs. Her plan was simple: to admit,
without a check, any mother nursing a child, and to serve her two
meals, morning and evening, as cheap but as substantial as possible.
In spite of modest resources, the service rapidly prospered. The
mothers who had been helped in this way expressed their gratitude.
One poor woman who had lost her little girl sent along five francs
which had been found in the dead child's money-box. One poor
old man used to go into the restaurant every day to offer a potato
he had saved. I opened three centers of this kind in Lyons. No
formalities, no conditions, no inquiries. Whoever a mother may be
or wherever she comes from, she may come in; and once in, she is
at home. The rules protect her against any indiscretion; she is surrounded by the secrecy that she is entitled to, and very naturally,
once the woman feels warm again and reassured, she very soon
starts to talk about herself eagerly, asks for advice, direction and
support. I have sometimes been told that the place is run too freely
and is almost anarchical. I admire and have adopted that fine maxim
of Orgon talking to his daughter in *Le Jeu de l'Amour et du
Hasard:* "Come now, in this world you have to be a little too good
to be good enough."

The law on workers' pensions was gradually becoming applicable. The town of Lyons put up a building for the Mutual
Insurance where it could work in complete independence. We
were also fighting for the right of the commune itself to erect
workers' houses, but the reactionary opposition refused. The
Government was still hostile to erecting houses under direct control; we had to limit ourselves to supporting private societies. We
increased communal holdings by the purchase of property; we had
given to the town ownership of the wealthy district of Grolée. Yet
in spite of these various enterprises, the budget of Lyons remained
perfectly healthy, with the receipts constantly in excess, and no
change in the total communal taxes. The rates had not varied for
the last thirty years. My colleagues and I thought that we should
demand the increase in our resources from the development of the
city itself.

At the Hôtel-de-Ville of Lyons we were also deciding on our
policy for the Rhône. We had before us the plan of Émile Harlé,
for the transport and distribution in Paris of the electric energy
produced by the river; this included the electrification of the Paris-

Lyons-Geneva railway line and the construction of a navigable waterway between the Rhône and the Rhine; a big dam would be built near Genissiat. The project had been studied by the Chamber of Commerce of our town and by its president, M. Coignet, and they expressed their approval of the scheme. I had corresponded with M. Harlé and he had promised us reduced rates and favorable allocation. I reserved judgment till the plan was publicly debated. But I remained intransigent about taking water to Paris; we had transformed our factories by bringing in electricity, increased our pumping capacity, reinforced our reservoirs and water mains, and sunk new wells. We did not intend to sacrifice the hygienic needs of Lyons by allowing the water level of the Rhône to be lowered. Moreover, it seemed to us quite unthinkable to allow the water supply of the capital to be dependent on an aqueduct 500 kilometers long, especially as we could take no possible action about making Lake Leman into a reservoir. I have always held that Lyons ought to be the great inland port of France, in accordance with the definition of the geographer Vidal-Lablache. I started up a service of pleasure boats again between our town and Avignon. I often said: "The future of Lyons is on the water."

Part II: The National Economy

As suggested in the Introduction, the development of nineteenth-century France may be seen as the result of two revolutions proceeding simultaneously: the political and the economic. Some of the long-term correlations between the two processes are indicated in the Chronology (at p. 23). The purpose of the present Part is to illustrate some of the basic economic changes in farming, trade, industry, and labor organizations. One of the recurrent themes is the interplay between State actions and social group actions. The paternalist and positive State which existed under Bonapartist rule did not die at Sedan. It persisted in attitudes and expectations, both of public authorities and of ordinary citizens. Had space permitted, many dramatic examples of capitalist enterprise might have been added—the formation of the *Crédit mobilier* in 1852 and its collapse only fifteen years later, or the *Union générale* which repeated the story between 1878 and 1881; or the sensational affairs of the Suez and Panama Canals; or the automobile and aviation enterprises between the world wars. Not only are such themes ill-suited to documentary treatment, but also, on the principle that attitudes and modes of action are no less important than formal organizations, more attention has been given to peasant and workers' activities.

Section A: Rural France

No economic problem more persistently haunted discussions of French social life throughout this period than that of peasant proprietorship. It is a problem made no less intractable by the shortage of reliable statistics and the prevalence of deep-seated prejudices and superstitions. The census of 1882 produced figures which could still be radically disputed. It showed that some 38 per cent of holdings were of less than 1 hectare (a hectare equalling 2.47 acres), but it could be argued that it was misleading to count these at all, since they were too small to constitute productive units and often represented gardens of wealthy town-dwellers. Even if they were omitted from the calculation altogether, the figures seemed to show that some 75 per cent of holdings were of more than 1 hectare but less than 10 hectares. But if calculated in terms of the proportion of the cultivable land of France worked by farmers owning medium-size holdings (i.e., between 10 and 50 hectares each), then it seemed that three-quarters of it was worked by medium-sized and large owners, leaving only one-quarter to be shared among the millions of little men who constituted three-quarters of the total number of farmers.

If such calculations left plenty of room for controversy, even more was opened up when it was asked whether prevailing trends made for yet further fragmentation (*morcellement*), whether productivity could be increased by integration, and whether the "democratic" advantages of having a wide distribution of landed property might outweigh the economic gains of greater concentration. One certainty was the political fact, under the Third Republic, that since most constituencies were rural in character and since the Constitution favored the countryside and overrepresented its interest as against the towns, the policies of any government must pay close attention to the opinions and rural interests of the 38,000 communes into which the electorate was divided.

The Second Empire, while fostering trade and public works, risked alienating the farmers by its commercial policy of free trade (see Document 38). In 1866 the government conducted a major inquiry into the state of farming. The 18th Commission, under the chairmanship of M. Granier de Cassagnac, was charged with a detailed inquiry into the area of the southwest, including the *départements* of Gers, Haute-Garonne, and Tarn-et-Garonne, around Toulouse. It discovered one striking feature. Most of the evidence it received came from the larger landowners, who lamented their own plight and the ill-effects of fragmentation. Yet the smaller landowners were clearly prosperous, and a common complaint against them was that they made more money and attracted away better workers. The Commission's report, part of which is given as Document 33, concluded that in Gers, particularly, landowning was breaking down into smaller units because it proved to be more efficient and more profitable, and the bigger proprietors were being forced to the wall, not, as they believed, by uneconomic fragmentation, but by a Darwinian process of natural selection, through competition from the more efficient medium-sized units of production (cf. Document 3).

The problems of French agriculture were tackled by a twofold approach: from above, by governmental action, and from below, by movements of self-help and association. When Gambetta formed his ministry in November, 1881, he decided to set up a separate Ministry of Agriculture, instead of merging it with Commerce as hitherto. Documents 34 and 35 give his reasons for doing so, and the Decree which implemented this. He appointed M. Paul Devès (1837–1899) to the new Ministry. The year before he had founded the National Society for the Encouragement of Agriculture to offset the influence of the Society of French Agriculturalists, founded in 1867, which was by social composition aristocratic and antirepublican. The approach of self-help was stimulated by the Law of March 21, 1884 (Document 45), which legalized occupational *syndicats*. From only five in 1884 these rose to more than 2,000 by 1900, to nearly 15,000 by 1930. Policies of integration (*remembrement*) and of redistribution (*remaniement*) were encouraged during the Third Republic; and Document 36 is a grass-roots

example of such a policy at work in 1884 in the commune of Jevoncourt in the area of Nancy, in Lorraine. The community of local
landowners formed a free "syndical association" and entered into a
treaty-agreement to make possible the more efficient rearrangement of
landholding in the commune. Having secured authority, they appointed
an arbitration committee of between ten and fifteen members, on whom
they conferred powers to proceed. M. Alfred de Foville, who prints the
French texts of Documents 33 and 36 as Appendices XII and XV of his
book *Le Morcellement* (Paris, Guillaumin, 1885), regards this agreement as a model of its kind. The French texts of Documents 34 and 35
are in *Bulletin des lois*, XII série, vol. 23, No. 11, 161 (pp. 727–9). The
farming policies of the Third Republic are discussed in detail in Michel
Augé-Laribé, *La politique agricole de la France de 1880 à 1940* (Paris,
1950).

33. *The Agricultural Inquiry of 1866:*
Granier de Cassagnac

. . . THE LARGE estates (50 hectares or over) are in real difficulty.
Medium-sized properties (10 to 40 hectares) are tolerably well off.
The small-holdings (½–10 hectares) enjoy a degree of prosperity
which clearly points to continuous development.

There are several reasons for the difficulties of the large estates.
The head of the family seldom has any knowledge of method, or
the habit of regular work. He farms with outside helpers, and because he does not supervise them constantly he does not get full
results. He is obliged by his rank to dress in a relatively costly
style; the education and settling of his children absorb, if they do
not exceed, income which ought to go into upkeep and cultivation.
Hence, he is faced with rising debts and the slow deterioration and
final breaking-up of the estate.

The medium-sized properties are in a better position. The owner
of the land usually works on it himself; he is the first to leave in
the morning, at the head of his workers, and the last to return in
the evening. This supervision, together with the fact that the
farmer himself does his share, encourages everybody to work to
better account. He eats at the same table as his workers, and so
is able to make domestic economies which nobody would think of
questioning, since he applies them to himself and his family. This
landowner makes a clear profit, which he invests annually, prefer-
ably in mortgage bonds. He not only has a maintenance fund, but
he also builds up savings, and is able to educate his family without
borrowing and even sometimes to set them up for themselves.

The small-holder is still better off. He is generally a retired servant, workman, or "*colon partiaire*," who has scraped together a modest capital of 1,000 to 1,500 francs. General custom in the Midi allows no hesitation as to the use to which this treasure should be devoted. Its owner knows no peace until he has fulfilled his dream by purchasing a small piece of land, on which he builds a modest dwelling.

If one compares Cassini's map, drawn more than a century ago, with the present official survey map of the Midi, one is struck by two remarkable features peculiar to this region. The first is that the humble laborers' families, who lived in the houses marked on Cassini's map, still live in the same houses marked on the ordnance survey map, thus demonstrating the religious zeal with which families preserve their inheritance. The second feature is the enormous number of those little houses we mentioned earlier, built by small-holders, which appear on the ordnance survey map and which are the result of the movement toward preserving the family started by the French Revolution.

This sketch of the small-holding would lack a final touch if we did not comment on the three important factors which result from its development. First, dividing up the land gives a greater impetus to cultivation, and by increasing total produce thereby increases national wealth. Secondly, competition among the small-holders maintains the market value of land at a high rate, thus benefiting large estates when they are parceled out. Third, and last, because they are worked with unabated enthusiasm, the small-holdings add to the elements of order and conservation of modern society. . . .

34. *The Ministry of Agriculture: Léon Gambetta to the President of the Republic, November 14, 1881*

Paris, 14 November 1881

DEAR MR. PRESIDENT,

The creation of a Ministry exclusively concerned with the study of the vast and complex questions arising from agriculture has long been desired by public opinion.

This most productive element of the national wealth must be developed, and the need to give special representation to this important interest in Government councils is self-evident.

Significant improvements have been obtained and successful results have been achieved, especially over the last few years. But it must be recognized that international exchanges, customs and colonial regulations, commercial treaties, etc., etc., will absorb more and more of the energies of the competent Minister. The two important departments of agriculture and commerce could no longer remain together without harmful consequences. Each of them requires in future a separate organization.

The same need has already persuaded several great nations to set up special departments for agriculture. We can see how this has been done in Germany; in the United States, after the War of Secession; in Austria, after Sadowa; and recently in Italy.

In our own country this reform is becoming really urgent, if we consider the difficult situation which French agriculture has been experiencing over the last few years.

Apart from foreign competition and the resultant economic changes, there have also been poor harvests and the disastrous inroads of phylloxera.

Such a state of affairs imposes the most pressing of obligations upon the Government of the Republic.

In order to ensure the legitimate and efficient control of its activities in this field, it is best to group together the different services which are concerned with agriculture in the schedule of State estimates.

Consequently this ministerial department, in addition to its already important attributions (veterinary schools and services, professional education in agriculture, inspection of agriculture and sericulture [breeding of silk worms], incentives for agriculture, drainage, phylloxera, doryphora [potato-beetle], stud farms, forests, sanitary establishments and services, statistics, etc.) should take over from the Ministry of Public Works the research department and grants for schemes of irrigation, reclamation and clearing of waterways, loans for irrigation and reclamation, water installation and drainage of communal marshlands.

If you give your approval to the views which I have the honor to lay before you, I beg you to sign the following decree.

I remain, Mr. President

Most respectfully yours,

The President of the Council

Minister for Foreign Affairs

Léon Gambetta

35. *Decree Setting up the Ministry of Agriculture, November 14, 1881*

THE PRESIDENT of the French Republic, on the proposal of the President of the Council, Minister for Foreign Affairs,
  Decrees:
Article 1—A Ministry of Agriculture is hereby established.
Article 2—The attributions of this Ministry include the administration of agriculture (Ordinary Budget, Part 2: General departments of ministries. Chaps. 1, 2, 3, 4, 5, 6, 7, 8, 8a, 9, 10, 11, 12, 17, 18, 19; Part 3: Chaps. 23, 24, 25, 26, 27; Part 4: Chap. 28. Budget for special resources. Chap. 1); the research department and grants for irrigation, reclamation and clearing waterways; agricultural improvements, drainage of communal marshlands, loans for irrigation and reclamation, guarantee of interest to concessionary companies undertaking irrigation canals or large-scale contracts for agricultural improvements, surveys and works appertaining to water installation (Chap. 19 of Section 1 of the Public Works Estimates; Chaps. 38, 40, 41, 42 of Section 2; Chap. 13 of the Estimates for nonrecurrent expenditure on public works).
Article 3—The President of the Council, Minister for Foreign Affairs, is made responsible for carrying out the present Decree.

Paris, November 14, 1881
                                          Jules Grévy
By the President of the Republic:
The President of the Council of Ministers
Minister for Foreign Affairs,
                                          Léon Gambetta

36. *The Syndical Society of Jevoncourt, June 22, 1884*

IN THE YEAR eighteen hundred and eighty-four, on June 22;
  We the undersigned, all landed proprietors in the district of Jevoncourt, canton of Haroué, *département* of Meurthe and Moselle, declare by these presents that we associate our interests in view of a scheme which will be set up as one of the collective proj-

ects for agricultural improvement as provided in paragraph 8 of Article I of the Law of 21 June, 1865, on syndical associations, and which will consist of:

1. The building of farm access roads;
2. Straightening of curved or irregular plots, and of narrow watercourses;
3. General *remembrement* of the area, with delimitation of cantons, *bènes* and *lieux-dits;*[1]
4. Renewal of the cadastral survey.

The association is formed on the following conditions, which we amicably and in good faith agree to observe in every particular:

Functions of the Managing Committee

A Committee shall be elected by all the undersigned landowners, by secret ballot and majority vote, composed of ten members, eight from the district and two from outside who have interests in the commune. The Committee shall have full powers:

1. To conclude an agreement laying down conditions for the schemes to be put in hand, with the assistance of a capable and conscientious surveyor who has already been approved by the board for the task of renewing the cadastral survey.
2. To direct the schemes detailed in the following articles:

Art. 1. Road-building. The Committee shall decide the number, siting and length of farm roads to be built or straightened.

If a proposed road is not acceptable to two-thirds of its members, the Committee shall summon to a meeting all landowners interested in the straightening or building of the proposed road. The proposal shall not be allowed unless it has received the vote of two-thirds of the members of this meeting.

Every road that has been voted for shall be delimited.

Art. 2. Straightening of furrows. The Committee shall decide in which cantons or *lieux-dits* curved furrows shall be maintained exceptionally. In principle, straightening should take place wherever possible.

Art. 3. Remembrement. The Committee shall decide if certain parts of the area, such as woods, vineyards, gardens or other enclosed spaces, shall become part of the scheme for *remembrement* or not. It shall also decide whether boundaries formerly fixed shall

---

[1] *Bènes* were customary units of land; *lieux-dits* were places large enough to have a recognized name, but were unregistered.

be maintained. If the answer is in the affirmative, the result shall be recorded exactly on the general plan and fitted into the overall scheme.

Art. 4. Delimitation of cantons. The Committee shall delimit, section by section, the cantons or *lieux-dits* which will be subject to separate proportional redistribution, taking care to increase the cantons in sufficient numbers to avoid too many displacements of land in soils of differing value.

Art. 5. Examination of title deeds. The Committee shall examine title deeds for all lands affected by the *démembrement,* and shall draw up a schedule which shall be given to the surveyor. Landowners will be asked to produce their title deeds on a day and at a time and place stated by the Committee. Any person who delays deliberately and for a long period the presentation of his deeds shall, where formal notice has been unsuccessful, be summonsed in the matter of boundaries before the magistrate, at his sole expense.

The undersigned also undertake:

1. To make all information available so as to allow the actual extent of their holdings to be decided where deeds are missing.
2. To give proof, by producing ancient deeds, of the extent of those lands over which the Committee might raise certain doubts.
3. To appear personally, or by a representative, on their lands, as often as shall be necessary, to indicate the boundaries, either to the Commission or to the Surveyor.

For land for which there are no title deeds at all, the Committee shall decide the area according either to the old cadastral survey, or to present tenure.

Art. 6. Proportional redistribution. When the Committee has laid down the principles of redistribution, the surveyor shall proceed with the measurement of the total area, canton by canton, and shall draw up a schedule of holdings which he will place with the Committee.

This schedule will be compared with that containing the examination of title deeds, and if there is a deficit in some cantons, the difference will be made up from neighboring cantons which have a surplus, but in such a way as to disturb the line of the furrows as little as possible. If the neighboring cantons have no surplus, or insufficient to balance the size of the holdings as shown in the deeds, the deficit shall be made up proportionally from the land-holdings of every person in the canton. When there is a surplus in a canton which will not be used for roads or to make good the deficit in a neighboring canton, it will be divided in the same proportions as above among the landowners of the canton.

The new delimitation which results from the proportional re-distribution described above shall be marked by strong oak stakes. The undersigned landowners will be requested to inspect these stakes within a week and to submit comments. If after this period no claim has been made, the redistribution shall be permanent.

Art. 7. Demarcation of cantons. The cantons or *lieux-dits* shall be marked out by the surveyor by means of strong boundary marks of hard stone with rounded head, at least 80 centimeters in length, of which the foot shall be 60 centimeters by 20, and 25 centimeters wide. There shall be no more than one hundred meters between those boundary stones which are used to mark the end of the plots. As regards marking out the plots, every owner may, during and after operations, compel his neighbor, through the law but in presence of the mayor, who shall have with him an extract of the plan, to set up boundary marks at joint expense dividing the plots, according to the dimensions shown on the said plan.

Art. 8. Entry into possession. Property shall be taken over as follows: In the fallow season, immediately after the stakes have been put in. When the stakes have not been put in before May 1, ground planted with peas, vetches, lentils and potatoes shall be free for October 1 following.

The first cutting only of artificial meadows, lucernes, clovers, etc., shall be made by the former owner. For the other seasons, possession shall become effective after the crops have been lifted. Trees, hedges or bushes shall be lifted by the former owner within a month of the stakes being put in. After this, the new owners may dispose of them.

Art. 9. Renewal of the cadastre. The Committee shall take all necessary measures to ask and obtain from the appropriate administrative authorities, i.e., the Director of Direct Taxation and the General Council, authority to complete the scheme for *remembrement* by the renewal of the *cadastre* and a new classification of property, when this renewal shall have been previously decided upon by the municipal council.

Art. 10. Establishment and effects of remembrement. The scheme for *remembrement* shall be established:

1) By a plan made out in duplicate, on a scale of one millimeter per meter in its subdivisions. This plan will show all the boundary marks for the cantons and the *lieux-dits* with the distances between them, the position of the stakes between the plots, the size and number of all the plots, the name of each canton or *lieu-dit*, the main roads, local roads and lanes, recognized footpaths and all watercourses of every size.

2) By a general table of all the definitive holdings or schedule of sections, which will show the number, type, and area of each plot, the name of the owner and that of the *lieu-dit*. An extract of this schedule containing all the above indications and the length and breadth of the plots shall be given to every landowner for all the lands which belong to him.

   The plan and schedule of sections will be deposited in the mayor's archives, and the undersigned undertake to recognize it as the sole deed of ownership with respect to the extent of holdings from the date of deposition. After that same date all conveyances, sales, exchanges, partitions and donations, etc., which shall be drawn up between the undersigned, whether by simple contract or by title deed, shall display the new area, together with the number on the plan and the section.

Art. 11. Disputes. The Committee shall, in the first instance, adjudge all difficulties which may arise between the undersigned, or which may be raised by one of them. Appeals against their decisions can only be made to the magistrate of the canton within three months after the decision. The Committee has full powers to serve summonses in the matter of boundaries, at all levels of jurisdiction, on all owners who do not adhere to the present agreement and who refuse to take part in the schemes it proposes.

Art. 12. Validity of decisions by the Commission. No decision of the Committee shall be valid unless two-thirds of its members are present and it is approved by at least half of the members present plus one. Where the votes are equal, the Chairman shall have a casting vote.

Art. 13. Costs of the scheme. The costs of all the schemes embodied in the present agreement shall be paid by the landowners, in proportion to the total amount of hectares and plots they possess in this district.

37. *Visits to Peasants in Central France,*
1907–1934: Daniel Halévy

Montluçon is a small industrial town in the very heart of France, in the *département* of Allier, on the edge of the Massif Central. Even now it has a population of barely 50,000. Rural life in the little villages around it has always been hard, and was much affected in the present century by "depopulation," as well as by economic depression and occasional disasters. The historian Daniel Halévy visited friends in the area at intervals between 1907 and 1934, and wrote vivid descriptions of the changing social and economic life of several villages, including the little village of Domérat, and its most enterprising resident, M. Rougeron. Both conditions and changes at Domérat were repeated thousands of times over, with local variations, in other villages of France.

The extracts come from Halévy's book, *Visites aux paysans du Centre (1907–1934)* (Paris, Grasset, 1935), between pages 48 and 248, and pages 340–342, and are here reproduced in translation by kind permission of the publisher, Bernard Grasset. On Halévy himself, as a man of letters whose life and work reveal interesting links between the culture and politics of the Third French Republic, see Alain Silvera, *Daniel Halévy and his Times: A Gentleman-Commoner in the Third Republic* (Ithaca, N.Y., 1966).

(i) Visit to Rougeron (1910)

"WHAT A lot of trouble he gives himself in his village of ruined vinegrowers!" This is what I was thinking on the road which rises from Montluçon to Domérat. What news should I get up there?

He is a brave man, and he never rests, and all he gets from his efforts is weariness, and the dislike of the very people he wants to help. When the vineyard had to be restored after the ravages of phylloxera, Rougeron managed to form a syndicate which bought the young plants, wire, vine-props, etc., wholesale, and was very useful to the vinegrowers. He hoped that the association would survive the crisis and continue to unite the enthusiasts. He was disappointed. Everybody left it and it came to an end.

For the past few years, with the falling prices and failure of crops bringing back hard times, Rougeron had seen some of his friends going off to Montluçon to seek work in the factories, and others selling off. Rougeron is a farmer to the depths of his being and disapproves of these departures. He will not admit ruin, and he will not give in so long as the land is there, ready to give so much. He cast around and came up with a new scheme: the commune owns very extensive common lands, which have been left untilled and provide only sparse grazing for a few cows. Rougeron wanted to set up an association to lease a section of these commons, plant them with vines and trees, and so create a source of wealth which would benefit everybody. He managed to get it going, and planted out the vineyard along with a few friends. But he could get no further; these good people, abetted by reactionary bourgeois, turned against him and destroyed his young plants and rented the lands that he had been wanting. A strange thing, love, steadfast as hate! Rougeron has a real vocation to devote himself and to conserve. His village persecutes him; he redoubles his ingenious efforts to save his village. He has a new dream and a new idea. The vinegrowers are complaining, and they have plenty of time to complain, for a vinegrower spends his winter gazing at his vines, fearing, hoping and grumbling. Why should they not work? This was Rougeron's idea: to discover some work that was seasonal, work to keep their hands busy during the winter, and to retain people in the village. He thought of cutlery and shoe-making, both ancient crafts spoiled by the machine. They would need capital, and continuous production. Basket-making was a better idea. He hoped he had found the answer, and he was right to have such hopes. France exports a great deal of fruit, more each year. Baskets are needed. Production is scarcely sufficient, it is entirely hand work. It was a wonderful idea.

Everyone Rougeron consulted gave him encouragement. He won over his neighbors, and a basket teacher was engaged. The last time Guillaumin and I were here, the teacher was just leaving after a month's instruction. He was pleased with his pupils, and the pupils were pleased with their master. A dance was held to mark the end of his course in the workroom still adorned with baskets—"English trunks," "sieves," and undressed osiers in long bundles. Eighteen months had gone by since then, when they would have had to produce and sell, a tricky business for isolated peasants. How far would they have succeeded?

There was Rougeron waiting for me at the edge of the village, never admitting defeat. I recognized from afar his tall figure, correct and simple, the sergeant major in civilian garb. He served for many years in the cavalry, and has retained a military bearing. He is a man of order, regularity and command. I believe he reads few books. His character is entirely practical yet sentimental,

painstaking yet dreamy. I have no doubt that Hoche or Moreau
would have made an admirable colonel of him, or perhaps a very
good corporal. Envious villagers nicknamed him the "Emperor."
Our age does not know what to make of these rare natures, and
abandons them at their place of birth.

He came toward me with hands outstretched, and led me to the
mayor's house, a huge building, startlingly massive beside the low
tumbledown houses. The vinegrowers of Domérat built it ten
years ago in a burst of pride and sudden wealth. Today they are
poorer than the tenant farmers of Ygrande and their fine monument is a mockery. Sale and slump, riches and rags, such is the lot
that the vine metes out to those who cultivate it.

"Come in," says Rougeron, "you shall see our school of basketwork. The commune is still helping us. It is paying two of our
youngsters for a month—for they are good workers—to teach
the others."

I went in. The school is installed in the big hall designed as a
theater. I could see the two young teachers, but I could see no
pupils. I realized that I was witnessing one last effort, and it was
not a success.

"No," Rougeron admits sorrowfully, "they are not attending,
at least, very few! It is laziness, lack of initiative. They don't want
to be bothered to learn a trade. They need a month's training, and
they won't do it. They prefer to go to Montluçon, with an hour
and a half walk morning and evening, to slave away in the chemi-
cal-products factory in a very unhealthy atmosphere, or to sign on
as laborers building the barracks, and what are their wages? To
begin with, the employer paid forty centimes an hour, but this
year all the peasants are feeling the pinch and try to get taken
on; the employer won't give more than thirty-five centimes. . . ."

We left the theater, decked with a dreadful pretentious curtain
all in tatters, and climbed the hill past the township.

"The poverty in these houses!" said Rougeron. "They suffer in
secret. They were rich once, and they are proud. The women
work very hard, sewing for the big shops in Paris. At one time a
carrier used to come up from Montluçon, distribute the work to
be done, and collect it when it was finished. But they realized
that the women here were very poor and glad to agree to anything.
They cut out the carrier and the women fetch and carry their
own loads. Their pay is one sou an hour. Sheer exploitation! We

have a school canteen. This year the children are eating twice as much as they ate last year. At home, they don't get enough."

"But if the vines bring in so little, couldn't they grow something else?"

"No. Holdings have been divided up, and now eight hundred families possess less than one hectare. Only vines make a profitable return on so small an area. So they must go without, wait and hope, or sell up and get out. If only they had shown themselves willing. A seasonal industry in the village which could have given work even to the children would have been their salvation. Basketwork was such a good idea. But they weren't keen. So our farmers send their fruit to England and have to buy their baskets in Switzerland or Holland!"

You could sense the simple, sincere sadness that lay behind these words. This man had conceived a bold dream. The creation of an industry is a difficult enterprise at the best of times. It requires the energy of a leader to produce capital, choose his associates and take on the risks. Rougeron had wanted to form a collective, ten to twenty workers joining to learn together, to run the risks together, produce and open up town markets all from their isolated village. It was asking a great deal, more than was reasonable. Cooperation is sometimes successful in established industries, but it cannot innovate and create.

We went past his house, which was unlike any other—newly built in stone cheerfully decorated with porcelain.

"I tried to show them," he explained, "that a farmworker's house could be as good as a civil servant's. It is because of my house that they call me the 'Emperor.'" The nickname is only superficially appropriate. Rougeron is the opposite of a despot. But there is something about his moral as well as his physical bearing, something pure and superior, even noble, which makes him different and is unexpected. He knows nothing about politics. That is sufficient to set him apart in this village of small property owners, where a strange socialism persists, entirely confined to its electoral role, nonexistent when it comes to action, but abusive and sectarian in its assertions. Rougeron is a socialist for the sake of socialism's teaching and aspirations, not for its committees, and he looks pityingly on these quarrels and long-windedness, which are always thwarting his carefully laid plans.

We continued to climb the hillside. Rougeron wanted to show

me his vineyard, his market garden, his watercress and his espaliers, which he uses every Thursday to give a lesson about arboriculture to the schoolchildren. He also wanted to show me the communal vineyard, the property called "The Hive." There it was, dominating the arid common land, the crops and all the other vineyards. It looked healthy and very well cared for. Rougeron surveyed it proudly. He believed it was safe. There were no more menaces from the envious. Last year they had pulled up ninety young plants, this year only three. A communal vineyard! The only one in the world.

"Do you know how the idea came to me?" said Rougeron. "I read one day in an agricultural journal that a schoolmaster had succeeded in setting up a school library with the proceeds of potato crops grown by his pupils. I thought: Let us do the same. We are on the right road. The credit bank of Montluçon made an advance for the initial outlay. We shall soon have paid them back, and our profits will be our own. We shall build a little room, install our books, and lay out an experimental ground to teach the children, and ourselves, too."

Rougeron became another man before my eyes. All sadness left him; his stubborn expression softened. His serious voice was charged with emotion. The practical man had disappeared, and a lone visionary stood and talked, contemplating the crops sloping down before him, the earth lying open to all his dreams, to all dreams.

"And then there is so much to be done! People here are poor because they want to be. Look how huge our communal lands are. They keep them like that out of sheer jealousy and inertia, and do nothing with them. If only they had listened to me! We would have clumps of trees here and over there — the grass would grow all the closer for the cows, as the soil would be firmer. Look at that hollow down there on the left. A stream goes through it. We only need a dam, which would not be very expensive, and we should have electric power all the year round. That would mean light and machinery."

He talked for a long time, and I realized that there existed in his imagination an idealized Domérat, transformed by the collective work of its inhabitants, more palpable and familiar to him than the dismal Domérat we had come through. He knew every detail of its amenities and attractions. He pointed out the exact sites where these would be built—where he had long ago built in imagination—the electric-power station, the wine-press, and the cooperative shop for the vineyard. He got excited as he talked. Night was falling.

"Rougeron," I said, "it is time to go down."

(ii) *Chronicle of Domérat* (*1920*)

I met Guillaumin in a hotel at Montluçon, and we went together to the station where Rougeron had arranged to meet us. There he was, with outstretched hands, pleased that he had taken a short holiday, the same brave, pleasant man that I remembered so well. Our greetings were brief. We ran to get the train and settled down, taking up the whole end of a compartment in full force.

"What about your vines?" asked Guillaumin. "Are you pleased?"

Rougeron's expression suddenly became thoughtful and strained.

"We had hail at Domérat," he said, "and this year there will be nothing."

All vinegrowers know this hazard of their calling. Rougeron explained the peculiar gravity of the event in his commune. Montluçon was near, the factories attracted the peasant, promising him high, steady wages. The temptation is always strong. It becomes irresistible when a fatal hazard has destroyed the harvest. The young men disappear and become laborers. Earnings from the factory are not subject to any risk, and they prefer it that way. With what scorn does Rougeron, the old country craftsman, vinegrower, tree-grower, and gardener, speak of these mechanical, servile earnings! You know nothing, you go into a workshop, you mind a machine, like a fool; that is all that is expected of you, and you earn your twenty francs in eight hours. You have in addition pleasures and privileges. The young men of Domérat who worked before the war in the factories were drafted back into them during the war, and saved their lives. Those that had not worked in them stayed in the trenches, and they are dead. Do you wonder, after that, if the land is abandoned? Rougeron loves his village and land passionately. He talks without discouragement or bitterness but with vigor and sadness. Guillaumin asks him:

"What has happened to your enterprises—your communal vineyard and the basketworks?"

"My enterprises? There is nothing left of the basketworks, or almost nothing. Yet they started off well. They had planted the osiers, and learned the craft with great good will. But our premises were not suitable. You need space, lots of space to work with osier withies, they are so long. Our rooms were not big enough. The men's work got in their wives' way, and they complained. We ought to have had a cooperative workshop; I was well aware of this, and I tried to raise funds by organizing and planting our communal vineyard. They had no faith in my vineyard. You yourself, Guillaumin, did not really believe in it. Yet it is the most lasting of my enterprises. During the war the women looked after it devotedly. They sprayed with sulphur, pruned and harvested it just like their husbands' vineyards. There are about ten thousand francs in the bank now. But what can we do with it? Today it would cost twenty thousand francs to buy a piece of land and build a workshop. Anyway, it is too late. We have waited too long. . . .

Our conversation took a less gloomy turn. We challenged Rougeron's pessimism. A district as fertile as Domérat, so near to Montluçon, would not be deserted. These same men who went to work in the factories, would they stop cultivating the land? Probably not. The short working day in the factory had the advantage of allowing them to take on a second job, in the open air, which would be so different that it would give relaxation as well as employment. Rougeron admitted this. He knew young men who would work among their crops morning and evening, before or after factory hours. We asked him whether a factory worker could look after a hectare of vineyard. No, replied Rougeron, a hectare would be too much, but he could certainly manage half a hectare. He knew some actual cases and mentioned them. That was one source of hope, and Rougeron, anxious for any sort of hope, clutched at it eagerly. In place of the former population of either peasants or factory workers, we should see a new population beginning, half peasant, half factory worker, and this would maintain some of the ingenious and reliable qualities of the peasants in our midst.

All right then, let us hope, but not hope too much. If the land is ingenious at keeping hold of men, industry is even more ingenious at getting them back. Rougeron told us that powerful companies in Montluçon were beginning to go out and pick up workhands at some distance, by means of trucks. These trucks went thirty or forty kilometers into the country, collecting the peasants in the morning and bringing them back at night, and the journeys are

so long that they only just manage to make the outward and return journeys in time. What will happen to their lands? What
will happen to the land? Industry is always a formidable enemy.
There is no respite to staving off the blows it delivers.

(iii) Domérat in 1934

Rougeron appeared, close at hand, waving to me. His vigorous
frame was lightly stooped, and his mustache was white. His step
was firm but slow. He was slowed down, anyway, by the heavy
baskets he carried, full of wonderful pears and peaches.

I have known him many years. I saw Rougeron when he was
still young, when he was at the height of his powers. Now he is
nearing a great old age. At least the pains he took have not been
wasted. Our old friend, dreamer, reformer, educator of Domérat,
once unknown beyond his village, has become one of the foremost
peasants of France. He is president of the Federation of the Allier,
and keeps it on a straight and narrow path, divorced from intrigue
and politics. They clamor for him and acclaim him at national
congresses, where his warm, pleasant manner of speaking is much
liked. He is too generous to remain unmoved by this popularity,
and too generous also to become vain as a result. He is always more
preoccupied with what remains to be done than with what has
been accomplished, for he still retains the fertile restlessness of
great spirits.

Here he was then; he put down his baskets and shook hands with
us.

"I have been admiring your flowers till you arrived."

"My flowers . . . come and see 'Mme Herriot.' It is growing
very well, and my hybrid teas. . . ."

He led me toward the rose garden, everything was thriving
and shooting up, more like a rose garden in June, in fact, and a tribute to the gardener's skill.

* * *

"Your rose garden is delightful," I said. "You can see it from a
long way off; it adds beauty to the landscape, and it is open to
everybody. . . . But now tell me what is happening among the
peasants. They say that there is grave discontent, and the young
people are communists."

Rougeron was in no hurry to reply, and his sturdy features
took on an anxious expression.

"We are restraining them as much as we can," he said. "Oh—
if we wanted to burn down the sub-prefectures, like at Saint-
Brieuc, it would not be difficult. We could just let these things
take their course. . . .

"The peasants are getting infuriated," he went on. "But if they
knew how to set about it, they would not suffer so much. Take
this question of prices. We are feeling the effect at Domérat. I say
it is partly our fault. Before the war, we had our regular clients
who came back to us every year, and everything rolled along
nicely. It is incredible what old customs there were. Before the
Revolution, a hundred and fifty years ago, our vineyard belonged
to some monks from Combrailles. These monks were used to our
wine, and people all around imitated them, and drank the wine of
Domérat. Well, this habit went on, and twenty years ago, before
the war, we still had our best customers in Combrailles. We used
to know one another, we would write, and they got their supplies
from us, and of course it was very convenient.

"Today it is all over. Business has altered, and now there is bulk
purchase. The isolated vinegrower cannot keep up his price. Of
course, we ought to do what is being done elsewhere, in Languedoc—form a group, and set up a winemaking cooperative. This
would mean better wine and consistent quality. The wholesale
buyer would know what he was buying. He could come along
and find somebody to talk to; the syndicate would be the seller.
What I have just been saying applied to wine and the sale of
wine. But there is more—far more to it. If the wine is not sold, and
the slump goes on, do they think that they can't do something
else with our grapes? The vinegrower is ignorant, the more's the
pity. Over in California, when there was a ban on wine, the Americans did not uproot their vines. Not one. They made wines without alcohol with their grapes, and juices and glucose, and the
Swiss are more alert than we. They, too, have been making wine
without alcohol, for America. They have sold seven million
bottles. Yet with all our vineyards, we sell seven hundred thousand.
You have to fight back, damn it, find a way around. The peasant
just stays put, without lifting a finger. He grumbles and on occasion gets angry. I've never seen what good that did, getting
angry.

"The peasant knows nothing. If he had some knowledge he
would have more courage. He makes wine and can't imagine making anything else. This antiquity I was talking about a while ago,

the sheer antiquity in these parts is incredible. It is true for industry as well as commerce. There is a wine press at Prunet which bears the date 1000. It was repaired in 1580, and they were still using it in 1870. The one at Aubeterre is still being used, and it is dated 1659. The one at le Gros has an inscription with a name and a date, François Couturier, 1762. All the cellars in our district are big and vaulted, six to eight meters deep, and date from the fourteenth and sixteenth centuries. They are good presses and fine cellars, I don't deny. I have nothing against the past, but I do wish that people were willing to learn. The soil around here is very good for fruit. I grow it and sell on my own terms. I am the only one, almost. The vinegrower is not used to it, doesn't know how, and doesn't dare. He is not really wrong, either; if you take a chance without the knowledge, you are taking a big risk. Fruit, flowers, sugar, perfumes, all that means work, and wealth—that is unknown. You have to admit that the peasant has plenty of excuses. He can just about read—he left school at thirteen. That is too early. He ought to study till he is sixteen. But it is not just a question of going to school; the school ought to provide for certain needs, and you should study what you need to study. These teachers they send us, do you think they know what we need? Do they teach them in their training colleges how to prune fruit trees, or the chemistry of fruit? I don't know what they do put into their heads, but I do know that what I should like to see isn't there. You would think they do it on purpose. I used to like teachers, but not now. Four years ago, I had fresh hopes. The teachers in our *département* had organized a society to study the problem of rural schools. At the Federation we voted them a pretty big grant, three thousand francs. I was at their first congress. I went in, with my arms full of flowers. I wanted to decorate their platform, to show what beautiful things we can get from the soil. But I didn't find their congress at all interesting. I was very disappointed. They talked among themselves, all about their petty affairs. Civil servants' chatter. The following year we cut the grant by a half, and gave only fifteen hundred francs. We went along to have a look, and the second congress was just like the first, gossip the whole time. After that, no more grant. It is so badly organized, rural schooling. I even wonder if it is organized at all, and if there is somebody at the top to organize, somebody who thinks about it—somebody who thinks at all. I don't believe there is anybody. By God, there ought to be somebody!" . . .

Then he began to talk about the land again. This is always at the back of his mind, and he thinks of politics only insofar as the land is affected, for better or for worse. He talked about this wretched dividing up of holdings, which makes their cultivation so difficult. In Domérat there were vinegrowers who worked a hectare of vines. It needed only two hands. But this hectare was divided into ten lots, more even, sometimes fifteen. It was impossible then to make anything of it. You needed to reassemble these dismembered lands. "*Re*-member" them, as they said. Of course, there is a law about it. We are never short of laws. But you needed an enforceable law, and a law which would be enforced. That was unusual in our country.

I listened, and my thoughts hovered over the problems which had been presented thus. "*Re*-membering" could not be enough. The evil that they were trying to remedy in this way had well-known causes; they were in our legal code. To "*re*-member" land, and stop at that, amounted to nothing. A farm that was "*re*-membered" today would inevitably, in forty years' time, be dismembered again. The evil lay in the injury imposed by equal partition, which was so harmful and in the end mortal, for the land. It is difficult to remedy. Just now, I blamed the code. But it is a more serious matter than that. The evil is in men's minds; the evil is this French tendency to put equality above everything else. It can be seen in our customs, which are even stricter than our code. Our code allows a certain amount of freedom to testators, free disposal of a certain part of their possessions. Our customs, however, are contrary to this freedom, and in practice they annul it. Equality before everything. It is a case of false evidence and powerful dogma. The land is the victim. It is obvious that the land is sick and suffering. The traveler need only use his eyes to see the marks of illness on the countryside. The land has been snipped into small fragments. The heirs have demanded not only their share of the family wealth, but each his share of wheatland, his share of pasture and his share of vineyard. There are walnuts in France which have been divided among four takers! The deed is done, the lawyer has worked well, human envy or mania is satisfied, but the land is stricken and torn apart. The day comes when it falls in shreds. Then it is menaced by desertion.

*   *   *

We had reached the little town and were not far from the town hall. Quite a good way to find out about a village is to read the list of births and deaths, and the household returns. All these would be at the town hall, and I asked to see them. We were shown the figures, and I made a note of them, for they were extremely interesting.

The first thing that struck me was the gap which existed between births and deaths. In the last twenty-five years births have been around thirty, or just over. Deaths varied between thirty and sixty. A rapid addition gives the total of this discrepancy. From 1910 to 1934 Domérat lost 650 inhabitants out of a total population of about 3,000. The second thing I noticed was the contrast which existed between the graph of births and that of deaths. The birth graph does decline, but gradually; the average between 1910 and 1914 is 36.8. Leaving out the war years, which were abnormal because of the absence of the men, if we calculate the average for the years 1920 to 1933, we get 32.5. The mortality curve, on the contrary, rises rapidly; from 1910 to 1913, the average is 46 and a fraction; from 1919 to 1933 it is 54 and a fraction. The figures for the war years are often equaled or exceeded: in 1920, 70 deaths, as many as in 1915; in 1922, 66 deaths, one more than in 1916. What is the explanation?

It was a new question for Rougeron. He did not know the annual loss sustained by his village, nor the rise in the death rate. This ignorance, a moral factor added to the material factor, seems to me remarkable in itself. We could even talk about double ignorance, since we are concerned with two quite distinct phenomena—birth and death. We can attribute ignorance of births to the fatalism with which the French allow an evil which threatens their future to develop. Ignorance of deaths is something quite different. Death is a personal menace for everybody, and the register of deaths gives information about good or bad conditions of public hygiene. But although the French worry about their health, public hygiene does not interest them. The English are the opposite. I remember reading in one of their propaganda leaflets: "Vote for our party. Every time you have returned us, we have lowered the death rate." It was at the time of a municipal election. Putting aside the electoral humor of this text, there still remains this very human preoccupation, so strange and unusual to us.

So there we were, Rougeron and I, bent over the figures, trying to understand them. It was not easy. To begin with, what was the population of Domérat? Everything depended on this changing datum. What had been the variable figures of this population over the last thirty years? In 1886 we found 3,680 inhabitants, a peak. Then a fall: in 1901, 3,327. In 1906 a surprise: the figure picks up, giving 3,447 inhabitants. Births show no influence, the opposite, rather. In the same space of time the number of households grew from 954 to 1,045. That meant that there had been some immigration. We must not forget that the factories of Montluçon were near and recruited labor at Domérat, and that the years 1901 to 1906 had been prosperous. Mobile industry made its fluctuation felt here, just as the sea sends its high and low tides to the head of its estuaries. Then there was another drop. In five years, from 1906 to 1911, Domérat lost 300 inhabitants, while the deficit in births was less than 100. So there was new emigration. Domérat was becoming depopulated, bleeding at every vein. From 1911 to 1921 the movement slowed down. In ten years Domérat lost 344 inhabitants, whereas the deficit of births, partly owing to the war, was 327. There was a difference of 17. There was very little emigration, therefore, or else it was counterbalanced by renewed immigration. After that the figures rose. In 1926 we find 2,823 inhabitants instead of the 2,814 of 1921. And in 1931, instead of 2,823, there were 3,044. There is the same rate in the number of households, which goes from 941 to 1,085. So colonization by the factory workers is taking place here, transforming and reanimating the village. Domérat may well find in some ten years' time that the peak of 1886 has been reached again, some 3,600 inhabitants.

In the light of these facts, we find that there is not a diminution but, on the contrary, a very slight increase in the birth rate. In fact, while the population decreases from 3,600 to 3,000, the births decrease only from 36 to 31. A very low figure, in fact—10 births per 1,000 inhabitants, while the French average is 17. What is somewhat difficult to explain is the rise in the death rate. Rougeron explains that in a village like this, where the young people are continually leaving, it is inevitable that the old people, that is to say, the dead and dying, are very numerous. Domérat is to a large extent not a very busy nursery and is a very active old people's home. This quite probably explains in some measure the deficit of births. But the growth in the number of deaths is not elucidated.

What with reading and commenting, it was getting late and time to go. A casual visitor can but skim the surface. I got the impression, nevertheless, that the pulse of Domérat is healthier. The population is expanding, and the abandoned land is being taken over again.

> (iv) Letter on the sanitary and demographic conditions in Domérat, from M. Rougeron to Daniel Halévy

Prunet, 31st October, 1934

My dear Friend,

In your last letter you gave me quite a turn when you suggested that the over-high death rate in my commune was perhaps due to wine-drinking, and I wondered for a moment if it were not true. I thought it over and decided that it was certainly not wine-drinking which caused far more deaths than births, nor epidemics. The cause was emigration to the towns, emigration which began about 1880, very slowly at first but much faster later on. All the young families who left the land to go and live in the towns had children in the towns where they lived, and many of them return to the country when they are old. They may have a pension, or have built up investments from business, and they come back to the country to wait for the end. That, in my opinion, is the principal cause for this over-large differential.

If we did not have the Dunlop factory which gives work to a large number of men in our commune and transport facilities—Dunlop has its own buses, which come out to all the villages in the Creuse to fetch the men, costing only three francs a week—there would be very few young people in my village. To give you some idea, I will give you the number of families and their ages at my end of the village, Prunet-le-Haut: 20 families from sixty to ninety years old; only 2 under fifty. Out of 20 families of more than sixty years of age, not one of the children has remained on the land.

If the population has a tendency to increase, that is because it is easy to go and work in Montluçon. The rise is not due to young people who remain on the land, but to young families who work in the town but live in the country. In recent years there have even been some young families who have come back to their village, where they often possess their own house, a small acreage of vineyard and a garden. There are also some families who do not come from these parts but who rent a house and a piece of land. The rent is less than in town. With the eight-hour day and weekends off, whether they own their house or rent it, they can work in their gardens and grow enough grapes and vegetables for their families, and they are happy. Their standard of life is higher than it is for their fellow factory workers, who often live in unhealthy hovels in insalubrious neighborhoods. Those who live in the country have also less occasion to frequent bistros, where they ruin their health with harmful aperitifs and enrich publicans and poison manufacturers with money which would far better be used for their families.

This part-time factory, part-time agricultural work, is surely one of the best and most rational uses of human activity!

Too often, alas, factory and field are set against each other, whereas, by jostling along together they will understand one another better. They will get on better and have a higher respect for one another. Shall we not find in this way not only one of the chief factors of the union, which is so necessary in periods of economic difficulty, but also one of the most indispensable factors, perhaps, in the balance which will have to be found one day, in order to harmonize the hours of work and the leisure hours of humanity?

Section B: Fiscal Policy

As a prevailingly rural society in which small farmers and small manufacturers predominated, France normally clung to a protectionist policy. By 1850 more than a hundred articles were on the list of prohibited imports. Food prices were kept high and, because iron, coal, and machinery could be imported only at great cost, industrial development (including railroads) was impeded. A few professional economists, some larger manufacturers, and some chambers of commerce, began to seek freer trade, but they aroused little response until the Second Empire. Measures of Napoléon III during the 1850's to reduce duties and suppress the prohibitions led to strong political resistance and to loud protests from farming and industrial interests. Influenced by the example of contemporary Britain, and by the arguments of free-trade economists such as Frédéric Bastiat (1801–1850) and Michel Chevalier (1806–1879), the emperor launched an attack on the tangle of commercial restrictions. The central aim was, while preserving some protection for certain industries, to shed many useless prohibitions and excessive barriers to trade.

The emperor set out his program in a letter to his Minister of State, Fould, which was then published in *Le Moniteur universel* on January 15, 1860. Its publication was intended to prepare opinion in France for the announcement of the signature of the important Treaty of Commerce with England eight days later (Document 38). The schedules of goods affected in Articles I and V are listed in full—they express vividly the main commercial interests in each country. The United Kingdom wants to sell chiefly textiles and cloth, iron and steel, machinery and ships. The French want to sell fine products and luxury goods (wines and brandies, silk, jewelry, clocks, tools, raw fruits and "feathers, dressed or not"), not to mention "canes, walking canes or sticks, umbrella or parasol sticks, mounted, painted, or otherwise ornamented."

The Treaty recalled, in aims and character, the Anglo-French Treaty of Commerce made during the interval between the American and French Revolutions in 1786. That had since been overwhelmed by the long wars and the protectionist measures of nineteenth-century governments seeking to control trade and to raise revenues. The Cobden-Chevalier Treaty of 1860 led, within the next decade, to a great expansion of trade between France and Britain, and to many measures of a similar kind in western Europe. The value of French imports from Britain increased, between 1859 and 1869, from 278 million francs to 549 million. Britain's imports from France in these same years grew from 591 million francs to 904 million. By chain reaction each country soon made similar agreements with other neighbors—with Belgium, the German *Zollverein*, Italy, Switzerland, Sweden, the Netherlands, Austria, and Portugal. *Article XIX*, "the most-favored-nation clause," was repeated in these other treaties and served to make western Europe, including its most advanced commercial nation, Britain, into one whole area within which trade in general flowed multilaterally more freely.

From these conditions British industrialists and traders were, however, better able to derive advantages than were the less concentrated and weaker industries of France. The Treaty was never generally popular in France, and was passed only because the emperor could use his personal power to do so. Most of the ensuing treaties, being made for ten years, were due to expire by 1878. In 1881 a new general tariff was devised, imposing duties some 24 per cent higher than under the treaties. But as the treaties were virtually renewed and their "most-favored-nation clause" was retained, and as the new general tariff operated only in the absence of such special agreements, protectionism remained more theoretical than substantial. In 1892 a further law imposed a new general tariff, operating on a double system of minima and maxima. Jules Méline (1838–1925), whose name is identified with the return to more severe protectionism by the end of the century, outlined his philosophy of it in the Committee's Report of 1891 (Document 39). See *Documents parlementaires*, No. 1257. Session 1891: *Rapport général fait au nom de la Commission des Douanes*, 12 and 13 May, 1891. The so-called "Méline

Tariffs" of 1892, with important variations in 1910 and again in 1927, remained the basis of the system throughout the Third Republic. Farming was specially provided for by the "Cadenas Law" of December 13, 1897, much invoked between 1930 and 1932 to give agricultural products speedy and special protection in the world economic depression. During the 1920's more than fifty special agreements about tariffs were made with other countries under the flexible Méline arrangements; and special arrangements were made concerning colonial trade. English and French texts of the Treaty in *Accounts and Papers: State Papers*, vol. LXVIII (1860), Session 24 January to 28 August, 1860, pp. 467–77.

38. *The Anglo-French Treaty of Commerce, January 23, 1860*

Art. I. His Majesty the Emperor of the French engages that on the following articles of British production and manufacture, imported from the United Kingdom into France, the duties shall in no case exceed 30 per cent *ad valorem*, the two additional decimes included.

The articles are as follows: refined sugar; turmeric in powder; rock crystal worked; iron forged in lumps or prisms; brass wire (copper alloyed with zinc), polished or unpolished, of every description; chemical productions, enumerated or nonenumerated; extracts of dye-woods; garancine; common soap of every description, and perfumed soap; stoneware and earthenware, fine and common; china and porcelain ware; glass, crystal, mirrors, and plate glass; cotton yarn; worsted and woollen yarn of every description; yarns of flax and hemp; yarns of hair, enumerated or nonenumerated; cotton manufacture; horse-hair manufactures, enumerated or nonenumerated; worsted and woollen manufactures, enumerated or nonenumerated; cloth list; manufactures of hair; silk manufactures; manufactures of waste and floss-silk; manufactures of bark and all other vegetable fibres, enumerated or nonenumerated; manufacturers of flax and hemp; mixed manufactures of every description; hosiery; haberdashery and small wares; manufactures of caoutchouc and gutta percha, pure or mixed; articles of clothing, wholly or in part made up; prepared skins; articles of every sort manufactured from leather or skins, included or not under the denomination of small wares, fine or common; plated articles of every description; cutlery; metal wares, whether enumerated or not; pig and cast iron of every description, without distinction of weight; bar and wrought iron, with the exception of the kinds specified in Article XVII; steel; machinery, tools, and mechanical instruments of every description; carriages on springs, lined and painted; cabinet ware, carved work, and turnery of every description; worked ivory and wood; brandies and spirits, including those not distilled from wine, cherries, molasses, or rice; ships and boats; with respect to refined sugar and chemical productions of which salt is the basis, the excise or inland duties shall be added to the amount of the above specified duties.

Art. II. His Imperial Majesty engages to reduce the import duties in France on British coal and coke, to the amount of fifteen centimes for the hundred kilogrammes, with the addition of the two decimes.

His Majesty the Emperor also engages, within four years from the date of the ratification of the present Treaty, to establish upon the importation of coal and coke by land and by sea, a uniform duty which shall not exceed that which is fixed by the preceding paragraph.

Art. III. It is understood that the rates of duty mentioned in the preceding Articles are independent of the differential duties in favour of French shipping, with which duties they shall not interfere.

Art. IV. The duties *ad valorem* stipulated in the present Treaty shall be calculated on the value at the place of production or fabrication of the object imported, with the addition of the cost of transport, insurance and commission necessary for the importation into France as far as the port of discharge.

For the levying of these duties, the importer shall make a written declaration at the Custom-house, stating the value and description of the goods imported. If the Custom-house authorities shall be of opinion that the declared value is insufficient, they shall be at liberty to take the goods on paying to the importer the price declared, with an addition of 5 per cent.

This payment, together with the restitution of any duty which may have been levied upon such goods, shall be made within the fifteen days following the declaration.

Art. V. Her Britannic Majesty engages to recommend to Parliament to enable her to abolish the duties of importation on the following articles: sulphuric acid, and other mineral acids; agates and cornelians, set; lucifers of every description; percussion caps; arms of every description; jewels, set; toys; corks; brocade of gold and silver; embroideries and needle-work of every description; brass and bronze manufactures, and bronzed metal; canes, walking canes or sticks, umbrella or parasol sticks, mounted, painted, or otherwise ornamented; hats, of whatever substance they may be made; gloves, stockings, socks, and other articles of cotton or linen, wholly or in part made up; leather manufactures; lace manufactured of cotton, wool, silk, or linen; manufactures of iron and steel; machinery and mechanical instruments; tools, and other instruments; cutlery, and other articles of steel, iron, or cast iron; fancy ornaments of steel and iron; articles covered with copper by galvanic process; millinery and artificial flowers; raw fruits; gloves, and other leather articles of clothing; manufactures of caoutchouc and gutta percha; oils; musical instruments; worsted and woollen shawls, plain, printed, or patterned; coverlids, woollen gloves, and other worsted and woollen manufactures not enumerated; handkerchiefs, and other manufactures not enumerated, of linen and hemp; perfumery, cabinetwork, carved work, and turnery of every description; clocks, watches, and opera glasses; manufactures of lead, enumerated or not enumerated; feathers, dressed or not; goat's, and other hair manufactures; china and porcelain ware; stone and earthenware; grapes, sulphate of quinine; salts of morphine; manufactures of silk, or of silk mixed with any other materials, of whatever description they may be; articles not enumerated in the tariff, now paying an *ad valorem* duty of 10 per cent; subject, however, to such measures of precaution as the protection of the public revenue may require, against the introduction of materials liable to Custom or Excise duties, in the composition of articles admitted duty free in virtue of the present paragraph. *Art. VI.* Her Britannic Majesty engages also to propose to Parliament that the duties on the importation of French wine be at once reduced to a rate not exceeding three shillings a gallon, and that from the 1st April, 1861, the duties on importation shall be regulated as follows:

1. On wine containing less than fifteen degrees of proof spirit verified by Sykes's hydrometer, the duty shall not exceed one shilling a gallon.

2. On wine containing from fifteen to twenty-six degrees, the duty shall not exceed one shilling and sixpence a gallon.

3. On wine containing from twenty-six to forty degrees, the duty shall not exceed two shillings a gallon.

4. On wine in bottles, the duty shall not exceed two shillings a gallon.

5. Wine shall not be imported at any other ports than those which shall be named for that purpose before the present Treaty shall come into force; Her Britannic Majesty reserving to herself the right of substituting other ports for those which shall have been originally named, or of increasing the number of them.

6. Her Britannic Majesty reserves to herself the power, notwithstanding the provisions of this Article, to fix the maximum amount of proof spirit which may be contained in liquor declared as wine, without, however, the maximum being lower than thirty-seven degrees.

Art. VII. Her Britannic Majesty promises to recommend to Parliament to admit into the United Kingdom merchandise imported from France, at a rate of duty equal to the excise duty which is or shall be imposed upon articles of the same description in the United Kingdom. At the same time, the duty chargeable upon the importation of such merchandise may be augmented by such sum as shall be an equivalent for the expenses which the system of excise may entail upon the British producer.

Art. VIII. In accordance with the preceding Article, Her Britannic Majesty undertakes to recommend to Parliament the admission into the United Kingdom of brandies and spirits imported from France, at a duty exactly equal to the excise duty levied upon home-made spirits, with the addition of a surtax of two pence a gallon,[1] which will make the actual duty payable on French brandies and spirits eight shillings and two pence the gallon.

Her Britannic Majesty also undertakes to recommend to Parliament the admission of rum and tafia imported from the French Colonies, at the same duty which is or shall be levied on these same articles imported from the British Colonies.

Her Britannic Majesty undertakes to recommend to Parliament the admission of paper-hangings imported from France, at a duty equal to the excise tax, that is to say, at fourteen shillings per hundredweight; and cardboard of the same origin, at a duty which shall not exceed fifteen shillings per hundredweight.

[1] Increased from two pence to five pence by the First Additional Article, signed at Paris on February 25, 1860.

Her Britannic Majesty further undertakes to recommend to Parliament the admission of gold and silver plate imported from France, at a duty equal to the stamp or excise duty which is charged on British gold and silver plate.

Art. IX. It is understood between the two High Contracting Powers, that if one of them thinks it necessary to establish an excise tax or inland duty upon any article of home production or manufacture which is comprised among the preceding enumerated articles, the foreign imported article of the same description may be immediately liable to an equivalent duty on importation.

It is equally understood between the High Contracting Powers, that in case the British Government should deem it necessary to increase the excise duties levied upon home-made spirits, the duties on the importation of wines may be modified in the following manner:

For every increase of a shilling per gallon of spirits on the excise duty, there may be, on wines which pay one shilling and sixpence duty, an augmentation not exceeding one penny halfpenny per gallon; and on wines which pay two shillings, an augmentation not exceeding two pence halfpenny per gallon.

Art. X. The two High Contracting Parties reserve to themselves the power of levying upon all articles mentioned in the present Treaty, or upon any other article, landing or shipping dues, in order to pay the expenses of all necessary establishments at the ports of importation and exportation.

But in all that relates to local treatment, the dues and charges in the ports, basins, docks, roadsteads, harbours, and rivers of the two countries, the privileges, favours, or advantages which are or shall be granted to national vessels generally, or to the goods imported or exported in them, shall be equally granted to the vessels of the other country, and to the goods imported or exported in them.

Art. XI. The two High Contracting Powers engage not to prohibit the exportation of coal, and to levy no duty upon such exportation.

Art. XII. The subjects of one of the two High Contracting Powers shall, in the dominions of the other, enjoy the same protection as native subjects in regard to the rights of property in trade-marks and in patterns of every description.

Art. XIII. The *ad valorem* duties established within the limits fixed by the preceding Articles shall be converted into specific duties by a Supplementary Convention, which shall be concluded before the 1st of July, 1860.[2] The medium prices during the six months preceding the date of the present Treaty shall be taken as the bases for this conversion.

Duties shall, however, be levied in conformity with the bases above established:

1. In the event of this Supplementary Convention not having come into force before the expiration of the period fixed for the execution by France of the present Treaty.

2. Upon those articles the specific duties on which shall not have been settled by common consent.

Art. XIV. The present Treaty shall be binding for the United Kingdom of Great Britain and Ireland, so soon as the necessary legislative sanction shall have been given by Parliament, with the reserve made in Article VI, respecting wines.

Further, Her Britannic Majesty reserves to herself the power of retaining, upon special grounds, and by way of exception, during a period not exceeding two years, dating from the 1st of April, 1860, half of the duties on those articles, the free admission of which is stipulated by the present Treaty.

This reserve, however, does not apply to articles of silk manufacture.

Art. XV. The engagements contracted by His Majesty the Emperor of the French shall be fulfilled, and the tariffs previously indicated as payable on British goods and manufactures shall be applied within the following periods:

1. For coal and coke, from the 1st July, 1860.

2. For bar and pig iron, and for steel of the kinds which are not subject to prohibition, from the 1st October, 1860.

3. For worked metals, machines, tools, and mechanical instruments of all sorts, within a period which shall not exceed the 31st December, 1860.

4. For yarns and manufactures in flax and hemp, from the 1st June, 1861.

5. And for all other articles from the 1st October, 1861.

[2] Modified by the Second Additional Article signed at Paris on June 27, 1860, and by Supplementary Conventions of October 12 and November 23, 1860.

Art. XVI. His Majesty the Emperor of the French engages that the *ad valorem* duties payable on the importation into France of merchandise of British production and manufacture shall not exceed a maximum of 25 per cent from the 1st October, 1864.

Art. XVII. It is understood between the two High Contracting Powers, as an element of the conversion of the *ad valorem* duties into specific duties, that for the kinds of bar iron which are at present subjected on importation into France to a duty of ten francs, not including the two additional decimes, the duty shall be seven francs on every hundred kilogrammes until the end of the 1st October, 1864, and six francs from that period, including in both cases the two additional decimes.

Art. XVIII. The arrangements of the present Treaty of Commerce are applicable to Algeria, both for the exportation of her produce, and for the importation of British goods.

Art. XIX. Each of the two High Contracting Powers engages to confer on the other any favour, privilege, or reduction in the tariff of duties of importation on the articles mentioned in the present Treaty, which the said Power may concede to any third Power. They further engage not to enforce one against the other any prohibition of importation or exportation, which shall not at the same time be applicable to all other nations.

Art. XX. The present Treaty shall not be valid unless Her Britannic Majesty shall be authorized, by the assent of Her Parliament, to execute the engagements contracted by Her in the Articles of the present Treaty.

Art. XXI. The present Treaty shall remain in force for the space of ten years, to date from the day of the exchange of ratifications; and in case neither of the High Contracting Powers shall have notified to the other, twelve months before the expiration of the said period of ten years, the intention to put an end to its operation, the Treaty shall continue in force for another year, and so on from year to year, until the expiration of a year, counting from the day on which one or other of the High Contracting Powers shall have announced its intention to put an end to it.

The High Contracting Powers reserve to themselves the right to introduce by common consent into this Treaty any modification which is not opposed to its spirit and principles, and the utility of which shall have been shown by experience.

Art. XXII. The present Treaty shall be ratified, and the ratifications shall be exchanged at Paris within the period of fifteen days, or sooner, if possible.

In faith whereof, the respective Plenipotentiaries have signed it, and affixed thereto the seal of their arms.

Done in duplicate, at Paris, the twenty-third day of January, in the year of our Lord one thousand eight hundred and sixty:

COWLEY   V. BAROCHE
R. COBDEN   F. ROUHER

39. The Case for Protection: Jules Méline, 1891

THE CAUSES which have brought about the agricultural crisis from which we have not yet emerged are today well-known, and nobody thinks of denying them.

There is first the considerable agricultural development among the nations of central and western Europe, such as Germany, Austria-Hungary, Russia and Rumania, whose agricultural products are increasingly flooding our markets, not to mention Italy and Spain, whose competition in wines has become so severe. But the principal cause is that the markets of Europe have now been entered by young nations, favored by nature and by the exceptional advantages of their financial situation, virgin land of very low value, unbelievably cheap labor, the absence of military burdens, and paltry taxes. In 1860 these peoples were lying dormant. That is the excuse made by the statesmen who neglected to take precautions for safeguarding the future of our agricultural production. But, suddenly, with the development of means of transport and communications, and the rapid drop in freight charges, within a few years the big markets have arrived on our doorstep, so that we have seen wheat from America and India reach Le Havre and Marseilles more cheaply than from our own principal centers of production. After wheat, it was cattle, even cattle on the hoof, which, thanks to ingenious improvements in the fitting out of the ships, is tending to replace French cattle; for slaughtered cattle the import facilities are even greater.

What we must protect by customs tariffs, therefore, is our manpower, bread and jobs for our workers. Our industrialists have made the greatest possible cuts in over-all costs; only the labor force can be reduced, and it would inevitably suffer if our new economic policy were inadequate.

Nobody can have the slightest inclination to reduce the wages of our workers, for in certain branches of production they are obviously insufficient. On the contrary, we ought to do our utmost to raise them and there is only one way: to maintain the price of our products at a profitable enough level, by preventing excessive cuts through foreign competition. That is how customs duties are linked to the social problem itself in its most acute form.

40. *Defense of the Franc: Raymond Poincaré, 1926*

One of France's grievous postwar burdens was an out-of-date and overstrained fiscal system. During the war her governments had abandoned any attempt to meet expenditure by taxation. They borrowed immense sums, either from the Bank of France or directly from the public, in the popular form of short-term *Bons de la Défense.* The system of taxation relied excessively on indirect taxes—income tax was introduced only in 1917, and then in a restricted form. Economies could not be strictly enforced in time of national urgency, and profiteering was rife. Yet the experience of Germany in 1923 showed the perils of unchecked inflation, and the series of unbalanced budgets in France meant fast depreciation of the franc. In this connection, France's political instability reinforced her financial instability. Weak governments and anxious parliamentarians would not incur the unpopularity of voting the taxes or enforcing the economies which were essential to balance and budget and so stabilize the franc.

Panic measures of increasing income tax and voting heavy new taxes, in 1925 and 1926, did not prevent the franc from falling in July, 1926, to 240 to the pound sterling, at which point the *Cartel des Gauches* gave way, and all parties—save the Socialists and Communists—formed a broad coalition under the former President of the Republic, Raymond Poincaré (1860–1934). This "National Union" ministry inspired confidence. Poincaré was known to be entirely honest and energetic, a dedicated republican, and a patriot. He took charge of the Ministry of Finance himself, leaving to the Radical leader Herriot the Ministry of Education. With an overwhelming majority in Parliament, he succeeded in saving the franc by means of drastic cuts in expenditure, higher taxes, and attracting capital from hiding or from abroad. The franc was stabilized at 124 to the pound (about one-fifth of its prewar value). Poincaré was, of course, bitterly hated by the Communists and by the more extreme Left, as is evident from the barrage of interruptions which greeted his "Declaration of the Government" on forming his ministry in July, 1926. Uproar in the Chamber of Deputies was to occur more frequently during the next decade—a sign of the widening schisms in French political life. French text in *Journal Officiel (Débats parlementaires, Chambre des Députés)*, No. 101 (July 27, 1926), pp. 3036–7.

Chamber of Deputies: Communication from the Government

PRESIDENT: I will now call upon the President of the Council for a communication from the Government.

(*Applause in the Center, on the Right, and on various benches of the Left. Interruptions on the extreme Communist Left. Prolonged noise*)

M. MARCEL CACHIN: Down with war!

M. MAURICE GAUTIER: There's your man of the Ruhr!

PRESIDENT: I must ask you to listen.

M. RAYMOND POINCARÉ, PRESIDENT OF THE COUNCIL, MINISTER OF FINANCE: Gentlemen, the Cabinet which is being presented to you has been formed in a spirit of national reconciliation, in order to ward off the dangers that threaten at one and the same time the value of our money, the freedom of our Treasury, and the equilibrium of our finances.

M. MARCEL CACHIN: We see you only when times are bad!

(*Applause on the extreme Communist Left. Exclamations in the Center, Right, and various benches on the Left*)

M. POITOU-DUPLESSEY: He is there to repair your mistakes!

(*The deputies sitting on the extreme Communist Left rise and sing the "Internationale"—lively protests on the Left, Center and Right. Prolonged noise*)

PRESIDENT (*addressing the extreme Communist Left*): Be good enough to listen to the President of the Council; if not I shall be obliged to penalize you according to standing orders.

(*Loud applause on the Center, Right, and numerous benches on the Left. Deputies sitting on these benches stand up and applaud the President of the Council*

On the benches of the extreme Communist Left—"Hou! Hou! Poincaré!" Loud protests on the Center, Right and various benches on the Left. Noise) . . .

PRESIDENT OF THE COUNCIL: Each one of the men who have come together with the same good will to work for the public safety considered that it was his duty to devote all his thought and energy to this end.

Later on, other questions may arise on which these men would have different opinions, but today they are of but one mind on the necessity, on the urgency, and on the means of achieving this financial salvage.

(*Interruptions on the extreme Communist Left*)

They therefore ask you to show your confidence in them and allow them to accomplish, with your assistance, the mission which the President of the Republic has thought fit to entrust to them.

After a close and conscientious appraisal of the situation, we hold the profound conviction, gentlemen, that it is possible rapidly to improve the state of French finances and to raise the rate of our currency. This result depends entirely on immediate and resolute collaboration between the Government and the Chambers.

(*Applause on the Center, Right, and some benches on the Left—interruptions on the extreme Communist Left*)

M. Reynaud Jean: What about the Cartel of the Left?

President of the Council: We are submitting to you right away a bill to cover the present inadequacy of our resources in relation to our expenses.

In order to avert once and for all new risks of inflation, we ask you to vote, together with the principle of important economies, supplementary funds which are indispensable.

If the pressing need to recover them without any delay compels us to increase, as the experts have suggested, certain indirect taxes . . .

(*Interruptions on the extreme Communist Left and on various benches of the extreme Left*)

M. Clamamus: Here we go!

President: Listen; you can debate later.

President of the Council: . . . we shall at the same time, through direct taxation, ask from acquired wealth the equitable participation which it is ready to provide . . . (*Exclamations from the extreme Communist Left and various benches on the extreme Left. Applause Center and Right*) . . . and part of which will be used as annual payments into a sinking fund for defense bonds.

We appeal to your clearsightedness and your patriotism to keep short, by voluntary discipline, debates which would aggravate instead of healing the trouble, if they were prolonged.

(*Applause at the Center, Right, and several benches of the Left—interruptions on the extreme Communist Left*)

M. Cornavin: You could still go to Bordeaux again.

President of the Council: The application of this first remedy will not free us from the need to keep perpetual watch over the state of our finances and to complete our initial effort by measures intended to maintain public confidence . . .

M. Henriet: And bread at three francs!

President of the Council: . . . to allow us to fulfill all State commitments punctually, to stimulate production at home and in the colonies, and to develop the vitality of the country.

(*Applause on Center and Right*)

We do not pretend to be able in a few weeks, or even in a few months, to solve all the economic and financial problems with which an almost universal malaise has confronted us. It is essential to go straight ahead as quickly as possible without turning aside or beating about the bush.

The nations who are our creditors and whom France has the firm intention of repaying to the best of her ability, have the same interest as ourselves in putting an end to this monetary crisis, which springs from numerous causes, although it is by no means impossible to calm its violence and annul its dangerous effects.

M. Desoblin: You have ruined the small savers.

President of the Council: France has known times more grave and painful than the present. She saved herself then by unity and energy. Now, once more, victory depends on those same conditions.

Gentlemen, let us take up our heavy task at once, for the sake of the Republic and for our country.

(*Loud applause at the Center, Right, and on several benches on the Left—loud interruptions on the extreme Communist Left*)

Section C: Capitalist Enterprise

41. *The Ironmasters' Trust, 1887*

The *Comité des Forges,* formed in the same year (1864) as the International Association of Working Men (the "First International"), was destined to become one of the most powerful industrial trusts in France; by 1914 it included nearly every iron and steel company in the country. The iron and steel industry expanded late in France, as compared with Britain or Belgium. The French sought this measure of self-defense after the Cobden Treaty (see Document 38). The loss of Alsace and Lorraine in 1871 inflicted a severe setback upon it. The works of the Wendel Company in Lorraine (employing 5,000 men) and of Dietrich in Alsace were in territory which became German. Schneiders of Le Creusot remained the biggest of the French companies, employing nearly 10,000 men. The Treaty of Frankfurt (Document 85) also proved to have cut France off from great iron deposits in the Moselle Basin, the full value of whose ore could be realized only after the Thomas and Gilchrist method of removing phosphorus was discovered in 1878. It may be noted, however, that Wendel's various establishments were still worked with French capital in 1914. Capitalist organization, even in these circumstances, transcended frontiers and national politics.

In 1887 the *Comité des Forges* took advantage of the new Law on *syndicats* (Document 45) to reorganize itself along more modern lines, and equipped itself with the Constitution given below (Document 41). Although in form "democratic," it was clearly designed to keep control in the hands of the half-dozen biggest companies. The considerable central funds were to be at the disposal of the Board of Directors (*Commission de direction*), which was given extremely wide powers (Art. 6). The trust was, of course, intended to be the protector and promoter of metullurgical interests in every way. Its able and energetic secretary, Robert Pinot, an adherent of the Catholic Socialist ideas of Le Play, was often accused of deliberately limiting industrial expansion for ideological reasons, while ensuring considerable profits from selling dear behind the protection of high tariffs. The recovery of Alsace and Lorraine in 1919, and sequestration of German ironworks built there meanwhile, compelled expansion in time to encounter the severe trade slump in 1921. Competition from the reconstituted German industry was partially offset by the occupation of the Ruhr in January, 1923 (a move to enforce payment of reparations which the *Comité des Forges* was suspected of encouraging). The *Comité* was viewed with the greatest distrust by the Left, not least because of the personal identity of its leading members with Regents of the Bank of France and other big insurance and financial bodies. Its sinister political influence was no doubt exaggerated, although it was indeed a central element in the financial oligarchy attacked by the measures of the Popular Front (see Document 76).

French text in *La sidérurgie française, 1864–1914* (Paris, 1920), published by the *Comité des Forges* to celebrate its fiftieth anniversary.

The *Comité des Forges de France* (1887)

FORMATION AND DESIGNATION OF THE ASSOCIATION

Article 1—In conformity with the Law of March 21, 1884, an Association is hereby established between all the metallurgical industries situated in French territory, to be known as the *Comité des Forges de France*.

Article 2—This Association has as its aim the study and defense of the economic, industrial, and commercial interests of the metallurgical industry. Its headquarters are in Paris.

Article 3—The duration of the Association, fixed until October 1, 1893, shall be prolonged beyond this date by tacit agreement for successive periods of three years, unless a decision to the contrary is taken by the General Meeting at least six months before the expiry of each period.

Article 4—So long as the Association is in being, members agree to pay an annual contribution calculated at the following rates:

(i) *Cast iron or steel industry*

One centime per ton of pig iron produced;

One centime per ton sold of ingots of steel, blooms, billets, and largets;

Two centimes per ton sold of finished products in cast iron or steel.

(ii) *Construction workshops and denaturation factories (wireworks, wire-nail works, bolt and nut works, etc.)*

Fifty centimes per workman.

Contributions must be not less than 100 francs.

They may not exceed 400 francs for workshops and denaturation factories.

The Board of Directors may further decide each year to make a levy of one or more tenths of the contribution in addition to the ordinary contribution.

In addition to the ordinary reserve fund, this will be set aside as a special reserve fund. The total amount will be fixed by the General Meeting and withdrawals will be made only with the sanction of the Board of Directors.

Article 5—The Association is administered by a *Board of Directors*. The Board of Directors is composed of not fewer than fifteen and not more than twenty members, nominated by all the subscribers.

Before each renewal the Board of Directors decides the number of members who shall be proposed for election by all the subscribers.

The Board has the right to co-opt up to *five* members of their choice from among subscribers or honorary members. They shall have the same powers as the original members.

The Board of Directors is appointed for the duration of the Association, as indicated by the present Articles.

If the Association is extended, members of the Board will have to seek re-election.

Article 6—The Board of Directors is endowed with the widest possible powers of administration of the Association.

The Board of Directors may delegate the whole or part of its powers by special mandate, either to members of the executive, or to committees of members of the Board.

NOMINATION OF MEMBERS OF THE BOARD OF DIRECTORS

Article 7—Nomination of members of the Board of Directors takes place by sealed postal ballot and by *scrutin de liste*.

Each member has as many votes as the amount by which his contribution multiplies the sum of 100 francs. No member may have more than ten votes.

GENERAL MEETING

Article 8—A General Meeting of the Association is held twice a year, in May and November.

The Chairman of this meeting is the President of the Board of Directors, or in his absence one of the Vice Presidents.

Notice of General Meetings is sent out two weeks in advance by separate letter enclosing the agenda and signed by the President.

The General Meeting in May shall be called to vote on the accounts of the previous financial year.

Members who are unable to be present may send a representative with full voting powers. . . . [Articles 9 to 11 concern Honorary Membership and Funds]

Article 12—The present Articles may be changed by the General Meeting on the proposal of the Board of Directors.

(New Constitution adopted on May 5, 1887, and March 8, 1888)

42. *Chambers of Commerce: Law of April 9, 1898*

Whereas the Revolution in 1791 suppressed those chambers of commerce which had grown up under the *ancien régime*, Bonaparte on December 24, 1802, created new ones in twenty-two major towns as well as a General Council of Commerce in Paris. The local prefect or mayor was *ex officio* a member, and it was the duty of the chambers to express the concerted opinion of businessmen on matters of trade, to keep the government informed of impediments to economic progress, and to concern themselves with any public works which affected trade. They were particularly concerned with ports and communications. Some twenty-three of them existed by 1812; a dozen more were added after the Restoration; and amid the economic expansion of the Second Empire they throve and multiplied.

By the end of the century it was decided to give them ampler official status as occupational interest groups. The Law of April 9, 1898, required that no *département* should be without a chamber of commerce. Their functions are adequately set out in the Articles here translated. French text in *Bulletin des lois*, XII série, vol. 57, No. 1971, pp. 425–31. A Decree of April 4, 1919, authorized the 136 chambers of commerce then existing to form 17 regional economic groups to perform for the region the tasks each chamber already, under the law, performed for its locality. Laws of January 3, 1924, and July 26, 1925, set up chambers of agriculture and of crafts to perform, for farmers and skilled artisans, the functions chambers of commerce had for so long fulfilled for wealthier businessmen.

Law of April 9, 1898, concerning Chambers of Commerce

Article 1—The Chambers of Commerce are the representatives, in relation to the public authority, of the commercial and industrial interests in their area.

They are public bodies.

There is at least one Chamber of Commerce for each *département*.

Article 2—The Chambers of Commerce are set up by decrees drawn up in the form of regulations of public administration, on the proposal of the Minister of Commerce. The advice of the municipal council of the commune designated as the headquarters of the new Chamber, of the General Council and of the Chambers of Commerce of the *département*, must first be obtained. . . .

Article 11—The functions of the Chambers of Commerce are:

1. To give advice and information to the Government when asked to do so, on industrial or commercial problems.

2. To present their views on means of increasing the prosperity of industry and commerce.
3. To be responsible, subject to the authorizations laid down in Articles 14 and 15, for carrying out work and administering the services necessary to the interests for which they are responsible.

Article 12—The advice of the Chambers of Commerce must be sought on:
1. Regulations relating to commercial practices;
2. the setting up in their district of new Chambers of Commerce, foreign-exchange offices and ship brokers, commercial tribunals, conciliation boards, branches of the Bank of France, general stores and public salesrooms for new merchandise by auction and wholesale;
3. taxes subsidizing transport services in the district which are under contract to the public authority;
4. all matters laid down by laws or special regulations, in particular, the advisability of public works to be carried out in their district, and taxes or tolls to be levied in order to finance these undertakings;
5. rates of pay for work done in prisons.

Article 13—Independently of the advice the Government always has the right to ask of them, the Chambers of Commerce may issue comments on their own initiative concerning:

Changes proposed in commercial, excise and economic legislation; Customs rates;

Fares and regulations of transport services contracted by the public authority outside their province but affecting their district;

Rates and regulations of establishments for the use of commerce opened in their district in connection with administrative licences.

Article 14—Chambers of Commerce may be authorized to set up and administer establishments for the purpose of commerce, such as general stores, public salesrooms, warehouses, testing-stands for weapons; bureaus for conditioning and titration; permanent exhibitions and commercial museums; schools of commerce, trade schools, courses for propagating commercial and industrial knowledge.

The administration of any of these establishments which have been founded by private enterprise can be handed over to the

Chambers of Commerce on the expressed desire of the subscribers or donors.

Finally, there may be delegated to them the administration of establishments of the same order which have been created by the State, the *département* or the commune.

Article 15—The Chambers of Commerce, by the procedure laid down by the Law of July 27, 1870, may be declared concessionaries for public works or be made responsible for public services, particularly those concerning maritime ports or navigable waterways in their districts. . . .

Article 20—When there exists in a town a Chamber of Commerce and one or more commercial exchanges, the administration of the exchange or exchanges belongs to the Chamber. . . . The stock exchange in Paris is not subject to the above provisions.

Article 21—Ordinary expenses of the Chambers of Commerce and commercial exchanges are to be met from an extra levy on the capital from the tax on patents. . . .

43. *The Bank of France: Law of July 24, 1936*

The Bank was founded on January 18, 1800, by Bonaparte and by those who had financed his *coup* of Brumaire, including the banker Perrégaux. Its initial capital was fixed at thirty million francs, divided into 30,000 shares of 1,000 francs each. Though this figure was frequently increased (it was trebled by 1806) and Bonaparte introduced several changes into the Bank's organization in 1806 and 1808, its original structure contained features that were to prove remarkably durable. It was a bank of deposits, of discounts, and of issue. From the outset it was provided that the two hundred largest shareholders who were also French citizens should act on behalf of all shareholders, and should form a General Assembly, which in turn would select fifteen Regents and three Auditors to serve as a General Council. The General Council, in turn, elected a Central Committee consisting of three of its own members, and its chairman served *ex officio* as chairman of both Council and Assembly. In 1806, Bonaparte replaced the Central Committee by a Governor and two Deputy-Governors, all appointed by himself; so a close link with the State and its financial policies was also established early. All these features survived both the Napoleonic reorganization in 1808 and further changes during subsequent régimes, and explain the terms of the Law of July 24, 1936, by which Léon Blum's Popular Front Government attempted to carry out its aim to "make the Bank of France into France's Bank." It aimed to break the stranglehold of the famous "two hundred families" who constituted the General Assembly.

Just as the original structure reflected its Bonapartist origins, and concentrated power into a hierarchical pyramid with three powerful men at the top, so the overhaul in 1936 reflected the democratic and socialistic ideas of the time. To the supporters of the Popular Front the Bank stood for a Bastille of financial privilege which remained to be captured. In the course of the nineteenth century the two hundred Regents of the Bank, originally the most representative men in the economic life of the country, had become a closed, often hereditary, and immensely powerful oligarchy, dominating the Governor, arrogantly browbeating governments (such as M. Flandin's in 1935), and extending their influence, through linked directorships, into a high proportion of the largest companies in engineering, insurance, shipping, and other major sectors of the national economy. It had, in the view of the Finance Committee of the Chamber which prepared the bill, "succeeded in ruling the country over the heads of its chosen representatives." It was, therefore, democratized by giving its 40,000 shareholders one vote each, regardless of his holdings, and by making the General Council predominantly representative of economic Departments of State and of such bodies as the General Confederation of Labor (C.G.T.) and the chambers of commerce (Art. 9). Both the General Council and the Governor were thus brought under the effective control of the State, but the share capital itself was not nationalized.

A Decree of December 31, 1936, codified the law concerning the Bank of France; the composition of the General Council was modified by a Vichy Law of November 24, 1940; and the Bank was eventually fully nationalized by the Ordinance of December 2, 1945. French texts of the Law of 1936 in *Journal officiel* (*Chambre des députés*) July 25, 1936.

Law of July 24, 1936, modifying and completing the laws and statutes governing the Bank of France

Article 1—The General Assembly is composed of all the shareholders of French nationality. Each member is entitled to one vote, however many shares he owns.

Article 2—The General Assembly nominates three auditors. It receives a yearly report on all operations of the Bank.

Article 3—The Governor and the two Deputy-Governors will not have to account for ownership of Bank shares.

Article 4—The Governor will take an oath, in the presence of the President of the Republic, to direct the affairs of the Bank well and faithfully, in conformity with the laws and statutes.

Article 5—The Governor shall receive from the Bank an annual salary equivalent to that of a vice president of the Council of

State; the two Deputy-Governors shall each receive a salary equivalent to that of a president of a division of the Council of State.

Article 6—The General Council shall decide the terms by which the Governor and two Deputy-Governors shall receive an entertainment allowance and reimbursement of exceptional expenses.

Article 7—During their term of office the Governor and Deputy-Governors are prohibited from holding or receiving any share or interest whatever for services or consultation in any private enterprise, industrial, commercial or financial.

Article 8—The Governor and Deputy-Governors who retire from office continue to receive their salaries for three years, on condition that they do not accept any public appointment during this period. Furthermore, they are prohibited for the same period from lending their support to any private enterprises and from receiving from them any remuneration for consultation or services.

Article 9—The Bank is administered by twenty councilors and supervised by three auditors. The Governor, Deputy-Governors, councilors and auditors form the General Council. The auditors have a consultative role on it.

Two councilors are to be drawn from the shareholders, nine represent economic and social interests, and nine represent the collective interests of the nation.

The councilors are designated as follows:

 I. Two are elected by the General Assembly from among mill owners, manufacturers, or tradespeople, other than persons assisting with services or consultation or as administrators in a banking house.

 II. One is nominated by the National Economic Council from its Vice Presidents.

One is nominated by the Higher Committee of the Savings Banks from its members.

One is elected by secret ballot by the personnel of the Bank of France.

Six are chosen by the Minister of Finance from lists of three names presented by each of the following organizations:

National Federation of Cooperative Supply Stores, General Confederation of French Artisans, Assembly of the Presidents of the Chambers of Commerce of France, General Confederation of Labor (C.G.T.), Permanent Assembly of the Presidents of Chambers of Agriculture, and commercial vocational sections of the National Economic Council.

The latter shall be provisionally chosen by the Minister of Commerce from the best qualified representatives of small tradesmen.

III. Three represent the Ministers of Finance, National Economy and the Colonies.

Six are members *ex officio: viz.*

The President of the Finance Division of the Council of State;

The Director of the general movement of Stocks [*mouvement général des Fonds*];

The Director-General of the Deposit and Consignment Office [*Caisse des Dépôts et Consignations*];

The Governor of the Loan Bank [*Crédit Foncier*];

The Director-General of the National Loan [*Crédit national*];

The Director-General of the National Bank for Agricultural Credit.

No member of Parliament may be a member of the General Council.

Article 10—Councilors elected or chosen by the Ministers upon presentation by interested parties may not sit for more than three consecutive years. One-third are replaced annually. The outgoing councilors may not be chosen or elected again within three years of leaving the Council.

Article 11—The General Council of the Bank may delegate all or part of its powers to a permanent committee comprising the Governor, the Deputy-Governors, and four councilors, one chosen by the Minister of Finance and three nominated by the General Council.

Article 12—The decrees issued before December 15, 1936, by the Council of Ministers, in conformity with the proposals of the General Council of the Bank of France, may modify the texts which control the internal administration of the Bank and decide the regulations for drawing up the balance sheet. . . .

Section D: Trade Unions

§ (a) The Law of Associations

The Le Chapelier Decree of June, 1791, banned occupational organizations of any kind. This total prohibition chimed with Jacobin doctrines of the State, derived from Jean-Jacques Rousseau, which regarded any groups or corporations intermediate between the individual and the State as undesirable. They produced, it was held, impediments and distortions to the "general will" of the community as a whole. Napoleon perpetuated this attitude in his Penal Code of 1810. Article 291, requiring governmental permission for any association of more than twenty persons meeting regularly for any purpose, "religious, literary, political, or other," was not rescinded until 1901. The Law of Associations of July 1, 1901, applied to all kinds of society other than those which had the aim of "sharing profits"–i.e., joint-stock companies, business partnerships, and all such economic enterprises. Its special Section III applied to religious congregations, and was invoked savagely against the churches and orders. But it marked the climax of trade-union recognition by the law (Document 46).

In France, as in other western European countries, labor organizations gained legal rights and status in the course of the nineteenth century. Article 291 of the Penal Code was invoked against trade unions. Articles 414 to 419 expressly banned combinations (*coalitions*), whether of employers or of workers, which aimed at fixing prices or wages, or at taking concerted industrial action. The two major advances came in Laws of 1864 and 1884 (Documents 44 and 45), and the process of emancipation reached its climax in the Law concerning Contract of Association of 1901. French texts in *Bulletin des lois*, XI série, vol. 23, No. 1206 (p. 733); XII série, vol. 28, No. 846 (pp. 617–9); and vol. 63, No. 2295 (pp. 1273–8).

The Law of May 25, 1864, was promoted by Émile Ollivier and, despite its restricted nature, was regarded by him as a major reform in social legislation. By omitting from his bill the very word "coalition," he ensured that merely combining for the purpose of improving working conditions ceased to be an offense in the eyes of the law. Strikes became legal so long as they were not conducted with violence and intimidation. His republican critics attacked the bill as inadequate, and denounced the phrase penalizing "fraudulent maneuvers" as too vague to be any safeguard. The law now permitted temporary combinations for strikes, but banned permanent association in trade unions. The anomaly was removed twenty years later. The Law of March 21, 1884, passed by Jules Ferry's ministry, legalized associations of employers and of workers and abolished most of the anti-unionist laws. It still, however, excluded religious and political associations and limited its concessions to occupational organizations alone. Partly as cause, partly as consequence of these changes in legal status, trade unions proliferated and grew in strength. Occupational groups became, in time, a vital element in the social and political structure of modern France.

44. Law of May 25, 1864, modifying Articles 414, 415, and 416 of the Penal Code (*concerning the offense of union*)

Article 1—Articles 414, 415, and 416 of the Penal Code are abolished. They are replaced by the following Articles:

Article 414—Whoever leads or maintains, attempts to lead or to maintain, an organized stoppage of work with the aim of forcing wages to be raised or lowered, or to interfere with the free practice of industry or work, by means of duress, assault, menaces or fraudulent maneuvers, shall be punished by imprisonment from six days to three years and a fine of from sixteen to three thousand francs, or by one of these penalties only.

Article 415—When the acts punished by the preceding Article shall have been committed as a result of a concerted plan, the convicted may be placed, either by order or by sentence of the court, under surveillance of the gendarmerie for from two years at least to five years at the most.

Article 416—All workers, employers, and contractors who, by means of fines, prohibitions, proscriptions, interdictions issued as the result of a concerted plan, shall have interfered with the free practice of industry or work, shall be punished by imprisonment from six days to three months, and a fine of from sixteen francs to three hundred francs, or by one of these penalties only.

Article 2—Articles 414, 415, and 416 above are applicable to landowners and farmers, as also to harvesters and country workers.

45. Law of March 21, 1884, concerning the formation of occupational syndicats

Article 1—The Law of June 14–17, 1791, and Article 416 of the Penal Code are abolished.

Articles 291, 292, 293, 294 of the Penal Code and the Law of April 10, 1834, do not apply to occupational *syndicats*.

Article 2—Occupational *syndicats* or associations, even exceeding twenty persons employed in the same occupation, similar trades or related occupations combining in the output of specific products, may combine without authorization from the Government.

Article 3—Occupational *syndicats* are exclusively concerned with the study and defense of economic, industrial, commercial, and agricultural interests.

Article 4—Founding members of every occupational *syndicat* shall produce the rules and names of those who, whatever their title, shall be in charge of the administration or management. . . .

Article 5—Occupational *syndicats*, duly constituted in accordance with the requirements of the present Law, may freely combine together for the study and defense of their economic, industrial, commercial, and agricultural interests.

These unions shall publish, in accordance with the second paragraph of Article 4, the names of the *syndicats* of which they are composed. They may not possess any building nor go to law.

Article 6—The occupational *syndicats* of employers or workers shall have the right to go to law.

They may use funds collected from subscriptions. However, they may not acquire buildings other than those which are necessary for their meetings, libraries, and courses of occupational instruction.

They may, without authorization but in accordance with other provisions of the law, set up among their members funds for mutual benefit and pensions.

They may freely set up and administer information offices for situations vacant and wanted.

They can be consulted on all disputes and on all questions connected with their own special field.

In contentious matters, the opinions of the *syndicat* shall be held at the disposition of the contending parties, who can receive them and take copies of them.

Article 7—Every member of an occupational *syndicat* can resign from the association at any time, notwithstanding any clause to the contrary, but without prejudice to the right of the *syndicat* to claim his subscription for the current year.

Every person who resigns from a *syndicat* retains the right to be a member of those societies for mutual benefit and retirement pensions in old age to whose funds he has contributed by contributions or deposits. . . .

46. *Law concerning Contract of Association,*
July 1, 1901

THE SENATE and the Chamber of Deputies have passed, The President of the Republic promulgates the Law in the following terms:

Section I

Article 1—Association is the agreement whereby two or more persons place in common, on a permanent footing, their knowledge or their activities with an aim other than that of sharing the profits. It is governed in its validity by the general principles of the law applicable to contracts and obligations.

Article 2—Associations of persons may be formed freely without authorization or prior declaration, but they will not possess legal competence unless they comply with the conditions of Article 5.

Article 3—Any association founded on an illegal basis or for an illegal purpose, contrary to law or to morality or which aims at impairing the integrity of the nation's territory and the Republican form of government, is null and void.

Article 4—Any member of an association which has not been formed for a specific period may resign at any time, after payment of subscriptions outstanding for the current year, notwithstanding any clause to the contrary.

Article 5—Any association which seeks to obtain legal competence as laid down in Article 6 must be made public on the initiative of its founders.

The preliminary declaration must be made at the prefecture of the *département* or the sub-prefecture of the *arrondissement* where the association will have its head office. It must state the title and object of the association, the location of its premises, and the names, occupations, and addresses of those persons responsible for its administration and management, in whatever capacity. A receipt will be given.

Two copies of the articles of association must accompany the declaration.

Associations must notify all changes in administration or management, as well as all alterations of the articles, within three months.

These alterations and changes cannot be objected to by a third

party before they have been notified. Furthermore, the alterations and changes shall be entered in a special register which must
be made available on demand to the administrative or judicial
authorities.

Article 6—Any association which has been declared in due form
may, without special authorization, go to law, and may purchase,
possess, and administer, apart from grants from the State, *départements*, or communes, the following:

  (i) Contributions from its members, or sums whereby such
       contributions have been commuted, such sums not exceed-
       ing five hundred francs;

 (ii) Premises to be used for the administration of the associa-
       tion and for meetings of its members;

(iii) Property strictly necessary for the fulfillment of the as-
       sociation's proposed aims.

Article 7—In cases of nullity as laid down in Article 3, dissolution
of the association shall be adjudged by the civil court, either at
the suit of any interested party, or on the initiative of the public
prosecutor.

Article 8—Any persons who contravene the provisions of Article 5
shall be liable to a fine of from sixteen to two hundred francs, or
a double fine in the case of a second offense.

The founders, directors, or managers of an association which
is continued or is re-formed illegally after an order of dissolution
shall be fined from sixteen to five thousand francs and sentenced
to between six days' and one year's imprisonment.

Any persons who encourage members of the dissolved association to meet, by agreeing to the use of premises at their disposal,
shall be liable to the same penalties.

Article 9—In cases of voluntary or statutory dissolution, or dissolution ordered by a court of law, the assets of the association
shall be disposed of in accordance with the articles or, in default
of statutory provision, according to the rules laid down at a general meeting.

Section II

Article 10—Associations may be recognized as serving a public
function by decrees published in the form of regulations of public
administration.

Article 11—Such associations can undertake all the activities of civil life which are not prohibited by their articles, but they may not possess or acquire movable assets other than those necessary for their proposed purpose. All stocks and shares of an association must be invested in registered securities.

Associations may receive gifts or legacies under the conditions laid down in Article 910 of the Civil Code and Article 5 of the Law of February 4, 1901. Real estate included in a deed of gift or in a testamentary clause, which is not essential for the functioning of the association, shall be sold within the time and in the form laid down by the decree or order which authorizes acceptance of the benefaction; the proceeds shall be paid into the association's funds.

Associations may not accept personal or real estate on which a life interest is reserved for the benefit of the donor.

Article 12—Associations composed of a majority of foreigners, and those which have foreign administrators or have head offices abroad, and whose activities are either such as to distort the normal working of the stock market or trade prices, or are such as to endanger the internal or external security of the State, under the terms of Articles 75 to 101 of the Penal Code, may be dissolved by decree of the President of the Republic issued in the Council of Ministers.

The founders, directors, or managers of an association which is continued or is re-formed illegally after the decree of dissolution shall be liable to the penalties quoted in Article 8, paragraph 2.

Section III

Article 13—No religious congregation may be formed without authorization made by a law which shall set out the terms on which it may function.

No congregation may found a new establishment except by virtue of a decree issued by the Council of State.

A congregation may be dissolved or any establishment may be closed down by a decree issued by the Council of Ministers. . . .

[*Articles 14 to 18* inclusive impose further restrictions on the activities of religious congregations; Articles 19 to 21 are concerned with tidying up juridical details, and the text ends (Art. 21) with the significant statement:

"Nothing is hereby derogated in future as regards special laws concerning occupational *syndicats*, commercial societies and friendly societies."]

§(b) Trade Union Movements and Ideas

Diverse movements, economic, social, and political, flowed together into French working-class organizations until in 1895 they achieved a degree of national unity in the formation of the C.G.T. (*Confédération Générale du Travail*, or General Confederation of Labor). Representatives of 28 federations of *syndicats*, of 18 *bourses du travail*, and of 126 separate trade-union bodies met at the Congress of Limoges in September, 1895. They agreed to set up a "unitary and collective organization under the name of the C.G.T.," and in the light of previous experience of political schism ruled that it should "stay outside all political schools of thought." Nevertheless, during the following decade, there were repeated conflicts and schisms within the movement. But both trade unions and *bourses* grew and multiplied in these years, while the political socialist parties fell apart even more. By 1905, Jean Jaurès headed a strong movement to attempt greater unification of the political socialist groups, and this raised for trade unionists the crucial issue whether they, too, like their colleagues in Britain and other European countries, could not strengthen themselves by collaborating more closely with political socialism. The issue came to the front in their Congress at Amiens in October, 1906: was a man a worker before he was a citizen, or did the recent success of the Unified Socialist Party in getting fifty-four members returned to parliament betoken a new phase in working-class politics? Was direct economic action against employers, or the winning of a majority in parliament by electoral action the right course now for trade unionists to pursue? The Federation of Textile Workers pressed for alliance with parliamentary socialism. Its secretary, M. Renard, scored a hit against the exponents of syndicalist separatism with the comment: "When antimilitarism is carried on, when antipatriotism is indulged in, when electoral abstention is preached, it is politics." But his resolution was defeated by 724 votes to 34, and the revolutionary syndicalists carried the day with the formulation below, proposed by Victor Griffuelhes and known as the Charter of Amiens, adopted by 830 votes to 8. It set the tone of trade-union conduct, and of trade-union relations with political parties and the State, until the time of the Popular Front; and it was reaffirmed at the Congress of Toulouse in 1936.

It should be noted that Georges Sorel's *Reflections on Violence* (Document 48) was a philosopher's exposition of principles which had meanwhile been reached, mainly on empirical grounds, by the French workers themselves; it had no important role in shaping them.

The French text of Document 47 is in *Revue politique et parlementaire* (Paris, Jan. 1907), pp. 171–72, and is reprinted in Jean Montreuil,

Histoire du mouvement ouvrier en France des origines à nos jours (Paris, Aubier, 1947), pp. 192–3, or in Paul Louis, *Histoire du Socialisme en France 1789–1945* (4th edn., Paris, Marcel Rivière, 1946), pp. 267–8.

47. *The Charter of Amiens, 1906*

THE CONFEDERAL CONGRESS of Amiens confirms Article 2 of the Constitution of the *Confédération Générale du Travail:* "The C.G.T. unites, independently of all schools of politics, all workers conscious of the need to strive for abolition of employers and wage earners."

The Congress holds that this declaration is a recognition of the class war which, in economic life, rallies workers in revolt against all the forms of exploitation and oppression, material as well as moral, practiced by the capitalist class against the working class.

The Congress adds to this affirmation of general principle the following specific points:

In the process of making its everyday demands syndicalism seeks to coordinate the efforts of the workers, to better their conditions through achieving such immediate improvements as shorter working hours, wage increases, etc.

But this activity is only one side of the work of syndicalism. It is preparing that complete emancipation, which can be accomplished only when the capitalist is expropriated; it commends the general strike as a means of action, and it believes that the *syndicat*, which is now the nucleus of resistance, will in future become the nucleus for production and distribution, the foundation of social reorganization.

The Congress declares that this double task of everyday life and of the future is the outcome of the conditions of wage earners which is burdensome to all workers and makes it the duty of the wage-earning class, whatever their political or philosophical inclinations, to belong to that essential group, the *syndicat;*

Accordingly, so far as individuals are concerned, the Congress declares that all members have complete freedom to take part outside the corporate group in any form of struggle which their political or philosophical beliefs may require, and it confines itself to asking them, in return, not to introduce into the *syndicat* opinions which they profess outside;

So far as organizations are concerned, the Congress decides that, for syndicalism to attain maximum effectiveness, economic action should be exercised directly against the employer class, and the Confederal Organizations must not, as syndicalist groups, pay heed to the parties and sects which, outside and by their side, are completely free to pursue their aims of social transformation.

48. *Revolutionary syndicalism: Georges Sorel, 1908*

Just as Karl Marx sought (e.g., *The Civil War in France*) to graft his own doctrines of world proletarian revolution onto the indigenous stock of the French revolutionary tradition, so his successors, even when critics and rivals of Marx, felt obliged also to state the relationship of their ideas to that central revolutionary legacy.

Georges Sorel (1847–1922), the engineer-philosopher whose debt to Marx was strongly colored by discordant ideas drawn from Proudhon, Nietzsche, and Henri Bergson, made a more fundamental break than Marx himself did with the French revolutionary "Jacobin" tradition. A friend of Charles Péguy, Daniel Halévy, and their circle, he had come out in favor of Dreyfus but was disenchanted by the outcome of the Affair. He gained from it, however, sharp insight into the nonrational forces in modern industrial society and was deeply impressed by their immense power in politics. He coupled with this view great impatience at the way in which even the socialists of his time, such as Jean Jaurès, perpetually looked back to the events of the French Revolution for the inspiration of their rhetoric, and for models of their behavior. He was in protest against the chronic political nostalgia of nineteenth-century France.

In defiance of the Jacobin tradition of political insurrection and of Blanquist conspiracy, Sorel emphasized the need for working-class organizations to be led and disciplined by an "audacious minority" manipulating a social "myth." (A "myth" for Sorel is any belief which produces action, regardless of whether or not the belief is objectively true). The myth he proposed as the activating faith for the modern proletariat was that of the "general strike," transforming every local dispute between workers and employers, every particular strike or lockout, into a skirmish in one of the series of battles involved in the "class war." If these battles are to be fought with any hope of success, the activating myth must be supported by an indispensable amount of violence. The leading élite should emerge from the workers' own groups, the trade unions. He therefore ridiculed the ideas and methods of parliamentary socialism, hopes of peaceful reform, and indeed all liberal-democratic government that relied on persuasion rather than "heroic" faith and coercion. Here is the case for "direct action," rather than political agitation. This attitude won his writings favor with Mussolini and the interwar fascists, who liked to claim that their ideas of the "Corporative State," as well as their "heroic activism," derived from Sorel. The anti-State revolutionary syndicalist thus, paradoxically, became an ideological founder of the totalitarian State.

Sorel's most famous work, *Reflections of Violence*, from which the two following extracts are taken, appeared as a series of articles in *Le Mouvement Socialiste* during the first half of the year 1906. They appeared as a book in May, 1908, and by 1946 it had run through ten French editions, as well as having been translated into Russian, Italian, Spanish, Japanese, German, and English. An English translation, by T. E. Hulme, appeared in 1916, and was reprinted in 1961 by Collier Books, with an Introduction by Edward A. Shils. The translation that follows has, however, been separately made from the French edition of *Réflexions sur la Violence* (Paris, Marcel Rivière, 1908, 10th edn., 1946), pp. 133–42 and 162–6.

THE PRESTIGE of the great revolutionary days has suffered directly in comparison with contemporary civil struggles. There was nothing during the Revolution which could bear comparison with the bloody battles fought in Paris in 1848 and 1871; the fourteenth of July and tenth of August would appear now to have been no more than affrays which could not have troubled a stable government.

There is yet another reason, still scarcely recognized by the professional writers on revolutionary history, which has contributed a great deal toward taking all the poetry out of these events. There can be no national epic about things if the people cannot imagine their being reproduced in the near future; popular poetry is more closely involved with the future than with the past. It is for this reason that the adventures of the Gauls, Charlemagne, the Crusaders, Joan of Arc, cannot form the subject of a narrative capable of interesting any but literary people. Once people adopted the view that contemporary governments could not be overthrown by riots such as those of July 14 and August 10, they ceased to look upon them as epic days. The parliamentary Socialists, who would like to use the memory of the Revolution to excite the ardor of the people but at the same time expect them to put all their confidence in parliamentarianism, are quite inconsistent, for they are themselves helping to ruin the very epic whose prestige they would wish in their speeches to maintain.

But then what remains of the Revolution, when we have removed the epic of the wars against the coalition and the epic of the Days of the People? What remains is somewhat unsavory:

police operations, proscriptions, and the meetings of servile tribunals. The use of State force against the vanquished shocks us the more because so many of the leaders of the Revolution were soon to be conspicuous among the servants of Napoleon, and were to employ the same police zeal on behalf of the Emperor as they had on behalf of the Terror. In a country convulsed by so many changes of régime, and which consequently has known so many recantations, political justice has something particularly odious about it, because the criminal of today may become the judge of tomorrow. General Malet could say before the council of war which condemned him in 1812 that had he succeeded he would have had as his accomplices the whole of France and his judges themselves.

It is pointless to enlarge on these reflections any further; the slightest observation will suffice to show that proletarian violence evokes a mass of painful memories of those past times; instinctively one starts to think of revolutionary committees, of the brutalities of suspicious agents, coarsened and panic-stricken, of the tragedies of the guillotine. It is understandable, therefore, why the parliamentary Socialists make such great efforts to persuade the public that they have the souls of sensitive shepherds, that their hearts are overflowing with goodness, and that they have but one passion: *hatred of violence*. They would like to pose as the protectors of the bourgeoisie against proletarian violence; and with the aim of raising their prestige as humanitarians, they never fail to repel all contact with the anarchists. Sometimes, even, they repel this contact with a brusqueness that is not unmixed with a certain amount of cowardice and hypocrisy.

When Millerand was the unchallenged head of the Socialist Party in Parliament, he advised them to "be afraid of causing fear," and, indeed, Socialist deputies would find few voters if they did not manage to convince the general public that they are very reasonable people, great enemies of the old practices, of the men of blood, and solely occupied in meditating on the philosophy of future law. In a long speech given at Limoges on October 8, 1905, Jaurès made a point of reassuring the bourgeoisie much more than had been done theretofore. He announced that triumphant Socialism would show princely bounty and that he was studying different ways of indemnifying former property owners. A few years back, Millerand had promised indemnities to the poor only; now everybody will be put on the same footing, and Jaurès assures that Vandervelde has written with great profundity on this subject. I am willing to take his word for it.

The social revolution is conceived by Jaurès as a sort of bankruptcy; large annuities will be given to the bourgeoisie today; then from generation to generation these annuities will decrease. These plans ought to appeal to financiers used to taking great advantage of bankruptcies. I do not doubt that the shareholders of *L'Humanité* think these ideas wonderful; they will become the trustees of this bankruptcy and will receive handsome fees which will compensate for the losses their paper has brought them.

In the view of the contemporary bourgeoisie everything is admirable which avoids the idea of acts of violence. Our bourgeois want to die in peace—after them the deluge. . . .

Syndicalism in France is engaged in antimilitarist propaganda, which clearly shows the immense distance that separates it from parliamentary Socialism on this question of the State. Many newspapers believe that it is merely an exaggerated humanitarian movement, provoked by the articles of Hervé; this is a gross mistake. It must not be thought that the protests are against the harsh discipline, or against the length of military service, or against the presence, in the higher ranks, of officers hostile to existing institutions; these are the reasons which led many bourgeois to applaud speeches against the army during the Dreyfus case, but they are not the Syndicalists' reasons.

The army is the clearest and most tangible of all possible manifestations of the State, and the one most firmly connected with its origins. The Syndicalists do not propose to reform the State as did the men of the eighteenth century. They would like to destroy it because they want to bring about this idea of Marx: that the Socialist revolution should not lead to the replacement of one governing minority by another minority. The Syndicalists emphasize their doctrine still more strongly when they give it a more ideological aspect and declare themselves antipatriotic—in line with the Communist Manifesto.

It is impossible for there to be the slightest agreement between the Syndicalists and the official Socialists on this subject. The latter do talk about breaking everything up, but they attack the men in power rather than the power itself. They hope to possess the forces of the State and they realize that the day they controlled the

government, they would need an army. They would carry on
foreign policy and, as a result, would have to encourage devotion
to one's country.

The parliamentary Socialists are well aware that antipatriotism is
very close to the hearts of the Socialist workers and they are making great efforts to reconcile the irreconcilable; they are anxious
not to oppose too vehemently ideas which have become dear to the
proletariat, but they are unable to abandon their beloved State,
which promises them so many benefits. They have been led into
the most comic oratorical acrobatics in order to get over the difficulty. For example, after the judgment of the Court of Assizes of
the Seine, condemning Hervé and the antimilitarists, the National
Council of the Socialist Party passed a resolution stigmatizing this
verdict, brought out of hatred and fear, declaring that class justice
could not respect liberty of opinion, protesting against the employment of troops in strikes and affirming publicly the necessity for
action, and international understanding among the workers for the
suppression of war. All this is very clever, but the fundamental
question is evaded.

Thus it can no longer be disputed that there is an absolute opposition between Revolutionary Syndicalism and the State; in
France this opposition takes the particularly harsh form of antipatriotism, because the politicians have used all known means to
spread confusion in men's minds about the essence of Socialism. On
the plane of patriotism there can be no compromises or intermediate position; it is therefore on this plane that the Syndicalists
have been forced to take their stand, while the bourgeois of every
shade have employed all their powers of seduction to corrupt
Socialism and to alienate the workers from the revolutionary idea.
They have been led to deny the idea of patriotism by one of those
necessities which are met with at all times in the course of history,
and which philosophers sometimes have great difficulty in explaining—because the choice is imposed by external conditions, and not
freely made for reasons drawn from the nature of things. This
character of historical necessity gives the present antipatriotic
movement a strength it would be useless to attempt to dissimulate
by means of sophistries.

We have the right to conclude from this that there must be no
confusion between Syndicalist violence perpetrated in the course
of strikes by proletarians who desire the overthrow of the State,

and those acts of savagery which superstition of the State suggested to the revolutionaries of '93, when they had power in their hands and were able to oppress the conquered—following the principles they had learned from the Church and the Monarchy. We have the right to hope that a Socialist revolution carried out by pure Syndicalists would not be defiled by the abominations which defiled the bourgeois revolutions.

49. *The Matignon Agreement, June 7, 1936*

On June 4, 1936, Léon Blum, at the head of the combination of parties and workers' organizations known as the "Popular Rally" (*Rassemblement populaire*), which was victorious in the May general elections, formed his famous "Popular Front" Government. It was faced, from the outset, with an epidemic of widespread strikes which was paralyzing the country. Given the extent of unemployment, which might have undermined the unity of the strikers, the strikes took the new form of "sitting-in" or occupying the factories, so preventing all work. On the night of June 6 to 7, after lengthy discussions between the delegations of the employers and of the C.G.T. under Blum's chairmanship at his new headquarters in the Hôtel Matignon, the following agreement was reached and signed. A spate of bills followed, constituting one of the greatest bursts of social-welfare legislation in French history before 1945. The French text was published in *Le Populaire*, June 8, 1936, and is reprinted in *L'Oeuvre de Léon Blum* (Paris, Albin Michel, 1964), Vol. III, pp. 291–2.

Article 1—The employers' delegation agrees to the immediate establishment of collective agreements of labor.

Article 2—These agreements must include especially the following Articles 3 to 5.

Article 3—As all citizens are under obligation to observe the law the employers recognize the freedom of opinion and the right of workers to join freely and belong to an occupational *syndicat* constituted in accordance with Book 3 of the Labor Code.

The employers undertake not to take into account whether or not a worker belongs to a *syndicat* in making their decisions about taking him on, or organizing or distributing work, or measures of discipline or dismissal.

If one of the contracting parties challenges the grounds for the dismissal of a worker as being in violation of the above-mentioned right, both parties will endeavor to establish the facts and to find an equitable solution for all disputes.

This intervention does not limit the right of the parties to obtain before the courts damages for injury to their interests. Exercise of the right to have a *syndicat* must not lead to contravention of the law.

Article 4—Actual wages paid to all workers on the date of May 25, 1936, will, from the day when work is resumed, be readjusted according to a diminishing scale, starting with a rise of 15 per cent for the lowest paid and amounting to a rise of 7 per cent for the highest-paid workers.

The total wages bill for any company must in no case be increased by more than 12 per cent; the increases already given since the above-mentioned date will be counted toward the readjustments defined above. But increases in excess of these readjustments will remain the right of the beneficiaries.

Negotiations for determining minimum wages by collective agreements, according to regions and by categories, which shall be begun at once, must deal in particular with the necessary readjustment of abnormally low wages.

The employers' delegation undertakes to proceed with any necessary readjustments to maintain a normal relationship between salaries and wages.

Article 5—Except in special cases already provided for by law, every factory employing more than ten workers, after agreement with the *syndicat* organizations or, in their absence, with the interested parties, will have two (titular) or several (titular and deputy) shop stewards, according to the importance of the factory. These shop stewards are entitled to lay before the management any individual claims that have not been satisfied directly and which have to do with application of the laws, decrees and regulations of the Labor Code, wage scales and measures of hygiene and safety.

All working men and women over eighteen shall have a vote, provided that they have at the time of the election been in the factory for more than three months and have not been deprived of their civil rights.

Those eligible for election shall be electors as defined above, of French nationality and aged at least twenty-five, who have worked in the factory for at least one year, but this time must be shortened if the number of candidates would be reduced to five.

Workers who themselves or whose wives keep a retail store, no matter of what kind, cannot be candidates.

Article 6—The employers' delegation undertakes that no sanctions will be taken against strike actions.

Article 7—The confederal workers' delegation will ask workers on strike to decide to resume work as soon as the managements have accepted the general agreement now made, and as soon as negotiations for its application have been begun between the managements and the staffs of the factories.

Paris, June 7, 1936

President of the Council (Prime Minister): Léon Blum.

For the C.G.T.:   Léon Jouhaux, René Belin, B. Frachon,
Semat, H. Cordier, Milan.

For the C.G.P.F.:   Duchemin, Dalbouze, Richemont,
Lambert-Ribot.

Part III: Conflicts Within Society

After 1879 conflicts about dynasty and régime subsided, and increasingly men accepted a Republic as inevitable. But if the hopes of monarchists and Bonapartists alike evaporated, there remained plenty of sources of deep division in the nation. If Frenchmen were divided a little less about the past, they were perhaps rather more divided about the future—the social future of an industrial nation. Extremes met, as democrats and antidemocrats agreed that liberty and authority are ultimately incompatible, so that while an "Alain" urged minimal government in the name of individual freedom, authoritarians urged the destruction of individual freedom in the name of a strong State. So, too, while monarchists, radicals and even some socialists favored decentralization and a diffusion of power from the center to a multiplicity of more autonomous units, the liberals and Bonapartists, strange allies, insisted upon centralized national sovereignty with only moderate delegation of self-government to other bodies. The chief pitfall of studying the political and social divisions of France of the Third Republic is to assume consistent alignments of parties.

The first three sections of this Part illustrate the three greatest sources of social and political division after 1870: the Paris Commune of 1871, which in legend, and partly in reality, assumed the character that Marx attributed to it, a "civil war in France"; the clash between civilian and military authority, which arose from the national need to maintain a large defense establishment based on universal military service; and the protracted clash between Church and State. In each case a powerful and influential section of the nation—the Capital, the Army, the Church—claimed rights and privileges which the parliamentary secular Republic was obliged to refuse. Although in each case the Republic secured a formal victory, in practice a certain element of compromise underlay the doctrinal assertion of supremacy. Nonetheless, disgruntled elements waited for a chance to reverse the decision, and many believed they had found it in 1940.

Section D, within the limits possible, attempts to trace the shifting meanings of "Right" versus "Left" between 1870 and 1940. The ideas and ideals of "socialism," variously interpreted, permeated nationalism by the end of the nineteenth century, radicalism by 1914, and national opinion in its resistance to both communism and fascism by 1940.

SECTION A: THE PARIS COMMUNE, 1871

Like so many other Paris insurrections, the Commune of 1871 took everyone by surprise. The city had surrendered after the war and the long siege. On January 27 the Prussians were about to enter the capital, but on the twenty-sixth some troops of the National Guard had seized forty guns and removed them, out of reach of the Prussians, to the top of the hills of Montmartre and Belleville. Two months later, Thiers decided to disarm the Parisians and to recover these guns. Since the proclamation of the Republic on September 4 (Document 5) the Mayor of Montmartre had been a local doctor, Georges Clemenceau. He intervened and pointed out to Thiers the dangers of provoking a riot. But on March 18, 1871, Thiers sent troops to seize the guns and to occupy the *Buttes* of Montmartre. The ill-advised move angered the National Guard, aroused the deepest suspicions of the populace, and precipitated the tragedy of the Commune. The day's events were vividly described by Clemenceau in an account he dictated to his secretary and corrected with his own hand. The climax of his account is given below (Document 50). The French text is in Jean Martet, *Le silence de M. Clemenceau* (Paris, Albin Michel, 1929, pages 293–299), here reproduced in translation by kind permission of the publishers. Generals Lecomte and Clément Thomas were taken prisoner by the National Guard and interned in the Château-Rouge. They were shot before Clemenceau could get there to prevent it. His story continues from that point.

50. *How the Uprising Began: Georges Clemenceau, March 18, 1871*

. . . WE HAD hardly turned the corner of the wall when a man ran up and said that the Generals had just been shot. We did not stop to answer him but ran even faster. He did not seem very sure of his facts, anyhow, and seemed to be repeating a rumor rather than something he had seen for himself.

The *Buttes* were covered with armed National Guards. We made our way into this crowd. My sash called everybody's attention to me, and I at once became the object of the most hostile demonstrations. They reproached me for having conspired with the Government to have the guns taken away, they accused me of betraying the National Guard, they insulted me.

Keeping between Mayer and Sabourdy, who were both fairly

well-known in the *arrondissement* and were my only safeguard, I continued on my way without answering.

As we went on, I heard people saying: "It's all over! Justice has been done! The traitors are punished! If anybody doesn't like it, we'll do the same to him! It's too late!"

I crossed the upper plateau, where I had met the General in the morning, and arrived in the Rue des Rosiers with Mayer and Sabourdy, having lost Garcin on the way. As we arrived opposite No. 6, a detachment of National Guards was coming out, in the midst of whom were a number of officers of the line. It was no longer possible to doubt the assassination of the Generals, for everyone was repeating the news with somber enthusiasm.

The detachment of National Guards was turning left when I cut across their path and asked where they were taking the officers.

M. Beugnot, who declares that I was wearing a tricolor sash—you can certainly believe that—declares that I was very pale. I do not doubt it, for I was extremely upset. As for him, he was livid, and so changed, that seeing him later at the trial [of the assassins] of the Generals, I scarcely recognized him.

The officer who led the detachment, Lieutenant Meyer, told me that he was going to save the officers, and he was taking them to the Vigilance Committee in the interest of their safety. I still hesitated a few seconds, for after the shock of the terrible news, I was afraid that they were trying to deceive me and that they wanted to shoot the officers.

Captain Beugnot spoke a few words to me, but I understood nothing, either because I was too upset to grasp their meaning, or because he was not in a fit state to express himself clearly. I understood from his attitude, however, more than anything else, that he approved of what Lieutenant Meyer was doing. So I stepped aside, and the detachment went on.

Momentarily there was an impression of emptiness in the street.

On the ground where the detachment which had just left had been standing, I went forward a few steps to J . . . ., that same member of the Central Committee who had reproached me that morning for betraying them. I expressed my horror of the crime which had just been committed. M. Sabourdy, cutting me short, spoke his mind in very vehement language. J . . . ., who seemed depressed and utterly bewildered, went on repeating "It's awful!"

Suddenly there was a great noise, and the mob which filled the courtyard of No. 6 burst into the street, in the grip of a kind of frenzy.

There were chasseurs, soldiers of the line, National Guards, women and children. They were all shrieking like wild beasts, without realizing what they were doing. I observed then that pathological phenomenon which could be called blood lust. A breath of madness seemed to have passed over this mob. From the top of a wall children were waving indescribable trophies, women with streaming hair and all disheveled twisted their bare arms and uttered raucous cries, bereft of any sense. I saw some of them weeping and shouting louder than the others. Men were dancing about and jostling one another in a kind of frenzied fury. It was one of those nervous phenomena so frequent in the Middle Ages, and occasionally occurring still among masses of human beings under the stress of some powerful emotion.

Suddenly a piece of artillery, drawn by four horses, arrived in front of the house. The confusion increased, if that was possible. Men clad in ill-matched uniforms, riding on the horses, swore and shouted. I saw one woman jump onto one of the horses. She was waving her bonnet and yelling, "Down with the traitors!"—a cry the crowd repeated and repeated.

The situation was becoming more and more dangerous for me. The mob looked at me in crazed defiance, shouting its cry of "Down with the traitors!" Several fists were raised.

I could do nothing more in this place. I had not been able to prevent the crime. It remained for me to look after the fate of the prisoners whom I had just seen go by, and to stop any misfortune befalling my prisoners at the Mairie, against whom there was very great hostility.

I did not go into the house, then, and I have a strong conviction that I would not have come out alive. I did not therefore see the corpses, as somebody alleges, saying that I saw some National Guards executing a sort of *danse macabre* round the bodies.

I decided to go to the Rue Château-Rouge to find out for myself the fate of the officers whom I had seen being taken away not long before, and about whom I was not completely satisfied.

M. Sabourdy, to whom I communicated this idea, started to go down the road taken by the prisoners. I stopped him, and without giving him any explanation, I told him that we must go down again by the *Butte*.

I have said how hostile the attitude of the National Guards had been toward me while I was climbing up the *Butte*. I had refrained from answering their threats because I still hoped to arrive at the Rue des Rosiers in time. Now, I thought that if I had to have it out with them, it would be better to do it there, right away, and gain the credit for appearing to invite this explanation, rather than to lay myself open at the Mairie to the risk of some hostile demonstration which might well lead to the massacre of the prisoners.

I therefore went down the *Butte* with M. Sabourdy. The feelings of hostility directed toward me by the National Guard were at once made evident. I soon became the target of very pointed threats. They accused me of plotting the removal of the guns; they were delighted at the murder which had just taken place; they shouted at me that there were other people who deserved the same fate, and repeated what had already been said to me, that if I did not like it, they would do the same to me. They accused me of wanting to give back the guns, and that I could not deny.

I extricated myself from this dangerous situation only by composure and coolness. Several men menaced me with their weapons. I retraced my steps and went right up to them, asking them to explain their grievances against me. I told them several times over that they had just disgraced the Republic, and that the murder on which they were congratulating themselves so loudly would inevitably have the most disastrous consequences, for them and for the country. My vigorous attitude made them fall back.

Yet it was with extreme difficulty, and by parleying at each step of the way, that I reached the lower platform of the *Butte*, where one of the guns was placed.

Here there was a group which displayed particularly strong hostility toward me. Most fortunately, M. Sabourdy was recognized by one of them, and as he vouched for my conduct they let us pass in the end, though not without difficulty.

The rest of the descent was accomplished with relative ease, although in the midst of a crowd of National Guards whose attitude toward me was hostile. If a single man had uttered to my face certain definite accusations which were in the minds of all, thousands of voices would have been raised against me, and it is my deep conviction, as also that of M. Sabourdy, that I would have suffered the fate of the Generals.

The first words that M. Sabourdy said when we had reached the foot of the *Butte* were: "Without your *sang-froid* you would have been lost!"

51. The Testament of the Commune, April 19, 1871

A month after its outbreak, the rising of the Commune had spent its first impetus and was torn by the eternal dilemma of revolutionaries—should their revolution be efficient or respectable? The national armies of Thiers were massing for a general attack on the beleaguered city, but the internal factions among the *communards* continued to dispute their aims. For its wilder doctrinaires, reforming the world took priority over meeting the desperate plight in which the whole city now found itself. From the Hôtel-de-Ville, where the Commune had established itself on March 28, poured a mass of "legislation" and proclamations, most of them incapable of implementation at any time. The nearest the Commune came to formulating any coherent program was the "Declaration to the French People" issued on April 19 in the form of immense placards posted all over Paris (Document 51). Its attempt to generalize and extend the principle of independent communes to the rest of France was successful in only a few of the larger towns—Marseilles, Lyons, Saint-Étienne—though there were also local risings, quickly crushed, at Toulouse, Narbonne, Le Creusot, and Limoges. The idea of the Republic as a "community of communes" took various forms in the political thinking of nineteenth-century France. It received substantial homage in the power accorded to the 38,000 communes in local administration, and extreme formulation in the ideas of regionalism and *fédéralisme* (see Document 25). French text of the placard is quoted in *Enquête parlementaire sur l'insurrection du 18 Mars* (Paris, 1872), vol. IX, p. 61.

DECLARATION TO THE FRENCH PEOPLE,

April 19, 1871

In this terrible, agonizing conflict which once more threatens Paris with the horrors of siege and bombardment the Commune has a duty to assert and to determine the aspirations and wishes of the population of Paris; to clarify the nature of the movement of the eighteenth of March, which has remained unknown, but has been misunderstood and misrepresented by the politicians meeting at Versailles. Yet once again, Paris labors and suffers for France as a whole. . . . What do we ask?

The recognition and strengthening of the Republic, which is the only government compatible with the rights of the people and the free and ordered development of society.

The absolute autonomy of the Commune extended to all districts of France, assuring integral rights to each district, and to every Frenchman the full exercise of his faculties and aptitudes, as man, citizen, and worker.

The autonomy of the Commune shall have no limits other than the right of autonomy equally enjoyed by all other communes adhering to the contract, and by whose association together French Unity will be preserved.

The rights inherent to the Commune are: voting for the Communal budget, receipts and expenditure; fixing and assessment of taxes; control of local services; organization of local magistrates, police and schools; administration of property belonging to the Commune.

Selection by ballot or competition with the responsibility and permanent right of control and dismissal of magistrates and all communal civil servants of all grades. Absolute guarantee of individual freedom, freedom of conscience, and freedom to work. Permanent intervention of citizens in communal affairs by the free expression of their ideas. Organization of urban defense and of the National Guard, which elects its leaders and is solely responsible for the maintenance of order in the city.

Paris asks nothing further in the way of local guarantees, on the understanding that the large central administration delegated by the federation of communes shall adopt and put into practice these same principles.

The Unity which has been imposed on us up to now by the Empire, the Monarchy, and Parliamentarianism is nothing but despotic centralization, and is unintelligent, arbitrary, and burdensome. The Political Unity which Paris desires is the voluntary association of all local initiatives.

The Communal Revolution, begun by popular initiative on March 18, ushers in a new era of experimental, positive, scientific policy.

It spells the end of the old world with its governments and its clerics, militarism, officialdom, exploitation, stock-jobbing, monopolies, and privileges, to which the proletariat owes its servitude, the country its ills and its disasters.

52. *Communards and Communists: Karl Marx, 1871*

The Commune was more important for the development of Marxism —and of socialist movements in France—than was Marxism for the genesis and course of the Commune. The insurrection began on March 18 as a spontaneous protest against the insensitive behavior of the Provisional Government of Adolphe Thiers toward the city, which was still reeling from its sufferings in the long siege by the Germans, the

humiliation of military collapse, and the entry of the Germans after
the armistice. Its mainspring was a mixture of deep social distress, with
wounded civic and patriotic pride. The rising was unplanned, the result
of no organized plot or far-reaching scheme. Friedrich Engels later
admitted, "The International did not raise a finger to initiate the Commune." Its aims had nothing to do with communism, but much to do with
left-wing Jacobinism, Louis Delescluze, and the ideas of Proudhon; and
even at its height there were never more than a score of adherents of
Marx's International among the ninety members of the Council in the
Commune. It was an episode in French history much more than in
European history.

But from his listening post in London, Marx was kept very well-
informed of the course of events once the outbreak came. He made
it his purpose to claim the epic story for the Marxist cause, its martyrs
as Marxist heroes, and its lessons as pointers to a new era in proletarian
revolutionary methods. Vincennes, the last fortress of the Commune,
fell to Thiers's troops on May 29. The next day, in London, Marx read
to the General Council of the International the text of *The Civil War in
France*. As an immediate historical record of the events and the facts,
it was (and remains) astonishingly accurate. It is Marx's interpretation
of the purport of the events that matters, and this was diametrically
contrary to the view all subsequent events would endorse, and that
most modern historians would accept. Far from being the model of a
new era of proletarian revolution, the Commune was the last dying
flicker of the old tradition. It looked not forward, but back. Never
again would Paris set the pace of revolutions by raising street barricades; and the severity used to crush the rising was to leave socialism
and working-class organization in France weak for a generation to
come.

Marx's ingenious, well-informed misinterpretation of what the Paris
Commune meant exerted considerable influence. He created a social and
revolutionary myth of far-reaching effect, which entitles *The Civil
War in France* to rank among all his tracts as second in power only to
the *Communist Manifesto* itself. It made the International better known;
for a time it grew in strength. But many of its friends and foes alike now
linked *communards* inseparably with *communists;* and many therefore
turned (as did social democrats in Germany, and parliamentary socialists everywhere) to seek socialism through the winning of elections and
peaceful capture of the State. For them the Commune demonstrated the
futility of spontaneous uprisings. But from Marx's interpretation Lenin
drew the contrary moral—that the Commune failed because of half-
measures and "unnecessary magnanimity." In his last brief exile to Fin-
land in 1917, on the eve of his successful management of the Bolshevik
Revolution from Petrograd, Lenin took with him his well-thumbed
copy of Marx's *The Civil War in France*. He did not risk failure
through half-measures, still less through any "unnecessary magnanimity." When Lenin died, January, 1924, his body was appropriately

shrouded in a *communard* flag—the term "Reds," long used of the Parisian Jacobin insurrectionists, being now firmly transferred to the Bolsheviks.

Because the pamphlet was a *tour de force* of first-hand, first-rate journalism, it was widely read and earned Marx great notoriety. It was written originally in English, and Marx claimed for a time to "have the honor to be the best calumniated man in London." Its first two sections recount the circumstances of the rising and pour vituperation upon the men who crushed it—Adolphe Thiers, Jules Favre, Jules Ferry, and the army leaders they employed. The men who had made peace with Bismarck he denounced as *"capitulards"* (capitulationists), a term which facilitated further confusion with "capitalists." The third section of the pamphlet, from which this excerpt comes, contains the arguments by which Marx sought to show the relevance of the Commune to his theories of communism. Full text in Karl Marx and Frederick Engels, *Selected Works* (2 vols., Moscow, Foreign Languages Publishing House, 1951), vol. I, pp. 468–77.

ON THE dawn of the 18th of March, Paris arose to the thunderburst of "Vive la Commune!" What is the Commune, that sphinx so tantalizing to the bourgeois mind?

"The proletarians of Paris," said the Central Committee in its manifesto of the 18th March, "amidst the failures and treasons of the ruling classes, have understood that the hour has struck for them to save the situation by taking into their own hands the direction of public affairs. . . . They have understood that it is their imperious duty and their absolute right to render themselves masters of their own destinies, by seizing upon the governmental power." But the working class cannot simply lay hold of the ready-made State machinery, and wield it for its own purposes.

The centralized State power, with its ubiquitous organs of standing army, police, bureaucracy, clergy, and judicature—organs wrought after the plan of a systematic and hierarchic division of labour—originates from the days of absolute monarchy, serving nascent middle-class society as a mighty weapon in its struggles against feudalism. Still, its development remained clogged by all manner of mediæval rubbish, seignorial rights, local privileges, municipal and guild monopolies and provincial constitutions. The gigantic broom of the French Revolution of the eighteenth century swept away all these relics of bygone times, thus clearing simultaneously the social soil of its last hindrances to the superstructure of the modern State edifice raised under the First Empire, itself the offspring of the coalition wars of old semi-feudal Europe against modern France. During the subsequent *régimes* the Government, placed under parliamentary control—that is, under the direct control of the propertied classes—became not only a hotbed of huge national debts and crushing taxes; with its irresistible allurements of place, pelf, and patronage, it became not only the bone of contention between the rival factions and adventurers of the ruling classes; but its political character changed simultaneously with the economic changes of society. At the same pace at which the progress of modern industry developed, widened, intensified the class antagonism between capital and labour, the State power assumed more and more the character of the national power of capital over labour, of a public force organized for social enslavement, of an engine of class despotism. After every revolution marking a progressive phase in the class struggle, the purely repressive character of the State power stands out in bolder and bolder relief. The revolution of 1830, resulting in the transfer of Government from the landlords to the capitalists, transferred it from the more remote to the more direct antagonists of the working men. The bourgeois Republicans, who, in the name of the Revolution of February, took the State power, used it for the June massacres, in order to convince the working class that "social" republic meant the republic ensuring their social subjection, and in order to convince the royalist bulk of the bourgeois and landlord class that they might safely leave the cares and emoluments of government to the bourgeois "Republicans." However, after their one heroic exploit of June, the bourgeois Republicans had, from the front, to fall back to the rear of the "Party of Order"—a combination formed by all the rival fractions and factions of the appropriating class in their now openly declared antagonism to the producing classes. The proper form of their joint stock Government was the *Parliamentary Republic*, with Louis Bonaparte for its President. Theirs was a *régime* of avowed class terrorism and deliberate insult towards the "vile multitude." If the Parliamentary Republic, as M. Thiers said, "divided them [the different fractions of the ruling class] least," it opened an abyss between that class and the whole body of society outside their spare ranks. The restraints by which their own divisions had under former *régimes* still checked the State power, were removed by their union; and in view of the threatening upheaval of the proletariat, they now used that State power mercilessly and ostentatiously as the national war engine of capital against labour. In their uninterrupted crusade against the producing masses they were, however, bound not only to invest the executive with continually increased powers of repression, but at the same time to divest their own parliamentary stronghold—the National Assembly —one by one, of all its own means of defence against the Executive. The Executive, in the person of Louis Bonaparte, turned them out. The natural offspring of the "Party-of-Order" Republic was the Second Empire.

The Empire, with the *coup d'état* for its certificate of birth, universal suffrage for its sanction, and the sword for its sceptre, professed to rest upon the peasantry, the large mass of producers not directly involved in the struggle of capital and labour. It professed to save the working class by breaking down Parliamentarism, and, with it, the undisguised subserviency of Government to the propertied classes. It professed to save the propertied classes by upholding their economic supremacy over the working class; and, finally, it professed to unite all classes by reviving for all the chimera of national glory. In reality, it was the only form of government possible at a time when the bourgeoisie had already lost, and the working class had not yet acquired the faculty of ruling the nation. It was acclaimed throughout the world as the saviour of society. Under its sway, bourgeois society, freed from political cares, attained a development unexpected even by itself. Its industry and commerce expanded to colossal dimensions; financial swindling celebrated cosmopolitan orgies; the misery of the masses was set off by a shameless display of gorgeous, meretricious, and debased luxury. The State power, apparently soaring high above society, was at the same time itself the greatest scandal of that society and the very hotbed of all its corruptions. Its own rottenness, and the rottenness of the society it had saved, were laid bare by the bayonet of Prussia, herself eagerly bent upon transferring the supreme seat of that *régime* from Paris to Berlin. Imperialism is, at the same time, the most prostitute and the ultimate form of the State power which nascent middle-class society had commenced to elaborate as a means of its own emancipation from feudalism, and which full-grown bourgeois society had finally transformed into a means for the enslavement of labour by capital.

The direct antithesis to the Empire was the Commune. The cry of "Social Republic," with which the revolution of February was ushered in by the Paris proletariat, did but express a vague aspiration after a Republic that was not only to supersede the monarchial form of class-rule, but class-rule itself. The Commune was the positive form of that Republic.

Paris, the central seat of the old governmental power, and, at the same time, the social stronghold of the French working class, had risen in arms against the attempt of Thiers and the Rurals to restore and perpetuate that old governmental power bequeathed to them by the Empire. Paris could resist only because, in consequence of the siege, it had got rid of the army, and replaced it by a National Guard, the bulk of which consisted of working men. This fact was now to be transformed into an institution. The first decree of the Commune, therefore, was the suppression of the standing army, and the substitution for it of the armed people.

The Commune was formed of the municipal councillors, chosen by universal suffrage in various wards of the town, responsible and revocable at short terms. The majority of its members were naturally working men, or acknowledged representatives of the working class. The Commune was to be a working, not a parliamentary body, executive and legislative at the same time. Instead of continuing to be the agent of the Central Government, the police was at once stripped of its political attributes, and turned into the responsible and at all times revocable agent of the Commune. So were the officials of all other branches of the Administration. From the members of the Commune downwards, the public service had to be done at *workmen's wages*. The vested interests and the representation allowances of the high dignitaries of State disappeared along with the high dignitaries themselves. Public functions ceased to be the private property of the tools of the Central Government. Not only municipal administration, but the whole initiative hitherto exercised by the State was laid into the hands of the Commune.

Having once got rid of the standing army and the police, the physical force elements of the old Government, the Commune was anxious to break the spiritual force of repression, the "parson-power," by the disestablishment and disendowment of all churches as proprietary bodies. The priests were sent back to the recesses of private life, there to feed upon the alms of the faithful in imitation of their predecessors, the Apostles. The whole of the educational institutions were opened to the people gratuitously, and at the same time cleared of all interference of Church and State. Thus, not only was education made accessible to all, but science itself freed from the fetters which class prejudice and governmental force had imposed upon it.

The judicial functionaries were to be divested of that sham independence which had but served to mask their abject subserviency to all succeeding governments to which in turn, they had taken, and broken, the oaths of allegiance. Like the rest of public servants, magistrates and judges were to be elective, responsible and revocable.

The Paris Commune was, of course, to serve as a model to all the great industrial centres of France. The communal *régime* once established in Paris and the secondary centres, the old centralized Government would in the provinces, too, have to give way to the self-government of the producers. In a rough sketch of national organization which the Commune had no time to develop, it states clearly that the Commune was to be the political form of even the smallest country hamlet, and that in the rural districts the standing army was to be replaced by a national militia, with an extremely short term of service. The rural communes of every district were to administer their common affairs by an assembly of delegates in the central town, and these district assemblies were again to send deputies to the National Delegation in Paris, each delegate to be at any time revocable and bound by the *mandat impératif* (formal instructions) of his constituents. The few but important functions which still would remain for a central government were not to be suppressed, as has been intentionally misstated, but were to be discharged by Communal, and therefore strictly responsible agents. The unity of the nation was not to be broken, but, on the contrary, to be organized by the Communal constitution, and to become a reality by the destruction of the State power which claimed to be the embodiment of that unity independent of, and superior to, the nation itself, from which it was but a parasitic excrescence. While the merely repressive organs of the old governmental power were to be amputated, its legitimate functions were to be wrested from an authority usurping preeminence over society itself, and restored to the responsible agents of society. Instead of deciding once in three or six years which member of the ruling class was to represent the people in Parliament, universal suffrage was to serve the people, constituted in Communes, as individual suffrage serves every other employer in the search for the workmen and managers in his business. And it is well known that companies, like individuals, in matters of real business generally know how to put the right man in the right place, and, if they for once make a mistake, to redress it promptly. On the other hand, nothing could be more foreign to the spirit of the Commune than to supersede universal suffrage by hierarchic investiture.

It is generally the fate of completely new historical creations to be mistaken for the counterpart of older and even defunct forms of social life, to which they may bear a certain likeness. Thus, this new Commune, which breaks the modern State power, has been mistaken for a reproduction of the mediæval Communes, which first preceded, and afterwards became the substratum of, that very State power. The communal constitution has been mistaken for an attempt to break up into a federation of small States, as dreamt of by Montesquieu and the Girondins, that unity of great nations which, if originally brought about by political force, has now become a powerful coefficient of social production. The antagonism of the Commune against the State power has been mistaken for an exaggerated form of the ancient struggle against over-centralization. Peculiar historical circumstances may have prevented the classical development, as in France, of the bourgeois form of government, and may have allowed, as in England, to complete the great central State organs by corrupt vestries, jobbing councillors, and ferocious poor-law guardians in the towns, and virtually hereditary magistrates in the counties. The Communal Constitution would have restored to the social body all the forces hitherto absorbed by the State parasite feeding upon, and clogging the free movement of, society. By this one act it would have initiated the regeneration of France. The provincial French middle-class saw in the Commune an attempt to restore the sway their order had held over the country under Louis Philippe, and which, under Louis Napoleon, was supplanted by the pretended rule of the country over the towns. In reality, the Communal Constitution brought the rural producers under the intellectual lead of the central towns of their districts, and there secured to them, in the working man, the natural trustees of their interests. The very existence of the Commune involved, as a matter of course, local municipal liberty, but no longer as a check upon the, now superseded, State power. It could only enter into the head of a Bismarck, who, when not engaged on his intrigues of blood and iron, always likes to resume his old trade, so befitting his mental calibre, of contributor to *Kladderadatsch* (the Berlin *Punch*), it could only enter in such a head, to ascribe to the Paris Commune aspirations after that caricature of the old French municipal organization of 1791, the Prussian municipal constitution which degrades the town governments to mere secondary wheels in the police machinery of the Prussian State. The Commune made that catchword of bourgeois revolutions, cheap government, a reality by destroying the two greatest sources of expenditure—the standing army and State functionarism. Its very existence presupposed the non-existence of monarchy, which, in Europe at least, is the normal incumbrance and indispensable cloak of class-rule. It supplied the Republic with the basis of really democratic institutions. But neither cheap government nor the "true Republic" was its ultimate aim; they were its mere concomitants.

The multiplicity of interpretations to which the Commune has been subjected, and the multiplicity of interests which construed it in their favour, show that it was a thoroughly expansive political form, while all previous forms of government had been emphatically repressive. Its true secret was this. It was essentially a working-class government, the produce of the struggle of the producing against the appropriating class, the political form at last discovered under which to work out the economical emancipation of labour.

Except on this last condition, the Communal Constitution would have been an impossibility and a delusion. The political rule of the producer cannot coexist with the perpetuation of his social slavery. The Commune was therefore to serve as a lever for uprooting the economical foundations upon which rests the existence of classes, and therefore of class rule. With labour emancipated, every man becomes a working man, and productive labour ceases to be a class attribute.

It is a strange fact. In spite of all the tall talk and all the immense literature, for the last sixty years, about Emancipation of Labour, no sooner do the working men anywhere take the subject into their own hands with a will, than uprises at once all the apologetic phraseology of the mouthpieces of present society with its two poles of Capital and Wages-slavery (the landlord now is but the sleeping partner of the capitalist), as if capitalist society was still in its purest state of virgin innocence, with its antagonisms still undeveloped, with its delusions still unexploded, with its prostitute realities not yet laid bare. The Commune, they exclaim, intends to abolish property, the basis of all civilization! Yes, gentlemen, the Commune intended to abolish that class-property which makes the labour of the many the wealth of the few. It aimed at the expropriation of the expropriators. It wanted to make individual property a truth by transforming the means of production, land and capital, now chiefly the means of enslaving and exploiting labour, into mere instruments of free and associated labour. But this is Communism, "impossible" Communism! Why, those members of the ruling classes who are intelligent enough to perceive the impossibility of continuing the present system—and they are many—have become the obtrusive and fullmouthed apostles of co-operative production. If co-operative production is not to remain a sham and a snare; if it is to supersede the Capitalist system; if united co-operative societies are to regulate national production upon a common plan, thus taking it under their own control, and putting an end to the constant anarchy and periodical convulsions which are the fatality of capitalist production—what else, gentlemen, would it be but Communism, "possible" Communism?

The working class did not expect miracles from the Commune. They have no ready-made utopias to introduce *par décret du peuple*. They know that in order to work out their own emancipation, and along with it that higher form to which present society is irresistibly tending, by its own economical agencies, they will have to pass through long struggles, through a series of historic processes, transforming circumstances and men. They have no ideals to realize, but to set free the elements of the new society with which old collapsing bourgeois society itself is pregnant. In the full consciousness of their historic mission, and with the heroic resolve to act up to it, the working class can afford to smile at the coarse invective of the gentlemen's gentlemen with the pen and inkhorn, and at the didactic patronage of well-wishing bourgeois-doctrinaires, pouring forth their ignorant platitudes and sectarian crochets in the oracular tone of scientific infallibility.

When the Paris Commune took the management of the revolution in its own hands; when plain working men for the first time dared to infringe upon the Governmental privilege of their "natural superiors," and, under circumstances of unexampled difficulty, performed their work modestly, conscientiously, and efficiently —performed it at salaries the highest of which barely amounted to one-fifth of what, according to high scientific authority, is the minimum required for a secretary to a certain metropolitan school board—the old world writhed in convulsions of rage at the sight of the Red Flag, the symbol of the Republic of Labour, floating over the Hôtel de Ville.

And yet, this was the first revolution in which the working class was openly acknowledged as the only class capable of social initiative, even by the great bulk of the Paris middle-class—shop-keepers, tradesmen, merchants—the wealthy capitalist alone excepted. The Commune had saved them by a sagacious settlement of that ever recurring cause of dispute among the middle class themselves—the debtor and creditor accounts. The same portion of the middle class, after they had assisted in putting down the working men's insurrection of June, 1848, had been at once unceremoniously sacrificed to their creditors by the then Constituent Assembly. But this was not their only motive for now rallying around the working class. They felt there was but one alternative—the Commune, or the Empire—under whatever name it might reappear. The Empire had ruined them economically by the havoc it made of public wealth, by the wholesale financial swindling it fostered, by the props it lent to the artificially accelerated centralization of capital, and the concomitant expropriation of their own ranks. It had suppressed them politically, it had shocked them morally by its orgies, it had insulted their Voltairianism by handing over the education of their children to the *frères Ignorantins*, it had revolted their national feeling as Frenchmen by precipitating them headlong into a war which left only one equivalent for the ruins it made—the disappearance of the Empire. In fact, after the exodus from Paris of the high Bonapartist and capitalist *Bohême*, the true middle class Party of Order came out in the shape of the "Union Républicaine," enrolling themselves under the colours of the Commune and defending it against the wilful misconstruction of Thiers. Whether the gratitude of this great body of the middle class will stand the present severe trial, time must show.

The Commune was perfectly right in telling the peasants that "its victory was their only hope." Of all the lies hatched at Versailles and re-echoed by the glorious European penny-a-liner, one of the most tremendous was that the Rurals represented the French peasantry. Think only of the love of the French peasant for the men to whom, after 1815, he had to pay the milliard of indemnity!

In the eyes of the French peasant, the very existence of a great landed proprietary is in itself an encroachment on his conquests of 1789. The bourgeoisie, in 1848, had burdened his plot of land with the additional tax of forty-five cents in the franc; but then he did so in the name of the revolution; while now he had fomented a civil war against the revolution, to shift on the peasant's shoulders the chief load of the five milliards of indemnity to be paid to the Prussians. The Commune, on the other hand, in one of its first proclamations, declared that the true originators of the war would be made to pay its cost. The Commune would have delivered the peasant of the blood tax, would have given him a cheap government, transformed his present blood-suckers, the notary, advocate, executor, and other judicial vampires, into salaried communal agents, elected by, and responsible to himself. It would have freed him of the tyranny of the *garde champêtre*, the gendarme, and the prefect; would have put enlightenment by the schoolmaster in the place of stultification by the priest. And the French peasant is, above all, a man of reckoning. He would find it extremely reasonable that the pay of the priest, instead of being extorted by the tax-gatherer, should only depend upon the spontaneous action of the parishioners' religious instincts. Such were the great immediate boons which the rule of the Commune—and that rule alone—held out to the French peasantry. It is, therefore, quite superfluous here to expatiate upon the more complicated but vital problems which the Commune alone was able, and at the same time compelled, to solve in favor of the peasant, viz., the hypothecary debt, lying like an incubus upon his parcel of soil, the *prolétariat foncier* (the rural proletariat), daily growing upon it, and his expropriation from it enforced, at a more and more rapid rate, by the very development of modern agriculture and the competition of capitalist farming.

The French peasant had elected Louis Bonaparte president of the Republic; but the Party of Order created the Empire. What the French peasant really wants he commenced to show in 1849 and 1850, by opposing his *maire* to the Government's prefect, his schoolmaster to the Government's priest, and himself to the Government's gendarme. All the laws made by the party of order in January and February, 1850, were avowed measures of repression against the peasant. The peasant was a Bonapartist, because the great Revolution, with all its benefits to him, was, in his eyes, personified in Napoleon. This delusion, rapidly breaking down under the Second Empire (and in its very nature hostile to the Rurals), this prejudice of the past, how could it have withstood the appeal of the Commune to the living interests and urgent wants of the peasantry?

The Rurals—this was, in fact, their chief apprehension—knew that three months' free communication of Communal Paris with the provinces would bring about a general rising of the peasants, and hence their anxiety to establish a police blockade around Paris, so as to stop the spread of the rinderpest.

If the Commune was thus the true representative of all the healthy elements of French society, and therefore the truly national Government, it was, at the same time, a working men's Government, as the bold champion of the emancipation of labour, emphatically international. Within sight of the Prussian army, that had annexed to Germany two French provinces, the Commune annexed to France the working people all over the world. . . .

53. *A* Communard *Looks Back: Lissagaray, 1896*

A journalist eye-witness of the Commune was Lissagaray, who contributed to the papers *L'Action* and *Tribun du peuple* and later wrote *Histoire de la Commune de 1871*, described by one modern historian as "the classic history of the Commune." There is no doubt where his sympathies lay in the struggle, but his account makes great efforts to do justice to the complexity of it and the sincerity of many of its participants, whom he knew personally. His book appeared first in Brussels in 1876, and Marx's daughter translated it into English in 1886. For the edition of it published in Paris by Dentu in 1896 Lissagaray wrote a brief epilogue, looking back on the event twenty-five years afterward: this is here translated as Document 53, and is an echo, even after the amnesty granted to the remaining *communards* so belatedly and grudgingly in 1880, of the old bitterness. See J. T. Joughin, *The Paris Commune in French Politics, 1871–1880* (Baltimore, 1955).

TWENTY-FIVE YEARS have passed over the Commune. The Gallifets are still there.[1] Were the people to be conquered, they would receive the same machine-gun fire. The old-time band of diehards

[1] General Gaston Gallifet, much hated by the Left for his role in crushing the Commune, was to serve as Minister of War in René Waldeck-Rousseau's Government of Republican Defense in June, 1899, along with the first Socialist minister, Alexandre Millerand.

has not one country squire fewer than in 1871, not one priest, not one slave-dealer fewer; it has even recruited a few bourgeois fife-players to smooth its way behind a democratic smoke-screen.

In 1848 they had said to the people: "Universal suffrage makes every insurrection criminal, the ballot has replaced the bullet." And when the people vote against their privileges, they jib; every Government is factious if it takes account of popular will. What remains to the people except the peremptory argument of force? This it has, at last. After trying a whole crowd of doctors, the worker in the towns and in the fields ended by producing an idea, and a desire of his own—to look after himself; after prolonged hesitations the lower middle class found itself thrown back into the proletariat by big business, and realized that their interests were identical. The union is almost complete between these two classes, which, because they are the only producers, are the real French people.

They have returned, after a long way around, to an under-standing of its origins. For a hundred years France has experi-mented with all forms of government, handed the instruments of power to all political parties, and all the State departments, ad-ministrations, and ministries have continued to drag in their wake their own world of creatures, their ever-mounting budgets, their vast parasitism, all of which is of profit to a caste, but is ruinous to the nation; for a hundred years France has made men of varied political hues and reputations responsible for framing its laws, and these laws have always brought about a diminution of national power, since they were always drawn up for the benefit of the few. The experiment lasted too long. The lion will no longer drag the ass after him.

Three times the French proletariat has made a Republic for other people; now it is ready for its own. The lights it lacked before now shine from it alone. Its handful of opponents can stir nothing but ashes, the remains of a world which was antimodern, anti-economic, and strong only in superannuated laws and administra-tion. Once they disappear the production of France will be increased a hundredfold, whereas today it is forced to waste away on the spot. The government of the people means harnessing a vast work reservoir which has accumulated and is today unproductive.

The nation has never had firmer muscles for taking over power.

A few dozen anemic ultra-modern dandies, who say that they are quite ill with *fin-de-siècle* uncertainty, are no more typical of France than the marquises before 1789. But the workers in the country and in the town—they are not uncertain of their ability. What generation for the past hundred years has been better equipped to understand its ideals?

What must we do to get rid of the hornets and stride victorious through the red horizons as they appear? Dare. As of old, "this word enshrines our whole outlook at this hour." Dare, and plough deeply. Audacity is the crowning splendor of faith. Because they dared, the people of 1789 tower above the heights of history. Because they did not falter, history will find due place for the people of 1870–71 who had faith unto death.

Section B: Antimilitarism

§(a) The Nation in Arms

From the wars of the French Revolution, France inherited the characteristic Jacobin notion of "the Nation in Arms," a doctrine hallowed by Valmy, utilized by Carnot, appropriated by Napoleon I. Deriving from the revolutionary *levée en masse*, it came to mean, in effect, universal, compulsory military service, held to be democratic because it saved the army from becoming a praetorian guard at the disposal of a dictator, and to be patriotic because it made all the nation's manpower available for national defense.

Between 1815 and the mid-1840's, however, the notion lost its popular appeal and went into eclipse. The restored Bourbons could not evoke so nationalistic a mood—they had been brought back in the baggage-trains of the Allies. Militarism, for a time, was favored by neither Right nor Left, and the soldier was not accorded the esteem he had enjoyed before Waterloo. From about 1840 onwards, the army, like the Bonapartist legend itself, regained some prestige. It conquered Algeria. It was increasingly valued by the July Monarchy and—after the June Days of 1848—by the Liberals, as a force of order. The professional armies, which most European governments increasingly relied on to crush revolution, were divorced in image from the democratic Jacobin tradition. In consequence, antimilitarism became an attitude of the Left, whereas a generation earlier it had been more characteristic of the Right.

The older revolutionary doctrine, of appealing for a great popular effort to save the nation in time of danger, continued under the Second

Empire to be heavily overlaid until 1866. To the republican Left, and even to the Liberal opposition, the army as it existed under Napoleon III was in essence a praetorian guard, the mainstay of military dictatorship. So long as armed forces were used more to shoot rioters and quell insurrection at home—their commonest function between 1815 and the mid-fifties—than to fight national enemies abroad, the Left was, perforce, antimilitarist. But a new era of major European conflict began in 1854, with the Crimean War. It continued through the nationalist wars of 1859 and 1866 against Austria-Hungary to the Franco-Prussian War of 1870. Armies resumed their more traditional external roles. Above all, the dramatic defeat of Austria-Hungary by the new-model Prussian army at Sadowa in 1866 compelled the French, both government and opposition, to rethink the defense system. As public interest in the army revived, it was inevitable that French Radicals should again speak of "the Nation in Arms," and see "the Nation in danger" from the new might of Bismarck's Prussia. Mirabeau had regarded Prussia as an army which possessed a State, rather than a State which had an army, and the relationship seemed little different now. The doctrine of "the Nation in Arms," which in variations was to dominate relations between Army and State in France for the next seventy-five years, owed its resuscitation first to Sadowa, and then to Sedan.

The military reorganization and re-equipment which Napoleon III and Émile Ollivier put through between 1867 and 1869 were designed to produce a modernized force based on more rigorous insistence on general obligations for service. These were principles the emperor's republican critics could hardly refuse to support, and Jules Simon in *La politique radicale* of 1868 expounded them clearly.

The defeat of the French armies in 1870, however, made the notion an indelible part of French republican ideology. When Paris fell to the Germans, the Government of National Defense sent out of the city, by balloon, its Minister of the Interior, Léon Gambetta. From Tours, Gambetta and his colleagues appealed to the whole of the rest of the nation to engage in a national war to the death against the German invader. The appeal recalled Danton and was the authentic voice of revolutionary Jacobinism (Document 54). Although the effort failed, it failed nobly and left an epic of desperate heroism to nourish the new republicanism. We can trace to such sources the origins of modern "total war," seen as struggle for national survival. (French text in *Enquête parlementaire sur les actes du gouvernement de la Défense nationale* (Versailles, 1875), No. 1416, Part II, p. 214.)

The Third Republic, nursing the country to recovery, again reorganized the armed forces on a basis of universal conscription and long-term service. Dominated by the aim of revenge, and faced with the implacable military power of the new German Empire, Republican governments of the 1870's and 1880's clung tenaciously to this ideal of a "Nation in Arms." But the new Left, the Socialists and Communists, had no love for the army since the national troops had so mercilessly crushed the Commune in May, 1871. They were ready to exploit popular dislike of the dreary life spent in barracks during lengthy periods of military service. And after the exploits of General Boulanger and the social upheavals of the Dreyfus Affairs, antimilitarism and even outright pacifism became, by the end of the century, strong ingredients of the Left. The journalist Urbain Gohier was one of the most effective and virulent writers in that cause. Document 55, excerpted from his book *L'Armée contre la Nation* (Paris, La revue blanche, 1899), pp. 15–20, is typical of these polemics.

Mounting international tensions in the twentieth century forced men like the Socialist leader, Jean Jaurès, to seek a new synthesis of nationalistic and socialistic aims in the combination of universal military training with short-term service, on the Swiss model. In his *L'Armée nouvelle* of 1911, he attacked the organization of the army not at all from pacifist principles, but from the patriotic standpoint of how to achieve the most economical use of national resources for effective national defense. He finished writing the book in 1910, and its famous tenth chapter on "The Army, the Nation, and the Proletariat" became a classic exposition of socialist theory. The book was republished during the First World War in a second edition of 1915. Jaurès himself was assassinated in 1914, but for four years France became indeed a "Nation in Arms," and its morale depended on conviction that it fought for national survival. The extract (Document 56) gives the opening pages of Chapter II, on the crucial distinction between the active and the reserve sectors of the army. French text in Jean Jaurès, *L'Armée nouvelle* (Paris, L'Humanité, 1915), pp. 17–22.

The immense losses of France in the First World War, and experience of the costliness of an offensive strategy, led military thinking after 1918 to preserve military conscription but to build the Maginot Line, a system of static defense in depth. Against this orthodoxy one military thinker of the 1930's urged the case of a smaller, specialized, and highly trained professional force, utilizing the advantages of great mobility and concentrated striking power made possible by tanks, aircraft, and motorized columns. Charles de Gaulle, in *L'Armée de métier* (1934), did not quite foresee the role of the dive-bomber in an offensive strategy, but he saw more perceptively than most of his contemporaries that new opportunities for *Blitzkrieg* warfare had been created. Document 57 consists of two brief extracts on this theme. French text in *L'Armée de métier* (Paris, Berger-Levrault, 1944), pp. 100–5 and 191–5. The extract is here reproduced in translation by kind permission of the publishers.

On this important theme in the history of modern France, see R. D. Challener, *The French Theory of the Nation in Arms, 1866–1939* (New York, 1955); R. Girardet, *La société militaire dans la France contemporaine, 1815–1939* (Paris, 1953); J.-P. Charnay, *Société militaire et suffrage politique en France depuis 1789* (Paris, 1964) and J. Monteilhet, *Les institutions militaires de la France 1814–1932* (Paris, 1932).

54. *Appeal for a National War: Léon Gambetta,*
October 9, 1870

CITIZENS OF THE *Départements:*

This situation imposes on you grave duties. First of all, do not allow yourselves to be diverted by any consideration but war— *le combat à outrance*—the fight to the finish. Secondly, accept, until peace comes, and in brotherly fashion, the commands of the Republican power, which has emerged out of necessity and of right. This power cannot be used to further private ambition without declining. It has but one desire and one justification: to snatch France from the abyss into which the monarchy has plunged her. After that, the Republic will be well-founded and protected against conspirators and reactionaries.

And so, since everything else has come to a halt, I have a mandate to rescue us from our plight, ignoring all difficulties or resistance, with the help of all free sources of energy, and, although time is short, to make up for this deficiency by speed of action. There is no shortage of men. What was lacking was resolution, decision, and the execution of plans to their conclusion.

After the shameful capitulation at Sedan it was arms that we lacked. All our supplies of this nature had been directed toward Sedan, Metz and Strasburg; you might almost think that the author of all our disasters tried, as he fell, to deprive us of all means of repairing our ruin by this final, criminal scheme. Now, thanks to the intervention of experts, arrangements have been made to buy up all available rifles on the world market. Great difficulties have been experienced in making these purchases; but now they have been overcome.

The number of factories for clothing and equipment will be increased and, if need be, raw materials will be requisitioned. We are not short of willing hands, and there will be no shortage of money either.

Finally, we must make full use of all our resources—and they are immense—rouse the countryside from its apathy, take firm measures against senseless panic, spread the war of the partisans, and in the face of an enemy so given to ambushes and surprise, we must prepare traps, harass his flanks, take his rear troops unawares, in a word, start a national war.

The Republic appeals to all for help; the Government pledges itself to make full use of all brave offers to fight, and to employ all men of ability. It is Republican tradition to arm the young leaders. We shall do so! The sky itself will no longer favor our enemies. The rains of autumn will come, and the Prussians, held, contained, by the capital, far from home, worried, troubled, and harried by a stirring population will be gradually decimated by our guns, by hunger, and by nature itself.

No, it is impossible that the genius of France should be obscured forever, that so great a nation should allow its place in the world to be taken from it.

So let us rise *en masse*, and die rather than submit to the shame of dismemberment. Throughout all our disasters, and beneath the blows of ill-fortune, there yet remains the knowledge of French unity, and the Republic undivided.

Beseiged Paris reaffirms with still more glory its immortal device, which shall be that of all France: "Long live the Nation! Long live the Republic, one and indivisible!"

The member of the Government of National Defense,
Minister of the Interior,
Léon Gambetta

55. The Barracks: Urbain Gohier, 1899

IN THE AUTUMN of every year more than two hundred thousand young Frenchmen put on their uniform, either as conscripts or as volunteers. The barracks are going to "moralize" them.

If the atrocious Vacher had butchered, mutilated, and violated five hundred thousand human creatures he would be a hero, an object of popular worship. If he had killed fifty thousand he would still be glorified as a great general or a great minister. If he had killed only one man, they would have chopped off his head. Because he killed nineteen people he will be shut up in a lunatic asylum. But if he had no army to enable him to become an Alexander or a Napoleon, he at least commanded two *escouades;* according to the evidence of his former colonel of the 60th regiment of the line, he was an excellent warrant officer. The barracks had "moralized" him.

"Moralization" by the barracks is the great argument used by the advocates of three years' service. Militarists raise scarcely any technical objection to proposals for reducing the period of service; they nearly all admit that the soldier can be got ready for the battlefield within a few months, especially if he has received some preliminary instruction. But they want to keep him in the barracks for three years, in order to inculcate the military spirit and the military virtues without which they consider no citizen to be complete.

Now a military spirit is not acquired in the barracks; it is acquired by war. The soldiers of the First Empire, who were models of the type, became imbued with the military spirit during their never-ending campaigns, not in the barracks, where they did not live anyhow. If, instead of being one of the most detestable forms of barbarism, the military spirit could really be esteemed a virtue, it would still be too high a price to pay if, in order to restore it, it meant waging war for ten years.

The barracks do not develop this spirit. They are simply a school for all the dissolute vices: laziness, lying, informing, lewdness, filth, debauchery, moral laxity, and drunkenness. Ever since the whole of Europe was brought under the scourge of militarism, the human species has deteriorated by several degrees. The surprising vitality and all-around progress of the Anglo-Saxon race, for which various ingenious explanations are sought, is certainly to be accounted for by the fact that its members escape the corrupting, degrading influence of the barracks.

A recent Grand-Master of the University, M. Rambaud, made the humorous remark that alcoholism "is a legacy of barbarism." The widespread alcoholism which is cankering the French race does not go back so far. It is a product of the barracks. The enormous increase in the number of bars and beerhalls, where the entire nation, without distinction of class, is poisoning itself now, coincides with putting the young men into barracks. Drinking is the only amusement in the regiment. The one aim is to drink more than the others. Paying for drinks brings all the respect there is. With this state of affairs, a people formerly praised for its sobriety has contracted Coupeau's disease. The French even need bars on the railway; they drink between Paris and Versailles.

The barracks are making France rotten with alcoholism and syphilis. And who forces all this on the people? *Those who are called up for either a very short time, or not at all.*

The answer is always the same.

Those who are in favor of three years' military service, that is
to say, a prolonged period in the barracks and compulsory degradation, are the following civilians: first, those who are exempted, or
invalided out, all those who avoid military service through fraud
or some infirmity, and who press for this imprisoning of able-
bodied men, just as they press for a war of extermination, to clear
the ground; then there are the fat politicians, those solemn members
of the middle class who have never paid their military debt and
who know all the ways of keeping their own offspring out too.

For them, and for their children, there is only one year's military
service. For the people, they insist on three years in the barracks.

One year of service at twenty years of age does no harm; it licks
the dear boy into shape and toughens him up. He is in no danger of
expeditions overseas. In France three years in barracks ruin a young
man, or deliver him up as prey to colonial slaughtering. One year
is for the apt sons of the middle class, for members of parliament,
and for journalists. Three years is for the sons of the people.

Prolonged military service for poor soldiers is also advocated by
many professional military men; not by all, for a number of
officers accept a reduction of time in the service, but by the leading
officers.

Who does this mean?

Those who got out of military service.

It must be noted that this is not just a paradox; this is a serious
subject and merits close reasoning.

Nearly all the officers who now hold or who will in the future
hold the highest ranks, those who have an important voice in legislative decisions bearing on military organization, and who resist
the reduction of time spent in barracks, have come from the big
Schools. They have not been in barracks at all.

It could be said that they have not done any military service.
Once they are officers, they continue their career just like civil
servants; they work for themselves. The *Polytechnicien* who goes
into the artillery works his way up and studies for promotion just
like a *Polytechnicien* who is going into the State Tobacco Department. The years spent in the School under enviable conditions,
with an elegant, popular uniform, in intelligent company, doing
work and getting teaching that is really worthwhile, do not re-
semble in the least a civil sacrifice. They have nothing in common
with service in the regiment.

In the Reserve, too, a very great number of officers come from the Schools: the School of Forestry, the Central School, and the Polytechnic School (for civil careers). They have never been soldiers but obtain their commission and do one year only of actual service with the rank of second lieutenant.

If military service was like this, there would not be one young Frenchman who would not be very keen to serve. An irresistible uniform, 2,500 francs in salary, a sword, a room in town, with a valet thrown in—what a dream for a twenty-year-old! But real military service means a gun, a terrible pack, awful hobnailed boots, filthy old clothes, alopecia, typhoid, repulsive duties, drunkard's vomit, a stinking barrack room, violence and swearing from your superior, with the alternative of letting yourself down if you submit, or wrecking your life if you hit back.

Most officers do not know this. They do not know what barracks are. How can they praise their virtues? They have never been in them. How do they dare insist that other people should be confined in them?

In France, in this democratic Republic, there is only one way of escaping from the barracks—get a commission. There is only one way of not being a soldier—become an officer.

56. The New Army: Jean Jaurès, 1911

THE ESSENTIAL defect in our military organization is that it has the appearance of being the nation in arms, whereas it is not, or hardly at all. It imposes a heavy burden on the nation, but does not obtain from it all the defensive resources a nation really armed and trained ought to be able to provide with less expenditure of time and energy. Compulsory, equal service is imposed by law on all citizens. No exceptions and no exemptions are allowed; all ablebodied men are liable for service during the greater part of their lives. By virtue of Article 32 of the law, every Frenchman considered fit for military service goes successively into active service for two years, the reserve of the active army for eleven years, the territorial army for six years, and the reserve of the territorial army for six years. All citizens spend two years in the barracks; after they are released from the regiment, all citizens are called up at regular intervals for maneuvers and exercises. Rich and poor, employers and workers, the most refined intellectuals and the most

ignorant of simple men are under the same obligation; they share as
soldiers in a common life and carry the same loads. All occupations
and all classes are merged beneath the same law and the same
discipline, with the same duty, the same sacrifice, the same peril.
Even physical weakness, if it is not below a certain standard, does
not exempt the citizen from all military effort; a weakling, if he is
not completely disabled, goes into the auxiliary services to pay off
his debt to the common motherland which has declared a common
obligation. Until forty-five years of age when, according to
Montaigne, a man has already walked for five years along "the
avenues of old age," military law keeps its hold on its citizens,
keeping them all under the same control, for the same length of
time, and for the same tasks. Could there be a vaster accumulation
of forces? Could there be more impressive equality? It is indeed
the Nation in Arms, the whole nation—at least in appearance. The
powerful shadow of an army of three million men is thrown as it
were on a screen. But it is nothing but a shadow. At the center of
our military system there is a deep-rooted prejudice which limits
its strength and opposes its effectiveness, the prejudice that the nation can really rely only on that part of the army which is in the
barracks.

The length of service in the barracks was reduced from seven to
five years, then to three, and then two. But M. Thiers's ideas have
survived, and he was suspicious of the masses. There are only two
classes in what is called the active army. And even leaving out the
whole of the territorial army, there are eleven classes in what is
called the reserve of the active army. So it is in the reserves that
the chief strength of the army lies. This is agreed—at least, people
think they agree. General Langlois goes so far as to say that the
French system is characterized by the preponderance of its reserves, as opposed to the German system. He writes in his substantial study, *Ten Days with the Swiss Army:*

> France and Germany have adopted two essentially different sys-
> tems in their organization of the nation in arms. According to our
> neighbors, the chief strength lies in the army of the first line, slightly
> reinforced by reserves from the youngest classes; in France, on the
> contrary, we rely principally on our reserves.
>
> It is not for us to examine here these two different conceptions.
> Ours is imposed by our political and social conditions, and we have
> to try to turn it to the best account.

But by using such terms we deceive ourselves, for our whole system presupposes the inferiority of the reserves. Although these reserves have been formed, with the framework of the statutory two years' service, from men who have undergone military instruction in barracks, and although, by suitable exercises, it is possible to prepare them and train them for the operations of war, they have never had more than a secondary, subordinate, or conditional importance within our whole institution. They are of value only when they form part of the active army. Everything conspires, even the very words, to disparage them and reduce them to a subordinate role.

Why should the assemblage of soldiers grouped in barracks be called "active army," and the distant, attenuated name of "reserve," a name of inferior meaning, be given to the mass of practiced soldiers who have returned to civilian life? They are enrolled in military units, will be called up on the day of mobilization, and in an authentic, realistic system of the nation in arms, would form the active army proper, the great mass organized for combat. The spotlight is concentrated entirely on the army in the barracks.

If the nation really had faith in its reserves, the barracks would be no more than the soldiers' preparatory school; it would not be the center of the French military force. What is called the active army would only be a course preparing soldiers to play their part in the real active army, the combat units, permanently established over the entire surface of the country. But the tiny fraction of the army in the barracks is thought of as the indispensable link, the necessary framework and base, the shining, resistant center of the dim, diffused and half-suspect forces scattered through the nation. The reserves are perceived but vaguely, in a sort of half-light, like soft, shapeless material, worthless until given form by the regimental army.

This mental reservation about the inferiority of the reserves in fact governs our whole military system. And by a natural consequence it inevitably reflects on the whole system, which tends to create this inferiority, and so to deaden and weaken the essential part of our defensive force.

This tacit conspiracy of old ideas, surviving after their apparent defeat, explains the unnecessary length of service spent in the barracks. Two years in the barracks is at least four times longer than is needed to teach the future soldier all he ought to know before entering the ranks of the nation in arms. I want to make it clear that by talking in this way I am not acceding to any temptation to win support from the masses. That will be clear from the serious obligations imposed on the citizens by the plan that is being proposed.

A party which did not have the courage to ask of the nation the sacrifices necessary for its life and liberty would be a poor sort of party, and would speedily be defeated by its own unworthiness.

But I am convinced that the long term of service in barracks is the result of a false notion. It is but one part of a deplorable system which, by neutralizing and degrading the reserves, the real active army, seriously impairs the defensive strength of France.

The need for the technical and individual education of the soldier did not dictate the two-year service. I do not advocate importing into France without modification the whole organization of the Swiss army. But when it is realized that the law for the Swiss army, and I am referring to the new law which has increased military duties, only requires for the instruction of recruits variable periods not exceeding three months, then it is impossible to explain this disproportion between three months and two years by the needs of military training. The Swiss Article 118 of the new law says forcibly:

> Schools for recruits are intended to train the soldier. They also carry out practical instruction for the ranks. The course for the infantry and engineers lasts sixty-five days; for the cavalry, ninety days; for artillery and fortifications, seventy-five days; for the medical corps, veterinary corps, and supply and transport corps, sixty days.

Whatever the alleged political, social, or moral differences between Switzerland and France, which we will be discussing later, it is impossible to say that three months, or even two months, is long enough to train a Swiss soldier and that two years is necessary for training the French soldier. If the barracks in France were merely the school for recruits and aimed only at training soldiers, they would have to stay just a few months. I expect it is no longer permissible to laugh at the Swiss army. Not only has the German army staff declared that it is excellent, not only has General

Langlois thought it worth his while to go and study its organization on the spot during the major maneuvers (and his findings, though not wholly uncritical, were nevertheless highly favorable), but also how could our professional patriots, who praised the patriotism and military spirit of this people at the time of the recent referendum in Switzerland, how could they ignore out of sheer disdain this model we are putting forward? The increases in the requirements the Swiss recently introduced are considered by a great many of their citizens to be useless. They claim that the new law was aimed much less at improving the defensive capacity of the army against an enemy from outside, than its offensive capacity against the enemy within, against the working class, which is growing in numbers and in power. Discussion on this topic is out of place here.

I am merely noting that these increases are considerable, since service in the school of recruits, which corresponds to our service in the barracks, has been raised from forty-five to sixty-five days for the infantry, from eighty to ninety days for the cavalry, and from fifty-five to seventy-five days for the artillery. It is almost a third as much again. The "militarists" won their vote by stirring up national feeling, and by appealing to their duty to safeguard their free and proud neutrality in all conflicts, through the forces of the Swiss people themselves. But during this period critical for patriotism none of them suggested that the system itself was bad; and with the deliberate conviction that they have a very reliable defense organization, capable of protecting that independence to which they are passionately attached, the Swiss people set a maximum limit of three months to this "formation of the soldier," for which the French system demands two years.

It will be said, perhaps, that Swiss citizens are prepared in advance for the activities of the soldier by the military education which they in fact call preparatory, and which the adolescents receive. It will be said, perhaps, that it is continued, and reinforced after the school for recruits, by regular important exercises. Certainly. But precisely because they take this truly national army seriously, and because they do not reduce military education to life in the barracks, they are interested in this vast, continuous education. The truly national and constant education of the army in the country is inevitably in inverse proportion to the importance given to the period spent in barracks.

One of the worst effects of a prolonged training in the barracks is to give the country the illusion that it is the most essential element in military education, and so to make people hostile to the vigorous, permanent endeavor which ought to maintain defensive power at a constant, normal level. Also, the French system itself is obliged to admit, if I can put it this way, that the Swiss system is satisfactory. For the French recruit is trained in five months. He enters the barracks in October, and by the beginning of March his course of instruction must be completed, in case war breaks out in the spring. At that moment he must be ready to start campaigning; and he is expected to go into the front line of the army, and so face the first attacks.

57. Technological Warfare: Charles de Gaulle, 1934

(a) Plea for a professional army

WORLD TENDENCIES, the conditions of an international peace organization, and, in any case, our own duty to help the weak and maintain order in the Empire, all combine to oblige us to establish professional forces. It might cause surprise that France had not already done so, if it were not realized how powerful is the prejudice against such a step. Above all, it must be admitted that the military conditions applied since Versailles against our principal adversary until recently ensured us such vast superiority that it seemed unnecessary to alter our institutions. Nobody was unaware, it is true, that this state of affairs could only be temporary, and that Germany, which had been created by arms and was eager to bear them, would some day insist that these restraints should cease. But at that time certain politicians hoped to prevent the unbridled rivalry of force by means of a new convention. If equality were established at a very low level, definite guarantees of security and control would have prevented any aggression.

This attempt at limitation seems clearly doomed to failure. Moreover, since it has been started under conditions of short-term service, it comes up against technical difficulties that are well-nigh insuperable. With only a mass system, real war power consists, in fact, much less in peace establishments, stocks and calibers of machine guns and cannon, or the number of airplanes classed as military; real war power means the number of men available for call-up, industrial potential, permanent active power in the air, public morale, all factors which, in practice, escape any common measure. And but for assurances of speedy and complete support from our other neighbors this so-called rule of equality would even have produced German superiority.

It is true that these drawbacks are considered unimportant by some people, who are convinced that short-service units most suitable for defense have the specific advantage of encouraging peace, whereas the professional army tends to make governments aggressive, since it excels in attack.

If this means that a State which has a *Reichswehr* will always have the initiative, compared with a neighbor which has only a militia, the assertion is irrefutable. But to draw an absolute conclusion, that the system of professional troops is in itself more deadly than mass levies, would be quite absurd. Clumsiness is never more than relative. If troops are unskilled, does it follow that they will not be used for attack? Did the volunteers and the conscripts of the Revolution hesitate to throw themselves on their enemies? There have never been rivals so relentlessly on the offensive as the improvised forces of North and South during the War of Secession. Bismarck and Moltke undertook three great wars with troops of conscripts and reservists. And we know the spirited attack of the novice Americans in Argonne and Champagne. Moreover, the same instincts of the people which encourage their leaders in peacetime to boast of their expectations, impel them to demand an offensive when war has been declared and passions are inflamed. At such a time Saint-Just says to Jourdan, "No prudence!"; Gambetta compels d'Aurelle to march against his will; and Briand appoints Nivelle in place of Joffre the procrastinator. In reality, the application of the principle of the nation in arms, providing inexhaustible resources, leads to wastefulness, and also greatly increases the sort of losses that are the price paid for inexperience in warfare. On the contrary, the professional army is smaller, difficult to reconstitute, and makes economy vital. All the wars of Louis XIV and Frederick the Great put together cost less than those of the Revolution alone. In three months Chanzy saw more men die on the Loire than Condé in his whole career. The sum total in French lives and property wiped out in battle from Joan of Arc to Rochambeau does not reach the sad proportions of the cost of the Great War.

If, therefore, the development which is giving an increasing superiority to regular armies were to bring about the more or less complete substitution of well-directed battles instead of furious clashes of the armed masses, it would bring priceless benefit to mankind.

War is, perhaps, an inescapable element in the general round, like birth or death. It may be indispensable for setting in motion downfalls and renewals; the ploughshare in the soil, the axe on the tree, the battering ram against the wall. The fact still remains that its horrors depend to a large extent on its dimensions. No struggle is in the aggregate more sanguinary than that of the nation in arms.

(b) Air power in modern war

In the conflict of the future we shall see fast-moving troops speeding far behind enemy lines, wherever there is a break in the front, striking at its sensitive spots, completely upsetting the entire system. Thus will be restored that strategical extension from results of a tactical nature, which neither Joffre nor Falkenhayn could achieve, any more than Hindenburg or Foch, through lack of appropriate means, but which in times gone by were considered the supreme aim and, so to speak, the noblest form of the art of war.

For if war is essentially destructive, the ideal of those who make war remains, nevertheless, economy, the least carnage for the greatest result, utilizing a combination of death, suffering, and terror to achieve the objective as soon as possible, and so put an end to all three.

What is more, this capacity for independent action, surprise, and exploitation, with which the motor will endow professional armies on the ground, will link up perfectly with the features of fighter aircraft, essential from now on. There can be no doubt, in fact, that air squadrons with long-range capability, lightning speed, three-dimensional maneuverability, striking vertically—the most impressive angle—will play a capital role in the war of the future. Till now they lacked comparable ground support. For the effects produced by bombers, however terrible they may be, are so to speak virtual. The flying machine cannot of itself turn its power to advantage. Of course, the ruins it piles up, the constant terror it inflicts, do tell on the enemy in the end, but only as after-effects. Like the artillery, of which it is, after all, the indefinite extension, aviation can destroy, but cannot constrain, conquer, or occupy.

So long as there is no ground force able to combine with the military aircraft, they have only two unsatisfactory alternatives:

either to restrict their action to the degree in which it can help
the ground forces, or else, by operating in isolation, contribute only
indirectly to the collective result. This is what happened to air
bombardment in the course of the World War. If it was directed
behind the enemy front at points that were close together, it
stopped far short of its capabilities.

If the bombers went any great distance against important objectives, such as industrial centers, ports, junctions of communications, the effect was massive but imponderable. After sorties over
Paris or Cologne, planes and airships would return, certain no
doubt that they had sown death and started fires, but there would
have been no advance of the lines toward the frontiers that were to
be liberated or territories to be seized which could justify this
massacre and destruction, no visible connection between such
episodes and the slow efforts of those who were conquering or
defending the land—land, which is the real objective of war, because men live on it.

But from the moment when extensive raids become once more
possible on land, this gap between war in the air and on the ground
will be closed. The material and moral damage produced by military aircraft will be immediately followed up. Throwing work in
the Ruhr basin into confusion by vertical bombing will influence
as before the overall fighting potential of the German people. But,
what is more, an army equipped for long-range enterprise will be
able to get there quickly. Cutting the Rhine bridges at Coblenz
and Mainz when there is fighting round Metz is certainly useful,
in any case. But how much more important if cannon and machine
guns then appear on the riverbanks! In short, somebody will be
there at the foot of the tree to pick up the fruit that has been
shaken down. Inversely, action by air forces will prolong that of
the shock troops. A rich field is being opened up for "combined
operations," a term that grammarians and committees waste their
time in discussing at the moment.

The World War saw the development of unparalleled power, but
it was brutal power and unselective. By adding speed, in the hands
of an élite, progress restores combined action.

§(b) The Dreyfus Affair

The Dreyfus Affair, the most burning issue in French national life for
a decade, began with the discovery of an undated, unsigned letter,
written in ink on flimsy paper, torn across and with no envelope. This

piece of paper (Document 58), known somewhat inaccurately as "the docket" (*bordereau*), was adduced as the main piece of evidence that Captain Alfred Dreyfus was betraying military information about the French army to Schwartzkoppen, the military *attaché* at the German Embassy in Paris. French text is in J. Reinach, *Histoire de l'affaire Dreyfus* (7 vols., Paris, La revue blanche, 1901–8), vol. 1 (1901), pp. 37–8. It was later shown to have been written by Major Esterhazy, but its discovery on September 27, 1894, started an astonishing train of events, lurid and sensational, leading not only to the unjust condemnation and punishment of Dreyfus and his eventual rehabilitation, but also to a major conflict between the Army (unwisely backed by some in the Church) and the Republican State. The conflict aroused violent passions throughout France and intense interest throughout the world. The cause of Dreyfus seemed to have been lost when, in January, 1898, the novelist Émile Zola breathed fresh life into it by publishing his famous indictment of the army leaders, in an open letter to the President of the Republic, Félix Faure (Document 59).

The indictment, with its refrain "I accuse . . . ," was published on January 13, 1898, in Georges Clemenceau's paper, *L'Aurore*. Since it named, in its charges, some of the highest-ranking officers, including General Boisdeffre, Chief of General Staff, and his assistant, General Gonse, as well as Generals Mercier and Billot who had been Ministers of War, it was intended to arouse the utmost sensation and to court legal action. The special edition of *L'Aurore* sold some 300,000 copies, and people fought for copies of it. French text in *Le Procès Zola devant la Cour d'Assises* (2 vols. Paris, Le Siècle et Stock, 1898), vol. 1, pp. 44–5.

Largely as a result of Zola's writing, and of the unwise support given to the army by some clerics, parties of the Left, especially the Radicals and Socialists, began to see Dreyfus as the victim of a plot of the forces of reaction, ranging from monarchists and clericalists to militarists and anti-Semites. Since Dreyfus was a Jew he attracted the denunciations of the violent anti-Semitic movements then active in France. The long, highly dramatic story has been told many times, yet seems inexhaustible in its interest. It has been given in careful detail by Guy Chapman, *The Dreyfus Case: A Reassessment* (London, 1955), and in briefer, livelier form by Douglas Johnson, *France and the Dreyfus Affair* (London, Blandford; New York, Walker and Company, 1966).

Before the story ended in 1906, with the complete vindication of the Dreyfusards and the rehabilitation of Dreyfus himself, its significance and repercussions had stretched far beyond a tussle between military and civilian authorities about one individual. It had prompted statements of basic moral principles on both sides of the controversy, and had won a place in French literature by reason of the writings of Charles Péguy, Anatole France, Georges Sorel, and others. Two contrasting comments a few years afterwards, one by a Christian, Péguy, and one by a freethinker, Anatole France, have therefore been included as Documents 60 and 61.

Péguy's essay "Our Youth" has already been quoted in Document 26. His reflections on the Affair in which, as a very young man, he had felt so passionately engaged, are quoted here as a memorable statement of the disillusionment felt by an idealist when harsh realities seem to reduce even the noblest ideas to matters of expediency. French text is in *Oeuvres complètes,* 4 vols. (Paris, Gallimard, 1916), vol. IV, pp. 88, 147–8, 197–200, 235–7, 240–4.

Two years earlier, the novelist Anatole France (Anatole François Thibault, 1844–1924) produced a satirical novel, *Penguin Island (L'Île des Pingouins)* which included in Book VI a brilliant skit on the whole Affair. Greatauk, Duke of Skull, is Minister for War. As a rabid anti-Semite he picks on a Jew called Pyrot, in the army, as scapegoat for all that goes wrong. When it is discovered that 80,000 bundles of hay, destined for the cavalry, have disappeared without trace, Greatauk exclaims automatically, "Pyrot must have stolen them." From then on, the only question is how to convict him. The satire hits at State, Army, Church, Socialism alike, and goes on to construct a whole fable of modern French history, with its social follies and personal tragedies. The very contrasts between these two documents, in style no less than in substance, suggest something of the heart-searching disruptiveness of the Affair. French text is in Anatole France, *L'Île des Pingouins* (Paris, Calmann-Lévy, 1908), pp. 242–7.

58. *The* "Bordereau," *1894*

ALTHOUGH I HAVE HAD NO WORD indicating that you want to see me I, nevertheless, Sir, send you some interesting information:

1. A note on the hydraulic buffer of the 120 and the way in which this gun behaves;

2. A note on the covering troops (some modifications will be introduced by the new plan);

3. A note on a modification in the artillery formations;

4. A note about Madagascar;

5. The preliminary Firing Manual of Field Artillery (March 14, 1894).

This last is extremely difficult to obtain, and I can have it at my disposal for only a very few days. The Ministry of War has sent a fixed number to the Corps, and the Corps is responsible for them. Each officer holding one has to return it after the maneuvers.

If, then, you wish to take from it whatever interests you and and then keep it for me, I shall fetch it. Unless you would like me to have it copied in full and send you only a copy.

I am just off on maneuvers.

59. "*J'Accuse*": Émile Zola, January 13, 1898

. . . I REPEAT with more vehement certainty: truth is on the march and nothing will stop it. It is only today that the affair begins, for only today are the positions clear: on one side, the guilty who do not wish the light to shine; on the other, the lovers of justice who would give their lives that it should. When the truth is buried under the earth it accumulates, it acquires the force of an explosion, so that on the day when it does burst forth it shakes everything. We shall see if there has not been prepared, for yet later, the most resounding of disasters. . . .

But, Mr. President, this letter is long, and it is time to bring it to an end.

I accuse Lieutenant Colonel du Paty de Clam of having been the diabolical worker of the judicial error, I would like to believe unconsciously, and of having afterwards defended his baneful work for three years by the most absurd and culpable machinations.

I accuse General Mercier of having been an accomplice, at least by reason of weakness of spirit, in one of the greatest iniquities of the century.

I accuse General Billot of having had in his hands certain proofs of the innocence of Dreyfus and of having suppressed them, of having incurred the guilt of this crime of betraying humanity and justice for a political end and to save the compromised General Staff.

I accuse General de Boisdeffre and General Gonse of being accomplices in the same crime, one no doubt from clericalist passion, the other perhaps from that *esprit de corps* which makes the offices of War an unassailable Holy Ark.

I accuse General Pellieux and Major Ravary of having conducted a criminal investigation. I mean by that an investigation of the most monstrous partiality, of which we have, in the latter's report, an imperishable monument of naïve audacity.

I accuse the three handwriting experts, Messrs. Belhomme, Varinard, and Couard, of having made lying and fraudulent reports, unless a medical examination finds them stricken by diseased views and judgment.

I accuse the offices of War of having led an abominable press campaign, especially in *L'Éclair* and in *L'Écho de Paris*, to mislead opinion and conceal their blame.

I accuse, finally, the first Court-Martial of having broken the law by condemning the accused on secret evidence, and I accuse the second Court-Martial of having hidden this illegality, on orders, and of committing in turn the juridical crime of knowingly acquitting a guilty man.

In bringing these accusations I am not unaware that I put myself under the penalty of Articles 30 and 31 of the Press Law of July 29, 1881, which punishes offenses of libel. And I willingly expose myself to it.

As for the people whom I accuse, I do not know them, I have never seen them, I bear them no bitterness nor hate. For me they are only entities, spirits of social evil-doing. And the act I am accomplishing here is only a revolutionary means to hasten the explosion of truth and justice.

I have only one passion, for the light, in the name of humanity that has suffered so much and has the right to happiness. My passionate protest is only the cry of my soul. So let me be brought before the court of assizes, and let the investigation proceed in full light of day!

I am waiting! Please accept, Mr. President, my deepest respects.

Émile Zola

60. *The Dreyfus Case: Charles Péguy, 1910*

I SHALL TRY to present the real truth about this immortal Dreyfus case. Like every self-respecting case, it was essentially mystical. It lived by its *mystique*. It died of its politics. That is the law and that the rule. It is on a par with men's lives. Every party lives by its *mystique* and dies of its politics. . . .

Our Dreyfusism was a religion. I use the word in its most exact, literal meaning. It was a religious upsurge, a religious crisis. . . . Justice and Truth, which we loved so much, to which we gave all, our youth, all, to which we gave ourselves completely during the whole of our youth, were not lifeless acts of justice and truth, they were not the justices and truths of books and libraries, they were not conceptual or intellectual justices and truths, justices and truths of an intellectual party. They were organic, they were Christian, they were in no wise modern, they were eternal, nor were they merely temporal. They were forms of justice and truth, a living justice and a living truth. And of all those emotions which combined to impel us, with what tremors, into this unique crisis, we can admit today, that of all those passions which impelled us into this seething fervor and into this swelling tumult, there was one virtue in our hearts, the virtue of charity. . . .

We were heroes. This must be said, quite bluntly, for I am quite sure no one will say it for us. This is precisely how and why we were heroes: everything in that environment in which we moved, in which we were working, in which we were still growing and coming to maturity, the question during two or three years of crescendo was not whether Dreyfus was *really* innocent (or guilty). It was to wonder if one would have the courage to acknowledge and declare him innocent. To proclaim him innocent. To wonder if one would have twofold courage. Firstly, the first courage, the exterior courage, crude courage, difficult enough, the social public courage, to proclaim him innocent to the world in full view of the public, to testify for him publicly. To gamble on it, to stake on him all one had, all one's hard-won money, all the money of the poor and the wretched, all the money of lesser folk, of misery and poverty; one's whole time, whole life, whole career; one's whole health, whole body, whole soul; ruin of the body, all ruins, heartbreak, families breaking up, relatives disowning one, eyes turned away, silent or furious reprobation, silent and furious, isolation, all kinds of ostracism. Friendships of twenty years' standing broken; for us, that meant lifelong friendships. All one's social life, all one's emotional life, everything. Secondly, the second, more difficult courage, inner courage, the secret courage to admit to oneself that he was innocent. To renounce for this man peace of the heart. Not only peace of the city, peace of the fireside. Peace of the family, peace of the home. But peace of the heart.

First of treasures, only treasure.

Courage to enter, for the sake of this man, into the kingdom of incurable anxiety.

And of bitterness which will never be dispelled. Our adversaries will never know, our enemies could not know, what we have sacrificed for this man, and with what courage we have sacrificed it. For him we have sacrificed our entire lives, since this case has marked us for life. Our enemies will never know, how we, who have convulsed and turned this country upside down, our enemies will never know how few we were and in what conditions we fought, thankless precarious conditions, in what conditions of misery and precariousness. . . . We had been, and were now once again, that handful of Frenchmen who, beneath withering fire, break through massed troops, lead an attack, and capture a position. . . .

Not only were we heroes. The Dreyfus case can only really be explained by that need for heroism which periodically seizes this people, this race, a need for heroism which at that moment seized upon an entire generation of us. These great movements, these great ordeals of an entire people, are like those other great ordeals —wars. Or, rather, there exists for peoples only one kind of great temporal ordeal, that of war, and these great ordeals are themselves wars. In all these great ordeals, in all these great sagas, it is far more the inner strength, the violence of eruption which produces the substance for history, than the substance which creates and produces the ordeal. When a great war breaks out, a great revolution, a war of this kind, it is because a great people, a great race, has an impulse to break out; it is bored; bored especially with peace. A great mass always feels a violent need, a great, profound need, a mysterious need for a great movement. . . . A mysterious need to inscribe a great story in eternal history. All other explanation is vain, reasonable, rational, unfruitful, unreal. In the same way, our Dreyfus case can only be explained by this very need, a need for heroism which seized an entire generation, ours, by a need for war, *military* war, and for military glory, by a need for sacrifice even unto martyrdom, perhaps (no doubt), by a need for sanctity. . . . If we were, once again, an army of lions led by asses, then we did indeed remain true to the purest French tradition. . . .

In reality, the true position for a long time of those who confronted us was not to say and believe that Dreyfus was guilty, but to believe and say that, innocent or guilty, they were not, for one man, for one man alone, going to trouble, they were not going to upset, they were not going to compromise, they were not going to set at risk the life and salvation of a people, the enormous salvation of a whole people. They meant by this *temporal* salvation, and it happened that our Christian *mystique* culminated so perfectly, so exactly, with our French *mystique*, with our patriotic *mystique* in our Dreyfusist *mystique*, that this must clearly be understood: *that we were taking our stand on nothing less than* <u>the eternal salvation of France</u>. What, indeed, did we say? Everything was against us, wisdom and law, meaning human wisdom, human law.

What we were doing was in the order of folly, or in the order of holiness, which are alike in so many ways, so many secret agreements, according to human wisdom, in human eyes. We were going, we were set, against wisdom, against the law. Against human wisdom, against human law. The others said: a people, a whole people, are an enormous amalgam of interests, of the most legitimate rights. The most sacred. Thousands, millions of lives are dependent thereto, in the present, the past (the future), thousands, millions, hundreds of millions of lives constitute it, in the present, the past (the future), through the chance of history, by the legacy of history, the task of safeguarding incalculable interests. Rights that are legitimate, sacred, incalculable. A whole people of men, a whole people of families: a whole people of rights, a whole people of interests, that are legitimate; a whole people of lives; a whole race; a whole people of memories; all history; all the ascent, all the expansion, all the past, all the future, the whole promise of a people and a race, all that is inestimable, incalculable, of infinite price, because it can only be done once, because it can only be obtained once, because it can never happen again; because it is an achievement which is unique; a people, this people in particular, is of unique worth, this ancient people; a people has not the right, and its first duty, the strict duty of a people, is not to expose all this, not to expose itself for one man, whoever he may be, however legitimate his interests and his rights. However sacred, even. A people never has this right. You do not lose a city, a city is not lost for one (single) citizen. It was the very language of true civism and of wisdom, it was wisdom itself, ancient wisdom. It was the language of reason.

From this point of view it was obvious that Dreyfus ought to sacrifice himself for France, not only for the tranquility of France, but for the very salvation of France, which he imperiled. And if he refused to sacrifice himself he should, if the need arose, be sacrificed. And what did we ourselves say? We said that one single injustice, one single crime, one single illegality, particularly if it is officially recorded and confirmed, one single wrong to humanity, one single wrong to justice and to right, particularly if it is accepted universally, legally, nationally and complacently, one single crime, shatters and suffices to shatter the whole social contract; one single breach, one single dishonor, suffices to ruin one's honor, to dishonor a whole people. It is a taint of gangrene that corrupts the whole body. We are defending not only our own honor. Not only the honor of our whole people, in the present, but the historic honor of our people, all the historic honor of our entire race, the honor of our forbears, the honor of our children. And the more we have a past, the more we have a memory (and therefore, you say, the more we have responsibility), so also the more we must here defend it thus. The more past we have behind us, the more (rightly) must we defend it thus and keep it pure. *I will give up my blood as pure as I received it.* That is the rule and the honor and the inspiration of Corneille, the old inspiration of Corneille. That is the rule and the honor and the Christian inspiration. One single spot defiles a whole family. It also defiles a whole people. One single mark blemishes the honor of a whole family. One single mark also blemishes the honor of a whole people. A people cannot ignore a wrong that has been suffered or imposed, a crime so solemnly, so definitively endorsed. The honor of a people is indivisible.

What would this mean, unless one did not know a word of French, but that our enemies were speaking the language of reason of State, which is not only the language of political and parliamentary interest, but which far more exactly, on a far higher plane, is the language—the very respectable language—of continuity, the temporal continuity of the people and the race, *of the temporal salvation of the people and the race.*

They would go no lower. And we, by a deep Christian urge, by a very deep pressure, at once revolutionary and Christian in tradition, following in this, a Christian tradition in the deepest, the liveliest sense, the most in line, in the mainstream, at the heart of Christianity, we would do no less than to raise ourselves, I do not say to the conception, but to the passion, to the anxiety of eternal salvation, the eternal salvation of this people. We were striving for nothing less than to live in constant anxiety, in mortal, eternal preoccupation and anguish, in constant solicitude for the eternal salvation of our people, for the eternal salvation of our race. Basically, we were the men of eternal salvation and our opponents were the men of temporal salvation. Such was the true, the real division in the Dreyfus case. Basically, we did not want France to be constituted in a state of mortal sin. In this world, in the modern world, in any world, only Christian doctrine insists so deliberately, so totally, so absolutely, that temporal death is as nothing, as insignificant, as nought, compared with eternal death, and the risk of temporal death is as nothing compared with sin, mortal sin.

61. "Penguin Island": Anatole France, 1908

Chapter II

PYROT

ALL PENGUINIA learned with horror of Pyrot's crime; at the same time they felt some satisfaction in knowing that this misappropriation, complicated by treason and bordering on sacrilege, had been committed by a little Jew. To appreciate this feeling you must understand the state of public opinion towards big and little Jews. As we have already had occasion to remark in this story, the financial caste, which was universally detested and supremely powerful, consisted of Christians and Jews. These Jews, on whom the nation vented all its hatred, were the big Jews; they possessed enormous wealth and held, it was said, more than a fifth of Penguinia's fortunes. Besides this formidable caste there were hordes of little Jews, in modest circumstances, who were no more popular than the big Jews and much less feared. In every police state wealth is held sacred; in democracies it alone is sacred. The Penguin State was democratic; three or four financial companies exercised power more widely, and above all more effectively and more continuously, than the ministers of the Republic. They governed these lordlings secretly, and forced them by intimidation or corruption to favor the companies at the expense of the State. If they remained honest, they were destroyed by slander in the press. In spite of the secrecy of the Bank, enough was known to arouse people's indignation, but all the Penguin bourgeoisie, greater and lesser alike, who had been conceived and brought forth with a respect for money, and who all had some means, large or small, were strongly aware of the solidarity of capital, and realized that modest wealth is ensured only by guaranteeing great wealth. Therefore they looked upon the Israelite millions, as on the Christian millions, with religious awe, and, since self-interest was stronger than aversion, they would have been scared to death to touch a single hair of the big Jews whom they detested. They were less diffident towards the little Jews, and if they saw one of them on the ground, they trampled on him. So the entire nation learned with grim satisfaction that the traitor was a Jew, but a little one. They would be revenged on him for the whole of Israel, without compromising public credit.

Hardly anybody hesitated one moment to believe that Pyrot had stolen the eighty thousand bundles of hay. They had no doubt, because lack of knowledge of this affair did not allow for doubt, which needs reason; for one does not doubt without reason as one believes without reason. They had no doubt because the story was being repeated everywhere, and as far as the public is concerned repetition is proof. They had no doubt because they wanted Pyrot to be guilty, and one believes what one wants, and because few men are capable of doubt; the minds of a tiny minority bear the germs of doubt within them, but these do not develop unless they are cultivated. Doubt is strange, exquisite, philosophic, immoral, transcendent, monstrous, full of malignity, damaging to people and property, contrary to the State police and the prosperity of empires, disastrous to humanity, a destroyer of the gods, hateful to heaven and earth. The great mass of Penguins knew nothing about doubt. They had faith in Pyrot's guilt, and this faith became one of the principal articles of the national beliefs and one of the essential truths of the patriotic creed.

Pyrot was secretly tried and found guilty. General Panther went at once to inform the Minister of War of the outcome of the trial. "Fortunately," he said, "the judges were certain, for there was no evidence."

"Evidence," murmured Greatauk, "evidence, what does that prove? There is only one certain irrefutable proof: confession of the guilty man. Has Pyrot confessed?"

"No, General."

"He will confess. He must. Panther, you must make him. Tell him it is in his own interest. Promise that if he confesses he will obtain concessions—a reduction of sentence, pardon; promise that if he confesses we will affirm his innocence and give him a medal. Appeal to his better nature. Get him to confess through patriotism, for the sake of the flag, by order, out of respect for the hierarchy, by special command of the Minister of War, on military grounds . . . But Panther, are you sure he hasn't confessed? There are tacit confessions; silence is a form of confession."

"But, General, he is not silent; he is squealing like a pig that he is innocent."

"Panther, the confessions of a guilty man sometimes stem from the vehemence of his denials. To deny desperately is to confess. Pyrot has confessed; we need witnesses of his confessions, in the interests of justice."

In West Penguinia there was a seaport called the Creek, consisting of three small coves, once open to shipping but now silted up and deserted; stagnant lagoons bordered the low-lying coast, exhaling a pestilential odor, and fever hovered over the sleeping waters. A high square tower stood at the water's edge like the ancient Campanile in Venice. On one flank, near the summit, suspended from a chain fastened to a crossbeam, hung an open cage in which the inquisitors at the time of the Draconides placed heretical clerics. In this cage, which had been empty for the last three hundred years, Pyrot was imprisoned under the guard of sixty warders who lived in the tower. They did not let him out of their sight day or night, on the watch for his confessions, so that they could take turns in reporting to the Minister of War. For Greatauk, who was scrupulous and prudent, wanted confessions and yet more confessions. Greatauk who was thought to be a fool was really full of wisdom and unusual perspicacity.

Meanwhile, Pyrot was burnt by the sun, bitten by mosquitoes, drenched with rain, hail and snow, frozen with cold, battered by storms, pestered by the sinister croaking of the crows perched on his cage. He wrote his declaration of innocence on pieces of his shirt with a toothpick dipped in blood. These rags got lost in the sea or fell into the hands of his jailers. A few, however, reached the public gaze. But Pyrot's protestations made no impression, for his confession had been published.

Section C: Anticlericalism

§ (a) The Struggle for the Schools

Throughout the whole period there was rivalry between secular and ecclesiastical powers for control over education. Bonapartists and republicans were at one in seeking to ensure secular control, though churches and other religious organizations were so strongly entrenched in the schools that a dual system usually had to be accepted as inevitable. Just as even the first Napoleon's Imperial University, whose Grand Master was in theory an absolute dictator of national education at all levels, produced rigidity rather than uniformity and permitted considerable Church control, so all subsequent systems became greatly modified in practice.

From the July Monarchy the Second Republic inherited a scheme of State elementary schools with teachers often under strong priestly influence. The Falloux Law of March 15, 1850, destroyed the University's monopoly even in principle, and permitted any private individual or authorized religious body to establish schools at any level. This frankly dual system was attacked, inevitably, by the Left as a surrender to clerical power, and by the extreme Right as a weak compromise with the ungodly doctrine of lay schools. But it survived into the Second Empire, and was never entirely overthrown by the Third Republic.

The story of clericalist pressures and anticlericalist counterattacks continued in the 1860's and 1870's, as a prelude to the great educational changes of Jules Ferry in the 1880's, which are too often presented as if they were a bolt from the blue. In 1863, Napoleon III appointed Victor Duruy, a liberal and anticlerical historian, as his Minister of Education. His reforms advanced the development of free, compulsory elementary education, equal educational opportunities for girls, vocational training, and adult education. Liberal Catholics who might have cooperated with him were heavily overshadowed by the Ultras who received Papal support in the 1860's—Louis Veuillot of *L'Univers* most vocal among them.

The national *débâcle* of 1870 produced a feverish quest for explanations, and these inevitably led not only to a reorganization of the army in 1872, but to anxious demands for overhaul of the whole educational system. The ex-priest Ernest Renan voiced national concern in his *Intellectual and Moral Reform* of 1871. Was the French defeat due to national decadence, or to bad institutions, or to shortcomings of education and public spirit? Or was it due, rather, to superior German organization and Protestant training, from which France could derive important lessons? Renan stated the case for educating an *élite*, which is here reproduced as Document 62. French text in E. Renan, *La réforme intellectuelle et morale de la France* (Paris, Michel Lévy, 1871), pp. 95–106.

Fired by the same spirit of republican regeneration, not unmixed with aims of *revanche*, Jules Ferry and the Radical governments of the 1880's set about equipping France with a complete network of free elementary schools in which lay teachers, specially trained, would inculcate positivist principles of civic morality and duty. The official program issued to elementary-school teachers within a year of the promulgation of the Law of March 28, 1882, postulated three kinds of education: physical, intellectual, and moral. The program for moral education is given as Document 63. It expresses vividly the essential aims of the Radical Republicans. To them—to the Masonic Lodges, societies of freethinkers, and the *Ligue de l'Enseignement*—the disaster was explained by illiteracy, by ignorance of science and technology, by subservience to the Jesuits and their allies. The remedy, then, was to destroy clericalist control over education, and this needed a corps of "lay missionaries" to carry the gospel of civic duty and republican patriotism into every village. The antithesis between village schoolteacher and parish *curé* was made personal in nearly every commune.

But again, human nature was less tidy than legislative enactment or political doctrine. Church secondary schools had to be authorized, however reluctantly and slowly, Document 64: *Bulletin des lois de la république française*, XII série, Vol. 22 (1881), No. 10, p. 748. During the school year 1911–1912 the *Manuel général de l'instruction primaire* asked teachers to send in statements of their experience and aspirations. Several hundreds replied, and a few of the replies are presented as Document 65. They tell their own diversified story. Documents 63 and 65 are taken from *French Educational Ideals of Today*, edited by F. Buisson and F. E. Farrington (New York, Harcourt, Brace and World Inc., 1920).

62. *Education for an Élite: Ernest Renan, 1871*

IN THE conflict which has just ended, the inferiority of France was mainly intellectual; what we lacked was not heart, but head. Public education is of paramount importance; French intelligence is enfeebled and must be fortified. Our greatest error is to believe that man is born already educated. The German, it is true, believes too much in teaching; he becomes a pedant. But we do not believe in it enough. Lack of faith in science is a grave failing in France; our military and political inferiority has no other cause. We are too distrustful of what reflection and informed cooperation can achieve. Our system of education needs radical reform; almost everything the First Empire did in this direction is bad. Public education cannot be given directly by the central authority. A Ministry of Public Education will always be a very mediocre education machine.

Primary schooling is the most difficult to organize. We envy the superiority of Germany in this respect; but it is not philosophical to want the fruit without the trunk and roots. In Germany, popular education came from Protestantism. Lutheranism made religion consist of reading a book, and later reduced Christian dogma to an intangible quintessence, thereby giving unusual importance to the schoolhouse; the illiterate have been almost driven away from Christianity, they are sometimes refused Holy Communion. Catholicism, on the other hand, made salvation depend on sacraments and supernatural beliefs, and so regards the school as of secondary importance. To excommunicate somebody who can neither read nor write seems to us impious. Since the school is not the annex to the Church, it is the Church's rival. The *curé* is suspicious of it, tries to keep it as poor as possible, and even prohibits it if it is not entirely clerical. And without the collaboration and good will of the *curé*, the village school will never flourish. We may well hope that Catholicism will reform itself and relax its old-fashioned rules! A *curé*, a Catholic pastor, could do so much, offering every village the model of a well-ordered family, looking after the school, almost a schoolmaster himself, giving to the education of the peasant the time that he spends in tedious repetition of his breviary! In truth, Church and school are equally necessary; a nation can no more do without one than the other. When Church and school oppose each other, everything goes badly.

We touch here on the problem which underlies all others. France wanted to remain Catholic, and is experiencing the consequences. Catholicism is too hieratic to provide intellectual and moral nourishment for the population. It permits transcendent mysticism to flourish side by side with ignorance. It has no moral effectiveness. It has a fatal influence on the development of the brain. A pupil of the Jesuits will never be an officer capable of opposing a Prussian officer; a pupil from the Catholic elementary schools will never be able to engage in a scientific war with improved weapons. The Catholic nations which do not reform themselves will always inevitably be beaten by the Protestant nations. Supernatural beliefs are like poison which kills if the dose is too strong. Protestantism does put a certain amount in its brew; but the proportion is small and therefore beneficial. The Middle Ages had created two controllers of the life of the spirit, the Church and the University. The Protestant countries have kept these two foundations; they created liberty in the Church and liberty in the University so that these countries can have Established Churches and official education, together with full liberty of conscience and education. The rest of us have had to have separation of the Church in order to obtain liberty; the Jesuits had long ago reduced our universities to a secondary role. And so our efforts have been feeble, for they are not linked to any tradition or to any institution of the past.

A liberal, such as we are, is in an acute dilemma; for it is our first principle that in anything affecting liberty of conscience the State has no right of interference. Faith, like all exquisite things, is sensitive; at the least touch it complains of violence. We should

aim at liberal reform of Catholicism, without State intervention.
Let the Church admit two categories of believers, those who hold
to the letter, and those who believe in the spirit. At a certain level
of rational culture, belief in the supernatural becomes for many an
impossibility; do not force them to wear a cope of lead. Do not
interfere with what we teach or what we write, and we will not
compete with you for the people; do not dispute our place in the
university and the academy, and we will leave you in sole possession of the village school. The human spirit is a ladder where
every rung is necessary. What is right at one level is not right at
another; what is harmful for one is not so for another. Keep for
the people their religious education, but leave us free. There is
no powerful development of the brain without liberty; moral
energy is the result not of any particular doctrine, but of the
race and the vigor of its education. There has been enough talk of
the decadence of Germany, presented as a hotbed of enervating
errors and dangerous subtleties. It was killed, they said, by sophism,
Protestantism, materialism, pantheism and fatalism. I would not
swear to it that M. de Moltke does not confess to one of these
errors; but one must concede that it does not prevent him from
being a very good staff officer. Let us renounce these fatuous
rantings. Liberty of thought allied to the highest culture, far from
weakening a country, is one condition for the full development of
the intelligence. No one particular solution strengthens the mind;
what does strengthen it is discussion and liberty. It could be said
that for the educated man there is no bad doctrine. For him every
doctrine is a striving toward the truth, a useful exercise for the
health of the mind. You want to keep your young men in a sort of
intellectual gynaeceum; you will make limited men of them. If you
want to turn out good scientists, and serious, dedicated officers,
you must have an education open to everything, without narrow-
ing dogma. Intellectual and military superiority will henceforth
belong to the nation which thinks freely. Everything which exercises the brain is salutary. Furthermore, liberty of thought in
the universities has the advantage that the free thinker is content
to reason unhampered from his chair, among people with the same
point of view as himself, and is therefore not tempted to make
propaganda among other people of high or low degree. The
German universities offer a very curious example in this respect.

Our secondary education, although open to criticism, is the best part of our system of teaching. Good pupils from a Paris lycée are better than young Germans in their talent for writing, the art of composition. They are better prepared to be lawyers or journalists; but they do not know enough facts. We must persuade ourselves to let science rank much higher than what we in France call "*lettres*."

Teaching ought to be mainly scientific; the result of education ought to be that the young man knows as much as possible of what the human mind has discovered about the reality of the universe. When I say scientific, I do not mean practical or professional; the State should not concern itself with occupational training, but it should take care that the education it gives is not limited to empty rhetoric, which does not strengthen the intelligence. We in this country esteem only brilliant gifts, talent, wit, genius. In Germany these gifts are rare, perhaps because they are not highly thought of. There are few good writers. Journalism and public speaking are not so brilliant as here. But brainpower, learning, balanced judgment, are much more widely spread, and result in a level of intellectual culture superior to anything that has yet been achieved in any nation.

It is in higher education that a reform is most urgent. The special schools thought up by the Revolution, the puny faculties created by the Empire, in no way replace the fine, great system of autonomous, rival universities, a system Paris created in the Middle Ages and which Europe has kept, except for France, in fact, which introduced it about 1200. By returning to this system we should not be imitating anyone, but merely renewing our own tradition. There must be created in France five or six universities, independent from one another, independent of the towns where they are established, and independent of the clergy. At the same time the special schools must be abolished: the Polytechnic, the *École Normale*, etc.—useless institutions if you possess a good system of universities and which impede the development of the universities. These schools skim the cream off the university students with disastrous consequences. The university teaches everything, prepares for everything, and within its walls all branches of the human mind touch and embrace. Beside the universities there must and should be schools of instruction; there must not be closed State schools in competition with the universities. There are complaints that the Faculties of Letters and Science have no diligent students. Is this surprising? Those who ought to be there are at the *École Normale*, or the Polytechnic, where they receive the same teaching, but without experiencing anything of the healthy interplay and community spirit created by a university.

Without prejudice, naturally, to the University of Paris and those great foundations which are unique, such as the *Collège de France*, and which are proper to Paris, universities set up in provincial towns seem to me to provide the best method of reawakening the French spirit. They would be schools founded on serious study, honesty and patriotism. Real liberty of thought would develop, which does not flourish without hard work. They would also effect a healthy change in the spirit of youth. They would encourage respect; they would adopt the idea of the importance of science. One factor which gives much cause for reflection is this: it is recognized that our schools are centers of irresponsible democratic thought and disbelief, tending to frivolous popular propaganda. It is quite the opposite in Germany, where the universities are centers of the aristocratic spirit, reactionary (as we would say), and almost feudal centers of free thought, but not of indiscreet proselytism. What is the reason for this difference? It is because in German universities liberty of discussion is absolute. Rationalism has very little bearing on democracy. Reflection teaches that reason is not the simple expression of the ideas and wishes of the masses, but the result of the apperceptions of a small number of privileged individuals. Far from being inclined to hand over the public administration to the whims of the mob, a generation which has been trained in this way will jealously preserve the privilege of reason, and will be hard-working, studious, and not very revolutionary. Science will be a title of nobility for this generation, which will not renounce it easily and which will even defend it with some ruthlessness. Young men educated to a sense of their own superiority will revolt if they count for no more than one, like just anybody. Filled with the just pride which is bestowed by awareness of knowing the truth of which the common herd is ignorant, they will not wish to be the interpreters of the superficial thoughts of the crowd. The universities will thus be nurseries of aristocrats. In that case, the sort of antipathy which the French conservative party entertains toward the highest culture of the mind will appear as the most inconceivable nonsense and the gravest of mistakes.

It goes without saying that beside these universities endowed by
the State, open to all opinions knowledgeably presented, complete
latitude will be left for the establishment of free universities. I believe that these free universities will produce but very mediocre
results; whenever liberty really exists within the university, liberty
outside the university is of little consequence, but by permitting
them to be set up you would have a clean conscience and you
would silence those naïve people who always tend to believe that
they would perform wonders if it were not for the tyranny of the
State. It is quite probable that the most fervent Catholics, like
Ozanam, for example, would prefer the wide range of the State
universities, where everything goes on in the open, to these little
universities behind closed doors founded by their own sect. In
any case, they would have the choice. What could these Catholics
most ready to rise against State monopoly complain about in such
an arrangement? Nobody would be excluded from university
chairs because of his opinions. Catholics would be appointed like
everybody else.

The system of *Privatdocent* would further permit all doctrines
to be expounded independently of the endowed chairs. Finally,
the free universities would remove the last remaining excuse for
recriminations. It would be the opposite of our French system,
which proceeds by the exclusion of brilliant people. We think that
we have done enough for impartiality if, when we have dismissed
or refused to appoint a freethinker, we dismiss or refuse to appoint
a Catholic. In Germany they set them face to face; instead of serving only mediocrity, their system serves the emulation and awaken-
ing of intelligence. By distinguishing the degrees carefully and the
right to exercise a profession, as they do in Germany, by laying
down that the university does not train doctors or lawyers, but
makes men fit to become doctors or lawyers, some of the difficulties would be removed which certain people object to in the con-
ferring of degrees by the State. In such a system the State does not
reward certain scientific or literary opinions; in the highest social
interests, and for the benefit of all kinds of opinion, it opens up
great fields, vast arenas, where different feelings can be expressed
and debated among themselves and can vie for the approbation
of the young people who attend these discussions, and who are
already matured by deep thought.

63. *Moral Education: The Program*

Infant section: Ages 5 to 7 years. Very simple talks mingled with all the exercises of the class and of recreation. Simple poems explained and learned by heart. Simple stories with a moral, related and followed by questions calculated to bring out their sense and ascertain if the children have understood them. Simple songs.

Special care should be given by the teacher to those children in whom she has observed any defect in character or any vicious tendency.

Primary section: Ages 7 to 9 years. Familiar talks. Reading with explanations (stories, examples, precepts, parables, and fables). Teaching through the emotions.

Practical exercises tending toward application of the moral training in the class itself:

1. By observation of individual character (taking account of the predispositions of the children to correct their defects or to develop their good qualities).

2. By intelligent application of school discipline as a means of education. (Distinguish carefully neglect of sense of duty from simple infraction of rules; show clearly the connection between the fault and its punishment; illustrate a scrupulous spirit of impartiality in the government of the class; inspire a horror of tale-bearing, dissimulation, and hypocrisy; put candor and uprightness above all else, and therefore never discourage frank speaking on the children's part, or refuse to listen to their complaints or their requests).

3. By constant appeal to the feelings and moral judgment of the child himself. (Frequently make the children judges of their own conduct, especially by having them evaluate moral and intellectual effort in themselves and in others; allow them to speak and act for themselves, but subsequently make them discover for themselves their errors or their faults.)

4. By correcting vulgar notions (popular superstitions and prejudices, belief in witchcraft, in ghosts, in the influence of certain numbers, foolish fears, etc.)

5. By instruction drawn from facts observed by the children themselves. It is advisable at times to make them feel the sad con-

sequences of the vices they sometimes have under their eyes; drunkenness, laziness, disorder, cruelty, brutal appetites, etc., while
inspiring in them as much compassion for the victims of the evil as
horror of the evil itself. It is also advisable to proceed in the same
way, through concrete examples and appeals to the immediate experience of the children, in order to initiate them into the moral
emotions, to develop in them, for instance, the feeling of admira-
tion for the order of the universe and of religious feeling by
making them contemplate their charitable impulses by calling their
attention to a misfortune to be relieved and giving them the opportunity of performing a practical act of charity discreetly; and to
arouse in them the feeling of gratitude and sympathy by the nar-
ration of an act of courage, by a visit to a charitable institution, etc.
Intermediate section: Ages 9 to 11 years. Talks, reading and interpretation, practical exercises. The same type and means of
teaching as before, save that instruction becomes somewhat more
methodical and precise. Coordination of lessons and readings so as
to omit no important point in the program below:

I. (a) The child in the family; duties toward parents and grand-
parents: obedience, respect, love, gratitude. Help the parents in their work; relieve them in their illness; come to
their aid in old age.

  (b) Duties of brothers and sisters: Love one another; protection of the younger children by the older; responsibility
for setting a good example.

  (c) Duties toward servants: Treat them politely and with
kindness.

  (d) Duties of the child at school: Regular attendance, obedience, industry, civility. Duties toward the teacher; duties
toward comrades.

  (e) The fatherland: France, her greatness and her misfortune.
Duties toward the fatherland and toward society.

II. (a) Duties toward oneself: Care of the body, cleanliness,
sobriety, and temperance. Dangers of alcoholism: weakening of the intelligence and of the will; ruin of the health.
Gymnastics.

  (b) Material goods: Economy, avoidance of debt, evil effects
of the passion for gambling; duty to avoid immoderate
desire for money and gain; prodigality; avarice. Work

(economy of time; obligation of all men to work; nobility of manual labor).

(c) The soul: Veracity and sincerity; never lie. Personal dignity, self-respect. Modesty; recognition of one's own faults. Evils of pride, vanity, coquetry, frivolity. Shame of ignorance and sloth. Courage in danger and misfortune; patience, spirit of initiative. Dangers of rage.

(d) Treat animals with gentleness. Do not let them suffer uselessly. The Grammont Law; societies for the protection of animals.

(e) Duties toward others: Justice and charity; the Golden Rule. Never injure the life, person, property, or reputation of another. Kindness, brotherhood. Tolerance, respect for the beliefs of others. Little by little alcoholism entails the violation of all duties toward others (laziness, violence, etc.).

(*NOTE*. In this whole course the teacher should assume the existence of conscience, of the moral law, and of moral obligation; he should appeal to the feeling and idea of responsibility. He does not undertake to demonstrate any of these by theoretical exposition.)

III. Duties toward God: The teacher is not required to give a course *ex professo* on the nature and attributes of God. The instruction which he should give to all without distinction is limited to two points:

First, he teaches his pupils not to speak the name of God thoughtlessly. He clearly associates in their minds a feeling of respect and veneration for the First Cause and the Perfect Being; and he accustoms each one to surround the idea of God with the same respect even when it is presented to him in a form different from that of his own religion.

Then, and without paying attention to the ordinances peculiar to the different religious beliefs, the teacher endeavors to make the child understand and feel that the first homage he owes the Divinity is obedience to the laws of God revealed to him by his conscience and his reason.

Higher Section: Ages 11 to 13 years. Talks, readings, practical exercises as in the two preceding sections. This course comprises, besides a regular series of lessons whose number and order may

vary, elementary instruction in ethics in general and more especially of one's duty toward society, according to the program below:

I. The family: Duties of parents and of children; reciprocal
   duties of masters and servants; the family spirit.

II. Society: Necessity and benefits of society. Justice, the con-
    dition of all society. Solidarity and human brotherhood. Al-
    coholism destroys these sentiments little by little by destroying
    the mainspring of will and of personal responsibility.

    Applications and development of the idea of justice: respect
    for human life and liberty; respect for property; respect for
    the pledged word; respect for the honor and reputation of
    others. Probity, equity, loyalty, delicacy. Respect for the
    opinions and beliefs of others.

    Applications and development of the idea of love or brother-
    hood. Its varying degrees; duties of benevolence, gratitude,
    tolerance, mercy, etc. Self-sacrifice, the highest form of love;
    show that it can find a place in everyday life.

III. The Fatherland: What a man owes his country: obedience to
     law, military service, discipline, devotion, fidelity to the flag.
     Taxes (condemnation of fraud toward the State). The ballot:
     a moral obligation, which should be free, conscientious, dis-
     interested, enlightened. Rights which correspond to these
     duties: personal freedom, liberty of conscience, freedom of
     contract and the right to work, right to organize. Guarantee
     of the security of life and property to all. National sovereignty.
     Explanation of the motto of the Republic: Liberty, Equality,
     Fraternity.

Under each of these heads in the course in social ethics, the
teacher should explain clearly, without entering into metaphysical
discussions:

1. The difference between duty and self-interest even when the
   two seem to be identified—that is to say, the imperative and
   disinterested nature of duty.

2. The distinction between the written and the moral law; the
   one fixes a minimum number of proscriptions which society
   imposes under penalty on all its members; the other imposes
   on each one in the secret of his conscience a duty which no
   one constrains him to fulfill, but in which he cannot fail without feeling a sense of wrong toward himself and toward God.

64. Decree authorizing the Bishop of Vannes to set up a Church Secondary School at Ploërmel (Morbihan), 1881

May 23, 1881

The President of the French Republic

Following the report of the Minister of the Interior and Churches,

Considering the request made on November 8, 1879, by the Bishop of Vannes to the effect that he be authorized to set up a Church Secondary School at Ploërmel,

Considering the favorable opinion of the Prefect of the Morbihan, dated January 15, 1880,

Considering the opinion of the Minister of Public Education of May 7, 1881, proposing with certain provisos that the request for authorization be granted,

Considering Article 70 of the Law of March 15, 1850:

DECREES

Article 1—The Bishop of Vannes be authorized to set up a Church Secondary School at Ploërmel (Morbihan) with the following provisos:

(i) The school shall in no circumstances admit more than two hundred and twenty pupils;

(ii) It shall not admit day pupils, primary pupils, or pupils of so-called special secondary education;

(iii) It shall not prepare pupils for admission to Government schools.

Article 2—The Minister of the Interior and Churches is responsible for the execution of the above Decree, which shall be published in the *Bulletin des lois*.

Signed: Jules Grévy
Paris, May 23, 1881

Minister of the Interior and Churches: Constans

65. The Teachers Speak

October, 1899. I have been appointed to a village forty miles from my family. My chief is an old, sweet-faced sister still in the service in spite of the laicization of the department. She received me with

a great deal of cordiality and animation, looked at me from behind her spectacles, and declared, "We shall get on well together,
I can see that." Sister Mélanie, her companion, is faded and as col-
orless as a tapestry figure.

My room, a closet about as big as a handkerchief, is hung in
blue paper covered with birds chasing each other. My classroom
is long and narrow, very low, with a worm-eaten, shaky door
which opens out on a sunken path. The desks are old and shaky,
too, but my enthusiasm is great, and my aspirations are boundless.
Monday. I have eighty-five pupils. Later on others will be coming
along, who are now picking potatoes. I feel bewildered in the
face of this crowd of little people. I have passed the day organizing my classes and getting things under way. The principal came
into my classroom this morning, made the sign of the cross, and
all the pupils chanted prayers for a half-hour. What could one
do? And this morning Sister Mélanie, coming in stealthily, took
a seat at the farther end of my classroom, gave me a friendly little
nod, and started the little ones on syllable exercises. Now I understand the words of the academy inspector when he gave me this
"position of responsibility," "You will need patience and tact,
Mademoiselle."

HAUTE-VIENNE

I am the only teacher in a little village near Lyons. Rising at six
in the morning, I put my little home in order. I have a clean, attractive apartment which the municipality has fitted out above the
classroom. There are four bright airy rooms, with fireplaces, running water in the kitchen sink, and electricity everywhere. In
short, I have all the modern conveniences, as well as a new school
that looks like a little villa, with beds of roses on either side of
the entrance door and flowering shrubs around the playground.

RHÔNE

In the eyes of the peasant and the working man the teacher, correctly dressed and decently lodged, is a lady, almost an aristocrat.
It should surely be a simple matter to keep children in a brilliantly
lighted, well-ventilated room that is heated in winter and kept cool
in summer! To have one rest day a week besides Sunday, to have
holidays at Christmas and Easter and two long months of liberty

in August and September—is not that an enviable existence? So a latent but real jealousy springs up among these workers, who have no idea of the exhausting labors of the school teachers.

RHÔNE

This is a country of large landholders. The town provides my lodging and my property is not negotiable: woods that thrive under the open sky, meadows where the grass touches the knees of the cattle, red-soil lands where the crops form green rivers. I have no *métayers* to call me "our gentleman," as in the olden times. I am far away, and that is a great objection. My mother came to see us. Her *coif* was not like those in this part of the country. These are important matters, things that help establish a reputation. Finally I have no horse and carriage, and since I read late into the night I am judged eccentric.

VIENNE

We must please everybody, and especially the good electors of Monsieur the Mayor; if not, look out for trouble! Please everybody, but how, especially when politics are involved?

Monsieur the Mayor comes into the school as if it were his own house, or rather as if it were a barn, to drag the teacher off to the town hall, while the pupils dance in the classroom. Another day he sends the teacher to the next hamlet for an entire afternoon in order to help the tax collector, who is allotting the firewood in the forest. Meanwhile the children, who have been set at liberty, gambol in the village streets, in the fields, or in the woods.

A small farmer said to me one day in speaking of his son, "I should like to make a teacher out of him but for the fact that he would have to be everybody's dog."

HAUTE LOIRE

The task is hard for us teachers in the Vendean country, where the priest and the squire are in league against us and our teaching. Think of being awakened with a start in the night by abusive noises made under your windows according to orders, of reading each morning on your door odious anonymous posters pasted there during your sleep. In the classroom itself you encounter the ill-will of the children, their apathy, and their indolence. Are you obliged to scold for careless work, for a lesson half learned, for vulgar language? The child sneers and says half aloud, "I will go over to the good sisters."

VENDÉE

From the moment of my arrival at B———, I turned my attention to making myself popular with the children and to winning the hearts of the mothers. The population sought to make things hard for me. I was spied upon, and the children were questioned to see if I had not been guilty of intolerance. The *curé* organized the campaign. He gave orders to close the doors in my face when I made my first round of visits. He used every means to make life unbearable for me and to keep me shut up at home. But I was not long in gaining a real influence over this community, and ever since I have been guarding it as a treasure. Established as it is in the popular confidence, my school is, so to speak, invulnerable. The violent attacks on the "schoolbooks" slipped by unnoticed. Not a single mother listened to the belligerent suggestions so freely made.

MAYENNE

My financial situation would be precarious enough if I were not secretary of the town council and treasurer of the savings bank. At forty-one years of age, with a salary of 1800 francs, I am grouped in the teachers of the third class.[1] I have four children, and truly we should be in misery but for my outside work. In fact, the teacher is a government employee who cannot earn his living at teaching. He is obliged to resort to other work in order to keep his family alive.

SARTHE

While adding a small sum to his slender income, the schoolmaster who serves as town clerk unquestionably increases his prestige in the community. Though he be ever so little conversant with his duties, he nevertheless quickly becomes indispensable to the village, and the mayor and the other inhabitants of the locality consult him daily.

LOT-ET-GARONNE

One teacher founded consecutively a savings bank, a school lunchroom, a school pharmacy, a museum, a library, a society for the prevention of cruelty to animals, a temperance society, an alumni

[1] I.e., who have served the State for at least ten years—Ed.

association, a loan fund for farmers, a farmers' syndicate, a mutual fire-insurance society, and a cattle-insurance society. Another teacher is the confidant of the peasants.

The peasant, surrounded by sharpers who prey upon his weakness and ignorance, is glad to have somebody in whom to confide. He becomes devoted body and soul to the schoolmaster who can win his affection. He makes the schoolmaster his counselor, his secretary, his confidant. Of all the compensations in my career, this was one of the greatest and most satisfactory. The good teacher has nothing to fear from pupils or parents; on the contrary, he derives his strength from them.

CORRÈZE

§(b) Church and State

Throughout the nineteenth century relations between Church and State in France were governed by Napoleon's Concordat of 1801. Designed to end the schisms caused by the Civil Constitution of the Clergy of 1790, the Concordat did much to stabilize French life. But one of its unexpected results was to weaken Gallicanism by compelling the French bishops to rely more and more on the Pope as their only protection against the secular authority, and by making parish clergy more completely dependent on the bishops. The basis was thus laid for the growth of Ultramontanism during the nineteenth century, and (by reaction) for the corresponding growth of anticlericalism. Napoleon III kept an unsteady balance between Catholics and Liberals both at home and abroad, but with the establishment of the Third Republic, and the triumph after 1876 of anticlerical Radicalism, renewed tensions arose to weaken the Concordat. Persistently the issue arose—can a good Roman Catholic be also a good republican? And every circumstance which associated the Catholic Church with enemies of the Republic— whether with monarchism in the 1870's, or with the army in the Dreyfus Affair, or with the *Action française* in the twentieth century, or with the men of Vichy after 1940—contributed to the breakdown of the Concordat.

The key document in the breakdown is the Law of December 9, 1905, concerning the Separation of the Churches and the State (Document 67). The English observer of France, J. E. C. Bodley, writing in 1906, summed up the two main effects of the Act as follows: "The abrogation of the Concordat is the first serious breach made in the administrative fabric constructed by Napoleon," and "the Separation Law, though the work of anticlericals, is an Ultramontane Act. For the first time since the French people became a nation the Pope is the absolute master of the Bishops and Clergy of France." It thus, in a curious way, extended the consequences of the Concordat even while abrogating it.

The intransigence of Ultramontane clericalists was matched by the fury of Republican anticlericals. The spread of positivist, socialist, and communist philosophies during the later nineteenth century produced a conflict of ideologies which, it seemed, could be resolved only by total separation of the State from all Churches, and of citizenship from all religious beliefs. Jules Ferry's education laws of the 1880's (see Section C (a)) rested on this belief, and on the doctrine proclaimed by Gambetta in the Chamber of Deputies on May 4, 1877: "Clericalism? —That is the enemy!"

The next decade brought repeated efforts by Pope Leo XIII and by some French Catholic leaders to seek reconciliation between Church and Republic, in the movement known as the *Ralliement*. Though inaugurated by Pope Leo XIII's Encyclical Letter *Immortale Dei* of November 1, 1885, its key document in France was—rather incongruously—the toast to the surprised monarchist officers of the French Mediterranean naval squadron commanded by the Bonapartist Admiral Duperré, given by Cardinal Lavigerie, Archbishop of Algiers, after lunch on November 12, 1890 (Document 66). The speech was completely premeditated and authorized, for it followed discussions in Rome and in Paris. It was designed—and was taken—as an official signal for Catholics to dissociate themselves from the extreme Right in French politics, and to come to terms with the lay Republic. For the next few years leaders of Church and State spasmodically followed policies of appeasement and *rapprochement*, though with only temporary and variable success. The passions aroused by the Dreyfus Affair undid much of the good.

In 1901 a new Law of Associations, applying to lay as well as to religious associations, and governing the terms of contract under which they could be formed, was passed by Waldeck-Rousseau (Document 46). His successor, the extremist anticlerical ex-priest Émile Combes (1835–1921), applied this Law with great rigor against the clergy, and passed new laws against the teaching Orders. In July, 1903, Leo XIII died; his successor, Pope Pius X, was unfamiliar with the situation in France and less anxious to effect a conciliation with the Republic; and in 1904 diplomatic relations were broken off between France and the Vatican. The Law of Separation was passed the following year, with no strong popular demand, though it received general support in the country after Aristide Briand (1862–1932), as "Reporter" of the Commission on the Law, had skillfully steered it through the Chamber.

The new arrangements were due to come into full effect on December 12, 1906. During a debate in the Chamber on November 7, Briand, now Minister of Public Instruction, Beaux-Arts, and Public Worship in the new Sarrien-Clemenceau ministry, spoke in defense of the Law. Part of his speech is given as Document 68. It expresses plainly the new mood in Church-State relations which was to last into the years between the wars. French text in *Journal officiel*.

There is a detailed study of events leading up to Cardinal Lavigerie's toast and the *Ralliement* by J. Tournier, *Le Cardinal Lavigerie et son*

action politique, 1863–1892 (Paris, Perrin, 1913), which contains the
full French text on pp. 287–9. The translation of the Law of Separation
is taken from *Church and State through the Centuries*, translated and
edited by Sidney Z. Ehler and John B. Morrall (London, Burns and
Oates, 1954), pp. 358–71, and is reproduced by kind permission of the
publishers. French text in *Bulletin des lois de la république française*,
XII série, vol. 71, No. 2663 (1905).

66. *The* Ralliement: *Toast of Cardinal Lavigerie,*
November 12, 1890

GENTLEMEN,

Before we break up, allow me to drink the health of the French
Navy, so nobly represented among us today. Our Navy recalls
to Algeria glorious and cherished memories; it contributed from
the very first to her conquest, and the name of its eminent leader,
who at this moment commands the Mediterranean squadron, seems
to bring back the noble, distant echo of her first songs of victory.

I am happy, my Lord Admiral, in the absence of our Governor-
General who is detained far fom us, to have been able to make
for you, as it were, a crown of honor, from all those who represent
the authority of France in Algeria: leaders of our administration,
our magistrature and our Army.

What I find most touching is that they are all here at this table
on the invitation of that old Archbishop who, like themselves, in
order to serve France the better, made Africa a second homeland.

Confronted with a past that is still bleeding, and an ever-menac-
ing future, we are in fact at this moment in supreme need of union.
The union of all good citizens is also, let me hasten to assure you,
the prime hope of the Church and its pastors of every rank in the
hierarchy.

Union does not demand that we should renounce the memories
of past glories, or the feelings of fidelity and gratitude which
honor all men; but when the will of a people has been clearly
stated, that the form of government, as Leo XIII recently proclaimed, contains nothing in itself contrary to the principles
which alone can give life to Christian civilized nations, when there
is no other way of saving one's country from the disaster that
threatens it than by adhering unreservedly to that form of government, then the moment has come to declare finally that the testing
time is over, and to put an end to our differences. The time has

come to sacrifice all that conscience and honor will permit. Each one of us must make sacrifice for the salvation of the country.

This is what I am teaching those around me, and what I hope to see imitated in France by all clergy, and by speaking out in this way, I am sure that no authorized voice will give the lie to me. Without this resignation and patriotic acceptance, nothing will be possible either to preserve peace and order, save the world from social danger, or to save that very religion of which we are ministers.

It would be madness to try to support the columns of a building without going inside the building itself, in order to prevent those who would like to destroy everything from achieving their end; madness above all to besiege it from without, as many still do in spite of the recent shameful events, letting our enemies witness our internal hatreds and driving into the heart of France the despair which is the forerunner of the worst of catastrophes.

The French Navy has been an example to us, whatever the feelings of a few of its members. It has never agreed to break with ancient tradition, or forswear the flag of the Fatherland, whatever the form of government, so long as it was in order, which that flag protects. That is one of the reasons why the Navy has remained strong and respected, even when times were worst, why it can bear its flag as a symbol of honor wherever the name of France must be maintained, and, allow a missionary-cardinal to say so with gratitude, to protect the Christian Missions which we have founded.

Gentlemen, to the French Navy!

(Algiers, November 12, 1890)

67. Law of December 9, 1905, concerning the Separation of the Churches and the State

The Senate and the Chamber of Deputies have adopted,
The President of the Republic promulgates the law as follows:

Section I

PRINCIPLES

Article 1—The Republic assures liberty of conscience. It guarantees the free exercise of religious worship, but with the restrictions enacted below in the interest of public order.

Article 2—The Republic does not recognize any salary or subsidy to any religious body. As a result, starting from 1st January following the promulgation of the present law, all expenses relating to the practice of religious worship shall be struck off the budgets of the State, the "départements" and the communes. There can, however, be included in the said budgets expenses relative to charitable organizations and those for the purpose of assuring the free exercise of religious worship in public establishments, such as high schools, colleges, schools, hospitals, asylums and prisons.

Public establishments for religious worship are suppressed, with modifying conditions laid down in Article 3.

Section II

ALLOCATION OF PROPERTY AND PENSIONS

Article 3—Establishments whose suppression is decreed by Article 2 shall continue provisionally to function in conformity with the arrangements now governing them, until the allocation of their goods to the associations, provided for by Section IV and at latest until the expiration of the periods fixed below. After the promulgation of the present law, the agents of the administration of property shall proceed to the descriptive and assessory inventory of:

   (i) movable and immovable goods of the said foundations.

   (ii) goods of the State, the "départements" and the communes of which the same foundations have the use.

This double inventory shall be drawn up in collaboration with the legal representatives of the ecclesiastical establishment; who, in any case, shall be duly summoned by a notification made in administrative form.

The agents entrusted with the inventory shall have the right of procuring the communication of all legal instruments and documents necessary for the proceedings.

Article 4—During the period of a year dating from the promulgation of the present law, the movable and immovable goods of clergy—houses, buildings, meeting places, assembly rooms and other public religious establishments—shall be transferred, with all the duties and obligations which rest on them and with due respect for the special purposes for which they are destined, by the legal representatives of these establishments to associations which, in conformity with the rules of the general organization of the religion of which they intend to ensure the practice, shall be legally formed, according to the requirements of Article 19, for the practice of this religion in the old delimitations of the said establishments.

Article 5—Those goods within the scope of the preceding Article, which have come from the State and which are not linked to a pious foundation created subsequently to the law of Germinal 18 of the year X, shall be returned to the State.

No disposal of goods shall be made by ecclesiastical establishments until a month after the promulgation of the ruling of the public administration provided for in Article 43. Failing this, the nullity of such disposal can be claimed before the civil Law Courts by every interested party or by the public ministry.

In case of alienation by the religious association of movable or immovable property forming part of the endowment of such a public establishment, the amount resulting from the sale should be invested in registered shares under the conditions provided for in paragraph 2 of Article 22.

The acquirer of the alienated goods shall be personally responsible for the regularity of this process.

Goods claimed by the State, the "départements" or the communes shall not be alienated, transformed or modified until a decision on the claim has been reached by the competent legal authorities.

Article 6—The associations disposing of the goods of suppressed ecclesiastical establishments shall be provisionally responsible for the assets as well as the debts of these establishments, according to the arrangements of the 3rd paragraph of the present Article; so long as they are not freed from this responsibility, they shall have the right to the enjoyment of the goods productive of revenues which should be returned to the State by virtue of Article 5.

The total revenue of the said goods remains subject to the payment of the balance of the customary and legal debts of the suppressed public establishment, when no religious association competent to receive the resources of this establishment shall be formed.

Annual payments from sums borrowed for expenses, relating to religious buildings, shall be borne by the associations in proportion to the time during which they shall have the use of these buildings by application of the arrangements of Section III.

In the case where the State, the "départements," or the communes

shall resume possession of the buildings of which they are proprietors, they shall be responsible for debts regularly contracted
and relating to the said buildings.

Article 7—The movable or immovable goods assigned to a charitable purpose or to any purpose other than the practice of religious
worship shall be transferred, by the legal representatives of ecclesiastical establishments, to public services or foundations or for
a public use whose purpose is in conformity with that of the said
goods. This transfer should be approved by the Prefect of the
"département" in which the ecclesiastical foundation is situated. In
case of non-approval, the case shall be decided by a decree issued
by the Council of State ("Conseil d'État," i.e. the Supreme Court
of Administration).

Any legal proceedings for restoration or re-possession should be
instituted within a period of six months, dating from the day when
the prefectorial order or decree approving the transfer shall have
been published in the *Journal Officiel*. Legal proceedings may
only be instituted in the case of gifts or bequests and only by the
donons and their heirs in the direct line.

Article 8—If an ecclesiastical establishment fails, within the period
fixed by Article 4, to effect the transfers prescribed above, the
matter shall be dealt with by decree.

On the expiration of the said period, the goods to be transferred
shall be placed in sequestration pending their transfer.

In the case where the goods transferred, by virtue of Article 4
and of par. 1 of the present Article, shall be either immediately or
later claimed by several associations formed for the practice of
the same religion, the transfer which shall have been made by the
representatives of the establishment or by decree may be contested by litigation before the Council of State ("Conseil d' État"),
by litigation, which shall give sentence after taking into account
all the circumstances of the case.

The appeal should be brought before the Council of State within the space of one year from the date of the decree or from the
notification made to the prefectorial authority, by the legal representatives of the public establishment of the religious body about
the transfer affected by them. This notification should be made
within the period of one month.

The transfer can, subsequently, be contested in case of a
schism in the association in possession of the property or of the

creation of a new association as a consequence of a modification in the territory of the ecclesiastical delimitation, or in the case where the association which has received the transfer is no longer capable of fulfilling its object.

Article 9—If there be no association to receive the goods of a public establishment of religious worship, these goods shall be transferred by decree to communal establishments for relief or charity, situated in the territorial limits of the ecclesiastical delimitation concerned.

In case of the dissolution of an association, the goods which shall have been assigned to it in virtue of Articles 4 and 8 shall be transferred, by a decree made in the Council of State ("Conseil d'État"), either to similar associations in the same district or neighbourhood or, if such do not exist, in the nearby district, or to the establishments mentioned in par. 1 of the present Article.

All proceedings for restoration or recovery of possession should be commenced within a period of six months dating from the day when the decree shall have been published in the *Journal Officiel*. The proceedings may only be instituted in the case of gifts or bequests and only by the donors and their heirs in the direct line.

Article 10—The allocations of property envisaged in the preceding Articles shall not permit of any appropriation for the profit of the Treasury.

Article 11—The ministers of religion who, after the promulgation of the present Law, shall be more than sixty years of age and who shall have, during at least thirty years, carried out ecclesiastical duties remunerated by the State, shall receive an annual pension and allowance equivalent to three-quarters of their salary.

Those who shall be more than forty-five years of age and who shall have, during at least twenty years, carried out ecclesiastical duties remunerated by the State, shall receive an annual pension and allowance equal to one-half of their salary.

The pensions allowed by the two preceding paragraphs may not exceed 1,500 francs.

In case of the decease of the holders, these pensions shall be payable to the value of half of their amount to the benefit of the widow and orphans, who are minors, left by the deceased, and to the value of one-quarter to the benefit of his widow without children who are minors. When the orphans attain their majority, the pension shall completely cease.

The ministers of religious bodies at present paid by the State, who shall not be included in the above provisions, shall receive, during four years beginning from the abolition of the budget for religious bodies, an allowance equal to the whole of their salary for the first year, to two-thirds of it for the second, to half for the third and to a third for the fourth.

In communes of less than 1,000 inhabitants and for ministers of religious bodies who shall continue to carry out their duties there, the duration of each of the four periods indicated above shall be doubled.

"Départements" and communes shall be able, under the same conditions as the State, to grant to ministers of religious bodies at present paid by them, pensions or allowances awarded on the same basis and for an equal period of time.

Exception is made of rights acquired in the matter of pensions by application of previous legislation, as well as of assistance granted to former ministers of different religious bodies or to their family.

The pensions mentioned in the two first paragraphs of the present Article cannot be held simultaneously with any other pension or any other allowance awarded, for whatever reason, by the State, the "départements" or the communes.

The law of June 27, 1885, regarding the personnel of the suppressed faculties of Catholic theology, is applicable to the professors in charge of courses, lecturers and students of faculties of Protestant theology.

The pensions and allowances mentioned above shall be forfeited, paid, or not paid, in the same conditions as civil pensions. They shall cease fully in case of condemnation for one of the offenses mentioned in Articles 34 and 35 of the present law.

The right to obtain or to enjoy a pension or allowance shall be suspended by circumstances leading to the loss of French citizenship; such suspension will last as long as the lack of citizenship persists.

Claims for a pension should, under penalty of disallowance, be submitted within the period of one year from the promulgation of the present law.

Section III

BUILDINGS OF RELIGIOUS BODIES

Article 12—Buildings which have been placed at the disposal of the nation and which, by virtue of the law of Germinal 18 of the year X, are used for the public worship of religious bodies or for the accommodation of their ministers (cathedrals, churches, chapels, temples, synagogues, archiepiscopal and episcopal residences, presbyteries and seminaries), as well as the immovable and movable property annexed thereto which was attached to them at the time when the said buildings were handed over to the religious bodies, are and remain properties of the State, the "départements" and the communes.

With regard to these buildings, as also with regard to those erected subsequently to the law Germinal 18 of the year X, of which the State, the "départements" and the communes shall be proprietors, including the faculties of Protestant theology, proceedings shall be taken in accordance with the provisions of the following Articles.

Article 13—Buildings used for the public worship of a religious body, as well as the movable objects attached to them, shall be left gratis at the disposal of the public establishments of the religious body, and afterwards of the associations called into being to replace them, to which the goods of these establishments shall have been assigned by application of the arrangements of Section II.

The cessation of this privilege and, if necessary, its transfer, shall be pronounced by decree, provision being made for appeal to the Council of State by litigation:

1. if the beneficiary association is dissolved;

2. if, apart from the case of *force majeure*, the public worship of the religious body ceases to be celebrated during more than six consecutive months;

3. if the preservation of the buildings, or that of the movable objects classified by virtue of the law of 1887 and of Article 16 of the present law, is compromised by insufficiency of attention, after warning duly notified by the municipal council or, failing it, the Prefect;

4. if the association ceases to fulfil its purpose or if the buildings are diverted from their rightful purpose;

5. if it does not satisfy the requirements of Article 6 or of the last paragraph of the present Article, or the provisions relative to historical monuments.

Decisions concerning deprivation of these immovable goods can be pronounced, in the cases mentioned above, by decree made by the Council of State ("Conseil d'État"). Apart from these cases, it cannot be pronounced, except by a law.

The immovable property sometimes attached to religious bodies, in which the ceremonies of the religious body have not been celebrated during the period of one year previously to the present Law, as well as those which shall not be claimed by a religious association within the period of two years after the present Law's promulgation, can be confiscated by decree.

The same applies to buildings whose confiscation shall have been requested before June 1, 1905.

The public establishments of the religious body, and afterwards the beneficiary associations, shall be responsible for repairs of any kind, as well as for costs of insurance and other charges relating to the buildings and the movable goods they contain.

Article 14—Archiepiscopal and episcopal residences, presbyteries and their annexes, Grand Seminaries and faculties of Protestant theology, shall be left freely at the disposal of the public establishments of the religious body and afterwards of the associations mentioned in Article 13, according to the following arrangement: archiepiscopal and episcopal residences during a period of two years; presbyteries in the communes where the minister of the religious body shall reside, Grand Seminaries and faculties of Protestant theology during five years, starting from the promulgation of the present Law.

The establishments and associations are subject, in matters pertaining to their buildings, to the obligations mentioned in the last paragraph of Article 13. However, they shall not be responsible for large works of repairing.

The cessation of occupancy of establishments and associations shall be pronounced in the conditions and modes determined by Article 13. The provisions of the third and fifth paragraphs of the same Article are applicable to buildings mentioned in par. 1 of the present Article.

The detachment of unnecessary portions of presbyteries left to the disposal of religious associations can, during the period mentioned in par. 1, be pronounced in favour of a public utility service by decree made in the Council of State ("Conseil d'État").

On the expiring of periods of occupancy free of charge, the free disposal of buildings shall pass to the State, the "départements" or the communes. The payments for lodgings at present falling upon the communes, failing a presbytery, by application of Article 136 of the law of April 5, 1884, shall remain chargeable to them during the period of five years. These shall cease fully in the event of dissolution of the association.

Article 15—In the "départements" of Savoy, Upper Savoy and the Maritime Alps, the occupancy of buildings erected previously to the law of Germinal 18 of the year X, for use in the public worship of religious bodies or for the accommodation of their ministers, shall be allocated by the communes of the territory in which the buildings exist, to religious associations, in the conditions indicated by Article 12 and the following Articles of the present law. Apart from this obligation, the communes shall be able to dispose freely of the property of buildings.

In these same "départements," the cemeteries shall remain the property of the communes.

Article 16—A detailed catalogue shall be made of buildings used for the public worship of a religious body (cathedrals, churches, chapels, temples, synagogues, archiepiscopal and episcopal residences, presbyteries, seminaries), in which catalogue should be included everything in these buildings, which possesses, in whole or in part, an artistic or historical value.

Objects, movable or immovable in purpose, mentioned in Article 13, which shall not have been placed on the list of the catalogue drawn up according to the law of March 30, 1887, are, as a result of the present law, added to the said list. The Ministry of Public Instruction and of Fine Arts shall proceed, within the period of three years, to the definite cataloguing of those of such objects whose preservation shall appear to be of sufficient importance, from the point of view of history or of art. At the expiration of this period, the other objects shall be removed finally from the catalogue *ex officio*.

In other cases, immovable and movable objects, allocated by virtue of the present law to associations, can be classified in the same conditions as if they belonged to public establishments.

There is no change otherwise in the arrangements of the law of March 30, 1887.

Ecclesiastical archives and libraries situated in archiepiscopal and episcopal residences. Grand Seminaries, parish churches, chapels of ease and their attached buildings shall be catalogued, and those which shall be recognized to be State property shall be restored to the State.

Article 17—Goods immovable in their purpose and catalogued by virtue of the law of March 30, 1887, or of the present law, are inalienable and imprescriptable.

In the event where the sale or exchange of a catalogued object should be authorized by the Ministry of Public Instruction and of Fine Arts, a right of pre-emption is granted (1) to religious associations; (2) to communes; (3) to "départements"; (4) to museums and societies of art and archaeology; (5) to the State. The price shall be decided by three experts to be designated by the seller, the buyer and the president of the civil tribunal.

If none of the buyers mentioned above makes use of the right of pre-emption, the sale shall be free; but the purchaser of a catalogued object is forbidden to take it out of France.

No work of repair, restoration, or upkeep, to be done to catalogued monuments or movable objects can be commenced without the authorization of the Minister of Fine Arts, nor carried out except under the supervision of his officials, under penalty against the proprietors, occupants or tenants who shall have ordered these works, of a fine of 1,000–1,500 francs.

Every infringement of the above arrangements, as well as of those of Article 16 of the present law and of Articles 4, 10, 11, 12 and 13 of the law of March 30, 1887, shall be punished with a fine of 100–10,000 francs and by an imprisonment from six days to three months, or by one of these penalties only.

Entrance to buildings and the exhibition of movable objects catalogued shall be free for the public without any liability to fiscal charges.

Section IV

ASSOCIATIONS FOR THE PRACTICE OF RELIGIOUS WORSHIP

Article 18—Associations formed to attend to expenses and upkeep of public worship of a religious body must be constituted in conformity with Articles 5 and the following of Section I of the law of July 1, 1901. They shall, in addition, be subject to the requirements of the present law.

Article 19—These associations shall have as their exclusive object the worship of a religious body and shall be composed of at least:
In communes of less than 1,000 inhabitants—7 persons;
In communes of 1,000–20,000 inhabitants—15 persons;

In communes where the number of inhabitants is more than 20,000
—25 persons
who are adult and domiciled or residing in the religious district in
question.

Each of their members shall be free to withdraw at any time,
after the payment of past rates and of those of the current year,
notwithstanding any contrary clause.

Notwithstanding any contrary clause of the statutes, the acts of
financial transactions and legal administration of goods carried out
by the directors or administrators shall be presented at least every
year to the scrutiny of the general assembly of members of the association and submitted to its approbation.

The associations can receive, in addition to the assessed amounts
mentioned in Article 6 of the law of July 1, 1901, the proceeds of
collections and contributions for expenses of religious worship; the
fees for religious ceremonies and services, even by endowment;
those for the occupation of benches and chairs; and for the supply-
ing of objects destined for use at funerals in religious buildings and
for the decoration of these buildings.

They shall be free to transfer the surplus of their assets, free of
tax to other associations constituted for the same purpose.

They shall not receive subsidies, in any form whatever from the
State, the "départements" or the communes. Sums allocated for
repairs to catalogued monuments are not considered as subsidies.
Article 20—These associations can, in the forms laid down by
Article 7 of the decree of August 16, 1901, establish unions having a
central administration or direction; these unions shall be regulated
by Article 18 and by the five last paragraphs of Article 19 of the
present law.
Article 21—Associations and unions shall keep a record of their
receipts and expenses; they shall present each year the financial
statement for the past year and the recorded inventory of their
goods, movable and immovable.

Financial control is exercised over the associations and unions by
the "Administration de l'enregistrement" [i.e. a public service in
France for registering private legal documents; as fees are collected
for this registering, the service is a part of the financial administra-
tion] and the "Inspection générale des finances" [i.e. a section of
the Ministry of Finance].
Article 22—Associations and unions can use their disposable re-

sources to set up a reserve fund sufficient to provide for the costs and upkeep of the religious body and not being allowed in any event to be directed to another purpose; the amount of this reserve shall never be allowed to exceed a sum equal to three times the annual average (in the case of unions and associations having a revenue of more than 5,000 francs) and six times the annual average (in the case of other associations) of sums spent by each of them for the expenses of the religious body during the five last financial years.

Independently of this reserve, which must be placed in registered investments, they shall be able to establish a special reserve, the funds of which should be deposited, in cash or in registered securities in deposit banks and in investments to be devoted exclusively, together with the interests thereof, to the purchase, building, decoration or repair of immovable or movable property destined for the needs of the association or union.

Article 23—The directors or administrators of an association or union which shall have contravened Articles 18, 19, 20, 21 and 22 shall be punished by a fine of 16–200 francs and, in the event of repetition, by a double fine.

The tribunals can, in the event of infringement of paragraph 1 of Article 22, condemn the association or union to transfer excess of the sum to communal establishments of assistance or of charity.

They can, furthermore, in all cases mentioned in paragraph 1 of the present Article, pronounce the dissolution of the association or of the union.

Article 24—The buildings which are intended for the worship of the religious body and which belong to the State, the "départements" or the communes shall continue to be exempt from ground rent and from the tax on doors and windows.

Buildings serving as the living quarters of ministers of religious bodies, as seminaries or as faculties of Protestant theology which belong to the State, the "départements" or the communes, and goods which are the property of associations and unions, are subject to the same taxes as those of individual persons.

Associations and unions are in no case subject to the subscription tax ("taxe d'abonnement") or to that imposed on clubs by Article 33 of the law of August 8, 1890, or to the tax of 4 per cent on revenue, enacted by the laws of December 28, 1880 and of December 29, 1884.

Section V

REGULATION OF RELIGIOUS WORSHIP

Article 25—Meetings for the celebration of public worship held in the property belonging to, or put at the disposal of, a religious association are public. They are dispensed from the formalities of Article 8 of the law of June 30, 1881, but remain placed under the supervision of the authorities in the interest of public order. They cannot take place except after a declaration made in the forms of Article 2 of the same law and indicating the place in which they will be held.

A single declaration is sufficient for the total number of permanent meetings, periodical or occasional, which shall take place during the year.

Article 26—It is forbidden to hold political meetings in the places regularly used for the public worship of a religious body.

Article 27—The ceremonies, processions and other external demonstrations of a religious body shall continue to be regulated in conformity with Articles 95 and 97 of the law of April 5, 1884, relating to municipalities.

The ringing of bells shall be regulated by municipal order and, in event of disagreement between the Mayor and the president or director of the religious association, by prefectorial decree. The ordinance of the public administration provided for by Article 43 of the present law shall determine the conditions and cases in which bellringings for civil purposes shall take place.

Article 28—It is forbidden in future to raise or place any religious sign or emblem on public edifices or in any public place whatsoever, with the exception of buildings used by a religious body, burial-grounds in cemeteries, funeral monuments and museums or exhibitions.

Article 29—Contraventions of the preceding Articles are punished by the ordinary legal penalties.

There are liable to these penalties, in the cases of Articles 25, 26 and 27, those who have organized the meeting or demonstration, those who have participated in it in the capacity of ministers of the religious body, and in the case of Articles 25 and 26, those who have provided the meeting place.

Article 30—In conformity with the provisions of Article 2 of the law of March 28, 1882, religious instruction cannot be given to children between the ages of six and thirteen years, enrolled in the public schools, except outside school hours.

The stipulations of Article 14 of the present law shall be applied to ministers of religion who infringe these provisions.

Article 31—Those who, whether by force, acts of violence or threats against an individual, by causing him to fear the loss of his employment or by exposing to injury his person, family or fortune, shall have coerced him into practising a form of religion, becoming a member or ceasing to be a member of a religious association, to contribute or to refrain from contributing to the expenses of a religious body, are to be punished by a fine of from 16 to 200 francs and by an imprisonment of from six days to two months, or by one of these two penalties only.

Article 32—Those who shall have hindered, delayed or interrupted the public worship of a religious body by disturbances or disorder caused in the place used for this public worship, shall be punished with the same penalties.

Article 33—The arrangements of the two preceding Articles are not applicable except to disturbances, outrages or acts of force, the nature or circumstances of which shall not demand more severe penalties according to the provisions of the Penal Code.

Article 34—Every minister of a religious body who, in the places where this religious body worships, shall have by spoken discourse, readings, writings distributed or notices exposed, publicly vilified or defamed a citizen entrusted with a public office, shall be punished with a fine of 500–3,000 francs and by an imprisonment of one month–one year, or by one of these two penalties only.

The truth of the defamatory act, but only if it is relevant to the functions (of the individual concerned), will have to be proved before the police court in the manner prescribed by Article 52 of the law of July 29, 1881. The requirements laid down by Article 65 of the same law, apply to offenses against the present Article and the Article which follows it.

Article 35—If a sermon delivered or a writing exposed or distributed publicly in places where a religious body worships contains a direct incitement to resist the execution of the laws or the legal acts of public authority, or if it tries to raise or arm one faction among the citizens against the others, the minister of the religious body who shall have been found guilty shall be punished by an imprisonment of three months — two years, without prejudice to the penalties for complicity in the case where the incitement shall have been followed by a sedition, revolt or civil war.

Article 36—In the event of condemnation by the ordinary tribunals or police courts in pursuance of Articles 25, 26, 34 and 35, the association formed for the worship of the religious body in the immovable property where the infringement has been committed shall be legally responsible.

Section VI

GENERAL PROVISIONS

Article 37—Article 463 of the Penal Code and the law of March 26, 1891, are applicable to all cases in which the present law decrees penalties.

Article 38—Religious congregations remain subject to the laws of July 1, 1901, December 4, 1902 and July 7, 1904.

Article 39—Boys who have obtained, on the ground of being ecclesiastical pupils, the exemption mentioned in Article 23 of the law of July 15, 1889, shall continue to do so according to Article 99 of the law of March 21, 1905, on condition that at the age of twenty-six they shall be provided with employment as ministers of a religious body, financed by a religious association and with reservation of requirements which shall be fixed by the ordinances of the public administration.

Article 40—During eight years, beginning from the promulgation of the present law, the ministers of a religious body shall be ineligible for the municipal council in the communes where they shall exercise their ecclesiastical ministry.

Article 41—The sums made available each year by the suppression of the budget for religious bodies shall be divided among the communes in proportion to the share of the land tax on unbuilt property which has been assigned to them during the financial year which shall precede the promulgation of the present law.

Article 42—The legal arrangements relating to present holidays are preserved.

Article 43—An ordinance of the public administration made within three months following the promulgation of the present law shall determine the measures necessary to ensure its application.

Ordinances of the public administration shall determine the conditions in which the present law shall be applicable to Algeria and the colonies.

Article 44—All arrangements relative to the public organization of religious bodies previously recognized by the State, as well as all arrangements contrary to the present law, are and remain abrogated. . . .

68. *Separation of Church and State: Aristide Briand, November 7, 1906*

THE LAW has not lapsed; it still applies, and what is more it has already produced its chief effects. What is separation? Separation is the neutrality, sanctioned by law, of the Republican State in confessional matters. It means in consequence, abrogation of the Concordat; the Concordat no longer exists. It means abolition of the Church budget; that budget has disappeared. Temporary indemnities are doubtless still paid; the Church budget, in principle and in essence, is in reality abolished. The law has had another result: the *curés* and priests in charge, and the bishops, who were public servants, official dignitaries, having by virtue of precedence a distinguished rank in the State, have lost this attribute; they have become citizens like everybody else. The separation has thus been carried into effect in its essentials; and if, in one of its parts, the law is not applied by the Catholic Church, it is, on the contrary, applied in its entirety by the other Churches. The Protestant, Israelite, and other Churches have accepted without reserve. As for the Catholic Church, one could not say that it has rejected the law; its own leader has not rejected it.

FROM THE RIGHT: What do you know about it?

THE MINISTER: I should have understood the Pope's saying, "A contract binds you to me; so long as we have not broken it by common consent, I do not know, and I do not want to know, whatever you do outside this pact. Any law which you can vote shall be held by me to be null and void, and I shall insist on regarding as still extant the contract which joins you to me and joins me to you."

The Pope might have spoken thus. But did he?

The Pope was among the first to agree to abrogation of the Concordat and to make use of the Law of 1905. ("Very good! very

good!" *from the Left—and extreme Left*) He was among the first
to come to terms with the arrangements for the separation. The
Concordat did not allow him to nominate bishops, and this was a
serious blow to his authority. As soon as the law was promulgated,
the Pope dealt with the vacant bishoprics; he himself nominated
bishops who at once took over their appointment. The Pope could
not proceed to these nominations without considering the Concordat as abrogated, and by making use of the rule of separation.
(*Loud applause on the Left and extreme Left*)

And that is not all, gentlemen! The Bishops have also agreed to
this arrangement. Under the Concordat, they had no right of assembly, or of discussion in common; they would have had to seek
authority to meet together, and I know many governments which
would have refused. But they have not had to ask any permission.
Thanks to this law of tyranny and persecution, as the Law of December 9, 1905, has been called, they did what has not been seen for
a great many years in this country, of their own accord, quite freely
and independently: they met together and freely deliberated, at
least in so far as concerns their relations with the law of their
country. (*Applause on the Left, extreme Left, and on various
Center benches*)

But even that is not all. You say that there are vexatious formalities in this law which compel you to oppose it. Yes there are. I
could tell you of some that the French priests agreed to from the
start with laudable haste: the formalities imposed on them by the
law and by the regulations of public administration to obtain their
pensions and grants. (*Loud applause and laughter on the Left and
extreme Left. Interruptions on the Right*)

SECTION D: RIGHT AND LEFT

§(a) Social Nationalism

It has already been suggested (Introduction, p. 16) that the labels
of "Right" and "Left" are particularly misleading in modern French
history, if only because parties and ideas once clearly of the Left may
later become those of the Right-Center or even the Right. Moreover
Bonapartism, with its blend of Jacobin democracy and monarchical
institutions, cut across conventional categories, as indeed does Gaullism
a century after the passing of the Second Empire. Document 69 is
Ernest Renan's assessment of the legacy of Bonapartism, and of its

interplay with other political movements as he saw them in the anxious mood of 1871. It comes (like Document 62) from Renan's *Intellectual and Moral Reform:* French text in E. Renan, *La réforme intellectuelle et morale de la France* (Paris, Michel Lévy, 1871), pp. 22–32.

By the end of the century the forces of assertive nationalism had been appropriated by movements of "integral nationalism" associated especially with the name of Maurice Barrès (1862–1923), the famous novelist. Barrès fostered a spirit of French nationalism with a special edge of provincial pride and regional patriotism deriving from his native Lorraine. Though saved from the violent royalism of Maurras by his own idiosyncratic personality, he was an eloquent voice of the Right in the days of Boulanger, Déroulède, and Dreyfus. He crystalized his conceptions of nationalism, regionalism, and social progress in the program he laid before the electorate of Nancy (in Lorraine) in 1898 (Document 70). He came out as a protectionist and something of a racist. Though successful in the Nancy election in 1898 he was then twice defeated, and from 1906 until the end of his life he sat in the Chamber for a Paris constituency. His program, here translated in full (save for one interpolation omitted), was praised by the *Action Française,* with whose ideas Barrès had some affinity. The French text is from Maurice Barrès, *Scènes et doctrines du nationalisme,* Appendix (Paris, Juven, no date). For the change of mood after 1905 see Eugen Weber, *Nationalist Revival in France 1905–1914* (Berkeley, 1959), and his *Action Française: Royalism and Reaction in Twentieth-century France* (Stanford, 1962).

69. National Spirit in Decline: Ernest Renan, 1871

. . . ANYBODY WHO knows France, indeed, in its entirety, and in its provincial variations, will not hesitate to recognize that the movement which has dominated the country for the last half century is essentially pacifist. The military generation, discouraged by the defeats of 1814 and 1815, had almost disappeared under the Restoration and the reign of Louis Philippe. A fundamentally honest but often superficial patriot related our former victories with an air of triumph which could often wound a foreigner; but this offensiveness daily became less common. It could be said to have stopped completely after 1848. Two movements began then, which were to put an end not only to all warlike spirit, but to all patriotism: I mean the extraordinary growth of material ambitions among the workers and peasants alike. It is obvious that the socialism of the workers is the antithesis of the military spirit; it is the denial, almost, of the fatherland. The doctrines of the International are there to prove it. The peasant, on the other hand, ever since the path to wealth was opened to him, and he was shown that his industry is the most certainly lucrative, the peasant has felt his horror of conscription redouble. I speak from experience. I took part in the electoral campaign in May, 1869, in a wholly rural constituency of Seine-et-Marne; I can give assurance that on my rounds I did not find a single element of the former military life of the country. An inexpensive government, unimposing, not interfering, an honest desire for liberty, a great thirsting for equality, a total indifference to the country's glory, the firm intention of making no sacrifice to intangible interests; this was the attitude of the peasant, as it seemed to me, in that part of France where the peasant, they say, is the most advanced.

I do not mean that there was no trace left of the old spirit which was nurtured on the memories of the First Empire. The very small party that could be called Bonapartist, in the literal sense, surrounded the Emperor with deplorable incitements. The Catholic party, with its mistaken commonplaces on the supposed decadence of the Protestant nations, was trying to rekindle a fire that was almost out. But this had no effect whatever on the country. The experience of 1870 was proof enough; the declaration of war was greeted with consternation. The stupid ranting of the newspapers, the bawling urchins on the boulevards, are facts that history will only take account of to show to what degree a thoughtless group can give a false impression of the real feelings of a country. The war proved only too clearly that we no longer had our former military ability. There is nothing in all this to surprise anybody who has fully grasped the philosophy underlying our history. France in the Middle Ages was a Germanic construction, raised by a Germanic military aristocracy with Gallo-Romanic materials. For centuries, France has labored to expel from within all those elements deposited by the Germanic invasion, right up to the Revolution, which was the last upheaval caused by these labors. The military spirit in France comes from what is German; by violently rejecting these Germanic elements and replacing them by a philosophic, egalitarian conception of society, France threw out at the same time all the military spirit she had. She has remained a rich country, and considers war as a stupid career, bringing very little remuneration. France has thus become the most pacifist country in the world; her entire activity is turned toward social problems, the acquisition of wealth and the progress of industry. The educated classes have not allowed their liking for art, science, literature, and elegant luxury to decline; but the military career has been abandoned. Few families from the wealthy middle class, when making a choice for their son's future, have shown preference for a profession of whose social importance they are unaware, instead of the rich perspectives of commerce and industry.

The school of Saint-Cyr had not much more than the throw-outs from among the young men, until the old nobility and the Catholic party began to send boys there. The consequences of this change have not yet had time to develop. This nation was formerly brilliant and warlike; but it was so by selection, if I dare say so. It maintained and produced an admirable nobility, full of courage and radiance. Now that this nobility is no more, there remains an ill-defined substratum of mediocrity, lacking originality or boldness, made up of commoners who understand neither the privilege of the mind nor of the sword. A nation so fashioned can reach the height of material prosperity; but it has no further role to play in the world, no more action abroad. Then again it is impossible to get out of such a state with universal suffrage; for you cannot overcome universal suffrage with universal suffrage, you can mislead it, and hoodwink it, but, so long as it exists, those who depend on it are obliged to come to terms with it and obey its law. It is a vicious circle to imagine that you can reform the mistakes of a public opinion which is beyond hope of conversion if you rely solely on that public opinion as your base of operations.

Besides, France has only followed the general movement of all European nations except Prussia and Russia. Mr. Cobden, whom I met about 1857, was delighted with us. England had preceded us along the path of industrial and commercial materialism; only, the English were wiser than we, and saw to it that their Government was in step with the nation, whereas we were so impolitic that the Government of our choice was able to involve us in war against our own wishes. I do not know if I am mistaken, but there is an interpretation of historical ethnography which recommends itself more and more to my liking. The similarity between England and Northern France strikes me more and more forcibly. Our thoughtlessness comes from the Midi, and if France had not involved the Languedoc and Provence in her circle of operations, we should be serious, active, Protestant and Parliamentary. Our racial origins are the same as those of the British Isles; although German influence was powerful enough in these islands to create a predominantly Germanic idiom, it was not more considerable over the whole of the three kingdoms than over the whole of France. Like France, England seems to me to be in process of expelling her Germanic element, that obstinate nobility, proud and intractable, which governed it in the time of Pitt, Castlereagh, and Wellington. How far is this pacifist and very Christian school of economists from the passion of those men of iron who imposed such great things on their country! English public opinion such as has developed in the last thirty years is in no way Germanic; you are conscious of the Celtic spirit in it, gentler, more sympathetic, more humane. This sort of appraisal should be made in very general terms; it can be claimed, nevertheless, that what still remains of the military spirit in the world is a Germanic achievement. It will probably be by the German race, in so far as it is feudal and military, that Socialism and egalitarian Democracy, which we Celts would find difficult to limit, will be finally brought under control. This would be in conformity with historical precedents, for one of the features of the German race has always been to keep the idea of conquest and the idea of guarantee in line with each other; in other words, to make the crude and material fact of property resulting from conquest override all considerations of the rights of man and abstract theories of social contract. The response to each progression of Socialism could be a similar progression of Germanism, and one can foresee the day when all socialist countries will be governed by Germans. The invasion of the fourth and fifth centuries was based on similar reasons, for the Roman countries had become incapable of producing good policemen or good managers of property.

In reality our country, especially in the provinces, was developing a social pattern which, in spite of differences in appearance, had more in common with America, a social pattern in which much that was once considered as within the purview of the State would be left to private initiative. It is true that such a future was not necessarily to be welcomed; it was clear that if France developed along these lines it would remain far inferior to America. Lack of education and distinction, the void that always occurs in a country which has no court, high society, or ancient institutions, America supplements in other ways: the vigor of young growth, patriotism, the confidence, maybe exaggerated, in her own strength, the conviction that she is working for the greatest good of humanity, her boldness and her spirit of enterprise, the almost complete absence of the seeds of socialism, the ease with which the difference between rich and poor is accepted, above all, the opportunity to spread her wings, in the infinity of space, without neighbors. France is deprived of these advantages, and conducts her experiment as it were inside a retort. She is too heavy and too light, too credulous and too mocking. She would never have been anything but a second-rate, paltry, mediocre America, perhaps more like Mexico or South America than the United States. Royalty retains in our ancient societies a mass of things worth preserving. Because of this idea that I have of ancient France and her genius, I should call this farewell to glory and to grandness: *Finis Franciae*. But in politics one must be careful not to reserve one's sympathy for what ought to be; success in this world is generally the opposite of our instincts, at least for us idealists. It is nearly always safe to assume that if we dislike something, it will prevail. This desire for a political state involving the least possible central government is the unanimous wish of the provinces. The antipathy shown toward Paris is not just righteous indignation against the outrages of a factious minority; it is not revolutionary Paris, but governing Paris that France does not like. Paris is for France a synonym for interfering demands. Paris levies the troops, absorbs the money and uses it in all manner of ways which the provinces do not understand. The most capable administrator of the last reign said to me, *à propos* of the elections of 1869, that the tax system seemed to him to be most endangered, for at each election the provinces forced their representatives to make certain promises, which would have to be honored to some extent, sooner or later, but if they were fulfilled it would mean the destruction of State finance. The first time I met Prévost-Paradol, on his return from his electoral campaign in the Loire-Inférieure, I asked him what was his chief impression. "We shall soon see the end of the State," he said. That is exactly what I should have replied, if he had asked me my impressions of Seine-et-Marne. The provinces will be quite happy if the Prefect interferes as little as possible, and if the taxes and military service are reduced as much as possible. Most people ask no more than to be left alone to make money in peace. Only the poor districts show some eagerness for posts; in the wealthy *départements* the Civil Service has no standing, and jobs in it are considered the least rewarding use of a man's activity.

This is the spirit of what might be called provincial democracy. Such a spirit, as can be seen, differs considerably from the Republican spirit. It can come to terms with the Empire and Constitutional Monarchy as well as it can with the Republic, if not better in some respects. It is as indifferent to any particular dynasty as to all that can be called glory or brilliance, but really prefers to have some sort of dynasty as the guarantee of order; but it is unwilling to make any sacrifice for the establishment of this dynasty. It is pure political materialism, the antithesis of that element of idealism which lies at the heart of Legitimist and Republican theories. A political party like this, which has the support of the immense majority of the French, is too superficial and narrow to be able to direct the destiny of a country. The enormous stupidity, from its own point of view, that it committed in taking on Prince Louis-Napoleon in 1848 to look after its affairs will be repeated twenty times over. Its fate is to be continually misled, for it is impossible for a man with mean interests to be clever; simple bourgeois platitudes cannot arouse the amount of devotion necessary to create and maintain an ordered whole.

70. *Integral Nationalism: The Nancy Program,*
Maurice Barrès, 1898

ELECTORS,

The nationalist and social ideas which we brought to a joint triumph for the first time in 1889, had at that time alarmed certain minds because of the popularity of General Boulanger. Today, whether because they seem to be more matured, or whether circumstances now justify them more, they attract many adherents even among the antagonists of the previous campaign, disabused by a party which has done nothing since we left it with a free field.

The "Nationalist Socialist Republican Committee of Meurthe-et-Moselle" and a large number of independent electors have asked me to take up again the electoral battle.

To a policy having for its aim only animosities to satisfy, and for its driving force only lust for power, I come anew to oppose those *national* and *social* ideas which already you have acclaimed and which you will not today repudiate.

I. We are Nationalists

In the top ranks of society, in the heart of the provinces, in the moral and in the material sphere, in commerce, industry, and agriculture, even in the shipyards where they are competing with French workers, foreigners are poisoning us like parasites.

One vital principle that should underlie the new French policy is to protect all its nationals against this invasion, and to beware of that brand of socialism that is so cosmopolitan, or rather so German, that it would weaken the country's defenses.

The Jewish problem is linked to the national problem. The Jews were assimilated to the native French by the Revolution, but have retained their peculiar characteristics and now, instead of being persecuted as they once were, are themselves the overlords. We believe in complete freedom of conscience; what is more, we should consider it highly dangerous to allow the Jews the chance of invoking (and so to appear to be defending) the principles of civil liberty promulgated by the Revolution. But they violate these principles by characteristically isolated behavior, by monopolies, speculation, and cosmopolitanism. There is, moreover, in the army, the magistracy, the ministries, in all branches of the administration, a far higher proportion of them than their numbers justify. They have been appointed prefects, judges, treasurers, officers—because they have money, which corrupts. We ought to destroy this dangerous disproportion, without even changing the law, by insisting on greater fairness on the part of those who govern, and so gain more consideration for our real nationals, the children of Gaul and not of Judea.

But the most urgent need is to make the process of naturalization more difficult. It is by this loophole that the worst Jews and many second-rate Frenchmen have slipped in.

Statistics show that 90 per cent of foreigners do not become naturalized until they have evaded active army service. We should insist that military service is a condition of nationality. What is more, a naturalized person (except those from Alsace-Lorraine) should be allowed just private rights, while only his descendants should be assimilated to French-born citizens and enjoy political rights.

The opportunist policy over the last twenty years has favored Jews, foreigners, cosmopolitans. The reason given by those who committed this criminal mistake was that these aliens would introduce a vigorous element into France. Fine elements these—Reinach, Cornelius Herz, Alfred Dreyfus, and the like—who have almost brought us to decay! This is the real position: French society does need vigorous new elements, it is true, but they can be found within that society, by encouraging the least privileged, the poorest, by raising their standard of living and improving their vocational training.

So nationalism leads inevitably to socialism. We define socialism as "the material and moral improvement of the largest and poorest classes."

It has taken some centuries for the French nation to give political security to its members. It must now protect them against that economic insecurity that prevails at all levels.

Let us define this insecurity.

II. We demand protection against economic insecurity

Insecurity of the worker—The elderly worker has not enough to eat. Even if he is able-bodied, he runs the risk of unemployment.

Wages are kept low by foreign competition.

Mechanization means that he is crowded into factories, subjected to military discipline under the arbitrary rule of the boss. In some districts he is reduced by certain economic organizations to real slavery.

He cannot get out. For one thing, you do not take your native earth with you on the soles of your boots, and for many of them exile is heartbreak. Again, materially speaking, if he goes, he and his family will probably starve to death for he will have no savings. Besides, where could he find work?

Insecurity of the small trader—The small trader has the same economic insecurity as the worker. They are interdependent. It is, in fact, the lower working class, black-coated and manual workers, who keep the small trader going, for the middle classes go to the big stores. The small trader helps the black-coated or manual worker to survive periods of unemployment by allowing credit. But the credit that the worker gets from the small trader—baker, butcher, grocer, or landlord—lays him open to ruin if unemployment is prolonged or too frequent.

Another cause of insecurity is that prime costs for small industrialists and tradespeople fluctuate arbitrarily, at the bidding of speculators.

We should note in passing that these traders and industrialists did not gain from the lowering of the bank rate. They still pay 8 per cent (6 per cent for three months with four renewals that

cost ½ per cent, making 8 per cent in all). Without going so far
as a State bank, which could be held to ransom in wartime, we
should like to have seen commerce profit by the renewal of the
charter of the Bank of France. But the Government and the
financial feudality thought otherwise.

Insecurity of the farmer—The price of wheat no longer depends
solely on the French harvest. At one time the producer used to get
compensation for a poor harvest in the higher prices charged to the
consumer. Nowadays these prices depend on the harvests of India
and the United States.

They have begun to remedy this situation by protection, which
is basically a socialist measure, intervention by the State in the
natural course of events. (Just as the same circumstances are sweep-
ing away parties, like a flood tide!)

We are in full agreement with the major aspects of protection.
It aims at guaranteeing a minimum price to the producer. But the
big middlemen absorb the profits with their fluctuations and specu-
lative maneuvers, which should be opposed with terrorist severity. . . .

Insecurity of the bourgeoisie—The bourgeoisie is menaced by the
international finance feudality, which turns financial securities into
bits of paper.

I will not go back as far as Panama—I could find ten examples
in the last twelve months. Take this one. The price of gold mines
launched on the French market was raised to the point where their
total value reached about 1.8 billion francs. Today they are worth
no more than 615 million. This means that in less than two years
national savings worth 1.2 billion was lost on securities held by
small French investors.

No investigation followed.

ELECTORS

It is for the defense of the ideas that I have just explained that I
propose for your approbation the following Program:

I. MEASURES TO BE TAKEN TO ENSURE THE UNION
OF ALL FRENCHMEN

Against foreign produce: the work of protectionism must be maintained;

Against the foreign worker who, being dispensed from military
service, draws every year a billion in wages from France and causes
poverty and destitution, through unemployment, among the fam-

ilies of French workers. In particular public works, financed from taxes, must be carried out by national workers;

Against the international financial feudality which, through its joint-stock association, eliminates the worker from the country and replaces him by undercutting with foreign workers, paralyzes the action of protective measures taken in support of agriculture and industry, organizes monopoly and speculation in the basic essentials, falsifies prices, sending them up and down, and in the end ruins the real producers of wealth—our farmers, our traders, our workers;

Against the naturalized foreigner, who claims to play a role in politics and to whom we would allow only private rights, reserving political rights for his descendants. This is the best way to get at the Jew, whose invasion of State functions the executive power would otherwise have to restrict.

II. INSTITUTION OF A SUPERANNUATION FUND for workers organized by the State.

The duties which must be levied on foreign workers and the customs duties levied on basic essential goods must be specifically allotted to this superannuation fund in order to simplify somewhat these taxes where strictly no levy should be imposed.

The matter of superannuation funds is one of the most important to settle for the sake of social peace. It is urgent. It forces itself upon us. But it is complicated by a grave financial problem which has to be solved. I shall give this all my attention and care. I declare myself in favor of the principle. I shall accept any solution likely to produce the quickest and most lasting results.

III. REFORM OF TAXATION TO PROMOTE DEMOCRATIC JUSTICE aiming at lowering taxes on consumer goods and charges which hit the small growers. The land tax is charged on an estimated income which often does not exist, on the basis of assessments which no longer correspond to reality. The tax on consumer goods is infinitely heavier on the poor than on the rich.

IV. ORGANIZATION OF AGRICULTURAL CREDIT, WHICH COULD INCLUDE THE FUNDS OF THE SAVINGS BANKS, today drained away from the whole province in order to BE CENTRALIZED and riskily used for the purchase of stocks.

V. FREEDOM OF ASSOCIATION. THIS IMPLIES EXTENSION OF THE CIVIL PERSONALITY OF THE TRADE UNIONS IN SUCH A WAY THAT WHETHER AGRICULTURAL OR INDUSTRIAL UNIONS, THEY CAN USE THE POWER

OF CREDIT, BECOME ASSOCIATIONS OF PRODUCERS and own the premises and working tools needed in industrial, commercial, or agricultural production.

VI. EXTENSION OF THE INDEPENDENT FREEDOMS AND THE CIVIL PERSONALITY OF THE COMMUNES, so as to permit them to achieve in part certain kinds of social progress—always provided they do not infringe the rights of the State.

VII. DEVELOPMENT OF PUBLIC EDUCATION IN THE DIRECTION OF OCCUPATIONAL TRAINING in order to allow all national aptitudes, all forms of intelligence to be developed.

VIII. REVISION OF THE CONSTITUTION with the aim of giving universal suffrage its full and complete sovereignty, particularly by means of the *municipal referendum.*

ELECTORS,

It is useful that, in this region of Lorraine, where day by day they become more numerous, the workers in factories and in the fields should be able to express their wishes; it would be dangerous to suppress them into silence, as the old opportunists wished to do.

This program of the "National Socialist Republican Committee" —what generous and just mind would wish to misunderstand it?— corresponds to the needs of our population; IT IS IN TUNE WITH THE SPECIAL SPIRIT OF OUR LORRAINE and of our frontier.

Articles IV, V, VI, VIII, which concern decentralization, strongly indicate the direction of our demands in our region, where the "School of Nancy" matches public feeling.

In all our Articles, as anyone can see who examines them in the light of our preliminary arguments, the path of the future is prepared, and at the same time immediate interests are guaranteed. I undertake to defend them with every means at my disposal, at the same time as I place myself completely at the service of the special interests of my compatriots.

Maurice Barrès

§(b) Radicals and Socialists

Modern French political parties, in the sense of nation-wide organizations based on local committees and concerned with getting candidates into the Chamber or Senate, mostly took shape around the turn of the century. The word "radical" itself was imported from English usage in the time of Louis Philippe, but Radicalism as a political force was identified in terms of the opposition to the Second Empire in the later 1860's. Jules Simon (1814–1896) in his *La politique radicale* of 1868, and Gambetta in his Belleville Manifesto (Document 21), gave it definition in terms of liberal representative institutions and practices and of the doctrine that social reforms "depend absolutely" on first achieving political democracy. It was also, in spirit, devoutly anti-clericalist, and by the end of the century had distinguished itself sharply from the older, more conservative "opportunist" republicanism of its founders and had moved on to press for such social reforms as greater provision of social security and regulation of working conditions. In the hands of Clemenceau and Camille Pelletan it found its characteristic pattern of organization in 1901 (Document 71) and at the Congress of Nancy in 1907 its more detailed programs (Document 72). Appealing strongly to middle-class traders, businessmen, farmers of moderate property, and to many professional people, it became the almost indispensable component of any ministerial coalition, and the "government party" *par excellence*.

To the so-called "Radical and Radical-Socialist Party" belonged many of the most familiar names in the frequently changing ministries of the Third Republic: Clemenceau, Herriot, Caillaux, Daladier. It gave the parliamentary system its special character, whether that be thought of as "The Republic of Committees" of which Daniel Halévy wrote, or "The Republic of Pals" which Robert de Jouvenel satirized. See Peter J. Larmour, *The French Radical Party in the 1930's* (Stanford, 1964) for an examination of its extraordinary elasticity. From the first it was challenged, on the Left, by the newly formed Socialist Party which, at the *Salle du Globe* in Paris in April, 1905, was founded as the French Section of the Workers' International (*Section française de l'internationale ouvrière*, or S.F.I.O.).

The S.F.I.O. was the triumph of Jean Jaurès and the moderate parliamentary Socialists, in their long efforts to bring some unity into the splintered Left. During the last quarter of the nineteenth century, various socialist movements, divided partly by doctrinal differences about ends or means, and partly by conflicting personalities, grew up in France. In addition to the Marxist group led by Jules Guesde and calling itself the French Labor Party, there appeared in the 1880's the group led by Paul Brousse, soon nicknamed the "Possibilists" because they were more empirical in method. They differed over the very conception of unity, for Guesde demanded adherence to a strict program and discipline, whereas Brousse aimed at a wide combination of all who wanted fundamental social change. Other groups emerged, based on yet finer distinctions, in addition to the trade unions (see Documents 47 and 49), the cooperative movements, and the *bourses du travail* or labor exchanges, concerned with welfare work and education as well as finding employment. The union effected by Jaurès bears all the signs of an uneasy compromise, and this was to break down in 1920 (Document 75) with the emergence of a Communist Party still further to the Left.

Meanwhile, the combination of Radical-Socialist and Socialist forces before 1914 produced important social legislation, two examples of which are given (in part) in Document 74. French texts in *Bulletin des lois*, XII série, vol. 47, No. 1583, pp. 841–8; *Journal officiel* (*Chambre des députés*) July 15 and 16, 1913.

French texts of Documents 71 and 72 are in Albert Milhaud, *Histoire du radicalisme* (Paris, Société d'Editions Françaises et internationales, 1951), Appendices; and in Jacques Kayser, *Les grandes batailles du radicalisme, des origines aux portes du pouvoir, 1820–1901* (Paris, 1962), will be found an interesting comparative table of Radical programs between 1849 and 1898, as well as the texts of the programs. The French text of the Socialist Party unification in 1905 (Document 73) is conveniently found in Georges Lefranc, *Le mouvement socialiste sous la troisième république, 1875–1940* (Paris, Payot 1963), pp. 124–5.

71. Declaration of the Republican Radical and Radical-Socialist Party, read at the close of the first Radical Congress (June 23, 1901) by M. Camille Pelletan, Deputy, and Chairman of the Organizing Committee

THE FIRST thought of a Republican Congress should be that of union against the common enemy. This has been forced upon the whole democracy in the face of open plots and intrigues for a *coup d'état*. This is what has brought us together in this hall, but it goes far beyond these walls, for it unites all the sons of the Revolution, whatever their differences of opinion, against the men of the counterrevolution whose numbers are swollen by accomplices drawn from the ranks of our former friends. Against this unshakable solidarity some have dared to invoke their concern for their country and the army, as if the heirs of the *émigrés* of '92 had some noble lesson to teach the descendants of the soldiers of Valmy and Quiberon. Others have tried to excuse their desertion by denouncing the attempt to unite the more moderate Republicans with the more ardent Socialists as being a mixture of incompatible elements, as if a similar alliance had not (already) been formed at all moments of peril, in the Great Days of 1830 and February, 1848, as well as on May 16, in face of the "Moral Order," and against Boulangism. Public good sense cannot be led astray like that. In the army of democracy, though each battalion keeps its own action and program distinct, all march in close formation in defense of the Republic. But is a policy of passive defense sufficient? France needs a bigger and bolder scheme.

The best way to defend the Republic is to make it really republican. Most of the promised reforms are yet to come. They should have been carried out long ago. There must be no more delay. First those against clericalism: the law against congregations has already been passed. The country expects it to be enforced with determination and will insist on this if necessary. The fight has begun and must be fought to the bitter end. The Falloux Law was pushed through in order to betray France to the Jesuits. It must be abrogated, once and for all. Nobody can maintain that the pact of alliance against liberty concluded between the Roman Papacy and the emergent Napoleonic dictatorship is a republican enactment. We can disagree only on the exact moment when we shall tear it up; universal suffrage will decide. Another danger is increasing daily in every country: the power that is falling into the hands of the big speculators through the concentration and manipulation of large capital funds. The general interests of the country, and the liberty and private means of all must be defended against their increasing domination, by means of legislation applied at long last against stock-jobbing maneuvers, and by legislative measures which return to the aegis of the State certain monopolies and public services in so far as the interests of national defense and agricultural and industrial production shall dictate. Social reforms must be the prime consideration of modern societies. What separates us from collectivist socialists in this respect in our passionate attachment to the principle of private property. We wish neither to begin nor even to prepare to abolish it. Precisely because this principle rests entirely on the inviolable right of each person to the product of his work, we do not intend to surrender it to anybody, either when it comes to making practical provision for old-age pensions, or if it involves the prevention of big industrial undertakings from assuming a new feudal character, or the speeding up of the peaceful evolution by which the worker shall own his own equipment, the legitimate reward of his labor. Fiscal reforms are no less urgent. Our tax system rests lightly on the rich and heavily upon the poor, and is most burdensome on the mass of agricultural workers, who form the majority and also the strength of the country. We want, first of all, to establish a graduated tax on income which will exempt all workers and bring relief to the villages in particular. We want, in general, to reform this archaic system, notably by the reform of the rates and those taxes which tie up rural property. In addition, real equality for military service reduced to two years.

So much for the program in broad outline. To carry it into effect we are relying completely on universal suffrage. Once it is securely armed with legitimate authority it will take the measures needed to free from pressure the liberty of the humblest voters, to put an end to the scandal of elections based on bribery and to modify the constitution so as to ensure its own full sovereignty. But there must be something more to democracy before it can feel that a truly Republican Government is completely in control. The deepest impression is made on the great majority in the country by daily routine business—the choice of civil servants, the weight carried by local influences, the countless questions of detail that confront a Government daily. If the solid masses of democracy, the unknown millions, whose devotion has never swerved from our cause, whose courage has resisted all persecution, and who, even more than the most famous politicians, are the true founders of the Republic, if they saw reactionary interests remaining indefinitely as powerful over the ministers whom they have brought to power as over those who formerly hunted them down, how could you prevent them from losing heart? Republican France is no longer disposed to tolerate a Government, however well intentioned, which lets itself be overpowered by those very influences it had made its mission to destroy, allowing its own civil service to betray it to begin with, and then to dominate it. Democracy has always claimed intentions of this sort. People have been talking like this for a long time, but so far the results have not come up to the country's expectations. A very powerful wish has emerged from the crowd of loyal citizens assembled here from all parts of France: to the effect that it is imperative to put an end to delays. We are not here seeking the causes that have prompted them. Our task is not recriminations about the past but to look to the future. The era of postponements must end. The era of resolutions must begin. Universal suffrage will insist on this. And so this union of all shades of Republicans against clericalism, against imperialist undertakings, against the power of money, in the cause of social justice, the union of which this Congress has been such an outstanding affirmation, will bring rich rewards to the Republic and to the Nation.

72. *Program of the Radical-Socialist Party adopted at the Congress of Nancy, 1907*

In Political Organization

The Radical and Radical-Socialist Party

1. Intends to revise the constitution in the most democratic direction possible, the *Republic* as such being no longer a subject for debate.
2. Affirms the sovereignty of universal suffrage, a sovereignty which insists that the Chamber of Deputies has the last word, particularly in budgetary matters.
3. Demands that the electoral system on which the Senate is based should be enlarged in a democratic direction, so as to make it more exactly proportional and to ensure more direct influence for universal suffrage.
4. Electoral reform, closely linked with the overhaul of our administrative system, must secure consultation with the people in conditions such that the electors shall reach decisions based on programs rather than on personalities. A new and equitable redistribution of legislative seats will secure for each region representatives numerically in proportion to the size of its population.

   Legislation regulating the method of voting will guarantee that voting shall be secret and genuine; all pressure from the employer on the citizens in his employment, whether he be a big industrialist or a big landed proprietor, will either be prevented, or severely reprimanded; corrupt practices will be inquired into or punished; legislative measures will be taken to restrict electoral expenses and to equalize the struggle between rich and poor.
5. The Radical and Radical-Socialist Party is in favor of far-reaching reforms which, without affecting the national unity achieved by the Revolution, will increase communal and departmental liberty, simplify administrative machinery, and reduce the cost and the number of civil servants, while improving the pay of minor officials. The country will be more closely organized through rapid means of communication and the transformations that have taken place during the last century.

6. The Party wants to extend to civil servants of all ranks a statute guaranteeing their civil liberty, and justice in promotion and in enjoyment of their rights, including the right of association. It demands that they should be required to pledge absolute devotion to the interests of the country and to republican institutions. It calls for firm sustained action from the Government to destroy influences in the public services which are hostile to democracy and which have too long held sway.

7. The Party wants justice to be swift and equal for all. Justice should also be free, and if it cannot be made free of charge in the near future, the Party considers it urgent to reduce the costs of litigation. It wants simplification of the codes by repeal of out-of-date laws that have fallen into disuse. It remains attached to the principle of electing judges; if this reform cannot be brought about in the near future, it demands new legislation for the recruitment, nomination and promotion of magistrates, ensuring their independence, loyalty and sincerity in applying republican law. Judicial reform must include extension of conciliation tribunals, suppression of lawyers' privileges and the transfer of ministerial offices to the public service.

8. The Radical and Radical-Socialist Party calls for the abolition of the death penalty.

9. *In matters of religion:*
Together with the preservation intact of the laws on secularity, the Radical and Radical-Socialist Party demands the effective suppression of congregations as yet nonexistent. Its formula, "Free churches within the sovereign State," ensures liberty of conscience, all forms of public worship and supremacy of the civil power.

10. *In matters of education:*
The Party considers that teaching is one of the most noble prerogatives of the State, which ought itself to provide lay teaching or should keep close control when private persons are allowed to make provision. All the children of the people have a right to full-time education according to ability. The system of national education must therefore guarantee this right. It must also allow the development of vocational training and adult refresher classes.

11. *In the sphere of fiscal and budgetary matters:*

In order to reestablish a true proportionality of levies according to the contributing capacity of each individual, the Radical and Radical-Socialist Party wants a global graduated tax on income to be set up, abolition of the four direct taxes, reduction in the duties on consumer goods, and on stamp duty and registration duties which impose a heavy burden of legal fees; reduction of the taxes which weigh heavily on agriculture, trade, and small industrialists. It will demand new sources of revenue for social reforms from a reform of probate duty or deeds of gift, based on the principle of graduation, either according to the degree of relationship or according to the total estate, and by reducing the degree of relationship through which the collateral line may inherit.

12. Financial reform implies strict control over all expenditure, military and civil alike, and gradual liquidation of the National Debt.

13. *In the social and economic sphere:*
Through all its moral, intellectual, and economic reforms, the Radical Party will try to give the proletariat full awareness of its rights and duties, and once it has achieved responsibility for its actions, endow it with the authority necessary to establish a more rational and equitable social system.

14. The Radical and Radical-Socialist Party holds firmly to the principle of private property and wants neither to begin to suppress it nor even to prepare for its suppression. But this is no blind attachment; it does not extend to abuses which would destroy the legitimacy and justification for private property. It is ready to propose all legal measures necessary to guarantee to every man the product of his work and to forestall the dangers presented by a constitution based on a capitalistic feudal system that holds workers and consumers to ransom.

15. The Party proposes the formation of unions and cooperative societies, and encourages all institutions through which the proletariat can exercise its rights, defend its interests, and improve its moral and material conditions, obtain ownership of equipment and a fair return for labor, end the servitude of a wage-earning class, and gain access to private property, the prerequisite of liberty and dignity.

16. Being firmly opposed to the selfish ideas of the laissez-faire

school, the Party maintains its individuality by reaffirming the right of the State to intervene in relations between capital and labor in order to establish the preconditions of justice.

17. The State must discharge society's debt toward children, the sick, the old, the disabled, and all those who need social assistance.

It must guarantee for the workers in towns, in factories, and in the country, when age or illness has broken their strength, the pensions solemnly pledged for all democracy. It must further continue the legislative task of social assistance undertaken by the Third Republic; improve the service for children receiving State relief and the system of medical help and relief for the old and infirm; it must build local hospitals, help antitubercular societies and the fight against alcoholism, etc.

18. The Radical and Radical-Socialist Party favors gradual extension of rights for women, who should be protected by law in all circumstances of life; communal, departmental or national assistance should be forthcoming for pregnant women who are in need; compulsory cessation of work six weeks before and after confinement is essential for women employed in factories, shops or offices.

19. The Labor Code and Social Insurance must be redrafted under the auspices of the Ministry of Labor to include the whole body of labor legislation: the employment of women and children in industry; work and apprenticeship contracts; the regulation of petty and major disputes between employees and employers through conciliatory and compulsory arbitration; accidents at work, occupational hazards and diseases and employers' responsibility; limitation of hours of work and weekly holidays; organization of insurance by the Nation for all workers in industry, trade and agriculture against risks of accident, illness, and unemployment; friendly societies and savings banks, which can improve the lot of the worker already safeguarded against destitution; healthy and hygienic conditions in industrial and commercial establishments, as also on all premises occupied by employees and workers.

20. The Radical and Radical-Socialist Party advocates that the State should take over virtual monopolies where they are powerful enough to warrant this step, more particularly in

order to gain control of big national services which exercise
a decisive influence on production, on the wealth of the country, and on its defense in the event of war; in order to prevent
certain industrial monopolies from taxing workers and consumers at will; and in order to use whatever resources are forthcoming from these monopolies either to lessen the taxpayers'
burden or to put through social reforms. First and foremost,
the party calls for acquisition of the railways and the insurance
monopoly. It is firmly resolved to protect public savings
against stock-jobbing and speculation.

21. In addition to the fiscal reforms already outlined with regard
to taxation, land tax on undeveloped property and conveyance
duties, including reform of mortgage, the Radical and Radical-
Socialist Party intends to support all those reforms already
undertaken to protect agriculture: development of agriculture,
technical education, and cooperative enterprise; agricultural
loans; insurance against fire, hail, frost, and death of cattle;
preventive measures against epizootic disease; rendering of
family property inalienable and immune from distraint; suppression of fraud; representation of small and medium as well
as large-scale farmers in chambers of agriculture, etc.

22. To encourage the growth of national wealth the Party will
give care to our harbor installations, inland navigation, our
canal system, which urgently needs to be completed and improved, the development of railroads, more systematic recruitment of our agents abroad and the widening of our commercial
activities.

23. *Foreign policy and defense:*
The Radical and Radical-Socialist Party is deeply patriotic
and resolutely devoted to peace. Its members' love for their
country is free from all feelings of hatred for other peoples;
they consider that patriotism is degraded when it is used as a
weapon in internal quarrels, and they oppose those parties
which try to exploit it for their own ends. The Radical Party's
foreign policy can be summed up in these words: friendly
understanding between peoples; extension of the practice of
international arbitration of serious disputes; the maintenance of
peace with dignity. It is opposed to any policy of foreign
adventures and opposes military expeditions whose aim,
avowed or concealed, would be the conquest of new colonies.

It demands development of the present vast French colonial territories, the setting up of a form of government that would have a civilizing role reflecting our national spirit and that would bear no trace of military domination or missionizing propaganda. It insists on respect for all the rights of humanity in our relations with the peoples of the regions which France has conquered.

24. The Party respects military duty but condemns abuses and prejudices of the military mentality. The army should be integrated more and more closely with the Nation. In order to allow reduction in the period of effective service with the colors, without endangering national security, schemes should be set on foot to prepare young Frenchmen for military service or to prolong service in the reserves.

25. Among the most urgent military reforms it advocates: those which will ensure conditions of democratic recruitment of a corps of officers loyal to the Republic; a law on *Cadres* guaranteeing promotion for officers; a law to bring about great economies by reduction in the number of officers on the active list and a better deployment of officers in the reserve and territorial army; abolition of councils of war in times of peace, and of disciplinary companies; shortening of the periods of instruction for reservists and territorials; retrenchment of the military and naval estimates, and reduction of waste by vigilant control.

73. *Socialists United, Paris, 1905*

THE DELEGATES of the French organizations—the Revolutionary Socialist Workers' Party, the Socialist Party of France, the French Socialist Party, the Independent Federations, etc.—declare that the action of the Unified Socialist Party must be based on the principles which have been established by the international congresses, especially the most recent ones at Paris in 1900 and at Amsterdam in 1904.

They state that the divergences of views and different interpretations of tactics, which have so far been able to appear, are due above all to circumstances peculiar to France and to the absence of a general organization.

They affirm their common desire to found a party of the class war which, even while it takes advantage for the workers of minor conflicts among the rich, or is by chance able to concert its action with that of a political party for the defense of the rights or interests of the proletariat, remains always a party of fundamental and unyielding opposition to the whole of the bourgeois class and to the State which is its instrument.

Consequently, the delegates declare that their organizations are ready to collaborate forthwith in this work of unifying the socialist forces on the following bases:

1. The Socialist Party is a class party whose aim is to socialize the means of production and distribution, that is to transform capitalist society into a collectivist or communist society, and to adopt as its means the economic or political organization of the proletariat. By its purpose, its ideal, by the means it adopts, the Socialist Party, while pursuing the achievement of the immediate reforms claimed by the working class, is not a party of reform but a party of class war and revolution.

2. Those whom it returns to Parliament form a single group as compared with all the bourgeois political sects. The Socialist group in Parliament must refuse the Government all the resources which ensure the power of the bourgeoisie and its domination, must refuse, therefore, military credits, credits for colonial conquests, secret funds and the whole of the budget.

Even in exceptional circumstances, those returned cannot commit the Party without its consent.

In Parliament the Socialist group must dedicate itself to the defense and the extension of the political liberties and rights of the workers, to the pursuit and realization of reforms such as will improve the conditions of life and advance the struggle of the working class.

Deputies, like all other selected members, must hold themselves at the disposition of the Party, to serve its action in the country, its general propaganda for organizing the proletariat, and the final ends of socialism. . . .

[Articles 3 to 7 assert the authority of the Party over all its elected representatives and over the Party press, exacting from deputies a portion of their parliamentary salaries and obedience to a *mandat impératif*—i.e., to prior instructions given to deputies by the Party organization. The statement also proposes a Congress of Unity to be held as soon as possible]

74. *Socialist Legislation Before 1914*

(i) Law of July 15, 1893, on free medical assistance

Article 1—Every French national who is sick and without resources receives free medical assistance from the commune, *département,* or State according to the place of residence at which outdoor relief is given, either at home or, if home circumstances are unsuitable, in a hospital.

The same conditions apply to women in confinement as to the sick. Foreigners who are taken ill and have no resources shall receive the same treatment as French nationals in every case in which the Government shall have concluded a treaty of reciprocal assistance with their country of origin.

Article 2—The commune, *département,* or State may always put in a claim, if necessary, either against one another, or against all persons, societies, or corporations responsible for medical assistance to the indigent sick, especially against members of the family of the assisted persons designated by Articles 205, 206, 207, and 212 of the Civil Code.

Article 3—Every commune is linked with one or more of the nearest hospitals for the treatment of its sick. . . .

(ii) Law of July 14, 1913, concerning allowances for large families

Article 1—For large families allowances are a compulsory service for all *départements,* with the participation of the communes and the State.

Article 2—Every head of a family of French nationality, who is responsible for more than three legitimate or acknowledged children and whose resources are insufficient for their upbringing, receives an annual allowance for each child under thirteen years of age, after the third child under thirteen years of age.

Article 3—The rate of allowance is determined for each commune by the municipal council, subject to the approval of the General Council and the Minister of the Interior.

It may not be less than 60 francs per year per child, and not more than 90 francs; if the allowance exceeds 90 francs, the difference is the exclusive responsibility of the commune.

§ (c) Communist Cleavage

The new element in French politics after 1919 was the existence of a
Bolshevik government in the Soviet Union and its success in enlisting
the allegiance of Communist Parties in European states. This doomed
both the uneasy compromise brought about within the French Socialist
Party in the decade before 1914, and the temporary unity forged by
World War I. The schism came at the Congress of Tours in 1920, with
the acceptance by a majority of the S.F.I.O. of the "Twenty-One Conditions" laid down for membership of the Communist International
(Document 75). Of the twenty-one conditions, nineteen had been
drafted by Lenin, and were then amended and supplemented by the
Party commission. They were intended to force the French and other
Socialist Parties to choose between subservience to the commands of
the Comintern and reformist elements within their ranks. Thenceforth
the former Socialist paper, *L'Humanité*, became the Communist organ,
Léon Blum and his followers founding *Le Populaire* as the new Socialist
paper. The split in the Left, irreparable even in the crucial days of the
Popular Front, weakened the whole of the French Left and gave
adventitious strength to the Center.

During 1934 tensions between Right and Left reached breaking
point in the "February Riots." The world economic depression was
at last affecting French life, bringing greater unemployment and lowering the standard of living for many families. Leagues and paramilitary
formations of the Right, intransigent in their denunciations of communism and of weak parliamentary government, were spoiling for
trouble in the streets. To the old *Action Française* of Maurras and
Daudet, dating from 1905, was added the *Croix de Feu* (Fiery Cross)
movement of Colonel de la Rocque, founded in 1927, and the *Jeunesses
Patriotes* (Patriotic Youth) of Pierre Taittinger, formed in 1924. More
recently, too, the perfumer Coty had formed a more openly Bonapartist
body, the *Solidarité Française* (French Solidarity) of 1933, recruiting
from the rowdy younger members of the *petite bourgeoisie*. When the
Stavisky scandal broke in the winter of 1933 to 1934, and exposed corruption at the heart of French government, fascist forces clashed in
the Paris streets with police and security guards, and Communists
counterdemonstrated and called for a general strike. The February Riots
challenged the régime enough to force temporary unity on the Left
to save the Republic. The result was the *Rassemblement populaire*,
claiming to be in the direct French revolutionary tradition and to be
"directly inspired by the watchwords of July 14." Its ten component
organizations issued a common election program on January 11, 1936
(Document 76). It was supported as a "minimum program" by the
Communist Party, but like the C.G.T. the Communists refused to take
part in the Popular Front Government which Blum formed in June
after his victory in the elections.

The Blum Government was, in effect, a Leftist coalition of Radical-Socialists and Socialists, supported by such traditional Radicals as the *Ligue des droits de l'homme*, by more recent anti-fascist groups, and by the main trade-union organizations, but harassed from the Left, as usual, by the Communists and their associated bodies. In 1937 there was a brief resurgence of scares of a Rightist *coup* with the exposure of the plot of the Hooded Men (*Cagoulards*)—apparently involving domestic extremists who were getting some foreign aid. Its wild and somewhat farcical character is demonstrated in the account given by a military officer whose aid the plotters tried to enlist (Document 77). This account appears in J.-R. Tournoux, *L'histoire secrète* (Paris, Librairie Plon, 1962), pages 94–96, and is here reproduced by kind permission of the publishers.

Thereafter, the extremists of the Right had to bide their time—distrusting France's ability to defend herself against the fascist dictators (in which they were correct) and ready to make terms with Hitler which would shake France free from her democratic heritage (in which they were wrong). Their supreme opportunity came after the defeat of France in June, 1940, when they either became avowed collaborators with the Germans (as did former men of the extreme Left, such as Marcel Déat and Jacques Doriot) or supporters of the Vichy régime of Marshal Pétain (as did Maurras and the Catholic banker, Paul Baudouin). Under these grim auspices they launched the so-called "National Revolution," for regeneration through devotion to the principles of Work, Family, Fatherland (*Travail, Famille, Patrie*). On October 11, 1940, the aged Marshal Pétain broadcast his Message to the French People (Document 78), which was presented as the manifesto of this National Revolution. Its emphasis on unity has pathos in the conditions of partition and disarray in which it was issued, but in its texture can be traced most of the antirepublican and traditionalist strands already described in French politics. The "French State" over which Pétain presided was meant to be the antithesis and the antidote to the central republican heritage.

The French text of the Twenty-One Conditions is printed in Georges Lefranc, *Le mouvement socialiste sous la troisième république, 1875–1940* (Paris, Payot 1963), pp. 399–403, and the English translation is printed in *The Communist International, 1919–1943: Documents selected and edited by Jane Degras*, Vol. I, 1919–1922 (London, Oxford University Press and Royal Institute of International Affairs, 1956), pp. 168 f., reproduced by kind permission of the publishers. French text of the Popular Front Program was published in *Le Populaire* on January 11, 1936, and is reprinted in *L'Oeuvre de Léon Blum, 1934–1937* (Paris, Albin Michel 1964), pp. 227–9; and of Pétain's Message in Philippe Pétain, *Quatre années au pouvoir* (Paris, La Couronne littéraire, 1949), pp. 59–68. There is a good account of the internal tensions of France in the 1930's in Alexander Werth, *The Twilight of France, 1933–1940* (London, 1942). See also David Caute, *Communism and the French*

Intellectuals, 1914–1960 (London, 1964); René Rémond, *La droite en France de la première restauration à la V e république* (Paris, 1963); and D. Shapiro, ed., *The Right in France 1890–1919* (London, 1962).

75. The Twenty-One Conditions of Communism, August 1920

. . . THE SECOND congress of the Communist International puts forward the following conditions of adherence to the Communist International:

1. *All propaganda and agitation* must be of a genuinely communist character and in conformity with the programme and decisions of the Communist International. The entire party press must be run by reliable communists who have proved their devotion to the cause of the proletariat. The dictatorship of the proletariat is to be treated not simply as a current formula learned by rote; it must be advocated in a way which makes its necessity comprehensible to every ordinary working man and woman, every soldier and peasant, from the facts of their daily life, which must be systematically noted in our press and made use of every day.

The periodical press and other publications, and all party publishing houses, must be completely subordinated to the party presidium, regardless of whether the party as a whole is at the given moment legal or illegal. Publishing houses must not be allowed to abuse their independence and pursue a policy which is not wholly in accordance with the policy of the party.

In the columns of the press, at popular meetings, in the trade unions and co-operatives, wherever the adherents of the Communist International have an entry, it is necessary to denounce, systematically and unrelentingly, not only the bourgeoisie, but also their assistants, the reformists of all shades.

2. Every organization which wishes to join the Communist International must, in an orderly and planned fashion, remove reformists and centrists from all responsible positions in the workers' movement (party organizations, editorial boards, trade unions, parliamentary fractions, cooperatives, local government bodies) and replace them by tried communists, even if, particularly at the beginning, "experienced" opportunists have to be replaced by ordinary rank and file workers.

3. In practically every country of Europe and America the class

struggle is entering the phase of civil war. In these circumstances communists can have no confidence in bourgeois legality. They are obliged everywhere to create a parallel illegal organization which at the decisive moment will help the Party to do its duty to the revolution. In all those countries where, because of a state of siege or of emergency laws, communists are unable to do all their work legally, it is absolutely essential to combine legal and illegal work.

4. The obligation to spread communist ideas includes the special obligation to carry on systematic and energetic propaganda in the army. Where such agitation is prevented by emergency laws, it must be carried on illegally. Refusal to undertake such work would be tantamount to a dereliction of revolutionary duty and is incompatible with membership of the Communist International.

5. Systematic and well-planned agitation must be carried on in the countryside. The working class cannot consolidate its victory if it has not by its policy assured itself of the support of at least part of the rural proletariat and the poorest peasants, and of the neutrality of part of the rest of the rural population. At the present time communist work in rural areas is acquiring first-rate importance. It should be conducted primarily with the help of revolutionary communist urban and rural workers who have close connections with the countryside. To neglect this work or to leave it in unreliable semi-reformist hands, is tantamount to renouncing the proletarian revolution.

6. Every party which wishes to join the Communist International is obliged to expose not only avowed social-patriotism, but also the insincerity and hypocrisy of social-pacifism; to bring home to the workers systematically that without the revolutionary overthrow of capitalism no international court of arbitration, no agreement to limit armaments, no "democratic" reorganization of the League of Nations, will be able to prevent new imperialist wars.

7. Parties which wish to join the Communist International are obliged to recognize the necessity for a complete and absolute break with reformism and with the policy of the "centre," and to advocate this break as widely as possible among their members. Without that no consistent communist policy is possible.

The Communist International demands unconditionally and categorically that this break be effected as quickly as possible. The Communist International is unable to agree that notorious opportunists, such as Turati, Modigliani, Kautsky, Hilferding, Hilquit, Longuet, MacDonald, etc., shall have the right to appear as members of the Communist International. That could only lead to the Communist International becoming in many respects similar to the Second International, which has gone to pieces.

8. A particularly explicit and clear attitude on the question of the colonies and the oppressed peoples is necessary for the parties in those countries where the bourgeoisie possess colonies and oppress other nations. Every party which wishes to join the Communist International is obliged to expose the tricks and dodges of "its" imperialists in the colonies, to support every colonial liberation movement not merely in words but in deeds, to demand the expulsion of their own imperialists from these colonies, to inculcate among the workers of their country a genuinely fraternal attitude to the working people of the colonies and the oppressed nations, and to carry on systematic agitation among the troops of their country against any oppression of the colonial peoples.

9. Every party which wishes to join the Communist International must carry on systematic and persistent communist activity inside the trade unions, the workers' councils and factory committees, the co-operatives, and other mass workers' organizations. Within these organizations communist cells must be organized which shall by persistent and unflagging work win the trade unions, etc., for the communist cause. In their daily work the cells must everywhere expose the treachery of the social-patriots and the instability of the "centre." The communist cells must be completely subordinate to the party as a whole.

10. Every party belonging to the Communist International is obliged to wage an unyielding struggle against the Amsterdam "International" of the yellow trade unions. It must conduct the most vigorous propaganda among trade unionists for the necessity of a break with the yellow Amsterdam International. It must do all it can to support the international association of red trade unions, adhering to the Communist International, which is being formed.

11. Parties which wish to join the Communist International are obliged to review the personnel of their parliamentary fractions and remove all unreliable elements, to make these fractions not only verbally but in fact subordinate to the party presidium, requiring of each individual communist member of parliament that

he subordinate his entire activity to the interests of genuinely revolutionary propaganda and agitation.

12. Parties belonging to the Communist International must be based on the principle of *democratic centralism*. In the present epoch of acute civil war the communist party will be able to fulfill its duty only if its organization is as centralized as possible, if iron discipline prevails, and if the party centre, upheld by the confidence of the party membership, has strength and authority and is equipped with the most comprehensive powers.

13. Communist parties in those countries where communists carry on their work legally must from time to time undertake cleansing (re-registration) of the membership of the party in order to get rid of any petty-bourgeois elements which have crept in.

14. Every party which wishes to join the Communist International is obliged to give unconditional support to any Soviet republic in its struggle against counter-revolutionary forces. Communist parties must carry on unambiguous propaganda to prevent the dispatch of munitions transports to the enemies of the Soviet republics; they must also carry on propaganda by every means, legal or illegal, among the troops sent to strangle workers' republics.

15. Parties which still retain their old social-democratic programmes are obliged to revise them as quickly as possible, and to draw up, in accordance with the special conditions of their country, a new communist programme in conformity with the decisions of the Communist International. As a rule the programme of every party belonging to the Communist International must be ratified by the regular congress of the Communist International or by the Executive Committee. Should the programme of a party not be ratified by the ECCI, the party concerned has the right to appeal to the congress on the Communist International.

16. All the decisions of the congresses of the Communist International, as well as the decisions of its Executive Committee, are binding on all parties belonging to the Communist International. The Communist International, working in conditions of acute civil war, must be far more centralized in its structure than was the Second International. Consideration must of course be given by the Communist International and Executive Committee in all their activities to the varying conditions in which the individual parties have to fight and work, and they must take decisions of general validity only when such decisions are possible.

17. In this connection, all parties which wish to join the Communist International must change their names. Every party which wishes to join the Communist International must be called: *Communist* party of such and such a country (section of the Communist International). This question of name is not merely a formal matter, but essentially a political question of great importance. The Communist International has declared war on the entire bourgeois world and on all yellow social-democratic parties. The difference between the communist parties and the old official "social-democratic" or "socialist" parties, which have betrayed the banner of the working class, must be brought home to every ordinary worker.

18. All leading party press organs in all countries are obliged to publish all important official documents of the Executive Committee of the Communist International.

19. All parties belonging to the Communist International and those which have applied for admission, are obliged to convene an extraordinary congress as soon as possible, and in any case not later than four months after the second congress of the Communist International, to examine all these conditions of admission. In this connection all party centres must see that the decisions of the second congress of the Communist International are made known to all local organizations.

20. Those parties which now wish to join the Communist International, but which have not radically changed their former tactics, must see to it that, before entering the Communist International, not less than two-thirds of the members of their central committee and of all their leading central bodies consist of comrades who publicly and unambiguously advocated the entry of their party into the Communist International before its second congress. Exceptions can be made with the consent of the Executive Committee of the Communist International. The ECCI also has the right to make exceptions in the case of representatives of the centre mentioned in paragraph 7.

21. Those members of the party who reject in principle the conditions and theses put forward by the Communist International are to be expelled from the party.

The same applies in particular to delegates to the extraordinary congresses.

76. *The Popular Front Program, 1936*

I. Defense of Freedom

1. A general amnesty.
2. Measures against the Fascist Leagues:
   (a) The effective disarmament and dissolution of all semi-military formations, in accordance with the law.
   (b) The enforcement of legal measures in cases of incitement to murder or any attempt against the safety of the State.
3. Measures for the cleansing of public life, especially by forbidding deputies to combine their parliamentary functions with certain other forms of activity.
4. The Press:
   (a) The repeal of the infamous laws and decrees restricting freedom of opinion.
   (b) Reform of the Press by the following legislative measures:
       (i) Measures effectively repressing libel and blackmail.
       (ii) Measures which will guarantee the normal means of existence to newspapers, and compel publication of their financial resources.
       (iii) Measures ending the private monopoly of commercial advertising and the scandals of financial advertising, and preventing the formation of newspaper trusts.
   (c) Organization by the State of radio broadcasts with a view to assuring the accuracy of news and equality of political and social organizations in radio programs.
5. Trade Union Liberties:
   (a) Application and observance of trade-union freedom for all.
   (b) Recognition of women's labor rights.
6. Education and freedom of conscience:
   (a) Measures safeguarding the development of public education by the necessary grants and by reforms such as the raising of the age for compulsory education to fourteen and, in secondary education, the proper selection of pupils as an essential accompaniment to free tuition.
   (b) Measures guaranteeing to all concerned, pupils and teachers, complete freedom of conscience, particularly by en-

suring the neutrality of education, its nonreligious character, and the civic rights of teachers.

7. Colonies: formation of a parliamentary committee of inquiry into the political, economic and cultural situation in France's territories overseas, especially French North Africa and Indochina.

II. Defense of Peace

1. Appeal to the people, and especially the working classes, for collaboration in the maintenance and organization of peace.

2. International collaboration within the framework of the League of Nations for collective security, by defining the aggressor and by joint application of automatic sanctions in cases of aggression.

3. Ceaseless endeavor to pass from armed peace to disarmed peace, first by a convention of limitation, and then by the general, simultaneous, and effectively controlled reduction of armaments.

4. Nationalization of war industries and suppression of private trade in armaments.

5. Repudiation of secret diplomacy; international action and public negotiation to bring back to Geneva the states which have left it, without weakening the essential principles of the League of Nations, which are the principles of collective security and indivisible peace.

6. Greater flexibility in the procedure provided by the League of Nations' Covenant for the peaceful adjustment of treaties which have become dangerous to the peace of the world.

7. Extension of the system of pacts open to all nations, particularly in eastern Europe, on the lines of the Franco-Soviet Pact.

III. Economic Demands

1. Restoration of purchasing power destroyed or reduced by the crisis.

  Against unemployment and the crisis in industry:

  Establishment of a national unemployment fund.

  Reduction of the working week without reduction of the weekly wage.

  Bringing young workers into employment by establishing a system of adequate pensions for aged workers.

Rapid execution of a public-works program, both urban and rural, linking local investments with schemes financed by the State and local authorities.

Against the agricultural and commercial crisis:

Revaluation of agricultural produce, combined with measures against speculation and high prices, in order to reduce the gap between wholesale and retail prices.

Establishment of a National Grain Board [*Office du Blé*] to abolish the tribute levied by speculators against both the producer and the consumer.

Strengthening of agricultural cooperatives, and supply of fertilizers at cost prices by the National Boards for Nitrogen and Potash, control and certification of sales of superphosphates and other fertilizers, extension of agricultural credits, reduction of farming leases.

Suspension of distraints and regulation of debt repayments. Completion of the revision of bills of credit.

Pending the complete and earliest possible removal of all unjust measures imposed by the economy decrees, immediate abolition of measures affecting those groups whose conditions of life have been most severely endangered by these decrees.

2. Against the robbery of investors and for the better organization of credit:

Regulation of banking business. Regulation of balance sheets issued by banks and joint-stock companies. Further regulation of the powers of directors of joint-stock companies.

State officials who have retired or are on the reserve list to be prohibited from joining the board of directors of a joint-stock company.

In order to remove credit and investment from the control of the economic oligarchy, the Bank of France must cease to be a private concern, and "The Bank of France" must become "France's Bank." The Council of Regents of the Bank of France must be abolished; the powers of the Governor of the Bank of France must be increased, under the permanent control of a council composed of representatives of Parliament, of the executive authority, and of the main organized forces of labor and of industrial, commercial, and agricultural activity. The capital of the Bank must be converted into debentures, with measures to safeguard the interests of small shareholders.

IV. Financial Purification

Control of the trade in armaments, in conjunction with the nationalization of armaments industries. Prevention of waste in the civil and military departments.

Establishment of a War Pensions Fund.

Democratic reform of the system of taxation so as to relax the fiscal burden blocking economic recovery, and raising revenue by measures against large fortunes. Rapid steepening of income tax on incomes above 75,000 francs a year. Reorganization of death duties. Special taxes on monopoly profits, but in such a way as to have no effects on retail prices. Suppression of fraud in connection with transferable securities by bringing into force the fiscal identity card which has been voted by Parliament, together with an amnesty on past tax evasions.

Control of export of capital, and punishment of evasion by rigorous measures, including confiscation of property concealed abroad or of its equivalent value in France.

77. *The Plot of the Hooded Men, 1937*

TWENTY-FIVE years after this abortive *putsch*, a retired general, who at that time held high office as colonel in an army headquarters in Paris, related the goings-on of that dramatic night of November 15–16.

The general belongs to the classic Right. He is a soldier by tradition, and faithful to the noble heritage of the French army: Honor and Country. He is worried and cannot help half-approving the measures of self-defense in the army. But he is disciplined and condemns the *Cagoule* unreservedly because the army is at the service of the State. Any other rule leads to adventure, and the army becomes the loser.

This general is given the code name of "Cold water" by the *Cagoule*.

"One evening," he relates, "Deloncle and his men get in touch with me. I am called to an apartment in the rue de Bourgogne. The hour has struck, explain Deloncle and General Duseigneur. The revolution is about to break out. At 1:30 A.M. tonight, after public transport has stopped, Communist troops will be on the move through the tunnels of the Métro. They will progress toward the vital centers, at the same time as surface troops.

" 'We have ready for you a battalion of our armed men to protect the *École Militaire*.'

" 'We are going to set up a battery of machine guns round the Élysée. The greater part of our troops are waiting round the gates into Paris. There is one minute to go. So there it is, Colonel. It is your duty to go to the Ministry for War, nearby, and warn Daladier that revolution has broken out. In any case, the Minister will not be surprised. This afternoon we sent him a first note of information by a politician. If Daladier refuses to put the plan of defense into operation, it will be our duty to arrest him immediately. For God's sake, don't delay. Any moment now it will be too late.'

"In front of me," the general goes on, "the *Cagoulard* leaders exchange mysterious telephonic communications. They assure me that gunfire can be heard in Paris! Although strongly affected, I refuse to make any official move before receiving categorical proof of a Communist march.

"All the same, I make contact with the officer on night duty at the rue Saint Dominique, to make sure that M. Daladier could be reached immediately if need be.

"The whole night is spent like this. The *Cagoulards* keep on coming back with 'We beg you to intervene. Inform Daladier. Sound the alarm!'

"I remain inflexible and reply, 'I shall wait for the first incidents. I shall act only then.'

"Dawn rises. Paris is absolutely quiet. I leave these gentlemen with a parting shot: 'I quite understand. Your story of a *putsch* was nothing but a lamentable farce.' "

78. *The National Revolution at Vichy, 1940*

Marshal Pétain: Message to the French People, October 11, 1940

FRENCHMEN!

Four months ago France received one of the biggest defeats in her history.

This defeat has many causes, but not all are of a technical nature. In reality the disaster is but the reflection in the military sphere of the weaknesses and blemishes of the old political régime.

Yet many of you were attached to that régime. As you voted every four years, you had the impression that you were free citizens in a free State, so you will be surprised when I say that never in the history of France has the State been more enslaved than in the course of the last twenty years.

Enslaved in various ways: successively, sometimes simultaneously, by coalitions of economic interests and by political or trade-union gangs claiming, fallaciously, to represent the working class. According to the predominance of one or the other of these two servitudes, majorities succeeded one another in power, too often bent only on defeating the rival minority. These struggles produced disasters. Then recourse was had to those vast groupings known as "National Unions," which were just another form of deception. For coherence is not achieved by bringing together divergent strands. "One will" is not obtained by adding up the number of men of good will.

The mark of these oscillations and this bondage was imprinted deeply in our way of life. Everything showed only too plainly the impotence of a régime which could survive the gravest circumstances only by renouncing itself and turning to *pleins pouvoirs* [plenary powers]. It was thus moving swiftly toward political revolution, and this was merely hastened by the war and the defeat.

And since the régime was a prisoner to this internal policy, it was usually unable to adopt a foreign policy worthy of France.

Inspired in turn first by touchy nationalism, then by unbridled pacificism, compounded of misunderstanding and weakness—at a time when our victory should have made us strong and generous—our foreign policy could only lead to the abyss. We have spent not more than fifteen years descending the slope that led to this abyss.

One day in September, 1939, without even daring to consult the Chambers, war was declared, a war almost lost already. We had not known how to avoid nor how to prepare for that war.

On this mound of ruins we must now reconstruct France.

The new order must not in any sense imply a return, even disguised, to the mistakes that have cost us so much; nor should we look for signs of a sort of "moral order," or revenge for the events of 1936.

The new order must not be a slavish imitation of other people's experiments. Some of these experiments are not without meaning or beauty. But every people should conceive a régime adapted to its climate and its national spirit.

The new order is a necessity for France. We must bring about in defeat, tragically, the revolution that in victory, in peace, in the voluntary alliance of equal peoples, we were unable to achieve.

External policy: a national régime

The task that France must accomplish is independent of the reverses of her arms, and must be independent also, and with even greater need, of the successes or reverses of other nations which have been her friends or enemies in the past.

The new régime, to be truly national, must free itself of these friendships or these enmities that have been called traditional but which in fact have gone on changing right through history to the greater profit of the moneylenders and traders in armaments.

The new régime will defend, first and foremost, national unity, which means close union of metropolitan France with France overseas.

It will maintain the heritage of its Greek and Latin culture and their effulgence in the world.

It will restore true nationalism, which refuses to concentrate on itself alone but goes beyond itself to attain international collaboration.

France is ready to seek this collaboration in every domain and with all her neighbors. She knows, moreover, whatever the political map of Europe and of the world, that the problem of Franco-German relations, which has been so criminally treated in the past, will continue to determine her future.

Germany can, without doubt, after her victory over our arms, choose between a traditional peace of oppression and an entirely new peace of collaboration.

Instead of the misery, the troubles, the repressions, and doubtless the conflicts that would be aroused by a new peace made in the old-fashioned style, Germany may prefer an invigorating peace for the victor, a peace that will engender the well-being of all.

The choice lies first of all with the victor; it depends also on the vanquished.

If all paths are closed to us, we shall know how to wait and how to suffer.

If, on the contrary, hope does rise over the world, we shall know how to dominate our humiliation, our mourning, our ruins. In the presence of a victor who has known how to dominate his victory, we shall know how to dominate our defeat.

Internal policy: a hierarchical social régime

The new régime will be a social hierarchy. It will not rest on the false idea of the material equality of men but on the necessary idea of the equality of opportunity given to all Frenchmen to prove their ability to serve.

Work and talent will become the sole bases of the French hierarchy. No unfavorable prejudice will count against any Frenchman on the score of his social origins, on the sole condition that he identifies himself with the new France and is prepared to help unreservedly. Class struggle, fatal to a nation, cannot be got rid of without getting rid of the causes that have made these classes, and raised one against the other.

So will arise the true élites, which the former régime spent years destroying, and which will form the *cadres* needed for the well-being and dignity of all.

Some may fear that the new hierarchy will destroy the liberty to which they cling and for which their fathers fought at the price of their blood.

They need have no fear.

Authority is necessary to safeguard the liberty of the State, the guarantee of individual liberties, against coalitions of private interests. A people is no longer free, in spite of its voting papers, when the government it has freely brought to power becomes the prisoner of its coalitions.

What does freedom, abstract freedom, mean in 1940 to the unemployed worker or the ruined small employer—except freedom to suffer helplessly in a vanquished nation?

We are really losing only some deceptive illusions of freedom, in order to make sure of saving the substance.

History is made up of alternations between periods of authority degenerating into tyranny, and periods of liberty generating licence. The hour has come for France to replace these powerful alternations by a harmonious union of authority and liberty.

The hierarchical character of the new régime is inseparable from its social character.

But this social character cannot be based on theoretical declarations. It must be made manifest in deeds. It must be turned into immediate practical measures.

It is the first duty of all Frenchmen—workers, farmers, civil servants, technicians, and employers—to work. Those who disregard this duty do not deserve to be called citizens. But all French people have also the right to work. It will be readily understood that to ensure that this right may be exercised and this duty enforced, a complete revolution of our old economic system must be carried out.

After a transition period when installation of new plants will be speeded up and spread over the whole country, we shall be able, in an organized economy, to create permanent centers of activity where each will have the job and the wage suited to his ability.

Schemes must be adapted to the various occupations if they are to be efficient. A scheme that is suitable for industry would certainly not suit family farming, which is the chief economic and social basis of France.

But there are some general principles which apply to all occupations.

These occupations will be organized and their organizations will apply to all.

Occupational organizations will deal with everything concerning the trade, but will be limited to a purely occupational sphere. With the authority of the State they will ensure that labor agreements are carried out. They will guarantee the dignity of the individual worker, by improving his standard of living right into his old age.

Economic policy: a coordinated economy and money in the service of that economy

They will avoid conflicts, by forbidding lockouts absolutely, and by forbidding strikes, by compulsory arbitration before labor tribunals.

The economic régime of the last years displayed the same imperfections and the same contradictions as the political régime.

On the parliamentary level there was a semblance of freedom. On the level of production and on the stock exchange there was a semblance of liberalism, but there was in reality servitude to the power of money and an ever greater recourse to State intervention.

This degradation of economic liberalism is easily explained.

Free competition was both the mainspring and the regulator of the liberal régime. From the moment when the coalitions and trusts smashed this essential mechanism, production and prices were abandoned defenseless to the spirit of profit and speculation.

And so the revolting drama was played out of millions of men in dire want, in the face of stocks unsold and even destroyed with the sole purpose of maintaining the markets in raw materials.

And so the world crisis crept nearer. Faced with the universal bankruptcy of economic liberalism, nearly every nation has started a new economic development. We, too, must start anew in this field and by exercise of our energy and faith make up for time lost.

Two essential principles will be our guides: the economy must be organized and controlled. Coordination of private activities by the State must break the influence of the trusts and their powers of corruption. Far from curbing individual initiative, the economy must free it from its present fetters by subordinating it to the national interest.

Money should be at the service of the economy. It should make possible the full development of production with stability of prices and wages.

Healthy money is primarily money which allows men's needs to be satisfied. Our new monetary system will not therefore affect gold except by the guarantee of external regulations. It will gauge interior circulation by the needs of production.

Such a system implies double control.

On the international plane, control of external commerce and stock exchanges so as to subordinate to national needs the use of monetary symbols on foreign markets.

Internally, vigilant control of consumption and prices, so as to curb the purchasing power of money, prevent excessive expenditure and produce a fairer distribution of production.

This system will not impair men's freedom except the freedom of those who speculate for personal or political gain.

It has been devised solely in the national interest. It must be administered with unyielding severity in these times of great hardship.

Let the working classes and the bourgeoisie together make an immense effort to escape from idle routine and become aware of their common interest as citizens in a nation henceforth united.

Conclusion

Frenchmen, that is the task I now ask you to perform.

We must reconstruct.

I want to achieve this reconstruction with your support.

The Constitution will be the legal expression of a Revolution already begun in fact, for institutions are of value only through the spirit which they embody.

A Revolution cannot be made only through laws and decrees. It can be successful only if the nation understands it, and asks for it, if the people accompanies the Government along the path of essential renewal.

Soon I shall ask you to come together, so that, assembled round me, in fellowship with the ex-servicemen already formed into a Legion, you may lead this Revolution to its conclusion, by rallying those who hesitate, breaking up hostile forces and combined interests, so that in this new France true national fraternity may reign supreme.

Part IV: External Relations

The first three Parts of this volume have dealt, in turn, with the State, the National Economy, and Social Conflicts. Their emphasis has been on internal conditions and events, and the attitudes of Frenchmen, individually or in groups, to these conditions and events. Even so, external relations, whether in religious, military, or economic matters, have been found to have constant relevance to internal affairs, and vice versa. Because France, throughout this period, rated as one of the major powers of Europe, and become one of the world's largest colonial powers, it would be possible to devote at least as much space to external as to internal developments. This will not be attempted in this final Part.

Documents have been selected with a simpler aim in mind: to illustrate the kinds of relation established by France with underdeveloped parts of the world, especially with Africa and Indochina, on the one hand, and with her main European neighbors on the other. The brief section on colonial history demonstrates the diversity of urges and considerations which lay behind French expansion overseas, and the tendency for tension to be generated between the administrator on the spot and public opinion and policy in Paris. Section B, on foreign relations, emphasizes the gulfs which came in 1871, 1919, and 1940, and indicates some of the problems and policies emerging in the intervals. And again, as with internal affairs, attention is concentrated on attitudes and conflicts of attitude toward national problems, rather than on any systematic survey of events.

SECTION A: COLONIAL RELATIONS

79. The White Fathers: Cardinal Lavigerie, October 29, 1874

Christian missionaries were ubiquitous and active throughout the nineteenth century, with Roman Catholic missions prominent among them. The French, it was estimated, provided some 40,000 out of the 60,000 Catholic missionaries of the 1870's. They were at work in India and China, Japan and Korea, Canada and the Pacific. But apart from Egypt and Ethiopia, they had made little impact upon Africa until the 1870's.

At the end of the Second Empire, Marshal MacMahon as Governor of Algeria and Cardinal Lavigerie, who became Archbishop of Algiers in 1868, clashed on the issue of whether to give a Christian education to the thousand orphans rescued from the famine, or restore them to Islam. Lavigerie won, and for the next seven years civil and ecclesiastical authorities cooperated to build hospitals and provide welfare in Algeria. In 1869 he founded the Society of African Missionaries (*Société des missionaires d'Afrique*), recruiting in France and the Low Countries and training especially for African conditions. Because they adopted the flowing Arab dress, they became known as the "White Fathers." His instructions were to go among the poor infidels and win first their affection, then their confidence, finally their souls. A female order of White Sisters—the *Soeurs missionaires de Notre-Dame d'Afrique*—was also formed. On October 29, 1874, in the presence of General Chanzy, then Governor of Algeria, Lavigerie inaugurated the motherhouse of la Maison Carrée near Algiers and addressed the novices in the terms given below. The famous address expresses precisely the conviction of the main missionary impulse, that in doing God's work in Africa they were also simultaneously advancing the aims and interests of France and the cause of civilization. It was the patriotic doctrine of France's "civilizing mission" in its purest form, and it proved most effective. No account of imperial expansion in this age should omit this dynamic element. The White Fathers spread throughout Tunisia and into the Sahara, often enduring the suffering and the fate of which Lavigerie had warned the novices. They warred against barbarism and the slave trade, and won converts by the force of example.

For the French text and other details, see Mgr. L. Baunard, *Le cardinal Lavigerie* (2 vols., Paris, J. de Gigord, 1922), Vol. I, Chapter XVI; and E. Lecanuet, *L'église de France sous la troisième république 1870–1878* (Paris, Ancienne librairie poussielgue, 1910), Chapter XI, p. 460.

I LOOK at you, my dear children, and see in your faces all the brightness and vigor of youth. I think of what you have left behind, family, country, and earthly hopes; and of all that awaits you in return: insults, suffering, cruel death. I look at you and think that you are the children of Catholic France. And I cannot refrain from thinking once more of our native land, and from feeling confidence in her, because God guards there so many hearts ready to be inspired to heroic and pure devotion.

No thought of self-interest or of glory spurs you on. You will lack food and shelter; you will die ignored by the world, maybe in frightful torture. This is the only promise I have made to you. But you know, and that suffices, that you serve a Master who can apportion his reward according to his servant's deserts.

Go forth, then, in the name of God and with His help. Succor the little ones, relieve the suffering, comfort them that weep, heal the sick. It will be the honor of the Church to see you spreading your work of charity step by step, right to the center of this immense continent. It will be the honor of France to see you completing her work, by carrying Christian civilization far beyond her conquests into this unknown world whose gates have been thrown open with such glory by the valor of her captains. And if, my dear sons, you find hostility in this country, as a result of the irreligious passions which unhappily lead astray a section of this colony, do not doubt that so long as you can combine devotion with wisdom, you will always find protectors among the eminent men whose noble qualities and impartial justice endow with such high honor the government, the army, the law, the magistrature and the administration of Algeria.

It is in their disinterested love of the good that I dare place my confidence, for the time, soon perhaps, when my voice can no longer defend you.

As for me, whether God calls me to him soon, or leaves me a little longer in this world, I shall not cease thanking Him for making me the father of your souls. I shall not cease asking Him to keep alive in you the pure flame which His Hands have kindled.

80. *Colonialism and Industrial Growth:* *Jules Ferry, 1890*

The name pre-eminently associated with the remarkable colonial expansion of France in the last quarter of the nineteenth century is that of Jules Ferry (1832–1893), a leading Republican opponent of the Second Empire, Mayor of Paris during the siege of 1870 and 1871, and champion of the anticlericalist laws on education during the 1880's. He would hardly seem to conform to the prototype of the great nineteenth-century imperialists—scarcely a Cecil Rhodes or a Theodore Roosevelt.

Ferry's views about colonialism looked like treachery to the more conventionally nationalistic Radicals, who held that any diversion of French strength or resources from the problem of security against Germany on the Rhine was simply unpatriotic. And he found himself an incongruous ally, on the other hand, of churchmen promoting missions and soldiers suppressing colonial uprisings. Here, again, divisions into Right and Left seemed to be uncomfortably scrambled. What prompted Ferry in these policies, which brought him intense unpopularity and brought down his ministry in 1885, is not made any easier to unravel by the fact that he seldom enunciated any clear principles or coherent philosophy of imperialism. He was content to act empirically as opportunities offered in Tunisia or Morocco, Madagascar or Tonkin. But on two occasions, at least, he came close to enunciating a general theory.

One occasion was during the debate in the Chamber of Deputies on July 28, 1885, on an appropriation for Madagascar. He ranged over the whole gamut of defenses for seeking to control colonial territories: Madagascar was primarily useful as a naval base and an addition to French prestige (the strategic-prestige argument); the value of Tonkin was that it gave access "to that enormous market of 400 million consumers . . . not poor blacks, like the inhabitants of equatorial Africa" (the industrial-economic argument); and as regards colonial expeditions in Africa and elsewhere, "we were led to them by that obligation and duty that are imposed on all civilized people to make the signature of their representatives respected by barbarous nations," and the work of a Brazza in equatorial Africa was surely a true civilizing mission (the humanitarian-civilizing argument). He placed special emphasis on economic purpose, linking it with the severe effects of the long industrial and commercial depression and presenting imperialism as an indispensable outlet for capital investment and as a market for industrial products. It is this argument that he emphasized even more strongly in his Preface to a book called *Tonkin et la Mère-Patrie* (Paris, 1890) by Léon Sentupéry. The extract translated below serves to illustrate his central theme, akin to Lenin's theory of a "glut of capital," and comes as close as may be possible to identifying Ferry's basic attitude. French text in Paul Robiquet, *Discours et opinions de Jules Ferry*, Vol. V (Paris, Armand Colin, 1897), pp. 557-9. See also T. F. Power, Jr., *Jules Ferry and the Renaissance of French Imperialism* (New York, 1944).

. . . COLONIAL POLICY is the daughter of industrial policy. For wealthy States, where capital abounds and accumulates rapidly, where the manufacturing element is growing continuously, attracting the most energetic and restless if not the most numerous section of that part of the population which lives by manual labor —where cultivation of the soil itself is forced to become mechanized in order to survive—exports are an essential factor of public prosperity. The spread of capital, like the demand for work, is measured by the extent of the foreign market. If manufacturing nations had been able to arrange a division of industrial labor, a systematic and rational allocation of industry according to the aptitudes, economic, natural, and social conditions of the different producer countries, setting the cotton industry here, metallurgy there, reserving alcohols and sugars for one, woolens and silks for the other, Europe might not have needed markets for its products beyond its own boundaries. But nowadays everybody wants to spin and weave, forge and distil. All Europe refines far too much sugar and wants to export it. The United States on one hand, and Germany on the other, have entered the stage as the last-comers to manufacturing industry. The starting of an industrial era in all its forms for the little states, from peoples who were dormant or exhausted, for Italy regenerated, for Spain enriched by French capital, for the Swiss who are so enterprising and so shrewd, all these factors have placed the whole of the West, except so far Russia, who is growing and nearly ready, on a slope which we shall not ascend again.

On the other side of the Vosges and across the Atlantic the protective-tariff system has increased manufactures, closed former outlets and introduced strong competition into the European market. Defending oneself by raising barriers in return is some help, but not enough. M. Torrens has very ably shown in his fine book on the colonization of Australia that if an increase in manufacturing capital was not accompanied by a proportionate extension of foreign outlets, it tended to produce a general decrease in prices, profits, and wages, as a result of internal competition. (Torrens, *Colonization of South Australia*)

The protective system is like a steam engine without a safety valve if it has no healthy, genuine colonial policy as a corrective and auxiliary. The plethora of capital invested in industry tends not only to diminish the profits from capital, but to halt the rise in wages, which is nevertheless the natural beneficent law of modern societies. Nor is it an abstract law, but a being compounded of flesh and bone, passion and will, which moves, complains and defends itself. In the industrial age of humanity, social peace is a question of outlets. The economic crisis which has weighed so heavily on working Europe since 1876 or 1877, the malaise which has resulted, of which long frequent strikes, often ill-advised but always significant, are the most painful symptom, has coincided in France, Germany, and even England, with a notable and persistent reduction in export figures. Europe can be compared to a commercial firm which has seen its business decreasing over a number of years. The European consumer market is saturated. New layers of consumers must be brought in from other parts of the globe. If this is not done, modern society will go bankrupt, and as the

twentieth century dawns, social liquidation will have been prepared by way of a cataclysm with incalculable consequences.

It is because England was the first to perceive those distant
horizons that she has headed the modern industrial movement. It is
because of possible setbacks which her industrial hegemony could
suffer through the detachment of Australia and India, after the
separation of the United States from North America, that she is
laying siege to Africa on four fronts: on the south, through the
Cape plateau and Bechuanaland; on the west through the Niger
and the Congo; on the northeast, through the valley of the Nile;
and on the east through Suakin, the Somali coast, and the basin of
the great equatorial lakes. In order to prevent British enterprise
from capturing for its exclusive profit the new markets that are
opening up for western products, Germany is opposing England at
all points of the globe with a rivalry which is as inconvenient as it
was unexpected. Colonial policy is an international manifestation
of the eternal laws of competition. . . .

81. *Lyautey in Morocco, 1913*

Greatest of all the colonial proconsuls of the Third Republic, who left
his mark on the administration of the whole of French North Africa,
was Marshal Hubert Lyautey (1854–1934). His career shows how interwoven were the roles of soldier and of colonial administrator, and the
translated excerpt from one of his despatches from Morocco as Resident-
General deals with this very combination of military and civil duties.
The tasks of conquest and pacification merged into those of keeping
order and of constructing the basic administrative services of a modern
State. Governments in Paris too rarely appreciated this, and parliamentary politicians temperamentally hostile to colonial expansion as
well as to militarism tried to enforce distinctions, both financial and
functional, which seemed entirely fictitious to the man on the spot.
Lyautey was never slow to voice his views on such failures to appreciate
realities. This is an example of such protest.

Morocco was by this time a familiar bone of international contention, as shown in Document 86. It was largely because of the work of
Lyautey and his staff that it held together at all as one unit. The dual
rôle of the French army, as military keeper of order and paternalist
provider of public services, remained important and was to assume crucial importance in the long but unavailing effort, between 1945 and
1962, to keep Algeria as part of France, "assimilated" in administration to metropolitan France itself. In company with Jules Ferry, political champion of modern colonialism, Lyautey insisted that far from

detracting (as its opponents held) from the defense and security of France, the overseas Empire was the best training ground for French troops and a powerful reinforcement of French manpower. As a son of Lorraine, he was never unaware of home defense. He it was who coined the conception that "France is a nation of 100 million." Even so, it was 1894 before a permanent Ministry of Colonies was created (with no authority over North Africa). Then frequent changes of minister prevented a coherent policy at the center, while leaving considerable independence to the proconsuls on the periphery.

French text in *Lyautey l'African: Textes et lettres du Maréchal Lyautey présentés par Pierre Lyautey*, Vol. I, pp. 238–41 and 243–4 (Paris, Librairie Plon, 1953), by whose permission the extracts are given. See also the popular biography by André Maurois (Eng. trans., London, 1931), *Marshal Lyautey;* and the "authorized life" by Sonia E. Howe, *Lyautey of Morocco* (London, 1931).

Role of the army in organizing the Protectorate
Rabat, June 2, 1913

. . . As REGARDS the credits in detail and discussion of them step by step, I am sending Colonel Pelle to Paris. He is in command of the Moroccan auxiliary troops and is acting as my chief of staff. He will be able to produce the necessary explanations and justifications.

But there is a question of principle on which I wish to express my point of view quite clearly: the argument that army outlay which appears not to be of a strictly military nature should be thrown out of the War Estimates.

I believe on the contrary that the proper rule, indeed the only one that meets the needs of the situation, is to start from exactly the opposite principle.

During the first years of occupation all installations are confined solely to military requirements.

If over the past year the conditions and facilities of this command have been radically changed, provisioning and transport of military supplies, and evacuation of the sick and wounded being carried out with an ease hitherto unknown, it is because there has been an over-all effort little short of a *tour de force* to provide tracks, roads, bridges, and telegraph systems. If forts, garrisons, and camps have become healthier, it is because a water supply has been installed.

As for construction of hospital buildings, the hutments in which civilian cases have been treated in the military hospitals of Casablanca and Rabat have been constructed at the expense of the Protectorate.

As far as organization of navigation services on certain *wadis* is concerned, I know only of the Sebou Wadi, which until now has been used exclusively for military transport.

Yes, I am proud to report that, thanks to the efforts of the troops and their officers, it is now possible to travel on tracks in good condition, open to horse-drawn and motor vehicles, from Rabat to Fez, Casablanca to Marrakesh, and from Mogador to Marrakesh, and which give access to the majority of military stations.

Bridges have been thrown over rivers which detachments of troops used to take hours to cross by ferry or to wade through with the water waist-deep.

There are scarcely any stations which are not connected by telegraph.

The command, troops, supplies, sick, and wounded receive the chief benefit of this situation.

It is obvious that the civilian native and European population also benefit, but is that a crime? Should a road or a bridge be closed to commerce, to the caravans, which are, in their turn, an element of pacification and in the forefront of those elements counterbalancing military strength, by the very fact that they have been set up with allocations from the War Office?

Moreover, there is no question at all of identical expenditure "drawn simultaneously from State funds and from the future loan."

TRACKS AND ROADS

It stands to reason that I establish a connection between my Public Works manager and my military services so that the strategic tracks which I have laid down as soon as I occupy a new country follow the line of the permanent road. This means that there is no waste of effort and all the work carried out on the strategic tracks can be used later for the permanent roads. I do not think anyone could reproach me for doing this and thus avoiding at all costs what I have seen in so many countries: military works parallel to public works, having the same purpose, but separated by a watertight compartment, ignoring yet duplicating each other.

If I try to avoid this stupid heresy, it is no less true that I am concerned with works of quite a different nature. Military tracks serve only one purpose, to provide immediate temporary viability by attending only to the most difficult sections with just occasional stretches of stone surfacing. It will be the task of the Public Works to complete the roads according to the permanent plan and carry out other important modifications, by means of the loan fund. Besides, tracks are laid down along a number of lines leading to military stations where there are no plans for roads coming out of the loan fund.

Bridges are erected temporarily and very seldom, and only when it is impossible to do without them until permanent bridges are erected out of the loan fund.

I think no one will question my duty to link all my military stations by telegraph, for it is of primary importance for their safety and for the smooth working of all the services. I fail to understand why any suggestion on this point should be made.

But I venture to draw your attention to another point. If the works for purely military use had not been carried out with War Office allocations they would not have been done at all. If they had had to come out of the Protectorate account, or from the loan fund, they would have had to run the gantlet of all the clauses in the Act of Algerciras and of the Franco-German agreement; they would have had to submit to tenders and delays and be laid before the diplomatic corps of Tangiers. Then again, the Protectorate has no money, the loan has not been voted, and consequently all the preliminary work of installation essential to the military penetration and occupation of this country would be suspended.

Given the fact that the least important public works in this unfortunate country are burdened by a terrible mortgage, and are seriously impeded by international clauses and obstructions that no other colony or Protectorate has had to bear in its beginnings, the French State ought to be only too happy to permit extensive development of military works, which would at least remove from the preliminary improvements essential to the life of the country the need for tenders and inspection.

I have heard that there was surprise that the service of Remounts should be made a charge on the War Budget, under the pretext that it is connected with horse-breeding, which can be considered a civilian service. What monkey tricks are these? We need cavalry most of all here. Algeria cannot supply any more horses, so we must find enough to remount our squadrons and to breed more. The setting up of the Service of Remounts has been pushed ahead so vigorously and intelligently that it has found great favor with the natives. It will certainly form the nucleus for experiments in scientific stud farming.

Shall we be reproached therefore that in this country, where everything has to be started from scratch, our military service should serve as a basis for institutions which will later benefit the Protectorate?

But without blowing my own trumpet, for my units and the regional commanders deserve all the praise, I can say full well that during the last year we have had incomparable achievements, and almost everywhere the troops are quartered in conditions that have not been reached elsewhere after several years. General health and medical statistics give striking proof of this. It is undeniable that such a result has only been obtained at a certain price, and the price is high owing to the high cost of labor, transport and materials. But this first outlay is essential and should on no account be niggardly.

Algeria took fifty years to conquer and pacify. It is only two years since we came out of the narrow limits of Chaouia to go to Fez.

It is one year since I took command, and I would just ask you to look at the map to realize the advance in pacified territories.

I have not asked for any reinforcements since the month of September, 1912. I know that there are none to send.

I am faced with a country and a population of at least four times what we found on arriving in Algeria, but fanatical in a quite different way, united, well-armed, and sustained by strange incitements which we never came across during the conquest of Algeria.

I am well aware that the European situation does not allow any more troops to be sent, and I said from the start that France must at least give me money to compensate for the men she cannot give.

It seemed then that this obligation was recognized without demur and accepted with enthusiasm.

But now I find that all the allocations on which I thought I could rely are being challenged.

First the loan: at the beginning of the year it looked as if it would be voted almost without discussion, and so allow me to start large-scale works, early in 1913, which would be spread over the country and attract local labor. These would have contributed in large measure to pacification and would have relieved my heavy military burden.

Now there are doubts about military credits. I might add that France has not given me one centime for political funds, and the only ones at my disposal are those I am authorized to levy on the Budget of the Protectorate, which is scarcely solvent. It is like telling somebody to put in his right pocket what is in his left pocket—and it is empty. Is there any operation in colonial history which has not been given large political funds in the early stages? Is it likely that the English would have succeeded in the Transvaal with such methods?

Coming nearer home—I am convinced that the Spaniards who were in charge of the business at Melilla were able to take advantage of a very different state of affairs.

I consider that I am burdened with the heaviest task imposed on any man for a long time; my troops have reached the limit of what they can be asked to do, voting for the loan appears to be receding daily and is meeting with new objections at every turn, the military credits are being subjected to more intense criticism and are threatened with reductions.

France cannot give me any men. If she can give me neither money nor means, I can but ask myself how I can accomplish my task.

82. *Colonial Defense in 1939:*
Admiral Decoux (*1949*)

The eternal tensions between service chiefs and colonial administrators on the outposts, and civilian and parliamentary rulers in Paris who accept advantages but are reluctant to pay for them in men and money, were apparent throughout all French colonial history. The extracts from General (later Marshal) Lyautey in Morocco (Document 81) are one example of this conflict. Another is the failure of the home government to think out and implement any coherent policy of imperial defense, here voiced in bitter tones by the man who was entrusted to defend Indochina from the Japanese in 1940, Admiral Decoux. Decoux succeeded General Catroux as Governor-General of Indochina soon after the Armistice in 1940 when, under the influence of Admiral Jean Darlan, it became normal to appoint admirals to key administrative posts in the overseas territories. (Other admirals went to Tunisia, Algeria, and Martinique, and in September Admiral Platon was made

Minister for the Colonies.) Decoux proved himself skillful at enacting reforms which kept the allegiance of many Indochinese for Pétainism, while limiting the effects of partial Japanese occupation. His achievement as administrator was parallel with Vichy's own subtle tightrope performance—essentially *attentisme*, or playing for time and awaiting the outcome of larger events. But in Indochina, as he argues, such a policy was dictated not by Hitler so much as by the inept defense strategy adopted by France before war had even begun.

Decoux's years of autocratic rule in Indochina were a strange mixture of benefits and disasters. Under pressure from Japan to cut off supplies to Chiang Kai-shek by closing the Indochinese border with China, he yielded what he regarded as "the unavoidable minimum," demanding in return Japan's recognition of French sovereignty. His reforms, including an attack on illiteracy and inefficient administration, made his rule more liberal than any under the Third Republic. But corruption also grew, there were huge rackets in currency and opium, and the net result was a surging desire for national independence, spurred by Japan's overthrow of the French régime for a brief spell in 1945. The chief beneficiary of the interlude was Ho Chi Minh and the Vietminh National Liberation Front.

The extract is a translation of pages from Decoux's memoirs, *À la barre de l'Indochine, 1940–1945* (Paris, Librairie Plon, 1949), pp. 74–6, by whose permission it is included. His account of his interview with General de Gaulle, on October 14, 1945, after his return to France (pp. 476–81) is a classic of mocking irony. It must be noted, of course, that the book was published in 1949 and was intended to be, retrospectively, a vindication of his own conduct as a proconsul of Vichy.

WHAT WERE the guiding lines of our colonial policy on the eve of the Second World War? I think they can be summed up as follows:

1. In the event of a new world conflict, the fate of the French Empire, and in particular that of Indochina, will be settled in Europe, or to be more exact, on the Rhine. Given the dearth of effectives, owing to the sparse years for conscription and the reduction of military service, the major part of the first-line troops must be concentrated in the home country, which has priority. The overseas territories will face the situation with the means at their disposal from peacetime. And if some "mobile forces," composed of 25,000 colonials and 22,000 North Africans, have been constituted in France to come to the help of the overseas territories in case of need, the underlying idea really is that these forces will not leave the home country in the event of war with Germany.

2. Therefore, in 1939 there is not only no question of sending reinforcements to Indochina at a time of danger, but on the contrary, the French command expects Indochina to send to the Mediterranean at the start of mobilization large contingents of nonspecialized colonial workmen (O.N.S.) or riflemen. And, in fact, as soon as the new conflict had begun instructions for war were given to this effect. We shall be coming back to these later.

3. The most urgent problems which ought to command our attention outside Europe are the maintenance of order in North Africa, safeguarding the North African—Black African block, and the firm re-establishment of French authority in the Near East. This directive is not my interpretation. It appears in full in note 852 DN3 of October 12, 1938, as "relative to the present situation," bearing the stamp of the general secretariat of the Superior Council of National Defense and signed by Gamelin. As can be seen, Indochina is not even mentioned.

4. The interests of France and Great Britain are, moreover, indissolubly linked in Asia as elsewhere. In the eventuality of a future conflict, our command can rely on the immediate assistance of Britain and accessory help from the United States.

5. Japan is dominated by her expansionist policy in China and has been bogged down in this immense continent since the beginning of the second incident in China (1937). In the course of the two years which have passed since this event, the Japanese forces have not achieved any decisive success in eastern Asia.

6. On the other hand, Japan is absorbed by surveillance of Russia, thus contributing to a large extent to keeping her in the Far East. As Japan is obliged to use all her resources in carrying out these two missions of prime importance, the Japanese Empire does not appear to be able at the moment to embark on any extensive land operation.

All these preconceived ideas appear, expressed more or less word for word, in the official documents, put out right through the year 1938 by the secretariat of the Superior Council for National Defense. I have already quoted certain characteristic passages.

Thus, in the minds of our rulers at that time, French Indochina seemed to be then, even more than formerly, a colony where nothing had ever happened, particularly during the First World

War, and where nothing would happen if there were a new war in Europe. What is more, the Government of the Third Republic based its policy for Indochina—I should say its lack of policy—on the fact that in the Far East the Anglo-Saxon powers were obviously in control. Accordingly, France could not thereupon help falling into step along the line of diplomatic action more or less pre-arranged between Washington and London. And if ever the situation became tense in eastern Asia or in the Pacific, French Indochina would probably not be directly threatened in the event of armed conflict in this part of the world. We could, then, defy Japan with impunity by sheltering behind England and the United States in the thorny controversy of the transit of merchandise to Nationalist China.

Until 1940 these over-simple concepts provided the French Government with a good excuse for their general directive, which consisted in not foreseeing anything serious happening in the Far East. Such a conception of the position of Indochina in time of war was frivolous and dangerous; all the more so when, during the first four months of 1939, Japanese forces occupied Hainan and the Spratley archipelago, which France claimed. A Japanese observation unit had meanwhile been installed on the orders of Tokyo in the Paracels, where we had recently maintained our sovereignty. From this moment French Indochina was threatened by the expansionist aims of Tokyo. This threat was to increase when, in November, 1939, three Japanese divisions disembarked in the Gulf of Tonkin to start operations in the Kwang-Si.

A few months earlier, in June, 1939, the Franco-British conference I have already mentioned had taken place in Singapore.

The weakness of the English defenses had been made clear on that occasion, but we had realized even more clearly, from that moment, that if there was a threat of war with Japan, our future allies were quite decided on holding a line of defense for their Empire consisting of Burma, Malaysia, the Dutch Indies, Australia, and New Zealand.

The Americans on their side seemed more and more convinced (as we shall see when we examine the conflict in the Pacific) that in such circumstances they would be likely to lose the Philippines soon after hostilities had begun.

Therefore, if there were suddenly grave events one day in Asia, and Great Britain and the United States found that they were unable to give France any substantial military or naval support in this theater of war on the periphery, Indochina ran the risk of being left in a dangerous vacuum, isolated on the line of outposts and therefore abandoned to Japanese offensives in this remote war area. This was exactly what did happen in 1940.

The Government of the Republic was completely convinced by the preconceived ideas we discussed earlier, and did not see the danger. Or if it did have an inkling it pretended in any case to be unaware of it. From the outset it was necessary to get the record straight about this moment in history.

SECTION B: FOREIGN RELATIONS

France's expansion overseas and her relations with her European neighbors were closely intertwined, and at points conflicted. Colonial rivalries in Africa with Great Britain cut across the need to secure British support against Germany. German policy could even encourage French colonialism as a diversion away from the urge to revenge defeat in 1871. Champions of the "lost provinces" of Alsace and Lorraine almost instinctively opposed extending French power into Indochina, and so on. For all these reasons colonial and foreign policies must be seen as merely different aspects of how the French State and nation regarded their dealings with the rest of the world.

Until 1919, French foreign policy, like that of all other powers, operated in a world of "international anarchy," in the sense that although a mesh of international agreements and undertakings had indeed come into existence, there was no organized system for promoting or keeping peace. Diplomacy operated according to certain agreed principles of balance of power and somewhat feverish rivalries in accumulating military and naval might, and constructing alliances. From 1919 onward the success of the new League of Nations, as its membership was composed, depended primarily on the concerted action of France and Britain to make it work. The step-by-step breakdown of the so-called system of "collective security" was the overriding fact of the 1930's, and led straight to the defeat of France by Germany in 1940, and the Armistice, which is the final document here, 91. It was a very far cry from the diplomatic insouciance which made the Pact of Plombières, Document 83.

§(a) Before 1919

83. *The Pact of Plombières, July 21, 1858*

The extraordinary bargain between Napoleon III and Count Camillo di Cavour, Premier of Piedmont, of which the crucial part is described below, was one of the diplomatic landmarks in the foreign policy of the

Second Empire. Napoleon was anxious to pose as the champion of liberal-nationalist causes in Europe, as the friend of Italian independence against Austria-Hungary, yet also as the protector of Papal rights. The political unification of Italy would, however, cause great difficulties for France, partly because of the "Roman Question," partly because Napoleon III had designs of his own upon Savoy and Nice. For these reasons, it seems certain he aimed not at unification, but only at limited federalization. He wanted an arrangement which would stop short of causing these difficulties, while leaving room for preponderant French influence throughout the Italian peninsula. This delicate operation was, in all likelihood, in his mind when he struck with Cavour an intricate bargain. It is described, by Cavour, in a long letter written from Baden to King Victor Emmanuel of Piedmont. The plotters met on July 21 for some eight hours.

The dynastic element in the deal, to which the second and longer portion of the letter (not translated here) was devoted, was the betrothal of Victor Emmanuel's daughter Clotilde, aged fifteen, to Napoleon's cousin Prince Jérôme Napoleon, popularly known as "Plon-Plon," notorious for his Jacobin anticlericalism but truly Napoleonic in his appearance and his dynastic enthusiasms. Two months later little Clotilde agreed to meet Jérôme and promised that "if he is not actually repulsive to me I have decided to marry him." He was not, so she did, though he was a roué of thirty-six, and an agnostic prince was a strange bridegroom for the devout Italian princess. The indelicacies of the marriage market were cynical enough, but no worse than the quest for convenient excuses to provoke war with Austria in order to seize Lombardy and Venetia for Piedmont, in return for the cession of Savoy and Nice to France.

The plot is the centerpiece in Napoleon's foreign policy, and was (as Professor Gordon Craig has suggested) "perhaps the first deliberate war-plot in the nineteenth century, but it was by no means an isolated case." Its antecedents were the Crimean War (in which Piedmont had staked a claim to be an ally of France), the Congress of Paris (in which it had become plain that Austria would yield to Italian claims only in defeat), and the Orsini plot of January, 1858, which had elicited Napoleon's avowed interest in Italian nationalism. It was itself the antecedent to a whole sequence of other important events: the secret Treaty of March, 1859, between France and Russia, which ensured Russian neutrality in the coming war with Austria, in return for France's promise to help in getting the Treaty of 1856 revised in Russia's favor; war with Austria in April, and the French-Piedmontese victories of Magenta and Solferino, which drove the Austrians out of Lombardy; Napoleon's hasty truce of Villafranca in July, whereby he tried to freeze Italian unification at an incomplete phase by coming to terms which left Austria in occupation of Venetia; then the events of 1860, which, surging beyond Napoleon's control and even, at times, of Cavour's, precipitated in 1861 the unification of the whole of Italy, with the exception of Venetia and the city of Rome.

Rome remained under Papal control, thanks to the presence of French troops stationed there since 1849. Napoleon knew that to withdraw them would outrage Catholic opinion. They remained until 1870, and so outraged Liberal opinion instead. Rather than placating both Catholics and Liberals, whether at home or abroad, he alienated each in turn by his tortuous policy.

The French text of Cavour's letter appears in *Il Carteggio Cavour-Nigra del 1858 al 1861* (Bologna, Nicola Zanichelli, 1926), Vol. I, pp. 103–8.

Cavour to King Victor Emmanuel
Baden, July 24, 1858

SIRE: THE letter which I sent in code to Your Majesty from Plombières could give Your Majesty only a very incomplete idea of the long conversations I have had with the Emperor. I believe he will consequently be impatient to receive an exact and detailed account. I am hastening to do this, having only just left France, by means of this letter, which I shall despatch to Your Majesty through M. Tosi, attaché at the Berne Legation.

As soon as I was shown into his study, the Emperor broached the question which was the reason for my journey. He began by saying that he had decided to support Sardinia with all his might in a war against Austria, provided that the war was undertaken for a nonrevolutionary cause, which could be justified in the view of diplomatic circles and still more of public opinion in France and Europe.

Since the search for such a cause presented the chief difficulty we had to resolve in order to reach agreement, I thought we ought to treat this question before all others. I first suggested that we take advantage of the grievances aroused by Austria's incomplete fulfillment of her commercial treaty with us. To this the Emperor replied that a commercial question of only minor importance could not give rise to a great war destined to change the map of Europe. I then proposed to bring up once more the issues which had persuaded us at the Congress of Paris to protest against the illegitimate extension of Austrian power in Italy, i.e., the Treaty of 1847 between Austria and the Dukes of Parma and Modena; the prolonged occupation of Romagna and the Legations; and the new fortifications built round Placentia.

The Emperor did not agree to this proposal. He observed that since the grievances we raised in 1856 had not been judged sufficient to bring French and English intervention in our favor, they would not see why they should now justify a call to arms. "Besides," he added, "so long as my troops are in Rome, I can hardly demand that Austria withdraws hers from Ancona and Bologna." This was a valid objection. I therefore had to give up my second proposal; I did so reluctantly, for there was something frank and bold about it, which went perfectly with the noble and generous character of Your Majesty and the People he governs.

My position was becoming embarrassing, for I had nothing else definite to suggest. The Emperor came to my help and together we began to go through the Italian States, in search of those grounds for war which were so difficult to find. After we had traveled the whole length of the peninsula without success, we came almost unawares upon Massa and Carrara, and there discovered what we had been trying so hard to find. When I had given the Emperor an exact description of that unfortunate country, of which he already had a pretty clear idea anyway, we agreed on getting in a petition from the inhabitants to Your Majesty asking for his protection and even requesting the annexation of these Duchies to Sardinia. Your Majesty would not accept the proposed surrender, but would support the cause of these oppressed populations by addressing a haughty and menacing note to the Duke of Modena. The Duke, confident of Austrian support, would reply in an impertinent manner. Thereupon, Your Majesty would occupy Massa, and the war would begin.

As the Duke of Modena would be the cause of it, the Emperor thinks that it would be popular not only in France but in England also, and in the rest of Europe, seeing that the Duke is considered, rightly or wrongly, as the scapegoat of despotism. Besides, since the Duke of Modena has not recognized any sovereign who has reigned in France since 1830, the Emperor has less need to be careful with him than with any other Prince.

This first question settled, the Emperor said: "Before going further we must consider two grave difficulties which we shall encounter in Italy: the Pope and the King of Naples. I must go carefully with them; the first, so as not to stir up the French Catholics against me, the second so as to preserve the sympathies of Russia, which makes it a point of honor for some reason to protect King Ferdinand."

I answered the Emperor that it would be easy to maintain the Pope in peaceful possession of Rome by means of the French garrison established there, while letting the provinces of Romagna revolt; that since the Pope had been unwilling to follow the advice he had been given in regard to them, he could not complain if these districts took the first favorable occasion to rid themselves of the detestable form of government the Court of Rome had stubbornly refused to reform. There was no need to worry about the King of Naples, unless he wanted to make common cause with Austria; and his subjects could be left free if they should seize the chance to throw off his paternal domination.

This reply satisfied the Emperor, and we passed on to the main question: What would be the aim of the war?

The Emperor freely agreed that the Austrians must be driven out of Italy altogether, leaving them not an inch of land this side of the Alps and the Isonzo. But after that, how would Italy be organized? After lengthy discourses, which I will spare Your Majesty, we more or less agreed to the following principles, while recognizing that they would be subject to modification by the course of the war. The Po valley, the Romagna and the Legations would be constituted the Kingdom of Upper Italy, under the rule of the House of Savoy. Rome and its surrounding territory would be left to the Pope. The rest of the Papal States together with Tuscany would form the Kingdom of Central Italy. The territorial boundaries of the Kingdom of Naples would remain untouched. The four Italian States would form a confederation on the pattern of the German Confederation, with the Pope as President to console him for the loss of the best part of his States.

This arrangement seems quite acceptable to me.

For Your Majesty, sovereign in law over the richest and most powerful part of Italy, would be sovereign in fact over the whole peninsula.

The question was left open of what sovereigns would be installed in Florence and Naples in the probable event that Your Majesty's uncle and his cousin would take the wise decision to retire to Austria; all the same, the Emperor did not hide the fact that he would with pleasure see Murat return to the throne of his father; and for my part I suggested that the Duchess of Parma, at least for the time being, might occupy the Pitti Palace. This last idea pleased the Emperor immensely. He seemed very anxious not to be accused of persecuting the Duchess of Parma, as she is a Princess of the Bourbon family.

After we had settled the future fate of Italy, the Emperor asked me what France would get, and if Your Majesty would cede Savoy and the County of Nice. I answered that Your Majesty believed in the principle of Nationalities, and realized accordingly that Savoy ought to be reunited with France; and that consequently you were ready to make this sacrifice, even though it would give you great pain to renounce the land which had been the cradle of your family, and the people who had given your ancestors so many proofs of their affection and devotion.

It was a different question for Nice, for the people of Nice belonged in origin, language, and habits more closely to Piedmont than to France, and consequently their incorporation into the Empire would be contrary to the very principle for whose triumph we were taking up arms. Thereupon, the Emperor stroked his mustache several times and contented himself with the remark that these were quite secondary questions for him, and there would be time for them later.

Passing on then to examine the means whereby there might be a happy outcome to the war, the Emperor observed that we should try to isolate Austria, and so have nobody else to deal with; that was why he was so insistent that the grounds for war should be such as not to alarm the other Continental powers, and would also be popular in England. The Emperor seemed convinced that what we had adopted did fulfill this double purpose. The Emperor counts positively on England's neutrality; he urged me to make every effort to work on public opinion in this country so as to force its government, which is a slave to opinion, not to undertake anything on behalf of Austria. He depends equally on the antipathy of the Prince of Prussia toward the Austrians to prevent Prussia from coming out against us. As for Russia, he has the formal and oft-repeated promise of the Emperor Alexander not to oppose his plans for Italy. So long as the Emperor is not deluding himself, which I am not inclined to believe after all he has told me, the question would be reduced to a war between France and ourselves on the one side and Austria on the other.

The Emperor believes nevertheless that, even reduced to these proportions, the matter is still of extreme importance and presents enormous difficulties. There is no disguising the fact that Austria has enormous military resources. The wars of the Empire were good proof of that. Although Napoleon beat her for fifteen years in Italy and Germany, although he destroyed a great many of her armies, seized provinces, and levied crushing war indemnities, he always found her on the battlefield once more ready to start the struggle again. And one is bound to recognize that at the end of the wars of the Empire, in the terrible battle of Leipzig, it was still the Austrian batallions which contributed most to the defeat of the French army. Therefore to force Austria to renounce Italy, two or three battles won in the valleys of the Po and the Tagliamento would not suffice. It would be necessary to penetrate to the center of the Empire and with our sword at its heart, i.e., in Vienna itself, force Austria to sign a peace on terms we have laid down in advance.

To attain this end, very considerable forces are essential. The Emperor estimates 300,000 men at least, and I think he is right. With 100,000 men the fortified places of Mincio and Adige could be blocked and the Tyrolean passes guarded. Two hundred thousand men would march on Vienna by way of Carinthia and Styria. France would furnish 200,000 men, Sardinia and the other provinces of Italy the other 100,000. The Italian contingent may appear small to Your Majesty; but if he reflects that we are talking of troops in action, troops of the line, he will realize that for 100,000 effectives, one needs 150,000 under arms.

The Emperor seemed to me to have very sound ideas on how to prosecute the war and what part the two countries must play. He recognized that France must make Spezia its marshalling area and concentrate especially on the right bank of the Po, until he has gained control of that river by forcing the Austrians to retire to their fortresses. There would therefore be two great armies, one commanded by Your Majesty and the other by the Emperor in person.

Once agreed on the military question, we were equally agreed on the financial question, which, I must inform Your Majesty, is what especially concerns the Emperor. Nevertheless, he has consented to provide us with what war materials we need, and to help us negotiate a loan in Paris. As for the contribution of the Italian provinces in money and material, the Emperor thinks we should make cautious use of it up to a point. The questions I have had the honor of summarizing for Your Majesty as briefly as possible were the topics of a conversation with the Emperor which lasted from eleven o'clock in the morning till three o'clock in the afternoon. At three o'clock the Emperor dismissed me but asked me to return at four o'clock to drive with him in his carriage. . . .

84. *American in Paris, 1869*

In the spring of 1869 a new United States minister, E. B. Washburne, arrived in Paris. He represented his country there for the next eight and a half years and his two volumes of *Recollections of a Minister to France, 1869–1877* (New York, Scribner's, 1887) provide a series of eye-witness accounts and first-hand evidence of the dramatic events of these years in Paris. Sympathetic to the Republicans, yet independent and often critical in his judgments, he wrote the kind of descriptions and narratives of events for which any historian is grateful. The following brief excerpt records his first impressions of Paris in the last days of the Second Empire. It comes from Vol. I, pp. 2–3 and 6–7, of his *Recollections*.

GENERAL DIX and the Marquis de La Valette arranged for the presentation of my letters of credence to the Emperor, on Sunday the twenty-third day of May, 1869. It was to me an entry upon a new career, and into a field in which I had never had any experience.

Paris, then the most attractive city in the world, was bright and beautiful, as it always is in that vernal season. The Emperor, residing at the Tuileries, was in the midst of a brilliant court, and was surrounded with glittering splendor. Princes and Dukes, Marquises, Counts and Barons, maintained their butterfly existence, and the *grandes dames*, in their splendid toilets, promenaded in their gilded phaetons on the magnificent Avenue of the Champs Elysées, or in the winding and shady alleys of the Forest of Boulogne. Milliners in the Rue de la Paix, tailors in the Chausée d'Antin, sober old merchants in the Rue St. Honoré, grand proprietors of immense establishments like the Bon Marché and the Louvre, the bankers on the Rue Laffitte, and the little shop-keepers and the barbers in the Boulevards, reaped rich harvests from the great outside world, which poured its gold into the lap of Paris, and, in return, carried to all lands and into every clime all that ingenuity and skill could invent to gratify the taste and tempt the appetite. The cry of *Vive l'Empereur*, uttered by the courtiers and parasites, was often heard in the streets, and was responded to by a giddy throng in Paris, which, flattered by the counterfeit consideration of the government, dazzled by the glitter of the court, or, fattening on the wealth of royalty, abandoned itself to the falsehood of pleasant dreams, and bowed down before the false glory and the material strength of the Empire. . . .

In Paris, during the last years of the Empire, and prior to the breaking out of the war in 1870, there were certain appearances of prosperity, happiness and content; but they were like the fruit of the Dead Sea, and to the last degree deceptive. Beneath all the outside show there was to be heard the deep rumbling of popular discontent. The people were dissatisfied, restless and uneasy. They considered that their rights and liberties had been trampled upon, and their discontent was often made manifest in Paris by their turbulent gatherings on the Boulevards, which had so often to be dispersed by the police and squadrons of cavalry, whose clashing sabres and sounding bugles were frequently heard in the streets. These gatherings were called *attroupements*. Thousands of individuals quickly assembling, idlers, laborers and loafers, sometimes completely blocked up the way for squares. Night after night large numbers would be arrested as rioters and revolutionists, and locked up in the prison of Mazas, or sent to the casemates of Fort Bicêtre. I had, at this time, a somewhat curious experience with an American who was one of the number "gobbled up." Though the Prefect of Police had issued a proclamation warning all peaceable people to keep out of the streets and not to mix up with the rioters, yet our American friend, his curiosity going beyond all reasonable bounds, found himself one night arrested, and with about eight hundred others taken to Fort Bicêtre, where he was obliged to sleep on straw, and had very little to eat, and that of the worst quality. He was soon, however, enabled to get a word to me; and upon my application to the authorities was immediately released, and came to tell me a pitiful story of abuse and even of robbery. The authorities did not deny that he had had a pretty hard time; but they did most strenuously deny that he had been robbed by the police authorities. Though he was altogether to blame for mixing himself up with the crowd of rioters, after having been warned of the consequences, he was very much dissatisfied with his treatment, and thought our government ought to take it up and "vindicate" him. This was often the case; and I found that whenever an American got into trouble, he thought that our country ought to go to war at once to vindicate him and its power and authority. . . .

85. *The Treaty of Frankfurt, May 10, 1871*

The Treaty which France and Germany signed at Frankfurt, and which restored peace after the Franco-Prussian War, is one of the major landmarks in modern French history, both for domestic and external relations. Its text is here given in full, and it was the centerpiece of protracted and immensely complicated diplomatic negotiations. So complete and sudden was the collapse of the French army in 1870 that Bismarck was, for a time, perplexed as to how to negotiate even an armistice convention. The abdication of Emperor Napoleon III and his replacement by the virtually self-appointed Government of National Defense; the need to conduct elections for a National Assembly which would be qualified to ratify the peace Treaty; the catastrophic intervention of the Paris Commune, which further delayed a peace settlement—all these circumstances made it possible for Bismarck to impose upon Jules Favre terms which inevitably fostered a mood of revenge, and led to deep chauvinistic desires for another war to retrieve the "lost provinces" of Alsace and Lorraine, annexed by the Treaty.

The Armistice Convention was at last signed on January 28, 1871, at Versailles; a "Preliminary Treaty of Peace" was signed, also at Versailles, on February 26, 1871. When this had been ratified by the National Assembly, negotiations continued to produce the "Definitive Treaty" of Frankfurt. In addition to the text here printed, three Additional Articles, mentioned in Article XVII of the Treaty, were also signed on May 10 at Frankfurt. The states of Baden, Bavaria, and Württemberg acceded to the Treaty on May 15, 1871. Further Conventions, based on the Treaty, were signed on October 12, 1871, at Berlin; on December 11, 1871, at Frankfurt; on June 29, 1872, at Frankfurt; and on March 15, 1873, at Berlin. The first two of these were concerned with precise details of the arrangements for the ceding of territory; the last two, mainly with the acceleration of the payment of the indemnity to Germany, negotiated by Thiers, in return for which German troops left French soil nearly two years early. For full details, see Robert I. Giesberg, *The Treaty of Frankfort: A Study in Diplomatic History, September 1870–September 1873* (Philadelphia, University of Pennsylvania Press, 1966). The French text appears in *Documents diplomatiques Français*, 1er. série (Paris, Imprimerie nationale, 1929), vol. 1, pp. 5–11.

The lessons that France—and Europe—drew from the Franco-Prussian War and from the Treaty which ended it were far-reaching. The dangers of a *Blitzkrieg* war, fought without allies, emphasized the need for alliances to gain security; the loss of territory, serious on both economic and strategic grounds, evoked intense nationalistic fervor because of the loss of French families now severed from the homeland; men from Lorraine—a Maurice Barrès and a Raymond Poincaré—were henceforth to rank among the most anti-German voices in French thinking about foreign affairs. The Treaty embodied decisions of momentous importance for both countries, and for the rest of mankind.

Art. I. The distance between the town of Belfort and the line of frontier, such as it had been proposed during the negotiations of Versailles, and such as it is marked on the map annexed to the ratifications of the Preliminaries of the twenty-sixth February, is considered as describing the radius which, by virtue of the clause relating thereto in Article 1 of the Preliminaries, is to remain to France with the town and fortifications of Belfort.

The German Government is disposed to extend that radius so as to include the Cantons of Belfort, Delle, and Giromagny, as well as the western part of the Canton of Fontaine, to the west of a line to be traced from the spot where the canal from the Rhône to the Rhine leaves the Canton of Delle to the south of Montreux-Château, to the northern limits of the Canton between Bourg and Felon where that line would join the eastern limit of the Canton of Giromagny.

The German Government will, nevertheless, not cede the above territories unless the French Republic agrees, on its part, to a rectification of frontier along the western limits of the Cantons of Cattenom and Thionville which will give to Germany the territory to the east of a line starting from the frontier of Luxemburg between Hussigny and Redingen, leaving to France the villages of Thil and Villerupt, extending between Erronville and Aumetz between Beuvilliers and Boulange, between Trieux and Lomeringen, and joining the ancient line of frontier between Avril and Moyeuvre.

The international commission, mentioned in Article 1 of the Preliminaries, shall proceed to the spot immediately after the ratifications of the present Treaty to execute the works entrusted to them and to trace the new frontier, in accordance with the preceding dispositions.

Art. II. French subjects, natives of the ceded territories, actually domiciled on that territory, who shall preserve their nationality, shall up to the first of October, 1872, and on their making a previous declaration to that effect to the competent authority, be allowed to change their domicile into France and to remain there, that right in no wise infringing on the laws of military service, in which case the title of French citizen shall be maintained.

They shall be at liberty to preserve their immovables situated in the territory united to Germany.

No inhabitant of the ceded territory shall be prosecuted, annoyed, or sought for, either in his person or his property, on account of his political or military acts previous to the war.

Art. III. The French Government shall deliver over to the German Government the archives, documents, and registers relating to the civil, military, and judicial administration of the ceded territories. Should any of the documents be found missing, they shall be restored by the French Government on the demand of the German Government.

Art. IV. The French Government shall make over to the Government of the Empire of Germany within the term of six months dating from the exchange of the ratifications of this Treaty:

1. The amount of the sum deposited by the *départements*, communes, and public establishments of the ceded territories.
2. The amount of the premium of enlistment and discharge belonging to soldiers and sailors natives of the ceded territory who shall have chosen German nationality.
3. The amount of security of responsible agents of the State.
4. The amount of sums deposited for judicial consignments on account of measures taken by the administrative or judicial authorities in the ceded territories.

Art. V. The two nations shall enjoy equal privileges as far as regards navigation on the Moselle, the canal of the Marne to the Rhine, the canal of the Rhône to the Rhine, the canal of the Sarre and the navigable waters communicating with those channels of navigation. The right of floatage shall be maintained.

Art. VI. The High Contracting Parties, being of the opinion that the diocesan circumscriptions of the territories ceded to the German Empire must agree with the new frontier determined upon by Article 1 above, will confer, without delay, after the ratification of the present Treaty, upon the measures to be taken in common on the subject.

The communities belonging either to the Reformed Church or to the Augsburg Confession, established on the territories ceded by France, shall cease to be under French ecclesiastical authority.

The communities of the Church of the Augsburg Confession established in the French territories shall cease to be under the Superior Consistories and the Directors residing at Strasburg.

The Jewish communities of the territories situated to the east of the new frontier shall cease to depend on the Central Jewish Consistory residing at Paris.

Art. VII. The payment of 500 million francs shall be made within thirty days after the re-establishment of the authority of the French Government in the City of Paris. One billion shall be paid in the course of the year, and 500 million on the first of May, 1872. The last three billion shall remain payable on the second of March, 1874, as stipulated in the Preliminary Treaty. From the second of March of the present year the interest on those three billion francs shall be paid each year on the third of March, at the rate of 5 per cent per annum.

All sums paid in advance of the last three billion shall cease to bear interest from the day on which the payment is made.

The payment can be made only in the principal German commercial towns, and shall be made in metal, gold, or silver, in Prussian Bank notes, in Netherlands Bank notes, in notes of the National Bank of Belgium, in first-class negotiable bills to order, or letters of exchange, payable at sight.

The German Government having fixed in France the value of a Prussian Thaler at 3 francs 75 centimes, the French Government accepts the conversion of the moneys of both countries at the rate above stated.

The French Government will inform the German Government, three months in advance, of all payments it intends to make into the Treasury of the German Empire.

After the payment of the first 500 million and the ratification of the definitive Treaty of Peace, the *départements* of the Somme, Seine Inférieure, and Eure shall be evacuated in so far as they shall be found to be still occupied by German troops. The evacuation of the *départements* of the Oise, Seine-et-Oise, Seine-et-Marne, and Seine, as well as the forts of Paris, shall take place so soon as the German Government shall consider the reestablishment of order, both in France and Germany, sufficient to ensure the execution of the engagements contracted by France.

Under all circumstances, the evacuation shall take place after the payment of the third 500 million.

The German troops, for their own security, shall have at their disposal the neutral zone between the German line of demarcation and the Paris enclosure on the Right Bank of the Seine.

The stipulations of the Treaty of February 26 relative to the occupation of French territories after the payment of the two billion shall remain in force. None of the deductions which the French Government might have a right to make shall be made on the payment of the first 500 million.

Art. VIII. German troops shall continue to abstain from levying contributions either in kind or money in the occupied territories; that obligation on their part being correlative to the obligations contracted for their maintenance by the French Government. Should the French Government, notwithstanding the reiterated demands of the German Government, fall behindhand in the execution of the said obligations, the German troops will have the right to procure what is necessary to their wants by levying taxes and contributions in the occupied *départements,* and even outside of them, should their resources not be sufficient.

With reference to the maintenance of the German troops, the system actually in force shall be continued until the evacuation of the Paris forts.

In virtue of the Convention of Ferrières, of March 11, 1871, the reductions pointed out by that Convention shall be put into force after the evacuation of the forts.

As soon as the effective strength of the German Army shall be reduced below the number of 500,000 men, account shall be taken of the reductions made below that number to establish a proportionate diminution in the price of the maintenance of the troops paid by the French Government.

Art. IX. The exceptional treatment at present granted to the produce of the industry of the ceded territories for imports into France shall be continued for six months, from the first of March, under the conditions made with the Commissioners of Alsace.

Art. X. The German Government shall continue to deliver up prisoners of war, making arrangements with the French Government. The French Government shall send to their homes such of the prisoners as can be discharged. As for those who shall not have completed their term of service, they shall be sent beyond the Loire. It is understood that the Army of Paris and Versailles, after the re-establishment of the authority of the French Government at Paris, and until the evacuation of the forts by German troops, shall not exceed 80,000 men. Until that evacuation, the French Government shall not concentrate troops on the Right

Bank of the Loire, but it shall provide garrisons in the towns within that circuit, according to the necessities of maintaining public order and peace.

As the evacuation shall proceed, the commanders of regiments shall agree together as to a neutral circuit between the Armies of the two nations.

Twenty thousand prisoners shall be sent without delay to Lyons on condition that they are immediately sent to Algiers, after their organization, to be employed in that colony.

Art. XI. The Treaties of Commerce with the different States of Germany having been annulled by the war, the French Government and the German Government will adopt as the basis of their commercial relations the system of reciprocal treatment on the footing of the most favored nation.

Are included therein import and export duties, transit dues, customs formalities, the admission and treatment of both nations as well as their agents.

Shall nevertheless be excepted from the above rule the favors which one of the Contracting Parties has granted or may grant, by treaties of commerce, to other States than the following: Great Britain, Belgium, the Netherlands, Switzerland, Austria, Russia.

The Treaties of Navigation as well as the Convention relative to the international service of railways in its relation with the Cantons, and the Convention for the reciprocal guarantee of literary work, shall be renewed.

The French Government nevertheless reserves to itself the right of levying tonnage and shipping duties [*droit de pavillon*] on German vessels and their cargoes, under the reservation that those duties shall not be higher than those imposed on vessels and cargoes of the above-mentioned nations.

Art. XII. All expelled Germans shall preserve the full and entire enjoyment of all property they may have acquired in France.

Such Germans who had obtained the authority required by French laws to establish their domicile in France shall be reinstated in all their rights, and may consequently again establish their domicile in French territory.

The delay stipulated by French laws to obtain naturalization shall be considered as not having been interrupted by the state of war for persons who shall take advantage of the above-mentioned facility of returning to France within six months after the exchange of the ratifications of this Treaty, and the time which has elapsed between their expulsion and their return to French territory shall be taken into account, as if they had never ceased to reside in France.

The above conditions shall be applicable in perfect reciprocity to the French subjects residing, or wishing to reside, in Germany.
Art. XIII. German vessels condemned by prize courts before the second of March, 1871, shall be considered as definitively condemned.

Those not condemned at the above-mentioned date shall be restored with their cargo in so far as it still exists. If the restoration of the vessels and cargo is no longer possible, their value, fixed according to the price of the sale, shall be restored to their owners.
Art. XIV. Each of the two Parties shall continue on his territory the works undertaken for the canalization of the Moselle. The common interests of the separate parts of the two *départements* of the Meurthe and the Moselle shall be liquidated.
Art. XV. The High Contracting Parties mutually engage to extend to their respective subjects the measures they may consider necessary to adopt in favor of those of their subjects who, in consequence of the events of the war, may have been prevented from arriving in time for the safety or the preservation of their rights.
Art. XVI. The two Governments, French and German, reciprocally engage to respect and preserve the tombs of soldiers buried in their respective territories.
Art. XVII. The regulation of additional stipulations upon which an understanding is to be come to in consequence of this Treaty and the Preliminary Treaty will be the object of further negotiations, which shall take place at Frankfurt.
Art. XVIII. The ratification of the present Treaty by the National Assembly and by the Chief of the Executive of the French Republic, on the one part, and on the other by the Emperor of Germany, shall be exchanged at Frankfurt, within not more than ten days, or sooner if possible.

In faith whereof the respective plenipotentiaries have signed it and affixed thereto the seal of their arms. Done at Frankfurt, May 10, 1871.

JULES FAVRE   BISMARCK
POUYER-QUERTIER   ARNIM
DE GOULARD

86. *The Resignation of Delcassé, June 6, 1905*

From his first becoming French Foreign Minister in June, 1898, Théophile Delcassé made it his purpose to undo the work of Bismarck in trying to keep France in friendless isolation in Europe. He was, naturally enough, bitterly disliked by the German Government, which hardly concealed its desire to get rid of him. Eventually, it achieved its end, but in circumstances which made his resignation one of the most typical saber-rattling incidents in the war of nerves in which the two states then indulged.

Morocco was one of the perennial points of Franco-German friction, and Delcassé weakened his position when, adopting a forward policy there, he consulted Spain, Italy, and Britain, but not Germany, before entering into secret agreements that ensured for France a major control when the crumbling sultanate of Morocco should be eventually partitioned. The deal was part of the Entente which France concluded with Britain in 1904. Chancellor Von Bülow pressed his advantage. He staged a dramatic visit of the German Emperor to Tangier, in Morocco, on March 31, 1905, to demonstrate Germany's interest in its future. But, in his clumsy way, he gave the impression that he intended to use the Moroccan dispute as a pretext to force France into war. His real aims were to gain compensation for Germany elsewhere in Africa, to get rid of Delcassé, and to disrupt the new Anglo-French Entente.

When the timid French Prime Minister, Rouvier, received the message from Bülow that "the Chancellor of the German Empire does not wish to have any further dealings with M. Delcassé," he interpreted it as almost an ultimatum, and the rest of the Council of Ministers supported him. Delcassé, who had previously (on April 22) offered his resignation, but had then withdrawn it at the request of both the President of the Republic and the Prime Minister, now felt compelled to offer it again. This time it was accepted with relief, in the circumstances dramatically described by the Minister of Justice, Chaumié, who was present. Delcassé had to go not because his colleagues disapproved of his foreign policy, but because France was not ready to fight Germany alone and could not rely on the help of others.

German behavior quickly turned the triumph sour. The kaiser made Bülow a prince on the following day, and the government decided to press for a settlement in Morocco. By the end of October the kaiser openly exulted ("Hurrah for dry powder and well-sharpened swords!") and a Conference of Powers was called at Algeciras in January, 1906. It became apparent, in the course of it, that whereas Germany's allies, Italy and Austria-Hungary, would not support her with any enthusiasm in Morocco, German antics were driving France and Britain closer together. The British Foreign Minister, Edward Grey, noted that "the French were humiliated because of an agreement we had with them," and authorized continued naval and military conversations with the French. German policy between the landing at Tangier and the Algeciras Conference clinched the Anglo-French Entente as nothing else could have done. Bülow thus succeeded in his lesser aim, getting rid of Delcassé, at the expense of total failure in his more important purpose, disrupting the Entente. And the ensuing naval agreements between Britain and France, which Grey always insisted were not fresh commitments, did much to ensure in practice that Britain stood by France in the crisis of 1914.

The French text appears in *Documents diplomatiques français, 2ᵉ série* (Paris, Imprimerie nationale, 1935), vol. VI, Annexe, pp. 601–4.

Note on the Cabinet meeting at which M. Delcassé handed in his resignation

THIS MORNING, June 6, 1905, nearly all the newspapers, if not all of them, reported that M. Delcassé would have to hand in his resignation to the Cabinet. The press had been talking for some days about serious differences of opinion between the Prime Minister and Delcassé. Yesterday evening Rouvier had said to Étienne, Dubief, and me in his office, after a meeting about the changes to be made in the Labor Exchange: "We will have it out with Delcassé in the Cabinet. What he wants to do is madness, he would be in danger of exposing the country to war, and in view of the present situation it would be a crime to run the risk."

Ten o'clock that morning. All the ministers have met in the Cabinet room, except Rouvier and Delcassé, who are in conference with the President of the Republic. This conference goes on till almost eleven o'clock. At last the usher announces the President of the Republic, who comes in, followed by Rouvier and Delcassé. We take our seats. Everybody is obviously very anxious. Rouvier and Delcassé are very pale. When the meeting has begun, Rouvier says that he thinks Delcassé should give his colleagues an account of the views he has just been expounding in the President's office. Delcassé then explains his policy. He tells us that England has made overtures about taking common action with France against Germany. These overtures have not been limited to diplomatic conversations. Written notes have already been exchanged. He reads the text of the latest note, which, without going into practical details, states quite clearly the offer by England of this common action. He considers that it is completely in our interest to conclude this alliance. No doubt Germany is uttering threats, just in case she should feel that some hostile act were being committed against her; but he believes that it is a hollow threat, that she is bluffing, that Germany does not want war and will not fight, according to the information he has received and the opinion of all our ambassadors abroad. "Let us be careful," he said, "if we refuse England's offer. She may want to make common cause with us just now, in order to destroy the German navy and ruin their trade, only to go over to Germany's side soon after, leaving us isolated, exposed to attack, in danger of losing the battle in Europe and being stripped of our colonies."

Rouvier replies. He tells us about the information he has received from the most reliable source. Germany has deeply resented the isolation created round her; the Moroccan affair was an opportunity for protest deliberately chosen by her. She was determined not to let this isolation tighten round her, or new hostile forces take shape. She knows of the conversations begun with England, and knows that it would be a good moment to attack us now. From all the communications that have been received, and there can be no doubt about their authenticity and gravity, it would appear that her threats are not idle, but, on the contrary, extremely serious. Rouvier has been warned that if we sign the agreement for common action with England, Germany will undoubtedly be informed and invade us without declaring war.

"But are we ready for war?" Obviously not. Our forts on the east need rebuilding and our armament must be overhauled. It has become clear as a result of General de Négrier's inspection that our covering troops in the east are not at total strength. Morale is low in the army, and anarchist propaganda is beginning to have some effect among the soldiers; elsewhere in the population, the strikes which have broken out at so many points in the country have revealed a state of opinion which raises fears that there may be difficulties over mobilization and, if there were initial setbacks in the campaign, possibly riots in Paris and other towns. We can quite well understand that England, who has no fear of invasion of her island, wants to throw us into the vanguard with her. Our united fleets would overcome the German fleet, and the German commercial ports would certainly be destroyed; but meanwhile, French territory would be invaded, and in land fighting against Germany there would be very heavy odds against us with perhaps disastrous results. The country would not understand why it should be involved in such a venture as a result of our dispute over Morocco.

To make war now in our present position of inferiority would be a more than foolhardy adventure; it would be criminal. If, later, they pick a quarrel with us and we are victims of aggression, we shall hit back, alone if need be, and with all our might, to defend the integrity of French soil; but Rouvier declares that he does not want to provoke aggression or open the door to such dangers to the country.

Delcassé resumes his argument, merely retorting to Rouvier's objections that his own information is reliable; Germany is bluffing and does not want war. Rouvier rejoins by revealing the sources of his information, which stem from declarations by the Chancellor, Von Bülow, and have been passed on by somebody whom he knows personally and who is very well-informed.

Certain ministers speak, notably Gauthier, who is of the same opinion as Rouvier, that the immediate danger must be averted. I ask Delcassé if it is essential to agree immediately to the overtures made by England, whose own interests are self-evident, and if it would not be possible, without committing ourselves to a formal resolution and a reciprocal promise of common action, to maintain our friendly agreement [*entente cordiale*] with England and an attitude of caution toward all.

Delcassé believes that we should accept the English proposals right away, whatever the consequences. He is insistent that we should not let slip this assistance and this alliance.

Rouvier again warns that England has everything to gain and little to lose if her proposals succeed, whereas France will face the greatest of dangers and, if defeated, risk such total collapse that it would be almost impossible for her to recover.

It should be noted that everybody agrees that if Germany's harsh threats of attack and invasion are serious, instead of just bluster, we are in a very dangerous situation at the moment, for the reasons already mentioned. A decision has to be made. Feeling is tense. Each minister is questioned in turn. We are all of Rouvier's opinion. Delcassé then states that he will resign. Rouvier says he accepts, but adds that the disagreement shown today can never make us forget the great services given by Delcassé since he has been at the Foreign Office, and assures him of our gratitude and constant friendship. Then, turning to the other ministers, he urges the Minister of War to prepare our frontier, our armament and our troops, assuring him that no funds that are necessary will be refused. Addressing us all, he urges us to help in the important task of opposing antipatriotic theories and indiscipline and of raising the morale of the country. Rouvier requests the President of the Republic to let him take over the Foreign Office for the time being. The meeting ends at a quarter to one o'clock. I have rarely, if ever, felt the responsibility of making a decision weigh more heavily. It was a truly tragic occasion.

(Note written at the time by the Minister of Justice, M. Chaumié)

87. *Armistice, 1918: Georges Clemenceau*

The warfare in which the European powers found themselves engaged between 1914 and 1918 was in nature utterly different from Bismarck's *Blitzkriegs* of the 1860's. In both aims and participants they had been highly selective. Their whole success depended upon swift knockout blows to accomplish limited objectives in a limited time, and then upon making a speedy bilateral peace settlement, without the intervention of nonbelligerent powers. Thus had Bismarck won the Franco-Prussian War and made the Treaty of Frankfurt. From the outset the Great War of 1914 (later sadly to be rechristened the First World War) was a general European war, which, since it involved the overseas empires of the Great Powers, was potentially a world war. It was general because of the system of great alliances, and potentially world-wide because of the prewar scramble for colonies. Since neither side had objectives other than winning the struggle for survival, and therefore engaged whole national communities in the battle, and since by 1917 the United States and other initially neutral powers had also been involved in it, discovering how to make an armistice was exceptionally difficult.

France stood at the very heart of this dilemma. She, along with Belgium, was the main battlefield of the Western Front. Every day more that the war went on meant more devastation of her national soil, as well as yet heavier loss of French lives. In 1917 the morale of her troops had temporarily wavered, bringing strikes and mutinies. She, more desperately than any of her allies, yearned for an end to the fighting. Yet the Treaty of Brest-Litovsk, which Germany had imposed on Russia in March, 1918, showed how exacting Germany's demands for peace could be, and with the arrival of the United States forces in strength allied aims were brought within reach of achievement. It was, therefore, almost inevitable that the timing and terms of an armistice should be controversial in France, and that in any subsequent peace settlement France should be continually anxious lest her own national interests would be in any way neglected or overlaid by the complex aims of her many allies.

Georges Clemenceau, "Father of Victory" and "Tiger" of the Peace, together with Marshal Ferdinand Foch (1851–1929), who since March, 1918, had been Generalissimo of the allied forces, were together responsible for determining the moment and the conditions of the Armistice. It was signed on November 11, 1918, in Foch's railway carriage at Rethondes, in the Forest of Compiègne. Though it brought the fighting in Europe to an end, the process of peacemaking was to last a further six years; the Treaty of Lausanne, by which Turkey at last made peace, did not come into operation until August 6, 1924. The Treaty of Versailles was signed by Germany on June 28, 1919. But although the Peace Conference of Paris, over which Clemenceau presided, came together only nine weeks after the Armistice, the process of peacemaking was sufficiently protracted and complex for the French to feel, with increasing intensity, that despite having won the war they were now losing the peace. For the arguments consult Sir Frederick Maurice, *The Armistices of 1918* (London, New York, Toronto, 1943) and Étienne Mantoux, *The Carthaginian Peace, or The Economic Consequences of Mr. Keynes* (London, New York, Toronto, 1946). Persistence of this feeling, that essential national interests had been sacrificed by the men who made the peace, underlay the obsession for "security" of all subsequent French governments, as well as the chauvinistic demands of the Leagues and the fatalistic mood of defeatism which evolved in certain military and ultra-Right circles.

The excerpt given below is a translation of part of Chapter VI of Georges Clemenceau's *Grandeurs et misères d'une victoire*, published in Paris in 1930, the year after his death. It is an old man's retrospective defense of his attitudes and actions, and may be compared with the book mentioned in the text, André Tardieu, *La Paix* (Paris, 1921), to which Clemenceau wrote a Preface dated September, 1920. The main line of self-defense for the peacemakers was, of course, that later mutilations of the treaties ruined the settlement. But cross-purposes at the time, among the French themselves and between them and their allies, bore some share of responsibility for the fragility of the settlement. The excerpt is published and translated by permission of the French publishers (Paris, Librairie Plon).

I HOPE that I may be forgiven for this brief attempt at an over-all picture of the moment when war was drawing to an end, on the threshold of a peace which had not yet been settled. I awaited that peace with confidence. I have kept alive its flower of aspiration. But aspirations, without the action they call for, are only vain words. Never have talkers talked so much. Never has so little been done.

Peace or war, we are in the throes of a relentless struggle of powers. Woe to the weak! Beware the opiate-mongers!

Who knows? Perhaps different groupings of humanity are preparing for unexpected effects. The reach of civilization is increasing, while to the strains of the Geneva guitar the field of violence is widening ready to reveal to us new echelons of humanity. The Armistice is, in fact, a door opening to the unknown. So in history, life's pendulum swings to and fro.

What I have to say on the preparation for the Armistice can be summed up in two phrases:

1. Complete agreement with Marshal Foch on all points, except on the total army strength left to Germany.
2. Complete disagreement with the President of the Republic about the preliminary negotiations between the Allies on the possibility of an armistice.

I do not know how M. Poincaré was led to intensify his opposition to this project. On October 8 he saw "a trap" in it, while October 4 was the date on which Prince Max of Baden telegraphed to Mr. Wilson with a view to calling the belligerents together *for peace negotiations based on the fourteen points, and* AT THE SAME TIME *for the immediate conclusion of an armistice*. Was it possible? THAT SAME October 8, M. Poincaré informed me yet again that "everyone hopes steadfastly" THAT THEY WILL NOT HAMSTRING OUR TROOPS BY AN ARMISTICE, HOWEVER SHORT.

The sequence of events is known. It has been told in many works, notably with exceptional clarity in M. Tardieu's book *La Paix*, and in General Mordacq's publication entitled *The Truth about the Armistice*.

Everyone knows today that, with the total collapse of the political world and of the Kaiser's army, the day came when no one cared to accept the burden of responsibility for that day any longer, save Prince Max of Baden, who courageously came forward for the period of transition.

Marshal Foch has declared that he had been informed long before of the general weakening in the ranks of the German army. He wanted to be seen playing with the opposite side like a cat with a mouse. In that case, why did he not inform me? And why did he leave the President of the Republic himself in complete ignorance of what was happening? At the first mention that the enemy had asked for an armistice, we in fact saw M. Poincaré making frenzied exertions to prevent the granting of even the briefest suspension of fighting.

If the President of the Republic, who was certainly no less

anxious to end the war than we were, refused to agree to the truce that was requested, it must have been that he was unaware of the morale of the German army and of the German people themselves at that moment, and it was the state of that morale which conditioned our reply in advance. He could only have formed his opinion from the same documents as we did. If he had had information from Foch, who claims that he himself knew everything, the attitude of M. Poincaré would be unaccountable. According to him, the Germans intended to divert us with false negotiations, so as to be able to outmaneuver us at the same time by marches planned to deal a final defeat. On what was this opinion founded? On facts? Or on the omens of a soothsayer?

In theory, some such military maneuver by the enemy would be conceivable. But during an armistice of a few days, a simple truce, that is, such as I decided to propose to the President of the Republic, the Germans would have been closely watched by us and could not have accomplished any successful maneuver.

What remains incomprehensible is why M. Poincaré, while disagreeing with his Government on whether to allow or refuse an armistice, did not draw upon the informed opinion of the chief of the allied armies. He was not unaware that in such a matter only the supreme military authority could decide. Everything that passed from him to me was submerged in those floods of ink to which he is addicted. Really, it was too much, when at that very hour, events in Germany had themselves settled whether there would be war or peace.

Nothing like that would have happened if Foch had fulfilled his first duty, which was to inform the Head of the State. It is true that the latter was equally bound to ask for information from the Commander in Chief, especially in such a case. There was no sign of any exchange of information between them. M. Poincaré vented his opposition to the armistice against me, with extreme violence, instead of asking for information from Foch, who let the Presidential wrath take its course without a single word of intervention. The simplest explanation perhaps is that Foch was only boasting when he claimed to know what was happening on the other side of the front. That would be the most likely. I dare not believe that, for it would be a very ugly trait of character.

Apart from all other factors, the most ordinary observer might have realized that the relative strength of the forces in the field, after four years of war during which the greatest battles in history had been fought, created inevitably on both sides a new situation, precipitated by the American intervention, which would inevitably incline the victory to our side. For it must be clearly recognized that it was the collapse of the German soldiers' resistance which produced the revolution in Berlin, with all its consequences, and not the civilian revolution which would have produced the military revolution, as it has vainly been attempted to establish.

On November 11, 1918, the fighting ceased.

I will not dispute the endurance of the German soldier. But he had been promised a *fresh and joyous* war, and for four years he had been held down beneath a sledgehammer. It was a famous German, Planck, who proposed the new *quantum theory*, according to which cosmic energy is not continuous, but proceeds in a series of definite shocks. Byzantium overcame Athens and Rome. Its *quantum* was soon exhausted. The *quantum* of a hypothetical German civilization would not lead us very far, because she is today still too close to barbarism, whereas the *quantum* of a Hellenic civilization, even though conquered, is nowhere near exhaustion. Our defeat would have inflicted on the civilization of the whole human species a relapse into violence and bloodshed. The question is to know what contribution to regeneration can and must be furnished by our victory, if it is maintained.

The truth is that the German soldier and the German civilian had both exhausted their efforts to conquer, simultaneously, whereas on the French side, with the magnificent combination of warlike virtues of our gallant Allies, we were fighting for our existence, always excepting the usual amount of degeneracy which in every country gained the stigma of "the dodger." The French fighter on the eve of the Armistice was as steadfast a soldier as at any moment of the war.

Yes! Yes! I know. There had been mutinies, when there was vacillation in the command. A few days of ugly words, not to hasten the end of the war, but to make all the leaders responsible for the few who had not given them victory. I saw these "mutineers." I talked to them. There was no need to do more than show them the Germans. The most dangerous man perhaps was the one who said nothing. There was never any question of an end of the war. I saw vague gestures of anger. All those "mutineers" were only waiting for a chance to return to the ranks. In general terms, it can be said that everything calmed down without repression at the mere cry of "Forward!"

Acts of violence against the civilization of man are repressed in the long run by their own excesses, and I discern in the psychological conditioning of the German soldier, with its theme of *Deutschland über alles*, the cause of the premature exhaustion which induced him to ask for an armistice sooner than the French soldier who was fighting for his independence. Orgies of crime pall more quickly than common cruelty until the day comes, distant still, no doubt, when the pendulum swings more gently.

That is one of the ways in which I explain the moral fatigue of the German on both fronts, while our Frenchman, with his exaggerated reputation of being superficial and volatile, kept smiling, with the same stout heart, till the end.

As far as I am concerned, there was no difference of opinion between Marshal Foch and myself, except about the number of troops allowed to the Germans, and I got the number considerably reduced with no difficulty. On this point I must say that Marshal Foch raised no objection. The question was probably not unimportant to him. But he realized that until the peace, at least, numbers that were impossible to check could have no effect in the anarchy of German disorganization.

I had to defend myself in the Chamber against the accusation of *"failing to disarm Germany."* It was the only point of disagreement that the opposition, in its confusion, had been able to find. To everything I could say, they replied *"Disarm Germany,"* and the Chambers re-echoed with applause. The deputy who succeeded me in the Ministry was among the most violent in this respect. When he was in my seat, Germany must have been disarmed by magic, for we heard no more about it.

But our journalist warriors had notebooks full of adventures to pursue. First we were reproached for not following the protocol observed under the monarchy for disarming the troops with the ceremony of a formal surrender. All arms were to be left behind on the field. The soldier advanced to the fixed frontier, laid down his rifle on the ground, and returned to his own country. I must admit that such protocol had not occurred to me.

Soon, another campaign was mounted to show that we had committed an unpardonable sin in accepting the Armistice instead of going to Berlin to get it signed. Marshal Foch, who was responsible for Rethondes, had not allowed himself to be tempted onto that road. I must say, to his credit, that I heard him protest vehemently against the wild notions of certain pen-pushers and reply that, with the military objective achieved, we had no right to gamble with *"the life of a single man"* over a question that had been settled in military terms.

As for me, my duty was very simple. When Mr. Wilson sent us the American army, he asked us the famous fourteen questions. Would we be ready to cease the fight on the day when the Germans tendered their submission on these different points? If I had refused to reply in the affirmative it would have been nothing less than a breach of faith, the country would have risen, unanimous against me, while our soldiers with good reason would have disowned me.

At home, and among our Allies, there was but one voice—Accept. It meant peace for France, peace for the Allies. We had no right to risk a single human life for any other result. It has been maintained that the brilliant military triumph would have made the Germans more resigned to defeat. They had seen the soldiers of Napoleon march through the Brandenburg Gate and, as we all know, they had forgotten it at Leipzig. To put the Treaty into effect, all we lacked later on was a statesman who had strength of purpose.

After I had promised, with everybody's approval, to agree to President Wilson's conditions, which were both wise and firm, was I likely to confront him with a refusal at the moment when he was asking me to fulfill our obligations? I was not the sort of man to betray myself and at the same time betray my country. Besides, nobody asked me to until the danger of refusal was past. That is what happened over the annexation of the Rhineland, where Foch's campaign found few adherents until all chance of its realization had disappeared.

To be quite frank, there was no serious opposition to the harshest clauses of the Armistice except from our British Allies who were briskly engaged in sparing Germany, for they feared nothing so much as that the balance of power might swing over too sharply to the advantage of her ally, France. In his book, *The World Crisis*, Mr. Winston Churchill, who is very far from being our enemy, relates how he dined with Mr. Lloyd George on the evening of the Armistice, and how the whole conversation revolved around the best way of helping Germany. At such a moment it might perhaps have been more natural to think first of helping France, so cruelly ravaged by the German soldiers.

On my return from India, as I was passing through London on my way to Oxford to receive an honorary degree, Mr. Lloyd George asked me to come and see him at the House of Commons. His first words were to ask me if I had anything to say to him.

"Yes indeed," I replied. "I have to tell you that from the very day after the Armistice I found you an enemy to France."

"Well," he replied, "was it not always our traditional policy?"

In conformity with this view, Mr. Lloyd George and Field-Marshal Sir Douglas Haig had sought to mitigate the conditions imposed on Germany. But throughout all discussions the French point of view was upheld. It was upon just this divergence of views that the Germans had speculated when they declared war on us. But they had grossly miscalculated the British mentality when they believed, with the simplicity of savages, that with Belgium violated the Briton would not at once shoulder arms.

Great Britain has not ceased to be an island defended by the waves, which is why she believes herself bound to multiply the causes of discord between the peoples of the continent in order to secure peace for her conquests. This policy has paid off handsomely in her interests, but against ours.

The new men across the Channel have not yet realized that since that time lots of things have changed. They were not unaware, however, that with the invasion of Belgium their shipping would be directly menaced by a Germany which announced that *"her future was on the water."* They decided to save England with our help, at the risk of freeing France at the same time. They did so gallantly, and we feel a gratitude to them, which they mistrust for fear that we should take it as a text for future advantages which still haunt the dreams of a few civilian warriors. The die seems to have been cast, for an invading America has taken it into her head to pay us visits with commercial interests in view, and Great Britain may suffer more from this than the genius of her up-to-date politicians yet allows her to suppose. How many question marks at the mere announcement of the first problems of peace!

§(b) Security and Disarmament, 1919–1939

Preservation of the settlement in Europe, and effective operation of the machinery provided by the Covenant of the League of Nations for increasing security and "organizing peace" depended equally upon successful cooperation between France and Great Britain. They alone had the joint power to achieve these aims, once the United States had withdrawn from the task and the Soviet Union (like Germany) had been excluded. The prolonged dialogue between France and Britain on these matters hinged, in the end, on divergent conceptions of how to accomplish them. Would security come only from general disarmament, as the British customarily held, or would general disarmament prove unattainable until security had been provided by material and diplomatic guarantees, as France maintained?

Because France continued to feel cheated of her most solid material guarantee—occupation of the Rhineland—which she had surrendered at the Paris Conference in expectation of a joint American-British diplomatic guarantee that never materialized, the policy of successive foreign ministers between the wars was to construct a system of alliances with states in eastern Europe. They hoped to find, in alliances which to the Germans could only look like "encirclement," a substitute for the security France had forfeited in the West, though the Locarno Pacts of 1925, whereby Germany, Belgium, France, Great Britain, and Italy entered into mutual guarantees against aggression, for a time eased French anxieties. The political agreement between France and Poland, reached at Paris on February 19, 1921, set the tone and model for a series of treaties with eastern European states—with the three powers of the Little Entente (Czechoslovakia, Rumania, and Yugoslavia), made between 1924 and 1927; and with the Soviet Union in 1935, after its entry into membership of the League of Nations (with French sponsorship) in 1934. The Polish agreement of 1921 is printed below (Document 88).

Meanwhile repeated attempts to secure agreed measures of disarmament in Europe came to little, though agreements about naval disarmament were reached by Britain, France, and United States, and Japan at the Washington Conference of 1921 and 1922. The normal French attitude toward military disarmament was well stated in the Memorandum on Disarmament which the French submitted on July 15, 1931, in preparation for the Disarmament Conference convened by the League of Nations. It is printed below (Document 89). It exemplifies the penetrating verdict of W. M. Jordan, in his study *Great Britain, France, and the German Problem, 1918–1939* (London, New York, Toronto, 1943), p. 169:

The real cleavage between France and Great Britain centred rather on the question whether European peace should continue to rest on the sanction of preponderant force. In the circumstances which resulted from the Treaty of Versailles, disarmament did not imply equal proportionate reduction in the armaments of all states; it implied the termination of the armed preponderance of France and her allies. For that preponderance, consecrated by the Treaty of Versailles, Great Britain sought to substitute a community of relatively disarmed states, the peace of which should be assured by the mutual confidence of each in the intentions of all.

Once Hitler came to power in Germany, the British dream had become quite unrealistic, and it was too late to fulfill the French.

French text of Document 88 reprinted in *Le livre jaune Français, Documents diplomatiques (1938–1939)* (Paris, Imprimerie nationale, 1939), Appendix 1. This agreement was supplemented by a military agreement on its execution signed the same day. Text of Document 89 from League of Nations Conference for the Reduction and Limitation of Armaments (Geneva, 1932). Documents IX, 9.

88. *Political Agreement of France and Poland, February 19, 1921*

THE POLISH GOVERNMENT and the French Government, both desirous of safeguarding, by the maintenance of the Treaties both have signed or which may in future be recognized by both Parties, the peace of Europe, the security of their territories, and their common political and economic interests, have agreed as follows:

(1) In order to coordinate their endeavors toward peace the two Governments undertake to consult each other on all questions of foreign policy which concern both States, so far as those questions affect the settlement of international relations in the spirit of the Treaties and in accordance with the Covenant of the League of Nations.

(2) In view of the fact that economic restoration is the essential preliminary condition of the reestablishment of international order and peace in Europe, the two Governments shall come to an understanding in this regard with a view to concerted action and mutual support.

They will endeavor to develop their economic relations, and for this purpose will conclude special agreements and a Commercial Treaty.

(3) If, notwithstanding the sincerely peaceful views and intentions of the two contracting States, either or both of them should be attacked without giving provocation, the two Governments

shall take concerted measures for the defense of their territory and the protection of their legitimate interests within the limits specified in the Preamble.

(4) The two Governments undertake to consult each other before concluding new agreements which will affect their policy in central and eastern Europe.

(5) The present Agreement shall not come into force until the commercial agreements now in course of negotiation have been signed.

Paris, February 19, 1921   (Signed)   ARISTIDE BRIAND
                                     (Signed)   E. SAPIEHA

89. *Memorandum on Disarmament, July 15, 1931*

THE GOVERNMENTS that are due to take part in the General Conference for the Limitation and Reduction of Armaments have been requested by the Council of the League of Nations to forward to the Secretariat before September 15 certain particulars concerning the state of their armaments and any information of a nature to enlighten the Conference of 1932 concerning them.

Without awaiting the complete compilation of the figures it is desired to communicate, the Government of the Republic considers it advisable to set forth the principles and methods of French policy as regards the limitation of armaments, the extent to which they have already applied them since signing the League Covenant, and, finally, those conditions whose fulfillment they deem necessary if the Conference of 1932 is not to disappoint the hopes it has awakened.

I

The general principles to be followed in the reduction and limitation of armaments were laid down both by Article 8 of the League Covenant and by Part V of the Peace Treaties.

By subscribing to Article 8 of the Pact, the Members of the League of Nations recognized "that the maintenance of peace requires the reduction of national armaments to the lowest point consistent with national safety and the enforcement by common action of international obligations."

They agreed, moreover, that the Council of the League of Nations, "taking account of the geographical situation and circumstances of each State, should formulate plans for such reduction for the consideration and action of the several Governments."

Article 8 of the Covenant is therefore based upon two fundamental conceptions, which it is important to emphasize.

The first is the idea of "common action."

In a system of international solidarity, like that of the League of Nations, each State must have sufficient armaments to protect itself against aggression until this "common action" can begin to function. If left to its own unaided resources, a State, unlawfully attacked, must be sufficiently armed not to be overwhelmed before having had time to mobilize the whole of its national forces. It will therefore be possible for the reduction of armaments to be the more substantial in proportion as the setting in motion of the contemplated "common action" is less uncertain and likely to be more prompt; (for this reason, successive Assemblies have urged since 1922 that such mutual assistance should be "immediate, effective, and in accordance with a prearranged plan" [Resolution XIV, 1922], if it be desired that "every State should be sure of not having to provide unaided for its security by means of its own armaments, and should be able to rely also upon the organized collective action of the League of Nations" [Resolution V, 1927]).

Viewed from this angle, the limitation of armaments, in conjunction with the development of the systems for the peaceful settlement of disputes and with mutual assistance, is a means of organizing peace. But, in order that it may be carried into effect, the principle of common action must supersede in the minds of the nations that of individual defense. It implies that the League is considered by them as a living reality, invested with positive responsibilities and possessed of effective power.

Concurrently—and this is the second essential idea upon which it is based—Article 8 of the Covenant clearly states that the point below which national armaments cannot be reduced depends upon the degree of security enjoyed by the nation concerned.

A proper estimate of this safety must take into account not only the manner in which the "common action" of the League will operate, but also the geographical situation and circumstances of each nation.

Article 8 of the Covenant therefore clearly lays down the principle that, as regards the reduction and limitation of armaments, there can be no hard and fast rules; the armaments of each State constitute an aggregate which must necessarily be adapted to its own particular case; the notion of diversity governs the work to be undertaken. Any leveling or automatic equalization of forces is, for this very reason, excluded *a priori*, for equality of armaments as between two States would only be justifiable in the unlikely event that their geographical situation and circumstances were identical.

In the midst of this diversity there is, however, one fixed element, which is supplied by Part V of the Peace Treaties in close conjunction with Article 8 of the Covenant.

The aim and purpose of Part V of the Treaties is indeed to lay down a definite standard for the armaments allotted to four Powers, which have formally pledged themselves to observe its military, naval, and air clauses.

By thus determining a certain standard of forces for the use of those four Powers, the framers of the Treaties make it clear that their purpose was to "render possible the initiation of a general limitation of the armaments of all nations."

Clearly, therefore, it is in relation to the armaments allotted by the Treaties to certain nations that it will be possible to prepare the limitation and reduction of the armaments of other nations.

It follows that the strict observance of the standards of forces thus laid down is one of the essential prerequisites of the limitation of armaments.

(This fact, indeed, the successive Assemblies of the League of Nations have not failed to recognize.) It by no means follows, however, that the Member States of the League, whose standards of forces have not been expressly defined by the Treaties, are under the obligation of adopting either the methods or the figures laid down in Part V of the Peace Treaties as regards the general limitation of armaments.

When the Treaties were framed, at no time and at no place was the argument advanced, either in speech or in writing, that other States should in their turn place their armaments on the level prescribed for certain States.

The Covenant stipulates, on the contrary, that the reduction of armaments is to be dealt with in a plan drawn up by the League Council and submitted to the several Governments for their con-

sideration and free decision. Account will be taken in this plan of
the requirements of national security, of the international obligations imposed by common action, and of the geographical situation
and circumstances of each State.

Were it to be admitted that the standards prescribed in Part V
of the Treaties for certain States should apply in an equal and uniform manner to other States, Article 8 of the League Covenant
would clearly be bereft of all value and all significance.

On this system of ideas are founded the principles to be followed
in the matter of the limitation and reduction of armaments, as laid
down in the Covenant of the League of Nations and in the Peace
Treaties.

This system has been expounded and consistently approved by
the successive Assemblies of the League of Nations.

The Government of the Republic has strictly conformed there-
with.

II

Since the coming into force of the Covenant, France has of her
own accord proceeded to reduce her armaments, taking into account, on the one hand, her geographical situation and the circumstances for which her armaments are intended to provide and, on
the other, the progress achieved in the organization of security.

The particular circumstances of French national defense are
well known.

Having thrice suffered invasion in the course of a hundred
years, and with extensive frontiers lying open to attack, more
particularly those frontiers in close proximity to which are concentrated the resources most essential to her economic life and national defense, France must have at her disposal land forces
sufficient to protect her as surely and as promptly as their sea
forces protect Naval Powers.

In addition, France is called upon to maintain order in an overseas Empire peopled by sixty million inhabitants, covering an area
equal to twenty-three times that of the home country, some parts
of which are not yet entirely pacified. She is therefore obliged to
maintain two specially trained forces, one in her dependencies, of
the smallest size compatible with assuring their security in normal
times, and a similar force in the home country, which would be
available in case of emergency.

In close conjunction with national defense on land, the protection of the sea frontiers, both at home and overseas, and of the essential communications between these various territories, requires the cooperation of a navy sufficiently powerful to dispense the Government of the Republic from the necessity of maintaining in every part of the Empire forces sufficient to cope alone with domestic disturbances which might conceivably coincide with a foreign aggression. The level, therefore, of the naval forces of France directly affects that of her land as well as that of her air forces.

Called upon to ensure the air defense of the home country, and to cooperate with the land and naval forces, the air service contributes in addition to the policing and protection of the overseas territories, which otherwise would require still larger land forces.

This interdependence of the three great categories of armaments is therefore extremely important for France; she must constantly consider them in combination with one another if she is properly to estimate the consequences which a measure adopted for one might have on the others.

As for security—an essential factor dominating the entire problem of the limitation and reduction of armaments and acting, one may say, as a mainspring for the functioning of Article 8 of the Covenant—the French Government has, in the last ten years, unceasingly striven to make clearer, stronger, and more tangible the conception of how this primary requisite is to be assured. It had all the more reason to devote its energies to this purpose that one of the foremost guarantees of French security, provided for and relied upon by the framers of the Peace Treaty, was from the very first nonexistent. In consequence, it has unreservedly associated itself with every effort undertaken at Geneva for the purpose of defining more clearly and developing on a general plane the principles of arbitration and mutual help laid down in the Covenant.

The value of those efforts it is by no means the French Government's intention to belittle today.

It must, however, be noted that the slow rate of progress hitherto achieved has not tended to speed up the task of reducing armaments. On the other hand, in a particularly sensitive European area, and one of vital interest to France, the signing of the Lacarno Agreement, based upon Articles 43 and 44 of the Treaty of Ver-

sailles, made for France, as well as for the other Powers adjacent
to that area, a great additional contribution to the guarantees of
security resulting from the strict observance of the Treaties.

90. *Manifesto of the Intellectuals, October 4, 1935*

After 1919, despite controversies about the details of the peace treaties,
there was a deep underlying unity in French opinion as regards the
essentials of foreign policy. Its aims, all agreed, must be to accumulate
ironclad guarantees for national security, particularly against any resurgence of German power. Most Frenchmen would have agreed,
further, that this involved preserving the treaties intact. The political
pendulum at home could swing from Poincaré to Herriot, Briand to
Tardieu, Barthou to Blum, but all alike sought the "organization of
peace," some system of collective action against any aggression which
could upset the broad pattern of the *status quo* in Europe.

Increasingly, however, parties and ministries differed about the means
by which this desirable end might best be achieved. By the mid-thirties
a sharper line had appeared between Left and Right, and the sharpen-
ing came mainly from the rise of Hitler to power in Germany. The
Covenant of the League, especially in Article 16, envisaged collective
and concerted action by the member states against any proved aggressor. Japan had successfully defied the League Powers in 1931, and had
evaded sanctions. The Soviet Union became a member of the League in
September, 1934. In 1935 Mussolini's fascist dictatorship in Italy forced
to the front the whole issue of "sanctions" by its attack on a fellow
member of the League, Abyssinia. In October, 1935, without declaring
war formally, Italy occupied Abyssinia; the Council of the League
declared Italy to be the aggressor; and the Assembly agreed to impose
limited economic sanctions against Italy, excluding coal and iron from
the goods to be denied to Italy. This situation divided French opinion
into those who (being of the Left) regarded the fascist states as the
enemy, and who therefore welcomed vigorous collective action; those
who (being of the Right) regarded communism as the major enemy
and so had considerable sympathy with the fascist dictators; and those
who (being unideological "realists") wished to resist Germany by
splitting away Italian support for her, and so were opposed to sanctions against Italy in the cause of Abyssinia. Outstandingly representative of this third view was Pierre Laval (1883–1945), who at the end
of 1935 colluded with the British Foreign Secretary, Sir Samuel Hoare,
to produce the "Hoare-Laval" proposals to appease Italy at the expense
of Abyssinia. In the event, France cooperated enough in the policy of
sanctions to alienate Italy, but sanctions were not rigorous enough to
check Italian aggression, and were abandoned by the Council of the
League in July, 1936.

These events excited extreme views in national opinion, and while in 1935 a manifesto signed by 140 parliamentarians supported sanctions against Italy, Charles Maurras and a host of right-wing leaders and intellectuals came out in favor of Italy. The Rightist manifesto, translated below, called itself a manifesto "for the defense of the West and for peace in Europe," and carried more than 850 signatures. (The original French text appeared in the French press [e.g. Gringoire] of October 4, 1935). The signatures comprised many it would have been surprising not to find attached to such a document, including Abel Bonnard, Fernand de Brinon, Charles Maurras, Henri Massis, and Léon Daudet. But they also included some that were more surprising, revealing how wide was the band of conservative opinion drawn into this camp: the historian Louis Madelin, Marcel Aymé, Maurice Maeterlinck, and several other eminent academicians and writers. It may be noted how strongly these intellectuals fall back upon the thesis of a "civilizing mission" and the doctrines of imperialism in their opposition to the policy of sanctions. See René Rémond, *La droite en France de la première restauration à la Ve république* (2nd edn., Paris, Aubier, 1963) pp. 360–1, where the "Manifesto" is conveniently reprinted. The Spanish Civil War, which began forthwith, brought this same schism in opinion to a new level of passion, and helped to produce that final paradox of Rightist attitudes—the slogan "Better Hitler than Blum."

AT A time when Italy is being threatened with sanctions which could lead to a war without precedent, we, as French intellectuals, wish to declare before world opinion that we want neither sanctions nor war.

Our refusal is dictated not only by our gratitude toward a nation which contributed to the defense of our soil when it was invaded; it is also prescribed by our profession.

When the actions of men to whom the destiny of nations is entrusted are likely to imperil the future of civilization, those who devote their labors to matters of intellect owe it to themselves vigorously to proclaim the voice of the spirit.

They wish to throw the European peoples against Rome.

They do not hesitate to treat Italy as guilty and, on the pretext of protecting the independence of a mixture of savage tribes, to tell the common people that this is the way to encourage the Great States to enter the lists.

If there were to be an offensive by a monstrous coalition, the rightful interests of the western community would be injured, and all civilization would assume the mantle of the fallen. Even to consider such action is the sign of a mental evil which betrays a real abandonment of the civilizing spirit.

Intelligence—where it has not already abdicated its authority—refuses to be an accessory to such a catastrophe. And so the undersigned believe that they should rise against so many causes of death, great enough to ruin forever that most precious part of our universe, which threaten not only the lives and spiritual and material possessions of thousands of individuals but the very idea of "Man," the legitimacy of what he holds and what he should hold—all things that the West has until now considered as superior, and to which it has owed its historic greatness with its creative virtues.

This idea, incarnating the ideals, honors, and humanity of the West, has been used by great peoples like those of England and France to justify their colonizing enterprise, which remains one of the highest and most fertile expressions of their vitality.

The Great Powers should surely have abandoned their own colonial mission from the outset, if they wished without hypocrisy to prevent Rome from pursuing the fulfillment of those projects which she honestly planned and openly prepared, in regions of Africa where she long ago acquired incontestable rights.

And so we see with some amazement a people, whose colonial empire covers one-fifth of the globe, oppose the justifiable ambitions of a young Italy, and thoughtlessly adopt the dangerous fiction of the absolute equality of nations; thus winning her the support at this juncture of all the revolutionary forces. For they invoke the same ideology in order to challenge the internal régime of Italy and at the same time to bring about the upheavals in Europe which they so desire.

Geneva provides powerful alibis to this disastrous alliance in the form of a false judicial universalism, which puts on an equal footing the superior and the inferior, civilized man and the barbarian. We can see for ourselves the results of this mania for equality, which throws together everything and everybody. For it is in the name of equality that sanctions are formulated which, in order to impede the civilizing conquest of one of the most backward countries in the world (where Christianity itself has remained inactive), would not hesitate to unleash a universal war, and to coalesce all kinds of anarchy and disorder against a nation in which some of the essential virtues of humanity at its highest level have been affirmed, revived, organized, and strengthened over the last fifteen years.

This fratricidal conflict would be not only a crime against peace but an unpardonable outrage against Western civilization, which was in the past and is now the only valid future open to the human race. As intellectuals we ought to protect that culture with all the more vigilance since we stand to gain more from its benefits; and we cannot let civilization choose against itself. We call upon all that is strong in the human spirit to prevent such suicide.

October 4, 1935

§ (c) Envoi

91. *The Franco-German Armistice, June, 1940*

On September 1, 1939, Germany invaded Poland. Two days later France and Britain declared war on Germany. The Polish War was soon over, partly because of Germany's superior military power, partly because on September 17 the Soviet Union also invaded Poland. Hitler and Stalin partitioned Poland. After the interlude of "phony war" (*drôle de guerre*) in the winter of 1939 to 1940, the Germans resumed their offensive in the West on May 10, with the invasion of the Low Countries. Within six weeks the British had been driven out of Europe at Dunkirk and the French armies had been routed.

On March 28, 1940, the British and French had made a mutual pledge "that during the present war they will neither negotiate nor conclude an armistice nor a treaty of peace except by mutual agreement." Although the French Prime Minister, Paul Reynaud, wished to fight on, he was surrounded by advisers (military, political, and purely personal) who urged the making of an armistice—without Britain's consent, if need be. On June 16 he resigned, and Marshal Pétain formed a ministry with the aim of asking Germany for the terms of an armistice. Deluding themselves with the thought that, should the terms be too severe, they could always resume the struggle, they were in some respects surprised to find that Hitler's terms were not even more stringent. The only reason they were not was that he deluded himself, similarly, with the conviction that Britain would have to surrender within a few weeks, and he could thereafter impose on both of them whatever conditions of peace he might think fit. Even so, the Armistice left Germany with a stranglehold over France as regards the financial costs of the occupation (Art. 18) and the 1.5 million French prisoners of war (Art. 20).

The Convention was signed by General Keitel, Chief of the German High Command, and General Huntziger, Head of the French Delegation, on June 22 at Rethondes in the Forest of Compiègne, in the very railway carriage (brought out of its museum) in which Foch had dictated the Armistice to Germany on November 11, 1918. Italy, Germany's "Axis" partner, had declared war on France only on June 10, but the French were now compelled to sign a comparable Convention with Italy on June 24. With France out of the war came two new developments. General de Gaulle fled to London and founded the Free French movement, in defiance of the Pétain Government and the Armistice; and Marshal Pétain, when the National Assembly met at Vichy to ratify the Convention, was granted full powers and authority to prepare a new Constitution. Thus the Armistice led directly to the end of the Third Republic and the establishment of the Vichy Government.

The territorial arrangements of the Convention, partitioning France into occupied and unoccupied zones (with the Vichy Government nominally responsible for the administration of both, Art. 3), lasted only until November 11, 1942, when the Anglo-American landings on French North Africa were countered by German occupation of the "unoccupied" zone.

One crucial item in the Convention was the disposition of the French fleet. To the British it was essential that the powerful French navy should not fall intact into German or Italian hands. But to Hitler, too, it was equally important that it should not escape intact into British control. Hence, his relatively mild stipulation (Art. 8) that it must be "demobilized and disarmed under German or Italian control" and his declaration that he had "no intention of using for the purposes of war the French Fleet. . . ." This might placate Admiral Darlan, who regarded the fleet as the basis of his own power and influence, and would suffice for the interim measure which the Armistice (and the Vichy régime itself) were intended to be. It was not expected or foreseen that both would last for a further four years, and that Vichy might even find some basis for precarious semi-independence in its control of the fleet, the Armistice army of 100,000 men, and the overseas territories, as well as in the increasing difficulties and losses encountered by the Axis partners at the hands of Britain and the Soviet Union. The Armistice Convention would have acquired an entirely different historical meaning—and one closer to what was intended by its makers—if Britain had really had its neck "wrung like a chicken's in three weeks," instead of winning the Battle of Britain during the next three summer months. Both German and French texts of the Convention were conveniently reprinted in *Politische Verträge, Traités politiques* (4 vols., Berlin, Carl Heymanns, 1941), vol. III. No. 111, pp. 1172–82.

The Franco-German Armistice
Convention, 1940

1. THE FRENCH GOVERNMENT proclaims the cessation of hostilities against the German Empire in France, in the French possessions, the colonies, the protectorates and the mandated territories, as well as on the sea. In orders those French units encircled by German troops immediately to lay down their arms.

2. In order to assure the protection of the interests of the German Reich, French territory will be occupied by German troops

to the north and to the west of a line drawn on the attached map.[1] The occupation of the territories which are to be occupied and which are not yet in German hands will start as soon as the Convention has been signed.

3. In those regions of France occupied by the Germans, the Reich is to exercise all the rights of an occupying power. The French Government undertakes to assist in all ways the carrying-out of orders made for the execution of these rights and to have them put into force with the help of the French administration. Consequently the French Government is immediately to notify the authorities and public services of the occupied territories that they will have to conform to the decisions of the German military commanders and to collaborate faithfully with them.

The German Government intends to limit the occupation of the west coast of France, after the cessation of hostilities with England, to the minimum extent which may be necessary.

The Seat of the French Government. The French Government is free to establish itself in a town of its own choice in unoccupied territory, or, if it so desires, to establish itself in Paris. In this case the German Government will give to the French Government and to the central administrations all facilities for putting into force the administration from Paris of occupied and unoccupied territory.

4. The French armed forces on land, sea, and in the air are to be disarmed and demobilized within a period later to be determined. This measure is not to be applied to those units which are necessary for the maintenance of internal order. Their numbers and their armament will be fixed by Germany and Italy. The French units to be found in the territories which are to be occupied by Germany must be brought back as quickly as possible into the territories which will not be occupied and are to be similarly liberated. Before setting out, these troops will lay down their arms and equipment on the exact spot where they happen to be at the moment of the entering into force of this Convention. They will be responsible for the handing over in good condition of these arms and of this material into the hands of the German troops.

5. As guarantee that the Armistice will be observed, France

[1] This line, starting to the east of the Franco-Swiss frontier near Geneva, ran through Dôle, Paray-le-Monial and Bourges to some twenty kilometers east of Tours: thence it ran southwards about twenty kilometers east of the Tours-Angoulême-Libourne railway, and on to the Spanish frontier, west of Pau.

will deliver in good condition all the guns, anti-tank guns, military aeroplanes, anti-aircraft guns, infantry armament, transport equipment and munitions of the French units which were fighting against Germany, and which happen to be, at the moment of the entering into force of the present Convention, in the territory which is not to be occupied by Germany. The extent of these deliveries will be fixed by the German Armistice Commission.

6. The remainder of the armaments, war material, and munitions of all kinds in the unoccupied region of France will be stored and put in safe custody under German or Italian control, with the exception of that which is to be left at the disposition of authorized French units. The German High Command reserves for itself the right in this matter to take all the necessary measures to prevent the incorrect usage of these stocks. The manufacture of new war material is immediately to cease in unoccupied territory.

7. In the territories which are to be occupied, all the ground and coastal fortifications with their armaments, munitions, material, stocks, and installations of all sorts are to be handed over in perfect condition. The plans of these fortifications, as well as those of the fortifications already taken by the German troops, must similarly be handed over. The exact situation of mines, mine-fields on land, etc., must be supplied to the German High Command. These obstructions must be removed by French forces at the request of the German authorities.

8. With the exception of that part which will be left to the French Government for the protection of its interests in its colonial empire, the French war fleet must be assembled in those ports which will later be designated. It will there be demobilized and disarmed under German or Italian control. The designation of the ports will be made according to the home bases of these ships in peace-time.

The German Government solemnly declares to the French Government that it has no intention of using for the purposes of war the French Fleet which will be found in the ports put under German control with, however, the exception of the units which will be necessary to guard the coasts and to remove mines. Moreover, the German Government solemnly and expressly declares that it does not intend to make any unreasonable claims on the French Fleet at the time of the conclusion of the peace. With the exception of that part of the French Fleet (it will be fixed later) which is to defend French interests in her colonial empire, all the warships to be found outside France must be brought back to France.

9. The French High Command must give to the German High Command precise directions concerning all the mines laid by France, all the minefields near to ports or off the coasts, and all defensive positions. If the German High Command so requests, the French forces must themselves remove the mines.

10. The French Government agrees not to undertake any hostile action whatsoever against the Reich with any part of the armed forces left at its disposition. Similarly the French Government will prevent members of the armed forces from leaving the country, as well as the transportation of arms, war material of any sort, warships and aeroplanes, to England or to any other foreign country whatsoever. The French Government will forbid French subjects from fighting against the Reich in the armies of the countries which are still at war with the latter. French subjects who do not conform to this law will be treated by German troops as *francs-tireurs*.

11. Merchant ships of all classes, comprising coastal small craft or those used in the ports which are in the hands of the French, must not until further notice put to sea. The recommencement of commercial navigation will be subject to the approval of the German Government or to that of the Italian Government. The French merchant ships which are outside French ports will receive from the French Government the order to return to France, or, if that is not possible, to enter neutral ports. All German merchant ships which have been captured and are in French ports are to be handed over intact on the demand of the German authorities.

12. All aircraft which are on French soil will be forthwith forbidden to take off. Any machine which takes off without German authorization will be considered as hostile and treated as such by the German Air Force. The aerodromes and installations of the air force which are in the unoccupied zone will be put under German or Italian control. Their being rendered useless may be demanded.

The French Government is bound to put at the disposition of the German authorities all foreign aircraft which are on unoccupied territory, or at least to prevent them from leaving. These aeroplanes are to be handed over to the German forces.

13. The French Government undertakes to see to it that in the

territories which are to be occupied by the German troops all the buildings, all the installations and stocks for the army are delivered intact to the German troops.

Moreover, it is to ensure that the ports, industrial installations, and shipbuilding yards are left as they are and that they be neither damaged nor destroyed. The same clause applies equally to the ways and means of communication, and in particular to the railways, roads and canals, to the telegraphic and telephonic networks, to maritime signalling devices, and to means of guiding ships off the coasts. The French Government similarly undertakes, on the decision of the German High Command, to put in hand all the reconditioning which will be necessary. They will see that there is in occupied territory the necessary personnel and rolling stock of sufficient quantity for means of transport, and in the same proportion as for a normal peace-time period.

14. With regard to the French broadcasting stations, a restriction on transmitting will immediately be put into force. The recommencement of wireless transmission in unoccupied territory will become the subject of a separate agreement.

15. The French Government binds itself to assure across unoccupied territory the transit of goods between the German Empire and Italy to the extent required by the German Government.

16. The French Government, in agreement with the German authorities, will undertake the repatriation of the population in the occupied regions.

17. The French Government binds itself to prevent all transport of securities and foodstuffs from territory which is to be occupied into unoccupied territory or abroad. The measures concerning these securities and foodstuffs are to be taken in agreement with the German Government. However, the German Government will take into consideration the vital needs of the population of the unoccupied regions.

18. The cost of maintaining German troops in French territory falls on the French Government.

19. All German military and all German civilian prisoners who are actually in the hands of the French, including persons arrested or condemned, who have been put into prison and tried for an act carried out in the interests of the German Empire, must be at once handed over to the German troops. The French Government is obliged to hand over on demand all the Germans who are either

in France or in French possessions, colonies, protectorates, and mandated territories who are demanded by name by the German Government.

The French Government binds itself to prevent German prisoners of war and civilian prisoners from being transferred from French possessions into foreign countries. A list of prisoners will be supplied who have been transported outside France, as well as of prisoners of war who are incapable of being moved owing to illness or wounds. The care of German prisoners of war who are either ill or wounded will be taken in hand by the German High Command.

20. The French military who are prisoners of war of the Germans will remain prisoners until the conclusion of a peace.

21. The French Government guarantees to keep in good condition and to hand over intact all chattels and securities which according to the treaty are to be put at the disposition of Germany, and which it is forbidden to transfer out of the country. The French Government is responsible for all destruction, damage, or removals of property which go contrary to the spirit of the Convention.

22. The execution of the Armistice Convention is regulated and controlled by a German Armistice Commission which will carry out its duties according to the instructions of the German High Command. In addition this Commission will carry out the duties of assuring the necessary concordance between the Convention and the Franco-Italian Armistice Convention. In order to represent French interests and to receive its executive orders from the German Armistice Commission, the French Government will send a delegation to the offices of the German Armistice Commission.

23. The present Armistice Convention will come into force as soon as the French Government has made with the Italian Government an agreement on the cessation of hostilities.[2] Hostilities will cease six hours after the time on which the Italian Government has made known to the Government of the Reich the conclusion of this agreement. The Government of the Reich will make this time known to the French Government by means of wireless.

[2] An Armistice Convention in substantially similar terms, with additional provisions for demilitarized zones between French and Italian territories in North Africa, was signed by General Huntziger and Marshal Badoglio on June 24, 1940 in Rome.

24. The Armistice Convention will remain in force until the conclusion of a peace treaty. It can be denounced at any moment and with immediate effect by the German Government if the French Government does not fulfil the obligations which it has assumed under this Convention.

This Armistice Convention has been signed in the Forest of Compiègne on June 22nd 1940 at 18 hours 50 German summer time.

Huntziger

Keitel

Select Bibliography

The more specialized studies available have been mentioned in connection with each document or group of documents, where it is most relevant to cite them. The lists which follow include general histories, works on political, economic, or social history that embrace several of the themes illustrated by the documents, and biographies and interpretative essays. The aim of the selection is to help the student wishing to pursue further (whether more deeply or more widely) the themes of the volume.

1. General Histories

Brogan, D. W.,   *The Development of Modern France, 1870–1939* (London, 1940; New York, 2 vols., revised 1966).

———,   *The French Nation from Napoleon to Pétain, 1814–1940* (London, 1957).

Bury, J. P. T.,   *France 1814–1940* (London, 1949; 3rd edn., 1959).

———,   *Napoleon III and the Second Empire* (London, 1964).

Campbell, P.,   *French Electoral Systems and Elections, 1789–1957* (London, 1958).

Chapman, G.,   *The Third Republic of France: The First Phase, 1871–1894* (London, 1962).

Chastenet, J.,   *Histoire de la troisième république* (Paris, 7 vols., 1952–1960).

Cobban, A.,   *A History of Modern France, 1715–1962* (Harmondsworth, Middlesex, 3 vols., 1965).

Gagnon, P. A.,   *France Since 1789* (New York, 1964).

Hanotaux, G.   *Histoire de la France contemporaine, 1870–1900* (Paris, 4 vols., 1908; Eng. trans. as *Contemporary France* [London, 4 vols., 1910]).

Wright, G., *France in Modern Times: 1760 to the Present* (Chicago and London, 1960).

2. *Political and Institutional*

Chapman, B., *The Prefects and Provincial France* (London, 1955).

Contamine, H., *La revanche 1871–1914* (Paris, 1957).

Dansette, A., *Le Boulangisme 1886–1890* (Paris, 1938).

———, *Histoire religieuse de la France contemporaine, 1789–1930* (Paris, 2 vols., 1951).

Fisher, H. A. L., *Bonapartism* (Oxford, 1908).

Frédérix, P., *État des forces en France* (Paris, 1939).

Goguel, F., *Géographie des élections françaises de 1870 à 1951* (Paris, 1951).

Lidderdale, D. W. S., *The Parliament of France* (London, 1951; rev. edn., 1954).

Scott, J. A., *Republican Ideas and the Liberal Tradition in France, 1870–1914* (New York, 1951).

Soltau, R., *French Political Thought in the Nineteenth Century* (London, 1931; New York, 1959).

Thibaudet, A., *Les idées politiques de la France* (Paris, 1932).

Thomson, D., *Democracy in France Since 1870* (London, New York, Toronto, 1946; 4th edn., 1964).

3. *Economic and Social*

Cameron, R. E., *France and the Economic Development of Europe 1800–1914* (Princeton, N.J., 1961).

Clapham, J. H., *The Economic Development of France and Germany, 1815–1914* (Cambridge, 1921).

Clough, S. B., *France: A History of National Economics, 1789–1939* (New York, 1939).

Dupeux, C., *La société française, 1789–1960* (Paris, 1964).

Duveau, G., *La vie ouvrière en France sous le second empire* (Paris, 1946).

Ehrmann, H. W., *French Labor from Popular Front to Liberation* (New York and Oxford, 1947).

Faure, M., *Les paysans dans la société française* (Paris, 1966).

Jeanneney, J. M., and Perrot, M. *Textes de droit économique et social français, 1789–1957* (Paris, 1957).

Kindleberger, C. P., *Economic Growth in France and Britain, 1851–1950* (Cambridge, Mass., and London, 1964).

Lorwin, V. R., *The French Labor Movement* (Cambridge, Mass., 1954).

4. Biographies

Binion, R., *Defeated Leaders: The Political Fate of Caillaux, Jouvenel and Tardieu* (New York, 1960).

Bruun, G., *Clemenceau* (Cambridge, Mass., 1943).

Chanlaine, P., *Gambetta, père de la république* (Paris, 1932).

Chapman, J. M. and B., *The Life and Times of Baron Haussmann* (New York, 1958).

Corley, T. A. B., *Democratic Despot: A Life of Napoleon III* (London, 1961).

Curtis, M., *Three Against the Third Republic: Sorel, Barrès, and Maurras* (Princeton, N.J., 1959).

Eubank, K., *Paul Cambon, Master Diplomatist* (Norman, Okla., 1960).

Goldberg, H., *The Life of Jean Jaurès* (Madison, Wis., 1962).

Gooch, G. P., *The Second Empire* (London, 1960).

Jackson, J. H., *Clemenceau and the Third Republic* (London, and New York, 1948).

Liddell Hart, B., *Foch: The Man of Orleans* (London, 1931).

Mallet, A., *Pierre Laval* (Paris, 2 vols, 1955).

Malo, H., *Thiers, 1797–1877* (Paris, 1932).

Neton, A.,   *Delcassé 1852–1923* (Paris, 1952).
Persil, R.,   *Alexandre Millerand* (Paris, 1949).
Rambaud, A.,   *Jules Ferry* (Paris, 1903).
Reclus, M.,   *Jules Ferry, 1832–1893* (Paris, 1947).
Soulié, M.,   *La vie politique d'Édouard Herriot* (Paris, 1962).
Stephens, W.,   *Madame Adam (Juliette Lamber): grande française* (London, 1917).
Thompson, J. M.,   *Louis Napoleon and the Second Empire* (Oxford, 1954).
Wormser, G.,   *La république de Clemenceau* (Paris, 1961).
Zeldin, T.,   *Émile Ollivier and the Liberal Empire of Napoleon III* (Oxford, 1963).

5. External Relations

Brunschwig, H.,   *Mythes et réalités de l'impérialisme colonial français 1871–1914* (Paris, 1960; Eng. trans. as *French Colonialism 1871–1914: Myths and Realities*, London, 1966).
Carroll, E. M.,   *French Public Opinion and Foreign Affairs 1870–1914* (New York, 1931).
Case, L. M.,   *French Opinion on War and Diplomacy During the Second Empire* (Philadelphia, 1954).
Duroselle, J. B.,   *Histoire diplomatique de 1919 à nos jours* (Paris, 1957).
Julien, C. A.,   *Les politiques d'expansion impérialiste* (Paris, 1949).
Schumann, F. L.,   *War and Diplomacy in the French Republic* (New York, 1931).

Index

DOCUMENTARY HISTORY OF WESTERN CIVILIZATION
edited by Eugene C. Black and Leonard W. Levy

ANCIENT AND MEDIEVAL HISTORY OF THE WEST

Morton Smith: ANCIENT GREECE

A. H. M. Jones: A HISTORY OF ROME THROUGH THE FIFTH CENTURY
Vol. I: The Republic
Vol. II: The Empire

Deno Geanakopolos: BYZANTINE EMPIRE

Marshall W. Baldwin: CHRISTIANITY THROUGH THE CRUSADES

Bernard Lewis: ISLAM THROUGH SULEIMAN THE MAGNIFICENT

David Herlihy: HISTORY OF FEUDALISM

William M. Bowsky: RISE OF COMMERCE AND TOWNS

David Herlihy: MEDIEVAL CULTURE AND SOCIETY

EARLY MODERN HISTORY

Hannah Gray: CULTURAL HISTORY OF THE RENAISSANCE

Florence Edler De Roover: MONEY, BANKING & COMMERCE, 13TH-16TH CENTURIES

V. J. Parry: THE OTTOMAN EMPIRE

Ralph E. Giesey: EVOLUTION OF THE DYNASTIC STATE

J. H. Parry: THE EUROPEAN RECONNAISSANCE

Hans J. Hillerbrand: THE PROTESTANT REFORMATION

John C. Olin: THE CATHOLIC COUNTER-REFORMATION

Orest Ranum: THE CENTURY OF LOUIS XIV

Thomas Hegarty: RUSSIAN HISTORY THROUGH PETER THE GREAT

Marie Boas-Hall: THE SCIENTIFIC REVOLUTION

Barry E. Supple: HISTORY OF MERCANTILISM

————: IMPERIALISM, WAR & DIPLOMACY,1550-1763

Herbert H. Rowen: THE LOW COUNTRIES

C. A. Macartney: THE EVOLUTION OF THE HABSBURG & HOHENZOLLERN DYNASTIES

Lester G. Crocker: THE ENLIGHTENMENT

Robert Forster: EIGHTEENTH CENTURY EUROPEAN SOCIETY